READINGS FOR
SOCIOLOGY
SECOND EDITION

READINGS FOR
SOCIOLOGY

SECOND EDITION

Edited by

Garth Massey
University of Wyoming

W. W. NORTON
NEW YORK LONDON

Cover art: Francine Seders Gallery, Seattle, WA. Jacob Lawrence, *Builders—Man on Scaffold*. 1985, 30 × 22¼". Photograph: Chris Eden

ISBN 0-393-96869-3 (pbk.)

W. W. Norton & Company, Inc., 500 Fifth Avenue, New York, N.Y. 10110
http://web.wwnorton.com

W. W. Norton & Company Ltd., 10 Coptic Street, London WC1A 1PU

1 2 3 4 5 6 7 8 9 0

Contents

PART I   The Study of Sociology

PART II   The Individual and Society

PART III   Structures of Power

Part IV   Social Institutions

PART V   Social Change in the Modern World

x   Contents

Preface

A sociology reader is a sampling of topics and perspectives that introduces students to the range and diversity of sociology. It should exhibit the excitement and relevance of doing sociology. In order to convey that excitement and relevance, I have incorporated well-known essays that have been effective in my classes along with new essays and portions of recently published books. Each reading repeats the sociological dictum that nothing is quite the way it appears. Sociologists revel in surprising the reader. They never tire of reminding students that what everyone else believes to be true may turn out to be quite wrong. Readings by non-sociologists, for example Leslie Silko ("The Border Patrol State"), further remind students both that sociological thinking is integral to critical thinking and that good sociology comes in many forms.

In most cases a reading applies to more than one topic. For example, Greta Foff Paule's " 'Getting' and 'Making' a Tip" uses participant observation to describe a work setting and the waitresses' strategies for coping with work, while revealing many aspects of gendered social structure. Sidney Blumenthal's "Christian Soldiers" has revelance for the study of religious trends in the United States today as well as political sociology and social movements. I have found that most sociology professors prefer to make their own decisions about the order for assigning readings and particular applications to topics. I hope this reader offers the kind of flexibility and choice that recognize the diverse preferences of sociology instructors.

In general, the reader follows the outline of topics presented in Anthony Giddens's second edition of *Introduction to Sociology*. Coverage of topics in this reader reflects the coverage Giddens has included in his text, as well as in most successful texts available for use in an introductory course in sociology. Giddens stresses the intersection of individuals and social structure. With few exceptions, students will find the readings in this volume also emphasize the way individuals experience their society, using the tools of culture and personality to navigate a course laid out by the structure of social relations. At the core of sociology is the study of social structure, most significantly expressed in the hierarchical structuring of social relations: race, gender, and class. The unifying concept in this reader is social inequality. An understanding of the sources, forms, and consequences of structured inequality is sociology's most important contribution to students. I have explicitly sought to include readings that exhibit unequal social relations which will help students develop insight into their own lives and the social life around them.

In selecting the readings for this volume I have benefitted from the advice and suggestions of many colleagues, including Randy Hodson of Indiana University and Quee-Young Kim of the University of Wyoming. Sheila Nyhus, teacher of Women's Studies and Sociology at the University of Wyoming, has been most directly helpful to me. I have relied on her judgment throughout the project. A special thanks goes to students in my own introductory courses over the past quarter century. They have been my most important source of guidance in the selection of these readings.

Garth Massey
October 1995

To the Instructor

If you are using this reader with Anthony Giddens's *Introduction to Sociology*, Second Edition, you may consider assigning the readings correlated to each text chapter below. If you are using this reader with another text, you can still follow this schema for most of the chapters.

CHAPTER	READINGS
1. What is Sociology?	1, 2, 3, 4, 29
2. Working with Sociology	1, 5, 6, 7, 35
3. Global Change and Modern Societies	8, 9, 10, 11, 26
4. Culture, Socialization, and the Individual	9, 12, 13, 14, 15, 18, 21, 22, 30, 43
5. Social Interaction and Everyday Life	6, 16, 17, 18, 33
6. Conformity, Deviance, and Crime	3, 6, 19
7. The Sociology of the Body	20, 21
8. Gender and Sexuality	7, 13, 17, 18, 20, 21, 22, 23, 24, 34, 38, 47
9. Stratification, Class, and Inequality	4, 11, 19, 25, 26, 27, 28, 29
10. Ethnicity and Race	3, 5, 28, 30, 31, 41
11. The Rise of Modern Organizations	32, 33
12. Government, Political Power, and War	11, 34, 40, 43, 45
13. Work and Economic Life	7, 16, 17, 26, 28, 35, 36, 37, 38, 44
14. Religion in Modern Society	10, 39, 40, 49
15. Marriage and the Family	15, 20, 24, 38, 41, 42, 43
16. Education, Popular Culture, and the Mass Media	25, 30, 37, 43, 44
17. Urbanism and Population Patterns	9, 31, 45, 46
18. Revolutions and Social Movements	14, 47, 49
19. Global Problems and Ecological Crises	11, 20, 36, 46, 48, 49

PART I

The Study of Sociology

1

What Is Obvious?

For decades sociologists have prided themselves on asking unpopular questions and challenging common sense beliefs. In this essay, written soon after World War II, one of sociology's most important practitioners shows how obvious conclusion may be contradicted by the facts. It is a good reminder that sociology is both an empirical science and a critical discipline.

The limitations of survey methods are obvious. They do not use experimental techniques; they rely primarily on what people say, and rarely include objective observations; they deal with aggregates of individuals rather than with integrated communities; they are restricted to contemporary problems—history can be studied only by the use of documents remaining from earlier periods.

In spite of these limitations survey methods provide one of the foundations upon which social science is being built. The finding of regularities is the beginning of any science, and surveys can make an important contribution in this respect. For it is necessary that we know what people usually do under many and different circumstances if we are to develop theories explaining their behavior. Furthermore, before we can devise an experiment we must know what problems are worthwhile; which should be investigated in greater detail. Here again surveys can be of service.

Finding regularities and determining criteria of significance are concerns the social sciences have in common with the natural sciences. But there are crucial differences between the two fields of inquiry. The world of social events is much less "visible" than the realm of nature. That bodies fall to the ground, that things are hot or cold, that iron becomes rusty, are all immediately obvious. It is much more difficult to realize that ideas of right and wrong vary in different cultures; that customs may serve a different function from the one which the people practising them believe they are serving; that the same person may show marked contrasts in his behavior as a member of a family and as a member of an occupational group. The mere description of human behavior, of its variation from group to group and of its changes in different situations, is a vast and difficult undertaking. It is this task of describing, sifting and ferreting out interrelationships which surveys perform for us. And yet this very function often leads to serious misunderstandings. For it is hard to find a form of human behavior that has not already been observed somewhere. Consequently, if a study reports a prevailing regularity, many readers respond to it by thinking "of course that is the way things are." Thus, from time to time, the argument is advanced that surveys only put into complicated form, observations which are already obvious to everyone.

Understanding the origin of this point of view is of importance far beyond the limits of the present discussion. The reader may be helped in recognizing this attitude if he looks over a few statements which are typical of many survey findings and carefully observes his own reaction. A short list of these, with brief interpretive comments, will be given here in order to bring into sharper focus probable reactions of many readers.

1. Better educated men showed more psycho-neurotic symptoms than those with less education. (The mental instability of the intellectual as compared to the more impassive psychology of the-man-in-the-street has often been commented on.)
2. Men from rural backgrounds were usually in better spirits during their Army life than soldiers from city backgrounds. (After all, they are more accustomed to hardships.)
3. Southern soldiers were better able to stand the climate in the hot South Sea Islands than Northern soldiers (of course, Southerners are more accustomed to hot weather).
4. White privates were more eager to become non-coms than Negroes. (The lack of ambition among Negroes is almost proverbial.)
5. Southern Negroes preferred Southern to Northern white officers. (Isn't it well known that Southern whites have a more fatherly attitude toward their "darkies"?)
6. As long as the fighting continued, men were more eager to be returned to the States than they were after the German surrender. (You cannot blame people for not wanting to be killed.)

We have in these examples a sample list of the simplest type of interrelationships which provide the "bricks" from which our empirical social science is being built. But why, since they are so obvious, is so much money and energy given to establish such findings? Would it not be wiser to take them for granted and proceed directly to a more sophisticated type of analysis? This might be so except for one interesting point about the list. *Every one of these statements is the direct opposite of what actually was found.* Poorly educated soldiers were more neurotic than those with high education; Southerners showed no greater ability than Northerners to adjust to a tropical climate; Negroes were more eager for promotion than whites; and so on. . . .

If we had mentioned the actual results of the investigation first, the reader would have labelled these "obvious" also. Obviously something is wrong with the entire argument of "obviousness." It should really be turned on its head. Since every kind of human reaction is conceivable, it is of great importance to know which reactions actually occur most frequently and under what conditions; only then will a more advanced social science develop.

2
The Sociological Imagination

C. WRIGHT MILLS

C. Wright Mills wrote of his own work, "I have tried to be objective; I do not claim to be detached." He argued that our questions as sociologists come from the same source as the questions everyone asks: their own experiences and the things that perplex, confuse, and inspire them. Sociology must make a connection between the individual and the social. It must allow the individual to see the larger context in which his or her life is lived, and in this way give both understanding and meaning to personal experiences.

Nowadays men often feel that their private lives are a series of traps. They sense that within their everyday worlds, they cannot overcome their troubles, and in this feeling, they are often quite correct: What ordinary men are directly aware of and what they try to do are bounded by the private orbits in which they live; their visions and their powers are limited to the close-up scenes of job, family, neighborhood; in other milieux, they move vicariously and remain spectators. And the more aware they become, however vaguely, of ambitions and of threats which transcend their immediate locales, the more trapped they seem to feel.

Underlying this sense of being trapped are seemingly impersonal changes in the very structure of continent-wide societies. The facts of contemporary history are also facts about the success and the failure of individual men and women. When a society is industrialized, a peasant becomes a worker; a feudal lord is liquidated or becomes a businessman. When classes rise or fall, a man is employed or unemployed; when the rate of investment goes up or down, a man takes new heart or goes broke. When wars happen, an insurance salesman becomes a rocket launcher; a store clerk, a radar man; a wife lives alone; a child grows up without a father. Neither the life of an individual nor the history of a society can be understood without understanding both.

Yet men do not usually define the troubles they endure in terms of historical change and institutional contradiction. The well-being they enjoy, they do not usually impute to the big ups and downs of the societies in which they live. Seldom aware of the intricate connection between the patterns of their own lives and the course of world history, ordinary men do not usually know what this connection means for the kinds of men they are becoming and for the kinds of history-making in which they might take part. They do not possess the quality of mind essential to grasp the interplay of man and society, of biography and history, of self and world. They cannot cope with their personal troubles in such ways as to control the structural transformations that usually lie behind them.

Surely it is no wonder. In what period have so many men been so totally exposed at so fast a pace to such earthquakes of change? That Americans have not known such catastrophic changes as have the men and women of other societies is due to historical facts that are now quickly becoming 'merely history.' The history that now affects every man is world history. Within this scene and this period, in the course of a single generation, one sixth of mankind is transformed from all that is feudal and backward into all that is modern, advanced, and fearful. Political colonies are freed; new and less visible forms of imperialism installed. Revolutions occur; men feel the intimate grip of new kinds of authority. Totalitarian societies rise, and are smashed to bits—or succeed fabulously. After two centuries of ascendancy, capitalism is shown up as only one way to make society into an industrial apparatus. After two centuries of hope, even formal democracy is restricted to a quite small portion of mankind. Everywhere in the underdeveloped world, ancient ways of life are broken up and vague expectations become urgent demands. Everywhere in the overdeveloped world, the means of authority and of violence become total in scope and bureaucratic in form. Humanity itself now lies before us, the super-nation at either pole concentrating its most co-ordinated and massive efforts upon the preparation of World War Three.

The very shaping of history now outpaces the ability of men to orient themselves in accordance with cherished values. And which values? Even when they do not panic, men often sense that older ways of feeling and thinking have collapsed and that newer beginnings are ambiguous to the point of moral stasis. Is it any wonder that ordinary men feel they cannot cope with the larger worlds with which they are so suddenly confronted? That they cannot understand the meaning of their epoch for their own lives? That—in defense of selfhood—they become morally insensible, trying to remain altogether private men? Is it any wonder that they come to be possessed by a sense of the trap?

It is not only information that they need—in this Age of Fact, information often dominates their attention and overwhelms their capacities to assimilate it. It is not only the skills of reason that they need—although their struggles to acquire these often exhaust their limited moral energy.

What they need, and what they feel they need, is a quality of mind that will help them to use information and to develop reason in order to achieve lucid summations of what is going on in the world and of what may be happening within themselves. It is this quality, I am going to contend, that journalists and scholars, artists and publics, scientists and editors are coming to expect of what may be called the sociological imagination.

1

The sociological imagination enables its possessor to understand the larger historical scene in terms of its meaning for the inner life and the external career of a variety of individuals. It enables him to take into account how individuals, in the welter of their daily experience, often become falsely conscious of their social positions. Within that welter, the framework of modern society is sought, and within that framework the psychologies of a variety of men and women are formulated. By such means the personal uneasiness of individuals is focused upon explicit troubles and the indifference of publics is transformed into involvement with public issues.

The first fruit of this imagination—and the first lesson of the social science that embodies it—is the idea that the individual can understand his own experience and gauge his own fate only by locating himself within his period, that he can know his own chances in life only by becoming aware of those of all individuals in his circumstances. In many ways it is a terrible lesson; in many ways a magnificent one. We do not know the limits of man's capacities for supreme effort or willing degradation, for agony or glee, for pleasurable brutality or the sweetness of reason. But in our time we have come to know that the limits of 'human nature' are frighteningly broad. We have come to know that every individual lives, from one generation to the next, in some society; that he lives out a biography, and that he lives it out within some historical sequence. By the fact of his living he contributes, however minutely, to the shaping of this society and to the course of its history, even as he is made by society and by its historical push and shove.

The sociological imagination enables us to grasp history and biography and the relations between the two within society. That is its task and its promise. To recognize this task and this promise is the mark of the classic social analyst. And it is the signal of what is best in contemporary studies of man and society.

No social study that does not come back to the problems of biography, of history and of their intersections within a society has completed its intellectual journey. Whatever the specific problems of the classic social analysts, however limited or however broad the features of social reality they have examined, those who have been imaginatively aware of the promise of their work have consistently asked three sorts of questions:

(1) What is the structure of this particular society as a whole? What are its essential components, and how are they related to one another? How does it differ from other varieties of social order? Within it, what is the meaning of any particular feature for its continuance and for its change?

(2) Where does this society stand in human history? What are the mechanics by which it is changing? What is its place within and its meaning for the development of humanity as a whole? How does any particular feature we are examining affect, and how is it affected by, the historical period in which it moves? And this period—what are its essential features? How does it differ from other periods? What are its characteristic ways of history-making?

(3) What varieties of men and women now prevail in this society and in this period? And what varieties are coming to prevail? In what ways are they selected and formed, liberated and repressed, made sensitive and blunted? What kinds of 'human nature' are revealed in the conduct and character we observe in this society in this period? And what is the meaning for 'human nature' of each and every feature of the society we are examining?

Whether the point of interest is a great power state or a minor literary mood, a family, a prison, a creed—these are the kinds of questions the best social analysts have asked. They are the intellectual pivots of classic studies of man in society—and they are the questions inevitably raised by any mind possessing the sociological imagination. For that imagination is the capacity to shift from one perspective to another—from the political to the psychological; from examination of a single family to comparative assessment of the national budgets of the world; from the theological school to the military establishment; from considerations of an oil industry to studies of contemporary poetry. It is the capacity to range from the most impersonal and remote transformations to the most intimate features of the human self—and to see the relations between the two. Back of its use there is always the urge to know the social and historical meaning of the individual in the society and in the period in which he has his quality and his being.

That, in brief, is why it is by means of the sociological imagination that men now hope to grasp what is going on in the world, and to understand what is happening in themselves as minute points of the intersections of biography and history within society. In large part, contemporary man's self-conscious view of himself as at least an outsider, if not a permanent stranger, rests upon an absorbed realization of social relativity and of the transformative power of history. The sociological imagination is the most fruitful form of this self-consciousness. By its use men whose mentalities have swept only a series of limited orbits often come to feel as if suddenly awakened in a house with which they had only supposed themselves to be familiar. Correctly or incorrectly, they often come to feel that they can now provide themselves with adequate summations, cohesive assessments, comprehensive orientations. Older decisions that once appeared sound now seem to them products of a mind unaccountably dense. Their capacity for astonishment is made lively again. They acquire a new way of thinking, they experience a transvaluation of values: in a word, by their reflection and by their sensibility, they realize the cultural meaning of the social sciences.

2

Perhaps the most fruitful distinction with which the sociological imagination works is between 'the personal troubles of milieu' and 'the public issues of social structure.' This distinction is an essential tool of the sociological imagination and a feature of all classic work in social science.

Troubles occur within the character of the individual and within the range of his immediate relations with others; they have to do with his self and with those limited areas of social life of which he is directly and personally aware. Accordingly, the statement and the resolution of troubles properly lie within the individual as a biographical entity and within the scope of his immediate milieu—the social setting that is directly open to his personal experience and to some extent his willful activity. A trouble is a private matter: values cherished by an individual are felt by him to be threatened.

Issues have to do with matters that transcend these local environments of the individual and the range of his inner life. They have to do with the organization of many such milieux into the institutions of an historical society as a whole, with the ways in which various milieux overlap and interpenetrate to form the larger structure of social and historical life. An issue is a public matter: some value cherished by publics is felt to be threatened. Often there is a debate about what that value really is and about what it is that really threatens it. This debate is often without focus if only because it is the very nature of an issue, unlike even widespread trouble, that it cannot very well be defined in terms of the immediate and everyday environments of ordinary men. An issue, in fact, often involves a crisis in institutional arrangements, and often too it involves what Marxists call 'contradictions' or 'antagonisms.'

In these terms, consider unemployment. When, in a city of 100,000, only one man is unemployed, that is his personal trouble, and for its relief we properly look to the character of the man, his skills, and his immediate opportunities. But when in a nation of 50 million employees, 15 million men are unemployed, that is an issue, and we may not hope to find its solution within the range of opportunities open to any one individual. The very structure of opportunities has collapsed. Both the correct statement of the problem and the range of possible solutions require us to consider the economic and political institutions of the society, and not merely the personal situation and character of a scatter of individuals.

Consider war. The personal problem of war, when it occurs, may be how to survive it or how to die in it with honor; how to make money out of it; how to climb into the higher safety of the military apparatus; or how to contribute to the war's termination. In short, according to one's values, to find a set of milieux and within it to survive the war or make one's death in it meaningful. But the structural issues of war have to do with its causes; with what types of men it throws up into command; with its effects upon economic and political, family and religious institutions, with the unorganized irresponsibility of a world of nation-states.

Consider marriage. Inside a marriage a man and a woman may experience personal troubles, but when the divorce rate during the first four years of marriage is 250 out of every 1,000 attempts, this is an indication of a structural issue having to do with the institutions of marriage and the family and other institutions that bear upon them.

Or consider the metropolis—the horrible, beautiful, ugly, magnificent sprawl of the great city. For many upper-class people, the personal solution to 'the problem of the city' is to have an apartment with private garage under it in the heart of the city, and forty miles out, a house by Henry Hill, garden by Garrett Eckbo, on a hundred acres of private land. In these two controlled environments—with a small staff at each end and a private helicopter connection—most people could solve many of the problems of personal milieux caused by the facts of the city. But all this, however splendid, does not solve the public issues that the structural fact of the city poses. What should be done with this wonderful monstrosity? Break it all up into scattered units, combining residence and work? Refurbish it as it stands? Or, after evacuation, dynamite it and build new cities according to new plans in new places? What should those plans be? And who is to decide and to accomplish whatever choice is made? These are structural issues; to confront them and to solve them requires us to consider political and economic issues that affect innumerable milieux.

In so far as an economy is so arranged that slumps occur, the problem of unemployment becomes incapable of personal solution. In so far as war is inherent in the nation-state system and in the uneven industrialization of the world, the ordinary individual in his restricted milieu will be powerless—with or without psychiatric aid—to solve the troubles this system or lack of system imposes upon him. In so far as the family as an institution turns women into darling little slaves and men into their chief providers and unweaned dependents, the problem of a satisfactory marriage remains incapable of purely private solution. In so far as the overdeveloped megalopolis and the overdeveloped automobile are built-in features of the overdeveloped society, the issues of urban living will not be solved by personal ingenuity and private wealth.

What we experience in various and specific milieux, I have noted, is often caused by structural changes. Accordingly, to understand the changes of many personal milieux we are required to look beyond them.

And the number and variety of such structural changes increase as the institutions within which we live become more embracing and more intricately connected with one another. To be aware of the idea of social structure and to use it with sensibility is to be capable of tracing such linkages among a great variety of milieux. To be able to do that is to possess the sociological imagination.

3
The Border Patrol State

LESLIE MARMON SILKO

A routine encounter with the police may reassure some people that the servants of the people are doing their job. For others, especially those for whom justice is not always dispensed equally, authorities can take on a hostile and alien quality. It depends on your perspective.

I used to travel the highways of New Mexico and Arizona with a wonderful sensation of absolute freedom as I cruised down the open road and across the vast desert plateaus. On the Laguna Pueblo reservation, where I was raised, the people were patriotic despite the way the U.S. government had treated Native Americans. As proud citizens, we grew up believing the freedom to travel was our inalienable right, a right that some Native Americans had been denied in the early twentieth century. Our cousin, old Bill Pratt, used to ride his horse 300 miles overland from Laguna, New Mexico, to Prescott, Arizona, every summer to work as a fire lookout.

In school in the 1950s, we were taught that our right to travel from state to state without special papers or threat of detainment was a right that citizens under communist and totalitarian governments did not possess. That wide open highway told us we were U.S. citizens; we were free. . . .

Not so long ago, my companion Gus and I were driving south from Albuquerque, returning to Tucson after a book promotion for the paperback edition of my novel *Almanac of the Dead*. I had settled back and gone to sleep while Gus drove, but I was awakened when I felt the car slowing to a stop. It was nearly midnight on New Mexico State Road 26, a dark, lonely stretch of two-lane highway between Hatch and Deming. When I sat up, I saw the headlights and emergency flashers of six vehicles—Border Patrol cars and a van were blocking both lanes of the highway. Gus stopped the car and rolled down the window to ask what was wrong. But the closest Border Patrolman and his companion did not reply; instead, the first agent ordered us to "step out of the car." Gus asked why, but his question seemed to set them off. Two more Border Patrol agents immediately approached our car, and one of them snapped, "Are you looking for trouble?" as if he would relish it.

I will never forget that night beside the highway. There was an awful feeling of menace and violence straining to break loose. It was clear that the uniformed men would be only too happy to drag us out of the car if we did not speedily comply with their request (asking a question is tantamount to resistance, it seems). So we stepped out of the car and they motioned for us to stand on the shoulder of the road. The night was very dark, and no other traffic had come down the road since we had been stopped. All I could think about was a book I had read—*Nunca Más*—the official report of a human rights commission that investigated and certified more than 12,000 "disappearances" during Argentina's "dirty war" in the late 1970s.

The weird anger of these Border Patrolmen made me think about descriptions in the report of Argentine police and military officers who became addicted to interrogation, torture and the murder that followed. When the military and police ran out of political suspects to torture and kill, they resorted to the random abduction of citizens off the streets. I thought how easy it would be for the Border Patrol to shoot us and leave our bodies and car beside the highway, like so many bodies found in these parts and ascribed to "drug runners."

Two other Border Patrolmen stood by the white van. The one who had asked if we were looking for trouble ordered his partner to "get the dog," and from the back of the van another patrolman brought a small female German shepherd on a leash. The dog apparently did not heel well enough to suit him, and the handler jerked the leash. They opened the doors of our car and pulled the dog's head into it, but I saw immediately from the expression in her eyes that the dog hated them, and that she would not serve them. When she showed no interest in the inside of our car, they brought her around back to the trunk, near where we were standing. They half-dragged her up into the trunk, but still she did not indicate any stowed-away human beings or illegal drugs.

Their mood got uglier; the officers seemed outraged that the dog could not find any contraband, and they dragged her over to us and commanded her to sniff our legs and feet. To my relief, the strange violence the Border Patrol agents had focused on us now seemed shifted to the dog. I no longer felt so strongly that we would be murdered. We exchanged looks—the dog and I. She was afraid of what they might do, just as I was. The dog's handler jerked the leash sharply as she sniffed us, as if to make her perform better, but the dog refused to accuse us: She had an innate dignity that did not permit her to serve the murderous impulses of those men. I can't forget the expression in the dog's eyes; it was as if she were embarrassed to be associated with them. I had a small amount of medicinal marijuana in my purse that night, but she refused to expose me. I am not partial to dogs, but I will always remember the small German shepherd that night.

Unfortunately, what happened to me is an everyday occurrence here now. Since the 1980s, on top of greatly expanding border checkpoints, the Immigration and Naturalization Service and the Border Patrol have implemented policies that interfere with the rights of U.S. citizens to travel freely within our borders. I.N.S. agents now patrol all interstate highways and roads that lead to or from the U.S.–Mexico border in Texas, New Mexico, Arizona and California. Now, when you drive east from Tucson on Interstate 10 toward El Paso, you encounter an I.N.S. check station outside Las Cruces, New Mexico. When you drive north from Las Cruces up Interstate 25, two miles north of the town of Truth or Consequences, the highway is blocked with orange emergency barriers, and all traffic is diverted into a two-lane Border Patrol checkpoint—ninety-five miles north of the U.S.–Mexico border.

I was detained once at Truth or Consequences, despite my and my companion's Arizona driver's licenses. Two men, both Chicanos, were detained at the same time, despite the fact that they too presented ID and spoke English without the thick Texas accents of the Border Patrol agents. While we were stopped, we watched as other vehicles—whose occupants were white—were waved through the checkpoint. White people traveling with brown people, however, can expect to be stopped on suspicion they work with the sanctuary movement, which shelters refugees. White people who appear to be clergy, those who wear ethnic clothing or jewelry and women with very long hair or very short hair (they could be nuns) are also frequently detained; white men with beards or men with long hair are likely to be detained, too, because Border Patrol agents have "profiles" of "those sorts" of white people who may help political refugees. (Most of the political refugees from Guatemala and El Salvador are Native American or mestizo because the indigenous people of the Americas have continued to resist efforts by invaders to displace them from their ancestral lands.) Alleged increases in illegal immigration by people of Asian ancestry means that the Border Patrol now routinely detains anyone who appears to be Asian or part Asian, as well.

Once your car is diverted from the Interstate Highway into the checkpoint area, you are under the control of the Border Patrol, which in practical terms exercises a power that no highway patrol or city patrolman possesses: They are willing to detain anyone, for no apparent reason. Other law-enforcement officers need a shred of probable cause in order to detain someone. On the books, so does the Border Patrol; but on the road, it's another matter. They'll order you to stop your car and step out; then they'll ask you to open the trunk. If you ask why or request a search warrant, you'll be told that they'll have to have a dog sniff the car before they can request a search warrant, and the dog might not get there for two or three hours. The search warrant might require an hour or two past that. They make it clear that if you force them to obtain a search warrant for the car, they will make you submit to a strip search as well.

Traveling in the open, though, the sense of violation can be even worse. Never mind high-profile cases like that of former Border Patrol agent Michael Elmer, acquitted of murder by claiming self-defense, despite admitting that as an officer he shot an "illegal" immigrant in the back and then hid the body, which remained undiscovered until another Border Patrolman reported the event. (Last month, Elmer was convicted of reckless endangerment in a separate incident, for shooting at least ten rounds from his M-16 too close to a group of immigrants as they were crossing illegally into Nogales in March 1992.) Or that in El Paso, a high school football coach driving a vanload of his players in full uniform was pulled over on the freeway and a Border Patrol agent put a cocked revolver to his head. (The football coach was Mexican-American, as were most of the players in his van; the incident eventually caused a federal judge to issue a restraining order against the Border Patrol.) We've a mountain of personal experiences like that which never make the newspapers. A history professor at U.C.L.A. told me she had been traveling by train from Los Angeles to Albuquerque twice a month doing research. On each of her trips, she had noticed that the Border Patrol agents were at the station in Albuquerque scrutinizing the passengers. Since she is six feet tall and of Irish and German ancestry, she was not particularly concerned. Then one day when she stepped off the train in Albuquerque, two Border Patrolmen accosted her, wanting to know what she was doing, and why she was traveling between Los Angeles and Albuquerque twice a month. She presented identification and an explanation deemed "suitable" by the agents, and was allowed to go about her business.

Just the other day, I mentioned to a friend that I was writing this article and he told me about his 73-year-old father, who is half Chinese and had set out alone by car from Tucson to Albuquerque the week before. His father had become confused by road construction and missed a turnoff from Interstate 10 to Interstate 25; when he turned around and circled back, he missed the turnoff a second time. But when he looped back for yet another try, Border Patrol agents stopped him and forced him to open his trunk. After they satisfied themselves that he was not smuggling Chinese immigrants, they sent him on his way. He was so rattled by the event that he had to be driven home by his daughter.

This is the police state that has developed in the southwestern United States since the 1980s. No person, no citizen, is free to travel without the scrutiny of the Border Patrol. In the city of South Tucson, where 80 percent of the respondents were Chicano or Mexicano, a joint research project by the University of Wisconsin and the University of Arizona recently concluded that one out of every five people there had been detained, mistreated verbally or nonverbally, or questioned by I.N.S. agents in the past two years.

Manifest Destiny may lack its old grandeur of theft and blood—"lock the door" is what it means now, with racism a trump card to be played again and again, shamelessly, by both major political parties. "Immigration," like "street crime" and "welfare fraud," is a political euphemism that refers to people of color. Politicians and media people talk about "illegal aliens" to dehumanize and demonize undocumented immigrants, who are for the most part people of color. Even in the days of Spanish and Mexican rule, no attempts were made to interfere with the flow of people and goods from south to north and north to south. It is the U.S. government that has continually attempted to sever contact between the tribal people north of the border and those to the south.[1]

Now that the "Iron Curtain" is gone, it is ironic that the U.S. government and its Border Patrol are constructing a steel wall ten feet high to span sections of the border with Mexico. While politicians and multinational corporations extol the virtues of NAFTA and "free trade" (in goods, not flesh), the ominous curtain is already up in a six-mile section at the border crossing at Mexicali; two miles are being erected but are not yet finished at Naco; and at Nogales, sixty miles south of Tucson, the steel wall has been all rubber-stamped and awaits construction likely to begin in March. Like the pathetic multimillion-dollar "antidrug" border surveillance balloons that were continually deflated by high winds and made only a couple of meager interceptions before they blew away, the fence along the border is a theatrical prop, a bit of pork for contractors. Border entrepreneurs have already used blowtorches to cut passageways through the fence to collect "tolls," and are doing a brisk business. Back in Washington, the I.N.S. announces a $300 million computer contract to modernize its record-keeping and Congress passes a crime bill that shunts $255 million to the I.N.S. for 1995, $181 million earmarked for border control, which is to include 700 new partners for the men who stopped Gus and me in our travels, and the history professor, and my friend's father, and as many as they could from South Tucson.

It is no use; borders haven't worked, and they won't work, not now, as the indigenous people of the Americas reassert their kinship and solidarity with one another. A mass migration is already under way; its roots are not simply economic. The Uto-Aztecan languages are spoken as far north as Taos Pueblo near the Colorado border, all the way south to Mexico City. Before the arrival of the Europeans, the indigenous communities throughout this region not only conducted commerce, the people shared cosmologies, and oral narratives about the Maize Mother, the Twin Brothers and their Grandmother, Spider Woman, as well as Quetzalcoatl the benevolent snake. The great human migration within the Americas cannot be stopped; human beings are natural forces of the Earth, just as rivers and winds are natural forces.

Deep down the issue is simple: The so-called "Indian Wars" from the days of Sitting Bull and Red Cloud have never really ended in the Amer-

---

1. The Treaty of Guadalupe Hidalgo, signed in 1848, recognizes the right of the Tohano O'Odom (Papago) people to move freely across the U.S.–Mexico border without documents. A treaty with Canada guarantees similar rights to those of the Iroquois nation in traversing the U.S.–Canada border.

icas. The Indian people of southern Mexico, of Guatemala and those left in El Salvador, too, are still fighting for their lives and for their land against the "cavalry" patrols sent out by the governments of those lands. The Americas are Indian country, and the "Indian problem" is not about to go away.

One evening at sundown, we were stopped in traffic at a railroad crossing in downtown Tucson while a freight train passed us, slowly gaining speed as it headed north to Phoenix. In the twilight I saw the most amazing sight: Dozens of human beings, mostly young men, were riding the train; everywhere, on flat cars, inside open boxcars, perched on top of boxcars, hanging off ladders on tank cars and between boxcars. I couldn't count fast enough, but I saw fifty or sixty people headed north. They were dark young men, Indian and mestizo; they were smiling and a few of them waved at us in our cars. I was reminded of the ancient story of Aztlán, told by the Aztecs but known in other Uto-Aztecan communities as well. Aztlán is the beautiful land to the north, the origin place of the Aztec people. I don't remember how or why the people left Aztlán to journey farther south, but the old story says that one day, they will return.

4

The Positive Functions of Poverty

Herbert J. Gans

The author is doing two things in this essay. He is demonstrating that the application of a functionalist perspective, popular in American sociology for many decades, is not incompatible with a conflict perspective. His second intention is to show us that, far from being inevitable or natural, poverty is the consequence of the intentions and actions of the non-poor who benefit from others' poverty.

Mertonian functional analysis is applied to explain the persistence of poverty, and fifteen functions which poverty and the poor perform for the rest of American society, particularly the affluent, are identified and described. Functional alternatives which would substitute for these functions and make poverty unnecessary are suggested, but the most important alternatives are themselves dysfunctional for the affluent, since they require some redistribution of income and power. A functional analysis of poverty thus comes to many of the same conclusions as radical sociological analysis, demonstrating anew [Robert] Merton's assertion that functionalism need not be conservative in ideological outlook or implication.

I

Over 20 years ago, Merton (1949, p. 71), analyzing the persistence of the urban political machine, wrote that because "we should ordinarily . . . expect persistent social patterns and social structures to perform positive functions which are at the time not adequately fulfilled by other existing patterns and structures . . . perhaps this publicly maligned organization is, under present conditions, satisfying basic latent functions." He pointed out how the machine provided central authority to get things done when a decentralized local government could not act, humanized the services of the impersonal bureaucracy for fearful citizens, offered concrete help (rather than law or justice) to the poor, and otherwise performed services needed or demanded by many people but considered unconventional or even illegal by formal public agencies.

This paper is not concerned with the political machine, however, but with poverty, a social phenomenon which is as maligned as and far more persistent than the machine. Consequently, there may be some merit in applying functional analysis to poverty, to ask whether it too has positive functions that explain its persistence. Since functional analysis has itself taken on a maligned status among some American sociologists, a secondary purpose of this paper is to ask whether it is still a useful approach.[1]

II

Merton (1949, p. 50) defined functions as "those observed consequences which make for the adaptation or adjustment of a given system; and dysfunctions, those observed consequences which lessen the adaptation or adjustment of the system." This definition does not specify the nature or scope of the system, but elsewhere in his classic paper "Manifest and Latent Functions," Merton indicated that social system was not a synonym for society, and that systems vary in size, requiring a functional analysis "to consider a *range* of units for which the item (or social phenomenon H.G.) has designated consequences: individuals in diverse statuses, subgroups, the larger social system and cultural systems" (1949, p. 51).

In discussing the functions of poverty, I shall identify functions for *groups* and *aggregates*; specifically, interest groups, socioeconomic classes, and other population aggregates, for example, those with shared values or similar statuses. This definitional approach is based on the assumption that almost every social system—and of course every society—is composed of groups or aggregates with different interests and values, so that, as Merton put it (1949, p. 51), "items may be functional for some individuals and subgroups and dysfunctional for others." Indeed, frequently one group's functions are another group's dysfunctions.[2] For example, the political machine analyzed by Merton was functional for the working class and business interests of the city but dysfunctional for many middle class and reform interests. Consequently, functions are defined as those observed consequences which are positive *as judged by the values of the group under analysis*; dysfunctions, as those which are negative by these values.[3] Because functions benefit the group in question and dysfunctions hurt it, I shall also describe functions and dysfunctions in the lan-

1. The paper also has the latent function, as S. M. Miller has suggested, of contributing to the long debate over the functional analysis of social stratification presented by Davis and Moore (1945).
2. Probably one of the few instances in which a phenomenon has the same function for two groups with different interests is when the survival of the system in which both participate is at stake. Thus, a wage increase can be functional for labor and dysfunctional for management (and consumers), but if the wage increase endangers the firm's survival, it is dysfunctional for labor as well. This assumes, however, that the firm's survival is valued by the workers, which may not always be the case, for example, when jobs are available elsewhere.
3. Merton (1949, p. 50) originally described functions and dysfunctions in terms of encouraging or hindering adaptation or adjustment to a system, although subsequently he has written that "dysfunction refers to the particular inadequacies of a particular part of the system for a designated requirement" (1961, p. 732). Since adaptation and adjustment to a system can have conservative ideological implications, Merton's later formulation and my own definitional approach make it easier to use functional analysis as an ideologically neutral or at least ideologically variable method, insofar as the researcher can decide for himself whether he supports the values of the group under analysis.

guage of economic planning and systems analysis as benefits and costs.[4]

Identifying functions and dysfunctions for groups and aggregates rather than systems reduces the possibility that what is functional for one group in a multigroup system will be seen as being functional for the whole system, making it more difficult, for example, to suggest that a given phenomenon is functional for a corporation or political regime when it may in fact only be functional for their officers or leaders. Also, this approach precludes reaching a priori conclusions about two other important empirical questions raised by Merton (1949, pp. 32–36), whether any phenomenon is ever functional or dysfunctional for an entire society, and, if functional, whether it is therefore indispensable to that society.

In a modern heterogeneous society, few phenomena are functional or dysfunctional for the society as a whole, and most result in benefits to some groups and costs to others. Given the level of differentiation in modern society, I am even skeptical whether one can empirically identify a social system called society. Society exists, of course, but it is closer to being a very large aggregate, and when sociologists talk about society as a system, they often really mean the nation, a system which, among other things, sets up boundaries and other distinguishing characteristics between societal aggregates.

I would also argue that no social phenomenon is indispensable; it may be too powerful or too highly valued to be eliminated, but in most instances, one can suggest what Merton calls "functional alternatives" or equivalents for a social phenomena, that is, other social patterns or policies which achieve the same functions but avoid the dysfunctions.

III

The conventional view of American poverty is so dedicated to identifying the dysfunctions of poverty, both for the poor and the nation, that at first glance it seems inconceivable to suggest that poverty could be functional for anyone. Of course, the slum lord and the loan shark are widely known to profit from the existence of poverty; but they are popularly viewed as evil men, and their activities are, at least in part, dysfunctional for the poor. However, what is less often recognized, at least in the conventional wisdom, is that poverty also makes possible the existence or expansion of "respectable" professions and occupations, for example, penology, criminology, social work, and public health. More

4. It should be noted, however, that there are no absolute benefits and costs just as there are no absolute functions and dysfunctions; not only are one group's benefits often another group's costs, but every group defines benefits by its own manifest and latent values, and a social scientist or planner who has determined that certain phenomena provide beneficial consequences for a group may find that the group thinks otherwise. For example, during the 1960s, advocates of racial integration discovered that a significant portion of the black community no longer considered it a benefit but saw it rather as a policy to assimilate blacks into white society and to decimate the political power of the black community.

recently, the poor have provided jobs for professional and paraprofessional "poverty warriors," as well as journalists and social scientists, this author included, who have supplied the information demanded when public curiosity about the poor developed in the 1960s.

Clearly, then, poverty and the poor may well serve a number of functions for many nonpoor groups in American society, and I shall describe 15 sets of such functions—economic, social, cultural, and political—that seem to me most significant.

First, the existence of poverty makes sure that "dirty work" is done. Every economy has such work: physically dirty or dangerous, temporary, dead-end and underpaid, undignified, and menial jobs. These jobs can be filled by paying higher wages than for "clean" work, or by requiring people who have no other choice to do the dirty work and at low wages. In America, poverty functions to provide a low-wage labor pool that is willing—or, rather, unable to be unwilling—to perform dirty work at low cost. Indeed, this function is so important that in some Southern states, welfare payments have been cut off during the summer months when the poor are needed to work in the fields. Moreover, the debate about welfare—and about proposed substitutes such as the negative income tax and the Family Assistance Plan—has emphasized the impact of income grants on work incentive, with opponents often arguing that such grants would reduce the incentive of—actually, the pressure on—the poor to carry out the needed dirty work if the wages therefore are no larger than the income grant. Furthermore, many economic activities which involve dirty work depend heavily on the poor; restaurants, hospitals, parts of the garment industry, and industrial agriculture, among others, could not persist in their present form without their dependence on the substandard wages which they pay to their employees.

Second, the poor subsidize, directly and indirectly, many activities that benefit the affluent.[5] For one thing, they have long supported both the consumption and investment activities of the private economy by virtue of the low wages which they receive. This was openly recognized at the beginning of the Industrial Revolution, when a French writer quoted by T. H. Marshall (forthcoming, p. 7) pointed out that "to assure and maintain the prosperities of our industries, it is necessary that the workers should never acquire wealth." Examples of this kind of subsidization abound even today; for example, domestics subsidize the upper middle and upper classes, making life easier for their employers and freeing affluent women for a variety of professional, cultural, civic, or social activities. In addition, as Barry Schwartz pointed out (personal communication), the low income of the poor enables the rich to divert a

---

5. Of course, the poor do not actually subsidize the affluent. Rather, by being forced to work for low wages, they enable the affluent to use the money saved in this fashion for other purposes. The concept of subsidy used here thus assumes belief in a "just wage."

higher proportion of their income to savings and investment, and thus to fuel economic growth. This, in turn, can produce higher incomes for everybody, including the poor, although it does not necessarily improve the position of the poor in the socioeconomic hierarchy, since the benefits of economic growth are also distributed unequally.

At the same time, the poor subsidize the governmental economy. Because local property and sales taxes and the ungraduated income taxes levied by many states are regressive, the poor pay a higher percentage of their income in taxes than the rest of the population, thus subsidizing the many state and local governmental programs that serve more affluent taxpayers.[6] In addition, the poor support medical innovation as patients in teaching and research hospitals, and as guinea pigs in medical experiments, subsidizing the more affluent patients who alone can afford these innovations once they are incorporated into medical practice.

Third, poverty creates jobs for a number of occupations and professions which serve the poor, or shield the rest of the population from them. As already noted, penology would be miniscule without the poor, as would the police, since the poor provide the majority of their "clients." Other activities which flourish because of the existence of poverty are the numbers game, the sale of heroin and cheap wines and liquors, pentecostal ministers, faith healers, prostitutes, pawn shops, and the peacetime army, which recruits its enlisted men mainly from among the poor.

Fourth, the poor buy goods which others do not want and thus prolong their economic usefulness, such as day-old bread, fruit and vegetables which would otherwise have to be thrown out, second-hand clothes, and deteriorating automobiles and buildings. They also provide incomes for doctors, lawyers, teachers, and others who are too old, poorly trained, or incompetent to attract more affluent clients.

In addition, the poor perform a number of social and cultural functions:

Fifth, the poor can be identified and punished as alleged or real deviants in order to uphold the legitimacy of dominant norms (Macarov 1970, pp. 31–33). The defenders of the desirability of hard work, thrift, honesty, and monogamy need people who can be accused of being lazy, spendthrift, dishonest, and promiscuous to justify these norms; and as Erikson (1964) and others following Durkheim have pointed out, the norms themselves are best legitimated by discovering violations.

Whether the poor actually violate these norms more than affluent people is still open to question. The working poor work harder and longer than high-status jobholders, and poor housewives must do more housework to keep their slum apartments clean than their middle-class peers

---

6. Pechman (1969) and Herriott and Miller (1971) found that the poor pay a higher proportion of their income in taxes than any other part of the population: 50% among people earning $2,000 or less according to the latter study.

in standard housing. The proportion of cheaters among welfare recipients is quite low and considerably lower than among income taxpayers.[7] Violent crime is higher among the poor, but the affluent commit a variety of white-collar crimes, and several studies of self-reported delinquency have concluded that middle-class youngsters are sometimes as delinquent as the poor. However, the poor are more likely to be caught when participating in deviant acts and, once caught, to be punished more often than middle-class transgressors. Moreover, they lack the political and cultural power to correct the stereotypes that affluent people hold of them, and thus continue to be thought of as lazy, spendthrift, etc., whatever the empirical evidence, by those who need living proof that deviance does not pay.[8] The actually or allegedly deviant poor have traditionally been described as undeserving and, in more recent terminology, culturally deprived or pathological.

Sixth, another group of poor, described as deserving because they are disabled or suffering from bad luck, provide the rest of the population with different emotional satisfactions; they evoke compassion, pity, and charity, thus allowing those who help them to feel that they are altruistic, moral, and practicing the Judeo-Christian ethic. The deserving poor also enable others to feel fortunate for being spared the deprivations that come with poverty.[9]

Seventh, as a converse of the fifth function described previously, the poor offer affluent people vicarious participation in the uninhibited sexual, alcoholic, and narcotic behavior in which many poor people are alleged to indulge, and which, being freed from the constraints of affluence and respectability, they are often thought to enjoy more than the middle classes. One of the popular beliefs about welfare recipients is that many are on a permanent sex-filled vacation. Although it may be true that the poor are more given to uninhibited behavior, studies by Rainwater (1970) and other observers of the lower class indicate that such behavior is as often motivated by despair as by lack of inhibition, and that it results less in pleasure than in a compulsive escape from grim reality. However, whether the poor actually have more sex and enjoy it more than affluent people is irrelevant; as long as the latter believe it to be so, they can share it vicariously and perhaps enviously when instances

7. Most official investigations of welfare cheating have concluded that less than 5% of recipients are on the rolls illegally, while it has been estimated that about a third of the population cheats in filing income tax returns.
8. Although this paper deals with the functions of poverty for other groups, poverty has often been described as a motivating or character-building device for the poor themselves; and economic conservatives have argued that by generating the incentive to work, poverty encourages the poor to escape poverty. For an argument that work incentive is more enhanced by income than lack of it, see Gans (1971, p. 96).
9. One psychiatrist (Chernus 1967) has even proposed the fantastic hypothesis that the rich and the poor are engaged in a sadomasochistic relationship, the latter being supported financially by the former so that they can gratify their sadistic needs.

are reported in fictional, journalistic, or sociological and anthropological formats.

Eighth, poverty helps to guarantee the status of those who are not poor. In a stratified society, where social mobility is an especially important goal and class boundaries are fuzzy, people need to know quite urgently where they stand. As a result, the poor function as a reliable and relatively permanent measuring rod for status comparison, particularly for the working class, which must find and maintain status distinctions between itself and the poor, much as the aristocracy must find ways of distinguishing itself from the *nouveau riche*.

Ninth, the poor also assist in the upward mobility of the nonpoor, for, as Goode has pointed out (1967, p. 5), "the privileged . . . try systematically to prevent the talent of the less privileged from being recognized or developed." By being denied educational opportunities or being stereotyped as stupid or unteachable, the poor thus enable others to obtain the better jobs. Also, an unknown number of people have moved themselves or their children up in the socioeconomic hierarchy through the incomes earned from the provision of goods and services in the slums: by becoming policemen and teachers, owning "Mom and Pop" stores, or working in the various rackets that flourish in the slums.

In fact, members of almost every immigrant group have financed their upward mobility by providing retail goods and services, housing, entertainment, gambling, narcotics, etc., to later arrivals in America (or in the city), most recently to blacks, Mexicans, and Puerto Ricans. Other Americans, of both European and native origin, have financed their entry into the upper middle and upper classes by owning or managing the illegal institutions that serve the poor, as well as the legal but not respectable ones, such as slum housing.

Tenth, just as the poor contribute to the economic viability of a number of businesses and professions (see function 3 above), they also add to the social viability of noneconomic groups. For one thing, they help to keep the aristocracy busy, thus justifying its continued existence. "Society" uses the poor as clients of settlement houses and charity benefits; indeed, it must have the poor to practice its public-mindedness so as to demonstrate its superiority over the *nouveaux riches* who devote themselves to conspicuous consumption. The poor play a similar function for philanthropic enterprises at other levels of the socioeconomic hierarchy, including the mass of middle-class civic organizations and women's clubs engaged in volunteer work and fundraising in almost every American community. Doing good among the poor has traditionally helped the church to find a method of expressing religious sentiments in action; in recent years, militant church activity among and for the poor has enabled the church to hold on to its more liberal and radical members who might otherwise have dropped out of organized religion altogether.

Eleventh, the poor perform several cultural functions. They have played an unsung role in the creation of "civilization," having supplied the construction labor for many of the monuments which are often identified as the noblest expressions and examples of civilization, for example, the Egyptian pyramids, Greek temples, and medieval churches.[10] Moreover, they have helped to create a goodly share of the surplus capital that funds the artists and intellectuals who make culture, and particularly "high" culture, possible in the first place.

Twelfth, the "low" culture created for or by the poor is often adopted by the more affluent. The rich collect artifacts from extinct folk cultures (although not only from poor ones), and almost all Americans listen to the jazz, blues, spirituals, and country music which originated among the Southern poor—as well as rock, which was derived from similar sources. The protest of the poor sometimes becomes literature; in 1970, for example, poetry written by ghetto children became popular in sophisticated literary circles. The poor also serve as culture heroes and literary subjects, particularly, of course, for the Left, but the hobo, cowboy, hipster, and the mythical prostitute with a heart of gold have performed this function for a variety of groups.

Finally, the poor carry out a number of important political functions:

Thirteenth, the poor serve as symbolic constituencies and opponents for several political groups. For example, parts of the revolutionary Left could not exist without the poor, particularly now that the working class can no longer be perceived as the vanguard of the revolution. Conversely, political groups of conservative bent need the "welfare chiselers" and others who "live off the taxpayer's hard-earned money" in order to justify their demands for reductions in welfare payments and tax relief. Moreover, the role of the poor in upholding dominant norms (see function 5 above) also has a significant political function. An economy based on the ideology of laissez faire requires a deprived population which is allegedly unwilling to work; not only does the alleged moral inferiority of the poor reduce the moral pressure on the present political economy to eliminate poverty, but redistributive alternatives can be made to look quite unattractive if those who will benefit from them most can be described as lazy, spendthrift, dishonest, and promiscuous. Thus, conservatives and classical liberals would find it difficult to justify many of their political beliefs without the poor; but then so would modern liberals and socialists who seek to eliminate poverty.

Fourteenth, the poor, being powerless, can be made to absorb the economic and political costs of change and growth in American society. During the 19th century, they did the backbreaking work that built the cities; today, they are pushed out of their neighborhoods to make room for "progress." Urban renewal projects to hold middle-class taxpayers and stores in the city and expressways to enable suburbanites to com-

10. Although this is not a contemporary function of poverty in America, it should be noted that today these monuments serve to attract and gratify American tourists.

mute downtown have typically been located in poor neighborhoods, since no other group will allow itself to be displaced. For much the same reason, urban universities, hospitals, and civic centers also expand into land occupied by the poor. The major costs of the industrialization of agriculture in America have been borne by the poor, who are pushed off the land without recompense, just as in earlier centuries in Europe, they bore the brunt of the transformation of agrarian societies into industrial ones. The poor have also paid a large share of the human cost of the growth of American power overseas, for they have provided many of the foot soldiers for Vietnam and other wars.

Fifteenth, the poor have played an important role in shaping the American political process; because they vote and participate less than other groups, the political system has often been free to ignore them. This has not only made American politics more centrist than would otherwise be the case, but it has also added to the stability of the political process. If the 15% of the population below the federal "poverty line" participated fully in the political process, they would almost certainly demand better jobs and higher incomes, which would require income redistribution and would thus generate further political conflict between the haves and the have-nots. Moreover, when the poor do participate, they often provide the Democrats with a captive constituency, for they can rarely support Republicans, lack parties of their own, and thus have no other place to go politically. This, in turn, has enabled the Democrats to count on the votes of the poor, allowing the party to be more responsive to voters who might otherwise switch to the Republicans, in recent years, for example, the white working class.

IV

I have described fifteen of the more important functions which the poor carry out in American society, enough to support the functionalist thesis that poverty survives in part because it is useful to a number of groups in society. This analysis is not intended to suggest that because it is functional, poverty *should* persist, or that it *must* persist. Whether it should persist is a normative question; whether it must, an analytic and empirical one, but the answer to both depends in part on whether the dysfunctions of poverty outweigh the functions. Obviously, poverty has many dysfunctions, mainly for the poor themselves but also for the more affluent. For example, their social order is upset by the pathology, crime, political protest, and disruption emanating from the poor, and the income of the affluent is affected by the taxes that must be levied to protect their social order. Whether the dysfunctions outweigh the functions is a question that clearly deserves study.

It is, however, possible to suggest alternatives for many of the functions of the poor. Thus, society's dirty work (function 1) could be done without poverty, some by automating it, the rest by paying the workers who do it decent wages, which would help considerably to cleanse that kind of work. Nor is it necessary for the poor to subsidize the activities they support through their low-wage jobs (function 2), for, like dirty work, many of these activities are essential enough to persist even if wages were raised. In both instances, however, costs would be driven up, resulting in higher prices to the customers and clients of dirty work and subsidized activity, with obvious dysfunctional consequences for more affluent people.

Alternative roles for the professionals who flourish because of the poor (function 3) are easy to suggest. Social workers could counsel the affluent, as most prefer to do anyway, and the police could devote themselves to traffic and organized crime. Fewer penologists would be employable, however, and pentecostal religion would probably not survive without the poor. Nor would parts of the second- and third-hand market (function 4), although even affluent people sometimes buy used goods. Other roles would have to be found for badly trained or incompetent professionals now relegated to serving the poor, and someone else would have to pay their salaries.

Alternatives for the deviance-connected social functions (functions 5–7) can be found more easily and cheaply than for the economic functions. Other groups are already available to serve as deviants to uphold traditional morality, for example, entertainers, hippies, and most recently, adolescents in general. These same groups are also available as alleged or real orgiasts to provide vicarious participation in sexual fantasies. The blind and disabled function as objects of pity and charity, and the poor may therefore not even be needed for functions 5–7.

The status and mobility functions of the poor (functions 8 and 9) are far more difficult to substitute, however. In a hierarchical society, some people must be defined as inferior to everyone else with respect to a variety of attributes, and the poor perform this function more adequately than others. They could, however, perform it without being as poverty-stricken as they are, and one can conceive of a stratification system in which the people below the federal "poverty line" would receive 75% of the median income rather than 40% or less, as is now the case—even though they would still be last in the pecking order.[11] Needless to say, such a reduction of economic inequality would also require income redistribution. Given the opposition to income redistribution among more affluent people, however, it seems unlikely that the status functions of poverty can be replaced, and they—together with the economic functions of the poor, which are equally expensive to replace—may turn out to be the major obstacles to the elimination of poverty.

11. In 1971, the median family income in the United States was about $10,000, and the federal poverty line for a family of four was set at just about $4,000. Of course, most of the poor were earning less than 40% of the median, and about a third of them, less than 20% of the median.

The role of the poor in the upward mobility of other groups could be maintained without their being so low in income. However, if their incomes were raised above subsistence levels, they would begin to generate capital so that their own entrepreneurs could supply them with goods and services, thus competing with and perhaps rejecting "outside" suppliers. Indeed, this is already happening in a number of ghettoes, where blacks are replacing white storeowners.

Similarly, if the poor were more affluent, they would make less willing clients for upper- and middle-class philanthropic and religious groups (function 10), although as long as they are economically and otherwise unequal, this function need not disappear altogether. Moreover, some would still use the settlement houses and other philanthropic institutions to pursue individual upward mobility, as they do now.

The cultural functions (11 and 12) may not need to be replaced. In America, the labor unions have rarely allowed the poor to help build cultural monuments anyway, and there is sufficient surplus capital from other sources to subsidize the unprofitable components of high culture. Similarly, other deviant groups are available to innovate in popular culture and supply new culture heroes, for example, the hippies and members of other counter-cultures.

Some of the political functions of the poor would, however, be as difficult to replace as their economic and status functions. Although the poor could probably continue to serve as symbolic constituencies and opponents (function 13) if their incomes were raised while they remained unequal in other respects, increases in income are generally accompanied by increases in power as well. Consequently, once they were no longer so poor, people would be likely to resist paying the costs of growth and change (function 14); and it is difficult to find alternative groups who can be displaced for urban renewal and technological "progress." Of course, it is possible to design city-rebuilding and highway projects which properly reimburse the displaced people, but such projects would then become considerably more expensive, thus raising the price for those now benefiting from urban renewal and expressways. Alternatively, many might never be built, thus reducing the comfort and convenience of those beneficiaries. Similarly, if the poor were subjected to less economic pressure, they would probably be less willing to serve in the army, except at considerably higher pay, in which case war would become yet more costly and thus less popular politically. Alternatively, more servicemen would have to be recruited from the middle and upper classes, but in that case war would also become less popular.

The political stabilizing and "centering" role of the poor (function 15) probably cannot be substituted for at all, since no other group is willing to be disenfranchised or likely enough to remain apathetic so as to reduce the fragility of the political system. Moreover, if the poor were given higher incomes, they would probably become more active politically, thus adding their demands for more to those of other groups already putting pressure on the political allocators of resources. The poor might continue to remain loyal to the Democratic party, but like other moderate-income voters, they could also be attracted to the Republicans or to third parties. While improving the economic status of the presently poor would not necessarily drive the political system far to the left, it would enlarge the constituencies now demanding higher wages and more public funds. It is of course possible to add new powerless groups who do not vote or otherwise participate to the political mix and can thus serve as "ballast" in the polity, for example, by encouraging the import of new poor immigrants from Europe and elsewhere, except that the labor unions are probably strong enough to veto such a policy.

In sum, then, several of the most important functions of the poor cannot be replaced with alternatives, while some could be replaced, but almost always only at higher costs to other people, particularly more affluent ones. Consequently, *a functional analysis must conclude that poverty persists not only because it satisfies a number of functions but also because many of the functional alternatives to poverty would be quite dysfunctional for the more affluent members of society.*[12]

V

I noted earlier that functional analysis had itself become a maligned phenomenon and that a secondary purpose of this paper was to demonstrate its continued usefulness. One reason for its presently low status is political; insofar as an analysis of functions, particularly latent functions, seems to justify what ought to be condemned, it appears to lend itself to the support of conservative ideological positions, although it can also have radical implications when it subverts the conventional wisdom. Still, as Merton has pointed out (1949, p. 43; 1961, pp. 736–37), functional analysis per se is ideologically neutral, and "like other forms of sociological analysis, it can be infused with any of a wide range of sociological values" (1949, p. 40). This infusion depends, of course, on the purposes —and even the functions—of the functional analysis, for as Wirth (1936, p. xvii) suggested long ago, "every assertion of a 'fact' about the social world touches the interests of some individual or group," and even if functional analyses are conceived and conducted in a neutral manner, they are rarely interpreted in an ideological vacuum.

In one sense, my analysis is, however, neutral; if one makes no judgment as to whether poverty ought to be eliminated—and if one can subsequently avoid being accused of acquiescing in poverty—then the analysis suggests only that poverty exists because it is useful to many

12. Or as Stein (1971, p. 171) puts it: "If the non-poor make the rules . . . antipoverty efforts will only be made up to the point where the needs of the non-poor are satisfied, rather than the needs of the poor."

groups in society.[13] If one favors the elimination of poverty, however, then the analysis can have a variety of political implications, *depending in part on how completely it is carried out.*

If functional analysis only identifies the functions of social phenomena without mentioning their dysfunctions, then it may, intentionally or otherwise, agree with or support holders of conservative values. Thus, to say that the poor perform many functions for the rich might be interpreted or used to justify poverty, just as Davis and Moore's argument (1945) that social stratification is functional because it provides society with highly trained professionals could be taken to justify inequality.

Actually, the Davis and Moore analysis was conservative because it was incomplete; it did not identify the dysfunctions of inequality and failed to suggest functional alternatives, as Tumin (1953) and Schwartz (1955) have pointed out.[14] Once a functional analysis is made more complete by the addition of functional alternatives, however, it can take on a liberal and reform cast, because the alternatives often provide ameliorative policies that do not require any drastic change in the existing social order.

Even so, to make functional analysis complete requires yet another step, an examination of the functional alternatives themselves. My analysis suggests that the alternatives for poverty are themselves dysfunctional for the affluent population, and it ultimately comes to a conclusion which is not very different from that of radical sociologists. To wit: *that social phenomena which are functional for affluent groups and dysfunctional for poor ones persist; that when the elimination of such phenomena through functional alternatives generates dysfunctions for the affluent, they will continue to persist; and that phenomena like poverty can be eliminated only when they either become sufficiently dysfunctional for the affluent or when the poor can obtain enough power to change the system of social stratification.*[15]

---

13. Of course, even in this case the analysis need not be purely neutral, but can be put to important policy uses, for example, by indicating more effectively than moral attacks on poverty the exact nature of the obstacles that must be overcome if poverty is to be eliminated. See also Merton (1961, pp. 709–12).

14. Functional analysis can, of course, be conservative in value or have conservative implications for a number of other reasons, principally in its overt or covert comparison of the advantages of functions and disadvantages of dysfunctions, or in its attitudes toward the groups that are benefiting and paying the costs. Thus, a conservatively inclined policy researcher could conclude that the dysfunctions of poverty far outnumber the functions, but still decide that the needs of the poor are simply not as important or worthy as those of other groups, or of the country as a whole.

15. On the possibility of radical functional analysis, see Merton (1949, pp. 40–43) and Gouldner (1970, p. 443). One difference between my analysis and the prevailing radical view is that most of the functions I have described are latent, whereas many radicals treat them as manifest: recognized and intended by an unjust economic system to oppress the poor. Practically speaking, however, this difference may be unimportant, for if unintended and unrecognized functions were recognized, many affluent people might then decide that they ought to be intended as well, so as to forestall a more expensive antipoverty effort that might be dysfunctional for the affluent.

References

Chernus, J. 1967. "Cities: A Study in Sadomasochism." *Medical Opinion and Review* (May), pp. 104–9.

Davis, K., and W. E. Moore. 1945. "Some Principles of Stratification." *American Sociological Review* 10 (April): 242–49.

Erikson, K. T. 1964. "Notes on the Sociology of Deviance." In *The Other Side*, edited by Howard S. Becker. New York: Free Press.

Gans, H. J. 1971. "Three Ways to Solve the Welfare Problem." *New York Times Magazine*, March 7, pp. 26–27, 94–100.

Goode, W. J. 1967. "The Protection of the Inept." *American Sociological Review* 32 (February): 5–19.

Gouldner, A. 1970. *The Coming Crisis of Western Sociology.* New York: Basic.

Herriot, A., and H. P. Miller. 1971. "Who Paid the Taxes in 1968." Paper prepared for the National Industrial Conference Board.

Macarov, D. 1970. *Incentives to Work.* San Francisco: Jossey-Bass.

Marshall, T. H. Forthcoming. "Poverty and Inequality." Paper prepared for the American Academy of Arts and Sciences volume on poverty and stratification.

Merton, R. K. 1949. "Manifest and Latent Functions." In *Social Theory and Social Structure.* Glencoe, Ill.: Free Press.

———. 1961. "Social Problems and Sociological Theory." In *Contemporary Social Problems*, edited by R. K. Merton and R. Nisbet. New York: Harcourt Brace.

Pechman, J. A. 1969. "The Rich, the Poor, and the Taxes They Pay." *Public Interest*, no. 17 (Fall), pp. 21–43.

Rainwater, L. 1970. *Behind Ghetto Walls.* Chicago: Aldine.

Schwartz, R. 1955. "Functional Alternatives to Inequality." *American Sociological Review* 20 (August): 424–30.

Stein, B. 1971. *On Relief.* New York: Basic.

Tumin, M. B. 1953. "Some Principles of Stratification: A Critical Analysis." *American Sociological Review* 18 (August): 387–93.

Wirth, L. 1936. "Preface." In *Ideology and Utopia*, by Karl Mannheim. New York: Harcourt Brace.

5

Racism and Research: The Case of the Tuskegee Syphilis Study

ALLAN M. BRANDT

Was it scientific zeal and the search for knowledge that led to this terrible episode in American scientific research? Or, was it a callous disregard for the lives and suffering of persons thought to be inferior in a racist society? Probably both, but the lessons remain important for everyone.

In 1932 the U.S. Public Health Service (USPHS) initiated an experiment in Macon County, Alabama, to determine the natural course of untreated, latent syphilis in black males. The test comprised 400 syphilitic men, as well as 200 uninfected men who served as controls. The first published report of the study appeared in 1936 with subsequent papers issued every four to six years, through the 1960s. When penicillin became widely available by the early 1950s as the preferred treatment for syphilis, the men did not receive therapy. In fact on several occasions, the USPHS actually sought to prevent treatment. Moreover, a committee at the federally operated Center for Disease Control decided in 1969 that the study should be continued. Only in 1972, when accounts of the study first appeared in the national press, did the Department of Health, Education, and Welfare halt the experiment. At that time seventy-four of the test subjects were still alive; at least twenty-eight, but perhaps more than 100 had died directly from advanced syphilitic lesions. In August 1972, HEW appointed an investigatory panel which issued a report the following year. The panel found the study to have been "ethically unjustified," and argued that penicillin should have been provided to the men.

This article attempts to place the Tuskegee Study in a historical context and to assess its ethical implications. Despite the media attention which the study received, the HEW *Final Report*, and the criticism expressed by several professional organizations, the experiment has been largely misunderstood. The most basic questions of *how* the study was undertaken in the first place and *why* it continued for forty years were never addressed by the HEW investigation. Moreover, the panel misconstrued the nature of the experiment, failing to consult important documents available at the National Archives which bear significantly on its ethical assessment. Only by examining the specific ways in which values are engaged in scientific research can the study be understood.

RACISM AND MEDICAL OPINION

A brief review of the prevailing scientific thought regarding race and heredity in the early twentieth century is fundamental for an understanding of the Tuskegee Study. By the turn of the century, Darwinism had provided a new rationale for American racism. Essentially primitive peoples, it was argued, could not be assimilated into a complex, white civilization. Scientists speculated that in the struggle for survival the Negro in America was doomed. Particularly prone to disease, vice, and crime, black Americans could not be helped by education or philanthropy. Social Darwinists analyzed census data to predict the virtual extinction of the Negro in the twentieth century, for they believed the Negro race in America was in the throes of a degenerative evolutionary process.

The medical profession supported these findings of late nineteenth- and early twentieth-century anthropologists, ethnologists, and biologists. Physicians studying the effects of emancipation on health concluded almost universally that freedom had caused the mental, moral, and physical deterioration of the black population. They substantiated this argument by citing examples in the comparative anatomy of the black and white races. As Dr. W. T. English wrote: "A careful inspection reveals the body of the negro a mass of minor defects and imperfections from the crown of the head to the soles of the feet. . . ." Cranial structures, wide nasal apertures, receding chins, projecting jaws, all typed the Negro as the lowest species in the Darwinian hierarchy.

Interest in racial differences centered on the sexual nature of blacks. The Negro, doctors explained, possessed an excessive sexual desire, which threatened the very foundations of white society. As one physician noted in the *Journal of the American Medical Association*, "The negro springs from a southern race, and as such his sexual appetite is strong; all of his environments stimulate this appetite, and as a general rule his emotional type of religion certainly does not decrease it." Doctors reported a complete lack of morality on the part of blacks:

> Virtue in the negro race is like angels' visits—few and far between. In a practice of sixteen years I have never examined a virgin negro over fourteen years of age.

A particularly ominous feature of this overzealous sexuality, doctors argued, was the black males' desire for white women. "A perversion from which most races are exempt," wrote Dr. English, "prompts the negro's inclination towards white women, whereas other races incline towards females of their own." Though English estimated the "gray matter of the negro brain" to be at least a thousand years behind that of the white races, his genital organs were overdeveloped. As Dr. William Lee Howard noted:

The attacks on defenseless white women are evidences of racial instincts that are about as amenable to ethical culture as is the inherent odor of the race. . . . When education will reduce the size of the negro's penis as well as bring about the sensitiveness of the terminal fibers which exist in the Caucasian, then will it also be able to prevent the African's birth-right to sexual madness and excess.

One southern medical journal proposed "Castration Instead of Lynching," as retribution for black sexual crimes. "An impressive trial by a ghost-like kuklux klan [sic] and a 'ghost' physician or surgeon to perform the operation would make it an event the 'patient' would never forget," noted the editorial.

According to these physicians, lust and immorality, unstable families, and reversion to barbaric tendencies made blacks especially prone to venereal diseases. One doctor estimated that over 50 percent of all Negroes over the age of twenty-five were syphilitic. Virtually free of disease as slaves, they were now overwhelmed by it, according to informed medical opinion. Moreover, doctors believed that treatment for venereal disease among blacks was impossible, particularly because in its latent stage the symptoms of syphilis become quiescent. As Dr. Thomas W. Murrell wrote:

They come for treatment at the beginning and at the end. When there are visible manifestations or when harried by pain, they readily come, for as a race they are not averse to physic; but tell them not, though they look well and feel well, that they are still diseased. Here ignorance rates science a fool. . . .

Even the best educated black, according to Murrell, could not be convinced to seek treatment for syphilis. Venereal disease, according to some doctors, threatened the future of the race. The medical profession attributed the low birth rate among blacks to the high prevalence of venereal disease which caused stillbirths and miscarriages. Moreover, the high rates of syphilis were thought to lead to increased insanity and crime. One doctor writing at the turn of the century estimated that the number of insane Negroes had increased thirteen-fold since the end of the Civil War. Dr. Murrell's conclusion echoed the most informed anthropological and ethnological data:

So the scourge sweeps among them. Those that are treated are only half cured, and the effort to assimilate a complex civilization driving their diseased minds until the results are criminal records. Perhaps here, in conjunction with tuberculosis, will be the end of the negro problem. Disease will accomplish what man cannot do.

This particular configuration of ideas formed the core of medical opinion concerning blacks, sex, and disease in the early twentieth century. Doctors generally discounted socioeconomic explanations of the state of black health, arguing that better medical care could not alter the evolutionary scheme. These assumptions provide the backdrop for examining the Tuskegee Syphilis Study.

THE ORIGINS OF THE EXPERIMENT

In 1929, under a grant from the Julius Rosenwald Fund, the USPHS conducted studies in the rural South to determine the prevalence of syphilis among blacks and explore possibilities for mass treatment. The USPHS found Macon County, Alabama, in which the town of Tuskegee is located to have the highest syphilis rate of the six counties surveyed. The Rosenwald Study concluded that mass treatment could be successfully implemented among rural blacks. Although it is doubtful that the necessary funds would have been allocated even in the best economic conditions, after the economy collapsed in 1929, the findings were ignored. It is, however, ironic that the Tuskegee Study came to be based on findings of the Rosenwald Study that demonstrated the possibilities of mass treatment.

Three years later, in 1932, Dr. Taliaferro Clark, Chief of the USPHS Venereal Disease Division and author of the Rosenwald Study report, decided that conditions in Macon County merited renewed attention. Clark believed the high prevalence of syphilis offered an "unusual opportunity" for observation. From its inception, the USPHS regarded the Tuskegee Study as a classic "study in nature,"[1] rather than an experiment. As long as syphilis was so prevalent in Macon and most of the blacks went untreated throughout life, it seemed only natural to Clark that it would be valuable to observe the consequences. He described it as a "ready-made situation." Surgeon General H. S. Cumming wrote to R. R. Moton, Director of the Tuskegee Institute:

> The recent syphilis control demonstration carried out in Macon County, with the financial assistance of the Julius Rosenwald Fund, revealed the presence of an unusually high rate in this county and, what is more remarkable, the fact that 99 per cent of this group was entirely without previous treatment. This combination, together with the expected cooperation of your hospital, offers an unparalleled opportunity for carrying on this piece of scientific research which probably cannot be duplicated anywhere else in the world.

Although no formal protocol appears to have been written, several letters of Clark and Cumming suggest what the USPHS hoped to find. Clark indicated that it would be important to see how disease affected the daily lives of the men:

1. In 1865, Claude Bernard, the famous French physiologist, outlined the distinction between a "study in nature" and experimentation. A study in nature required simple observation, an essentially passive act, while experimentation demanded intervention which altered the original condition. The Tuskegee Study was thus clearly not a study in nature. The very act of diagnosis altered the original conditions. "It is on this very possibility of acting or not acting on a body," wrote Bernard, "that the distinction will exclusively rest between sciences called sciences of observation and sciences called experimental."

The results of these studies of case records suggest the desirability of making a further study of the effect of untreated syphilis on the human economy among people now living and engaged in their daily pursuits.

It also seems that the USPHS believed the experiment might demonstrate that antisyphilitic treatment was unnecessary. As Cumming noted: "It is expected the results of this study may have a marked bearing on the treatment, or conversely the non-necessity of treatment, of cases of latent syphilis." . . .

Selecting the Subjects

Clark sent Dr. Raymond Vonderlehr to Tuskegee in September 1932 to assemble a sample of men with latent syphilis for the experiment. The basic design of the study called for the selection of syphilitic black males between the ages of twenty-five and sixty, a thorough physical examination including x-rays, and finally, a spinal tap to determine the incidence of neuro-syphilis. They had no intention of providing any treatment for the infected men. The USPHS originally scheduled the whole experiment to last six months; it seemed to be both a simple and inexpensive project.

The task of collecting the sample, however, proved to be more difficult than the USPHS had supposed. Vonderlehr canvassed the largely illiterate, poverty-stricken population of sharecroppers and tenant farmers in search of test subjects. If his circulars requested only men over twenty-five to attend his clinics, none would appear, suspecting he was conducting draft physicals. Therefore, he was forced to test large numbers of women and men who did not fit the experiment's specifications. This involved considerable expense since the USPHS had promised the Macon County Board of Health that it would treat those who were infected, but not included in the study. Clark wrote to Vonderlehr about the situation: "It never once occurred to me that we would be called upon to treat a large part of the county as return for the privilege of making this study. . . . I am anxious to keep the expenditures for treatment down to the lowest possible point because it is the one item of expenditure in connection with the study most difficult to defend despite our knowledge of the need therefor." Vonderlehr responded: "If we could find from 100 to 200 cases . . . we would not have to do another Wassermann on useless individuals. . . ."

Significantly, the attempt to develop the sample contradicted the prediction the USPHS had made initially regarding the prevalence of the disease in Macon County. Overall rates of syphilis fell well below expectations; as opposed to the USPHS projection of 35 percent, 20 percent of those tested were actually diseased. Moreover, those who had sought and received previous treatment far exceeded the expectations of the USPHS. Clark noted in a letter to Vonderlehr:

> I find your report of March 6th quite interesting but regret the necessity for Wassermanning [sic] . . . such a large number of individuals in order to uncover this relatively limited number of untreated cases.

Further difficulties arose in enlisting the subjects to participate in the experiment, to be "Wassermanned," and to return for a subsequent series of examinations. Vonderlehr found that only the offer of treatment elicited the cooperation of the men. They were told they were ill and were promised free care. Offered therapy, they became willing subjects. The USPHS did not tell the men that they were participants in an experiment; on the contrary, the subjects believed they were being treated for "bad blood"—the rural South's colloquialism for syphilis. They thought they were participating in a public health demonstration similar to the one that had been conducted by the Julius Rosenwald Fund in Tuskegee several years earlier. In the end, the men were so eager for medical care that the number of defaulters in the experiment proved to be insignificant.

To preserve the subjects' interest, Vonderlehr gave most of the men mercurial ointment, a noneffective drug, while some of the younger men apparently received inadequate dosages of neoarsphenamine. This required Vonderlehr to write frequently to Clark requesting supplies. He feared the experiment would fail if the men were not offered treatment. . . .

The readiness of the test subjects to participate of course contradicted the notion that blacks would not seek or continue therapy.

The final procedure of the experiment was to be a spinal tap to test for evidence of neuro-syphilis. The USPHS presented this purely diagnostic exam, which often entails considerable pain and complications, to the men as a "special treatment." Clark explained to Moore:

> We have not yet commenced the spinal punctures. This operation will be deferred to the last in order not to unduly disturb our field work by any adverse reports by the patients subjected to spinal puncture because of some disagreeable sensations following this procedure. These negroes are very ignorant and easily influenced by things that would be of minor significance in a more intelligent group.

The letter to the subjects announcing the spinal tap read:

> Some time ago you were given a thorough examination and since that time we hope you have gotten a great deal of treatment for bad blood. You will now be given your last chance to get a second examination. This examination is a very special one and after it is finished you will be given a special treatment if it is believed you are in a condition to stand it. . . .
> REMEMBER THIS IS YOUR LAST CHANCE FOR SPECIAL FREE TREATMENT. BE SURE TO MEET THE NURSE.

The HEW investigation did not uncover this crucial fact: the men participated in the study under the guise of treatment.

Despite the fact that their assumption regarding prevalence and black attitudes toward treatment had proved wrong, the USPHS decided in the summer of 1933 to continue the study. Once again, it seemed only "natural" to pursue the research since the sample already existed, and with a depressed economy, the cost of treatment appeared prohibitive— although there is no indication it was ever considered. Vonderlehr first suggested extending the study in letters to Clark and Wenger:

> At the end of this project we shall have a considerable number of cases presenting various complications of syphilis, who have received only mercury and may still be considered untreated in the modern sense of therapy. Should these cases be followed over a period of from five to ten years many interesting facts could be learned regarding the course and complications of untreated syphilis.

"As I see it," responded Wenger, "we have no further interest in these patients *until they die*." Apparently, the physicians engaged in the experiment believed that only autopsies could scientifically confirm the findings of the study.

Bringing the men to autopsy required the USPHS to devise a further series of deceptions and inducements. Wenger warned Vonderlehr that the men must not realize that they would be autopsied:

> There is one danger in the latter plan and that is if the colored population become aware that accepting free hospital care means a post-mortem, every darkey will leave Macon County and it will hurt [Dr. Eugene] Dibble's hospital.

The USPHS offered several inducements to maintain contact and to procure the continued cooperation of the men. Eunice Rivers, a black nurse, was hired to follow their health and to secure approval for autopsies. She gave the men non-effective medicines—"spring tonic" and aspirin—as well as transportation and hot meals on the days of their examinations. More important, Nurse Rivers provided continuity to the project over the entire forty-year period. By supplying "medicinals," the USPHS was able to continue to deceive the participants, who believed that they were receiving therapy from the government doctors. Deceit was integral to the study. When the test subjects complained about spinal taps one doctor wrote:

> They simply do not like spinal punctures. A few of those who were tapped are enthusiastic over the results but to most, the suggestion causes violent shaking of the head; others claim they were robbed of their procreative powers (regardless of the fact that I claim it stimulates them).

Letters to the subjects announcing an impending USPHS visit to Tuskegee explained: "[The doctor] wants to make a special examination to find out how you have been feeling and whether the treatment has improved your health." In fact, after the first six months of the study, the USPHS had furnished no treatment whatsoever.

Finally, because it proved difficult to persuade the men to come to the hospital when they became severely ill, the USPHS promised to cover their burial expenses. The Milbank Memorial Fund provided approximately $50 per man for this purpose beginning in 1935. This was a particularly strong inducement as funeral rites constituted an important component of the cultural life of rural blacks. One report of the study concluded. "Without this suasion it would, we believe, have been impossible to secure the cooperation of the group and their families."

Reports of the study's findings, which appeared regularly in the medical press beginning in 1936, consistently cited the ravages of untreated syphilis. The first paper, read at the 1936 American Medical Association annual meeting, found "that syphilis in this period [latency] tends to greatly increase the frequency of manifestations of cardiovascular disease." Only 16 percent of the subjects gave no sign of morbidity as opposed to 61 percent of the controls. Ten years later, a report noted coldly, "The fact that nearly twice as large a proportion of the syphilitic individuals as of the control group has died is a very striking one." Life expectancy, concluded the doctors, is reduced by about 20 percent.

A 1955 article found that slightly more than 30 percent of the test group autopsied had died *directly* from advanced syphilitic lesions of either the cardiovascular or the central nervous system. Another published account stated, "Review of those still living reveals that an appreciable number have late complications of syphilis which probably will result, for some at least, in contributing materially to the ultimate cause of death." In 1950, Dr. Wenger had concluded, "We now know, where we could only surmise before, that we have contributed to their ailments and shortened their lives." As black physician Vernal Cave, a member of the HEW panel, later wrote, "They proved a point, then proved a point, then proved a point."

During the forty years of the experiment the USPHS had sought on several occasions to ensure that the subjects did not receive treatment from other sources. To this end, Vonderlehr met with groups of local black doctors in 1934, to ask their cooperation in not treating the men. Lists of subjects were distributed to Macon County physicians along with letters requesting them to refer these men back to the USPHS if they sought care. The USPHS warned the Alabama Health Department not to treat the test subjects when they took a mobile VD unit into Tuskegee in the early 1940s. In 1941, the Army drafted several subjects and told them to begin antisyphilitic treatment immediately. The USPHS supplied the draft board with a list of 256 names they desired to have excluded from treatment, and the board complied.

In spite of these efforts, by the early 1950s many of the men had secured some treatment on their own. By 1952, almost 30 percent of the test subjects had received some penicillin, although only 7.5 percent had received what could be considered adequate doses. Vonderlehr wrote to one of the participating physicians, "I hope that the availability of antibiotics has not interfered too much with this project." A report published in 1955 considered whether the treatment that some of the men had obtained had "defeated" the study. The article attempted to explain the relatively low exposure to penicillin in an age of antibiotics, suggesting as a reason: "the stoicism of these men as a group; they still regard hospitals and medicines with suspicion and prefer an occasional dose of time-honored herbs or tonics to modern drugs." The authors failed to note that the men believed they already were under the care of the government doctors and thus saw no need to seek treatment elsewhere. Any treatment which the men might have received, concluded the report, had been insufficient to compromise the experiment.

When the USPHS evaluated the status of the study in the 1960s they continued to rationalize the racial aspects of the experiment. For example, the minutes of a 1965 meeting at the Center for Disease Control recorded:

> Racial issue was mentioned briefly. Will not affect the study. Any questions can be handled by saying these people were at the point that therapy would no longer help them. They are getting better medical care than they would under any other circumstances.

A group of physicians met again at the CDC in 1969 to decide whether or not to terminate the study. Although one doctor argued that the study should be stopped and the men treated, the consensus was to continue. Dr. J. Lawton Smith remarked, "You will never have another study like this; take advantage of it." A memo prepared by Dr. James B. Lucas, Assistant Chief of the Venereal Disease Branch, stated: "Nothing learned will prevent, find, or cure a single case of infectious syphilis or bring us closer to our basic mission of controlling venereal disease in the United States." He concluded, however, that the study should be continued "along its present lines." When the first accounts of the experiment appeared in the national press in July 1972, data were still being collected and autopsies performed.

THE HEW FINAL REPORT

HEW finally formed the Tuskegee Syphilis Study Ad Hoc Advisory Panel on August 28, 1972, in response to criticism that the press descriptions of the experiment had triggered. The panel, composed of nine members, five of them black, concentrated on two issues. First, was the study justified in 1932 and had the men given their informed consent? Second, should penicillin have been provided when it became available in the early 1950s? The panel was also charged with determining if the study should be terminated and assessing current policies regarding experimentation with human subjects. The group issued their report in June 1973.

By focusing on the issues of penicillin therapy and informed consent, the *Final Report* and the investigation betrayed a basic misunderstanding of the experiment's purposes and design. The HEW report implied that the failure to provide penicillin constituted the study's major ethical misjudgment; implicit was the assumption that no adequate therapy existed prior to penicillin. Nonetheless medical authorities firmly believed in the efficacy of arsenotherapy for treating syphilis at the time of the experiment's inception in 1932. The panel further failed to recognize that the entire study had been predicated on nontreatment. Provision of effective medication would have violated the rationale of the experiment—to study the natural course of the disease until death. On several occasions, in fact, the USPHS had prevented the men from receiving proper treatment. Indeed, there is no evidence that the USPHS ever considered providing penicillin.

The other focus of the *Final Report*—informed consent—also served to obscure the historical facts of the experiment. In light of the deceptions and exploitations which the experiment perpetrated, it is an understatement to declare, as the *Report* did, that the experiment was "ethically unjustified," because it failed to obtain informed consent from the subjects. The *Final Report's* statement, "Submitting voluntarily is not informed consent," indicated that the panel believed that the men had volunteered *for the experiment*. The records in the National Archives make clear that the men did not submit voluntarily to an experiment; they were told and they believed that they were getting free treatment from expert government doctors for a serious disease. The failure of the HEW *Final Report* to expose this critical fact—that the USPHS lied to the subjects—calls into question the thoroughness and credibility of their investigation.

Failure to place the study in a historical context also made it impossible for the investigation to deal with the essentially racist nature of the experiment. The panel treated the study as an aberration, well-intentioned but misguided. Moreover, concern that the *Final Report* might be viewed as a critique of human experimentation in general seems to have severely limited the scope of the inquiry. The *Final Report* is quick to remind the reader on two occasions: "The position of the Panel must not be construed to be a general repudiation of scientific research with human subjects." The *Report* assures as that a better designed experiment could have been justified:

> It is possible that a scientific study in 1932 of untreated syphilis, properly conceived with a clear protocol and conducted with suitable subjects who fully understood the implications of their involvement, might have been justified in the pre-penicillin era. This is especially true when one considers the uncertain nature of the results of treatment of late latent syphilis and the highly toxic nature of therapeutic agents then available.

This statement is questionable in view of the proven dangers of untreated syphilis known in 1932.

Since the publication of the HEW *Final Report*, a defense of the Tuskegee Study has emerged. These arguments, most clearly articulated by Dr. R. H. Kampmeier in the *Southern Medical Journal*, center on the limited knowledge of effective therapy for latent syphilis when the experiment began. Kampmeier argues that by 1950, penicillin would have been of no value for these men. Others have suggested that the men were fortunate to have been spared the highly toxic treatments of the earlier period. Moreover, even these contemporary defenses assume that the men never would have been treated anyway. As Dr. Charles Barnett of Stanford University wrote in 1974, "The lack of treatment was not contrived by the USPHS but was an established fact of which they proposed to take advantage." Several doctors who participated in the study continued to justify the experiment. Dr. J. R. Heller, who on one occasion had referred to the test subjects as the "Ethiopian population," told reporters in 1972:

> I don't see why they should be shocked or horrified. There was no racial side to this. It just happened to be in a black community. I feel this was a perfectly straightforward study, perfectly ethical, with controls. Part of our mission as physicians is to find out what happens to individuals with disease and without disease.

These apologies, as well as the HEW *Final Report*, ignore many of the essential ethical issues which the study poses, The Tuskegee Study reveals the persistence of beliefs within the medical profession about the nature of blacks, sex, and disease—beliefs that had tragic repercussions long after their alleged "scientific" bases were known to be incorrect. Most strikingly, the entire health of a community was jeopardized by leaving a communicable disease untreated. There can be little doubt that the Tuskegee researchers regarded their subjects as less than human. As a result, the ethical canons of experimenting on human subjects were completely disregarded.

The study also raises significant questions about professional self-regulation and scientific bureaucracy. Once the USPHS decided to extend the experiment in the summer of 1933, it was unlikely that the test would be halted short of the men's deaths. The experiment was widely reported for forty years without evoking any significant protest within the medical community. Nor did any bureaucratic mechanism exist within the government for the periodic reassessment of the Tuskegee experiment's ethics and scientific value. The USPHS sent physicians to Tuskegee every several years to check on the study's progress, but never subjected the morality or usefulness of the experiment to serious scrutiny. Only the press accounts of 1972 finally punctured the continued rationalizations of the USPHS and brought the study to an end. Even the HEW investigation was compromised by fear that it would be considered a threat to future human experimentation.

In retrospect the Tuskegee Study revealed more about the pathology of racism than it did about the pathology of syphilis; more about the nature of scientific inquiry than the nature of the disease process. The injustice committed by the experiment went well beyond the facts outlined in the press and the HEW *Final Report*. The degree of deception and damages have been seriously underestimated. As this history of the study suggests, the notion that science is a value-free discipline must be rejected. The need for greater vigilance in assessing the specific ways in which social values and attitudes affect professional behavior is clearly indicated.

6
The World of Pool Hustling

NED POLSKY

Many sociology students are lucky enough to recognize that nothing the sociologist does or sees is without some sociological value. Polsky's description of people he knew and things he was a part of uses the research method of participant-as-observer to show the often hidden and obscure interaction strategies of the serious poolroom.

METHOD AND SAMPLE

My study of poolroom hustling extended over eight months in 1962 and 1963. It proceeded by a combination of: (a) direct observation of hustlers as they hustled; (b) informal talks, sometimes hours long, with hustlers; (c) participant observation—as hustler's opponent, as hustler's backer, and as hustler. Since methods (b) and (c) drew heavily on my personal involvement with the poolroom world, indeed are inseparable from it, I summarize aspects of that involvement below.

Billiard playing is my chief recreation. I have frequented poolrooms for over 20 years, and at one poolroom game, three-cushion billiards, am considered a far better than average player. In recent years I have played an average of more than six hours per week in various New York poolrooms, and played as much in the poolrooms of Chicago for most of the eight years I lived there. In the course of traveling I have played occasionally in the major rooms of other cities, such as the poolrooms on Market Street in San Francisco, West 25th Street in Cleveland, West Lexington in Baltimore, and the room on 4th and Main in Los Angeles.

My social background is different from that of the overwhelming majority of adult poolroom players. The latter are of lower-class origin. As with many American sports (e.g., baseball), pool and billiards are played by teenagers from all classes but only the players of lower-class background tend to continue far into adulthood. (And as far as poolroom games are concerned, even at the teenage level the lower class contributes a disproportionately large share of players.) But such differences—the fact that I went to college, do highbrow work, etc.—create no problems of acceptance. In most good-sized poolrooms the adult regulars usually include a few people like myself who are in the poolroom world but not of it. They are there because they like to play, and are readily accepted because they like to play.

The poolroom I play in most regularly is the principal "action room" in New York and perhaps in the country, the room in which heavy betting on games occurs most often; sometimes, particularly after 1:00 A.M., the hustlers in the room well outnumber the non-hustlers. Frequently I play hustlers for money (nearly always on a handicap basis) and occasionally I hustle some non-hustlers, undertaking the latter activity primarily to recoup losses on the former. I have been a backer for two hustlers.

I know six hustlers well, and during the eight months of the study I talked or played with over 50 more. All are now usually based in New York, except for two in Chicago, two in Cleveland, one in Philadelphia, one itinerant hustler whose home base is Boston and another whose home base is in North Carolina. However, the hustlers based in New York are of diverse regional origins; almost a third grew up and started their hustling careers in other states.

It is not possible to demonstrate the representativeness of this sample because the universe (all U.S. pool and billiard hustlers) is not known exactly. But the hustlers I asked about the number of real hustlers in America, i.e., the number of people whose exclusive or primary occupation is hustling, generally agree that today the number is quite small. In response to my queries about the total number of poolroom hustlers, one hustler said "thousands" and another said "there must be a thousand," but the next highest estimate was "maybe 400" and somewhat lesser estimates were made by nineteen hustlers. Moreover, the three hustlers making the highest estimates have rarely been out of New York, whereas over half the others either come from other parts of the country or have made several road trips. It seems safe to assume that the sample is at least representative of big-city hustlers. Also, it is probable that it includes the majority of part-time hustlers in New York, and certain that it includes a good majority of the full-time hustlers in New York.

POOLROOM BETTING: THE STRUCTURE OF "ACTION"

Hustling involves betting against one's opponent, by definition. But the converse is not true. The majority of poolroom contests on which opponents bet do not involve any element of hustling. In order to understand how hustling enters the picture, one must first establish a perspective that encompasses all betting on poolroom games, hustled or not.

In pool or billiard games, the betting relationship has three possible modes: (1) player bets against player; (2) player against spectator; (3) spectator against spectator. In most contests only the first mode occurs, but combinations of the first and second are frequent, and slightly less so are combinations of the first and third. Combinations of all three are uncommon, but do occur when there is more "ready action" offered to the players by the spectators than the players can or wish to absorb. I have never seen the second mode occur alone, nor a combination of second and third. I have seen the third mode occur alone only twice—

at professional tournaments. The betting relationship, then, involves the mode player-vs.-player, whatever additional modes there may be.

If two mediocre players are betting, say, upward of $15 per game, and at another table two excellent players are playing for only a token amount, the first table will invariably draw many more people around it. The great majority of spectators, whether or not they bet much and whatever their own degree of playing skill, are attracted more by the size of the action than the quality of the performance. (A visiting Danish billiardist tells me this is not so in Europe, and also that betting on pool-room games is far less frequent there than in America.)

There is an old American poolroom tradition that players should make some kind of bet with each other, if only a small one. This tradition remains strong in every public poolroom I know. (It is weak in the pool or billiard rooms of private men's clubs and YMCAs, weaker still in student unions, and virtually nonexistent in faculty clubs.) When one player says to another, "Let's just play sociable," as often as not he means that they should play for only a dollar or two, and at the very least means that they should play "for the time" (the loser paying the check). It is only some of the newer and least skilled players who refuse to bet at all (who want to "split the time"), and nearly always they rapidly become socialized to the betting tradition by a carrot-and-stick process—the stick being that it is often hard to get a game otherwise, the carrot that better players are always willing to give poorer ones a handicap (a "spot"). Most of the regular players will not even play for the check only, but insist on a little money changing hands "just to make the game interesting." The player who claims that just playing the game is interesting enough in itself is regarded as something of a freak.

Few serious bettors, hustlers excepted, care for big action; but nearly all, including hustlers, want fast action. Although they may not want to bet much per game, they want the cash to change hands fairly quickly. Consequently, in an action room the standard games are redesigned for this purpose. Some are simply shortened: players gambling at snooker will remove all the red balls but one; or three-cushion billiard players will play games of 15, 20, or 25 points instead of the usual 30, 40, or 50. In straight pool (pocket billiards), where the standard game is 125 or 150 points, good players are usually reluctant to play a much shorter game because scoring is so easy—any really good player can occasionally run more than 50 balls—that shortening the game makes it too much a matter of chance. Therefore, in an action room one finds most of the pool players playing some variant of the game that not only requires high skill but also minimizes chance, and that therefore can be short (taking only 5 to 20 minutes per game). Today the chief of these variants are "nine ball" and "one pocket" (also called "pocket apiece"), although there are several others, such as "eight ball," "bank pool," and "rotation."

Every poolroom has at least one "No Gambling" sign on display, but no poolroom enforces it. The sign is merely a formal gesture for the eyes of the law (and in some cities required by law). It is enforced only in that the proprietor sometimes may ask players to keep payoffs out of sight—not to toss the money on the table after the game—if the room is currently "heaty," e.g., if an arrest has recently been made there. Police are hardly ever concerned to stop the gambling on poolroom games, and everyone knows it. (But police sometimes check to see that the minimum age law is observed, so proprietors will often ask youths for identification.) Betting is so taken for granted that in most poolrooms the proprietor—the very man who displays a "No Gambling" sign over his desk—will on request hold the players' stake money.

However, in no poolroom does the house take a cut of the action; the proprietor gets no fee for permitting gambling or holding stake money, and wouldn't dream of asking for one. His payment from bettors is simply that they comprise most of his custom in equipment rental. And hustlers, as he and they well know, count in this regard far beyond their numbers, for they play much oftener and longer than other customers; indeed, they virtually live in the poolroom.

The only non-bettor whose payment is somewhat related to the size of the action is the rack boy (if one is used), the person who racks up the balls for the players after each frame. The bigger the action, the larger the tip he can expect, and if one player comes out very much ahead he tips the rack boy lavishly. The rack boy's position is thus analogous to that of the golf caddie, except that a rack boy is used in only about half of hustler-vs.-hustler contests and in but a tiny fraction of other contests. Sometimes he is an employee (sweeper, etc.) of the poolroom, but more often he is a spectator performing as rack boy on an *ad hoc* basis.

NON-HUSTLED POOLROOM GAMBLING

Hustling is *not* involved when the games played for money are any of the following:

(a) *Non-hustler vs. non-hustler.* A "sociable" game in which the bet is a token one. The only betting is player vs. player.

(b) *Non-hustler vs. non-hustler.* A game for significantly more than a token amount. The players play even-up if they are fairly equal. If they are aware of a significant difference in skill levels, the weaker player is given an appropriate handicap. Usually the betting is just between players; rarely, one or both players will bet spectators; spectators do not bet each other.

(c) *Hustler vs. non-hustler.* The players are aware of the difference in skills, and this is properly taken into account via an appropriate spot. Usually the betting is only player vs. player, though sometimes spectators bet players or each other. The hustler tries to avoid this type of game, and agrees to it only when he has nothing better to do.

(d) *Hustler vs. hustler.* Each player knows the other's mettle, if only by reputation ("Minnesota Fats" vs. "Fast Eddy" in *The Hustler*, for example). The hustler, contrary to the impression given by the movie, does *not* prefer this type of game (though he does prefer it to the foregoing type) and does *not* regard it as hustling. But he plays it often because he often can't get the kind of game he wants (a true "hustle") and this alternative does offer him excitement—not only the greatest challenge to his playing skill, but the most action. The average bet between two hustlers is much higher than in any other type of poolroom contest.[1] And betting modes 2 and 3 (player vs. spectator, spectator vs. spectator) occur much more often.

Be that as it may, the hustler much prefers to hustle, which means to be in a game set up so as to be pretty much a sure thing for him, a game that "you're not allowed to lose" as the hustler puts it. In order to achieve this, to truly hustle, he engages in deception. The centrality of deception in pool or billiard hustling is perhaps best indicated by the fact that the poolroom hustler's argot originated that widespread American slang dictum, "never give a sucker an even break."

THE HUSTLER'S METHODS OF DECEPTION

The structure of a gambling game determines what methods of deception, if any, may be used in it. In many games (dice, cards, etc.) one can deceive one's opponent by various techniques of cheating. Pool and billiard games are so structured that this method is virtually impossible. (Once in a great while, against a particularly unalert opponent, one can surreptitiously add a point or two to one's score—but such opportunity is rare, usually involves risk of discovery that is judged to be too great, and seldom means the difference between winning and losing anyway; so no player counts on it.) One's every move and play is completely visible, easily watched by one's opponent and by spectators; nor is it possible to achieve anything via previous tampering with the equipment.

However, one structural feature of pool or billiards readily lends itself to deceit: on each shot, the difference between success and failure is a matter of a small fraction of an inch. In pool or billiards it is peculiarly easy, even for the average player, to miss one's shot deliberately and still look good (unlike, say, nearly all card games, where if one does not play one's cards correctly this is soon apparent). On all shots except the easiest ones, it is impossible to tell if a player is deliberately not trying his best.

The hustler exploits this fact so as to deceive his opponent as to his (the hustler's) true level of skill (true "speed"). It is so easily exploited that, when playing good opponents, usually the better hustlers even disdain it, pocket nearly every shot they have (intentionally miss only some

---

1. When two high-rolling hustlers agree to play each other there is often a real race among poorer spectators to offer rack-boy services because, as previously noted, if one is engaged for such a session he can expect a good tip. I witnessed one six-hour session between hustlers in which the winning hustler came out $800 ahead and tipped the rack boy $50.

very difficult shots), and rely chiefly on related but subtler techniques of failure beyond the remotest suspicion of most players. For example, such a hustler may strike his cue ball hard and with too much spin ("english"), so that the spin is transferred to the object ball and the object ball goes into the pocket but jumps out again; or he may scratch (losing a point and his turn), either by "accidentally" caroming his cue ball into a pocket or by hitting his cue ball hard and with too much top-spin so that it jumps off the table; or, most commonly, he pockets his shot but, by striking his cue ball just a wee bit too hard or too softly or with too much or too little english, he leaves himself "safe" (ends up with his cue ball out of position, so that he hasn't another shot). In such wise the hustler feigns less competence than he has.

Hustling, then, involves not merely the ability to play well, but the use of a kind of "short con." Sometimes the hustler doesn't need to employ any con to get his opponent to the table, sometimes he does; but he always employs it in attempting to keep his opponent there.

The best hustler is not necessarily the best player among the hustlers. He has to be a very good player, true, but beyond a certain point his playing ability is not nearly so important as his skill at various kinds of conning. Also, he has to possess personality traits that make him "rocklike," able to exploit fully his various skills—playing, conning, others— in the face of assorted pressures and temptations not to exploit them fully.

THE HUSTLER'S CARDINAL RULE

As the foregoing indicates, the hustler's cardinal rule is: *don't show your real speed.* Of course, an exception is permitted if by some miracle the hustler finds himself hustled, finds himself in a game with someone he thought would be easy but who turns out to be tough. But this is not supposed to happen, and it rarely does. For one thing, hustlers generally know each other, or of each other, and their respective skill levels. Secondly, any pool or billiard game is overwhelmingly a game of skill rather than luck—even in the chanciest type of poolroom game the element of skill counts for much more than in any card game whatsoever—and this means it is possible to rate the skill levels of various players (to "handicap" them) along small gradations with a high degree of accuracy. For example, if one has seen the three-cushion billiard players X and Y play various people over a period of time, it is possible to arrive at the judgment "On a 30-point game, X is two or three points better than Y" and to be dead right about it in at least eight out of ten contests between them.

The corollaries of the hustler's chief rule are: (a) The hustler must restrain himself from making many of the extremely difficult shots. Such restraint is not easy, because the thrill of making a fancy shot that brings applause from the audience is hard to resist. But the hustler must resist, or else it would make less believable his misses on more ordinary shots. (b) He must play so that the games he wins are won by only a small margin. (c) He must let his opponent win an occasional game.

It may be thought that once a hustler has engaged an opponent, a bet has been agreed upon and the stake money put up, and the game has started, the hustler might safely let out all the stops. This would be terribly short-sighted.

In the first place, as noted earlier, the typical non-hustler bets only a small amount on the game. The hustler's only hope of making real money, therefore, is to extend the first game into a series of games, entice his opponent into doubling up when he is behind, etc. If the hustler does this well, the opponent will hang on for a long time, may even come back after the first session to play him on another day, turn into a real "fish" (the poolroom term for an inferior opponent who doesn't catch on that he's outclassed, and keeps coming back for more). And when the opponent starts demanding a spot, as sooner or later he will, the hustler can offer him his (the hustler's) average winning margin, or even a little better, and still have a safe game.

Secondly, there are spectators to take into account. Some of them will bet the hustler if he offers the non-hustler a seemingly fair spot. More importantly, some of them are potential opponents. Nearly all poolroom spectators are also players. The hustler doesn't want to look too good to spectators either.

He knows that as he beats various opponents his reputation will rise, and that increasingly he'll have to offer spots to people, but he wants to keep his reputation as low as possible as long as possible with as many people as possible. He also knows that he has to play superbly on occasion—that he will play fellow hustlers when there's no other action around, and that then he must show more skill—but he wants to keep these occasions few. (It helps considerably, by the way, that because hustler-vs.-hustler games occur when hustlers give up hope of finding other action, these games usually take place after midnight when there aren't so many non-hustler potential victims around to watch.)

The sooner everyone in the poolroom knows the hustler's true speed, the sooner he exhausts the real hustling possibilities among the room's regular players. Such a situation constitutes one of the career crises that every hustler has to face. (For reasons which will become apparent below, he now has to face it earlier in his career than hustlers formerly did.) When it occurs, either he must move on to a room where he's less known or, if he stays in the room, he has to take games he shouldn't take or else restrict his pickings to strangers who wander in.

Job-Related Skills and Traits

Although the hallmarks of the good hustler are playing skill and the temperamental ability to consistently look poorer than he is, there are other skills and traits that aid him in hustling. Some are related to deceiving his opponent, some not.

Chief of these is argumentative skill in arranging the terms of the match, the ability to "make a game." The prospective opponent, if he has seen the hustler play, may when approached claim that the hustler is too good for him or ask for too high a spot, i.e., one that is fair or even better. The hustler, like the salesman, is supposed to be familiar with standard objections and "propositions" for overcoming them.

Another side of the ability to make a game reveals itself when the prospective opponent simply can't be argued out of demanding a spot that is unfair to the hustler, or can be convinced to play only if the hustler offers such a spot. At that point the hustler should of course refuse to play. There is often a temptation to do otherwise, not only because the hustler is proud of his skill but because action is his lifeblood (which is why he plays other hustlers when he can't find a hustle), and there may be no other action around. He must resist the temptation. In the good hustler's view, no matter how badly you want action, it is better not to play at all than to play when you are disadvantaged; otherwise you are just hustling yourself. (But the hustler often will, albeit with much argument and the greatest reluctance, agree to give a fair spot if that's the only way he can get action.)

The hustler, when faced, as he very often is, with an opponent who knows him as such, of course finds that his ability to make a game assumes greater importance than his ability to feign lack of skill. In such situations, indeed, his game-making ability is just as important as his actual playing ability.

On the other hand, the hustler must have "heart" (courage). The *sine qua non* is that he is a good "money player," can play his best when heavy action is riding on the game (as many non-hustlers can't). Also, he is not supposed to let a bad break or distractions in the audience upset him. (He may pretend to get rattled on such occasions, but that's just part of his con.) Nor should the quality of his game deteriorate when, whether by miscalculation on his part or otherwise, he finds himself much further behind than he would like to be. Finally, if it is necessary to get action, he should not be afraid to tackle an opponent whom he knows to be just about as good as he is.

A trait often working for the hustler is stamina. As a result of thousands of hours of play, all the right muscles are toughened up. He is used to playing many hours at a time, certainly much more used to it than the non-hustler is. This is valuable because sometimes, if the hustler works it right, he can make his opponent forget about quitting for such a "silly" reason as being tired, can extend their session through the night and into the next day. In such sessions it is most often in the last couple of hours, when the betting per game is usually highest, that the hustler makes his biggest killing.

Additional short-con techniques are sometimes used. One hustler, for example, entices opponents by the ancient device of pretending to be sloppy-drunk. Other techniques show more imagination. For example, a hustler preparing for a road trip mentioned to me that before leaving town he was going to buy a soldier's uniform: "I walk into a strange room in uniform and I've got it made. Everybody likes to grab a soldier."

Finally, the hustler—the superior hustler at any rate—has enough flexibility and good sense to break the "rules" when the occasion demands it, will modify standard techniques when he encounters non-standard situations. An example: Once I entered a poolroom just as a hustler I know, X, was finishing a game with non-hustler Y. X beat Y soundly, by a higher margin than a hustler should beat anyone, and at that for only $3. Y went to the bathroom, whereupon I admonished X, "What's the matter with you? You know you're not allowed to win that big." X replied:

> Yeah, sure, but you see that motherfucking S over there? [nodding discreetly in the direction of one of the spectators]. Well, about an hour ago when I came in he and Y were talking, and when S saw me he whispered something to Y. So I had a hunch he was giving him the wire [tipping him off] that I was pretty good. And then in his middle game it looked like Y was stalling a little [missing deliberately] to see what I would do, so then I was sure he got the wire on me. I had to beat him big so he'll think he knows my top speed. But naturally I didn't beat him as big as I *could* beat him. Now he'll come back cryin' for a spot and bigger action, and I'll nail him.

And he did nail him.

7

Sociological Explanations for Failure to Seek Sexual Harassment Remedies

Patricia A. Gwartney-Gibbs and Denise H. Lach

One of the most difficult things for students studying sociology is to recognize how situations and social structures organize many of the choices people make. The world is not made up of good people and bad, the brave and the weak, the ambitious and the lazy. Anita Hill's seemingly contradictory behavior can be best understood by looking into the situation that urged her to show hesitancy, as well as the situation where she showed great bravery.

Public and private debate over whether Supreme Court nominee Clarence Thomas sexually harassed former employee Anita Hill—and, if he did, why Hill would wait ten years to reveal his behavior publicly—has centered on psychological explanations of the state of mind of Thomas and Hill. This article provides an alternative sociological explanation, emphasizing the effects of gender and race in the social organization of work, and the links between workplace dispute resolution and employment inequality.

In October 1991, U.S. Senate Judiciary Committee hearings on the nomination of Judge Clarence Thomas to the Supreme Court erupted amid allegations that he had sexually harassed his former employee Anita Hill. Thomas denied Hill's claim. Intense debate ensued both in public and private arenas over whether Thomas *really* harassed Hill sexually and, if he did, why she did not do something immediately, such as change jobs or report his actions, and why she waited ten years to reveal his behavior publicly. These debates have centered on the psychology of the situation and Hill's state of mind in particular. In commenting on the Senate testimony, leading psychologists and psychiatrists have invoked explanations concerning the dynamics of the human memory (particularly selective recall), delusions (for example, erotomania), and purposive, self-serving deception (Barringer, 1991).

No psychological explanation, however, takes into account the influence of social structural conditions or the work setting on Hill's actions. What mechanisms for dispute resolution, for example, were available in the workplace, under which Hill could have brought her claims? If she had brought a claim against Thomas at the time of the alleged sexual harassment, what formal and informal processes would she have encountered and how might she have fared under them? Moreover, individualized psychological explanations do not account for the normative influences of gender roles and race on behavior. How does being a woman, and a black woman at that, influence one's ability or willingness to bring a claim and pursue it to resolution? Sociological theory predicts that roles and tokenism in the workplace are part of the social organization of work that affects women's access to effective means of dispute resolution in the workplace, independently of their individual propensities to pursue a workplace problem. We invoke sociological theory to argue that if Anita Hill experienced sexual harassment from Clarence Thomas ten years ago, it would have been reasonable, not psychologically aberrant, for her to not pursue a sexual harassment claim.

CONCEPTUAL AND THEORETICAL BASES

Dispute resolution in the workplace is any attempt by an employee to resolve a problem in the employment relationship. In earlier work (Gwartney-Gibbs and Lach, 1991), we have developed a tripartite conceptual model of dispute resolution in which we argue that workplace disputes comprise origins, processes, and outcomes. That is, in the course of ordinary work day activities, disputes arise over such issues as sexual harassment, wages, discipline, parental or family leave, discrimination, job posting, job performance, and hours. Once a dispute is articulated, it can be resolved in various formal and informal processes, including a grievance procedure, peer review forum, open door policy, employee assistance program, or simple conversation between disputants. The outcomes of workplace dispute resolution have both behavioral and attitudinal components that include dispute settlement, continuing problems, transfer and quitting, as well as job satisfaction and performance (Lewin and Peterson, 1988).

We postulate that these three components of workplace dispute resolution—origins, processes, and outcomes—are patterned by gender roles and by the sex and race composition of jobs (that is, tokenism). Thus we argue that women and incumbents of highly sex- and race-segregated jobs have distinctive workplace disputes, processing of disputes, and outcomes in the settlement of disputes. In developing this model, we utilize gender role theory and stratification theories from sociology. We then assess the extent to which these perspectives are useful in explaining why Anita Hill did not pursue her sexual harassment allegations earlier. (For greater theoretical development and empirical evidence for this theoretical and conceptual model, see Gwartney-Gibbs and Lach, 1990, 1991, forthcoming).

GENDER AND WORKPLACE DISPUTING

Gender role theory tells us that sexual harassment is only one of many potential sources of dispute women encounter in the workplace. Sociologists and economists have documented the interference of gender roles in women's employment (Abel, 1991; Berk, 1985). For example, many full-time women workers also have primary responsibility for children, homes, and the care of aging parents. These responsibilities can lead to workplace problems concerning family leave, absenteeism (due to family illness), and scheduling (shifts, compulsory overtime, weekend hours) that women experience more often than men. Researchers have also documented typical gender roles in sexual behavior: women tend to be passive receivers of attention, whereas men tend to be aggressive initiators of encounters (Nieva and Gutek, 1981). To the extent that sexuality is in the workplace, women are more likely to sustain uninvited sexual attention than men, and this may be defined as sexual harassment (Stanko, 1985; MacKinnon, 1979).

When workplace disputes arise, gender role theory suggests that women workers will be unlikely to pursue them to resolution. Women's socialization is often associated with avoidance of conflict and confrontation with authority and lack of self-confidence (Stockard and Johnson, 1992). These patterns suggest that women with workplace disputes will be unlikely to act on them, and that if they do act they will forbear at every stage of informal and formal dispute resolution. (Technically, unions may pursue grievances without grievants' continued involvement, but the extent to which they do this on behalf of women members or women's issues is unknown.)

Not acting on workplace disputes can, however, be a rational response to conditions of the workplace, the available processes of dispute resolution, and the legal system. Collective bargaining agreements and in-house dispute resolution procedures in nonunionized firms may have no provisions for female-typed disputes, such as family emergency leave, so women with those types of disputes will not have access to a venue in which to pursue their complaints. Even if workplace dispute resolution procedures contain provisions for female-typed disputes, women employees may perceive a lack of support or sympathy for them from supervisors, personnel managers, union stewards, and attorneys—the "gatekeepers" responsible for implementing these procedures (Costello, 1985; Gannage, 1986; Stanko, 1985). The gatekeepers of workplace dispute resolution forums play critical roles in forming employees' attitudes toward these forums and willingness to use them (Clark, 1988; also see Reskin and Padavic, 1988). Gatekeepers may practice sex discrimination, consciously or not, in hearing and actively pursuing the workplace disputes more often experienced by women. These gatekeepers may simply be less practiced in dealing with them than with the complaints typically expressed by male workers (such as job assignment). The economic and noneconomic costs of filing complaints may also dissuade women, given the historical disregard for female-typed disputes in labor law (Hoyman and Stallworth, 1986). These factors, singly or in concert, may cause women to perceive a lack of access to dispute resolution forums for their unique workplace difficulties. Under such conditions, it makes sense for women not to pursue workplace disputes, such as sexual harassment, to resolution.

The unique origins and processes of women's workplace dispute resolution suggest several outcomes. The less women use formal dispute resolution forums, the less often female-typed disputes, or women workers with any type of dispute, will reach formal settlement. To the extent that women attempt to use workplace dispute resolution forums and fail (whether because of the weakness of their cases, inadequate representation, or lack of will), there will be fewer role models for women pursuing future complaints. Rather, women workers will drop their complaints or exit the employment setting (by transferring or quitting) and thus will not appear in the formal records of arbitration, litigation, or government agency actions. Consequently, cases that do have formal outcomes are likely to be unusually strong and not representative of working women's daily workplace problems. Moreover, to the extent that women's employment disputes go unresolved, women workers will exhibit greater job turnover, lower job satisfaction, and poorer performance evaluations (Lewin, 1987; Lewin and Peterson, 1988). When repeated across time, place, and circumstance, gender differences in dispute resolution may contribute to, or be precursors of, aggregate patterns of gender inequality in employment (in earnings and promotions, for example).

TOKENISM AND WORKPLACE DISPUTING

Sex segregation in occupations and firms is well established. In 1985, 60 percent of all women workers would have had to change occupations to have the same occupational distribution as men, and over two-thirds were employed in occupations in which 70 percent or more of workers are women (Jacobs, 1989). Within firms, occupational sex segregation is virtually 100 percent (Bielby and Baron, 1984).

Occupational race segregation has declined significantly since World War II (Jacobs, 1989). Although there has been a considerable reduction in the occupational segregation index between white women and women of color, the gap between minority women and white men remains high (Reskin and Roos, 1990). The existence of occupational race and sex segregation creates a very narrow range of occupations in which minority women are proportionately represented. In most occupations, minority women are a numerical minority.

Segregation is most likely to become a disputable issue for tokens, that is, for women in male-typed jobs and nonwhites in white-typed jobs. Tokens experience discrimination in evaluation, task assignment, scheduling, pay, and promotion, as well as teasing, condescension, social isolation, and exclusion on the job (Kanter, 1977a, 1977b; Roos and Reskin, 1984; Segura, 1989; Swerdlow, 1989). On these bases, tokenism can serve as a point of origin for workplace disputes involving discrimination and harassment. (In Gwartney-Gibbs and Lach, 1990, we argue that sex segregation can also relate to the origins of workplace disputes for nontokens, from gender role spillover theory; Nieva and Gutek, 1981).

Tokenism may also be related to the processes of pursuing workplace disputes to resolution (Kanter, 1977a, 1977b). Tokens' high visibility generates pressure to conform to role expectations. Moreover, their social isolation on the job results in powerlessness and conformity to the dominant workplace culture. When tokens experience workplace disputes associated with tokenism, therefore, they simultaneously experience pressure not to voice these disputes, in an attempt to gain acceptance from the dominant group. Even if they do voice workplace difficulties, Kanter's research suggests they will receive little sympathy or support from nontoken co-workers or the gatekeepers of formal dispute resolution procedures. This lack of support is in turn associated with a lack of access to informal support networks and information needed to pursue workplace disputes through formal channels. Thus we expect that tokens are pressured to conform to stereotypical roles and will less often articulate their workplace disputes. When disputes are voiced, we expect that tokens will be heard less often and their disputes resolved not by the gatekeepers of formal dispute resolution forums (who we expect are predominantly white men), but informally, not at all, or by quitting (Segura, 1989). (Note that this argument should apply equally to men in jobs predominantly held by women; that is, because of a tendency to conform to gender roles, men tokens should aggressively pursue their workplace disputes through formal channels, with roadblocks related more to the nature of the claim than to the person.)

These different origins and processes of workplace disputes, related to the sex and race composition of jobs, suggest at least one important outcome. That is, if nontokens experience fewer workplace disputes, receive greater understanding or support from coworkers and supervisors for their disputes, and perceive more fairness in the processes and outcomes of dispute resolution than tokens, then use of and satisfaction with a dispute resolution process is patterned by both gender and race.

ANITA HILL'S CASE

Anita Hill's case illustrates many of the points in the foregoing discussion. Her workplace dispute originated in an alleged series of experiences with sexual harassment. From our theory of gender and dispute resolution, we recognize sexual harassment as an employment problem women are more likely to sustain than men. Such an issue is also related to authority relationships in the workplace, in which men tend, like Clarence Thomas, to be supervisors and women tend, like Hill, to be subordinates. Hill's allegation of sexual harassment also is consistent with gender roles and the social construction of sexuality, in which men are sexual initiators and dominant.

Both Hill and Thomas, as African-Americans, were also tokens in the workplace. They were black in historically white positions of power in Washington, D.C. Moreover, it could be argued that the School Employment Opportunity Commission at the Department of Education and the Equal Employment Opportunity Commission (EEOC), where they worked, were token offices within the federal bureaucracy. Theory and previous empirical findings lead us to expect that the behavior of tokens is highly scrutinized and evaluated by their peers. Everything tokens say or do is assumed to show what all African-Americans, or all women, or all black women, will do in general in their positions. Both Hill and Thomas, as African-American lawyers with significant policy-implementing authority in the federal government, must have experienced a great deal of pressure from their social structural positions as tokens.

We can also predict from theory and previous empirical research that Hill's and Thomas's nontoken co-workers engaged in boundary-heightening behaviors, for example, nor including them in after-hours socializing. Contradictory feelings of scrutiny would be the result, on one hand, and social exclusion and isolation on the other. Such isolation in turn should result in greater conformity to the dominant workplace culture and to stereotypical race and sex roles. This pattern is, in fact, consistent with Hill's actions. She conformed to her gender role by not challenging her supervisor, by doing all she could to avoid interpersonal conflict and confrontation, and by attempting to maintain a semblance of normalcy in her social relations with Thomas. When that proved impossible, Anita Hill left her position at the EEOC to pursue an academic career. Leaving a job without confronting a problem is gender-specific behavior consistent with both theory and empirical findings.

Co-workers and colleagues often provide informal networks of support and information, helping others to "name" their workplace disputes, and affirming that their experiences are not trivial or ridiculous. If Hill is at all like women we have interviewed, we speculate that she distrusted her own feelings at first and may have had difficulty naming her experience sexual harassment. But as a black female attorney, Hill was a token in the workplace, and tokens often lack critical informal support networks. Two or three of Hill's friends and acquaintances testified that she mentioned her difficulties with Thomas to them; but from her office staff's testimony, Hill appeared to lack a dense network of confidantes, consistent with token theory.

Hill also lacked structural access to formal dispute resolution mechanisms concerning sexual harassment. Although the issue of sexual harassment in the workplace was named in the scholarly literature with MacKinnon's influential book in 1979, and the EEOC published guidelines that defined sexual harassment (Equal Employment Opportunity

Commission, 1980), when the alleged encounters occurred in the early 1980s, the Supreme Court had not yet defined sexual harassment to include the alleged behaviors of Clarence Thomas. Not until 1986, well after Hill had left her employment with Thomas, did the Supreme Court hold that an employer could be held liable for sex discrimination when sexual harassment created a "hostile work environment" (*Meritor Savings Bank v. Vinson*, 1986). Thus, even if she had been able to name her experience as sexual harassment, Hill lacked formal legal mechanisms by which to pursue her complaint.

Earlier in this article we discussed the importance of gatekeepers—for example, union stewards, managers, and human resources personnel whose job it is to help workers identify their workplace disputes and find routes to deal with them. In the best of circumstances, it can be difficult for women and tokens to approach these gatekeepers. But what is a woman to do when her harasser is the chief gatekeeper in the nation, the head of the EEOC? From our theory of gender, tokenism, and workplace dispute resolution, it is not at all surprising that Hill did not pursue her complaint through the gatekeeper in her workplace.

During the Senate hearing much was made of the fact that Anita Hill left employment at the EEOC without ever mentioning the harassment from Clarence Thomas. Exit from a problematic work setting is consistent, however, with our theory and previous research. In many situations women workers feel that leaving a problem behind and moving to a new job or new firm is preferable to entering into a nonresponsive dispute forum. Such action is consistent with gender role theory, but it is also a rational response to a work setting that lacks avenues in which women could pursue their specific complaints. By leaving the EEOC without voicing her complaint, Hill joined the legions of other women who have chosen exit over voicing their disputes.

Finally, workplace legends may function to dispel women's desire to pursue workplace disputes (Gwartney-Gibbs and Lach, 1991). In in-depth interviews with sixty workers in two large firms, we found that women who pursued female-type disputes such as sexual harassment through formal dispute resolution mechanisms became legendary in the workplace. Stories about what they had to go through in attempting to resolve the disputes were told and retold. The processes were often humiliating (for example, a clerical worker endured psychiatric evaluations of her childhood and sex life as part of a mental harassment case against her supervisor). Even when the workplace legends involved women who won their cases, we found that the stories served to deter women workers further from pursuing resolution of the daily workplace difficulties associated with roles and tokenism that confronted them. This leads us to wonder what sort of legend will Anita Hill's case create. Although the media are full of stories about men's increased caution and self-censoring in the workplace, we wonder what woman would now pursue a similar complaint—particularly with Clarence Thomas seated on the Supreme Court.

CONCLUSIONS

This article applies our conceptual and theoretical framework of gender, tokenism, and workplace dispute resolution to explain why a woman, particularly a minority woman, would wait a decade to pursue a sexual harassment claim. We argue that gender roles and tokenism are related to the origins, processes, and outcomes of workplace disputes in both formal and informal proceedings. We argue that few women employees or female-typed disputes proceed to formal resolution; most instead drop out along the way to formal resolution. Moreover, we suggest that women are often in workplace positions lacking a venue to pursue their unique disputes.

The fact that Anita Hill did not pursue her claims of sexual harassment is predicted from our synthesis of theory on gender roles, tokenism, and dispute resolution. This explanation is unique in that it appears well able to explain Hill's behaviors by relying on the tenets of sociological theory, without requiring speculation about her personal psychology or the psychology of the situation. Moreover, our argument suggests that Hill's case is not unique. We suspect that the majority of women's workplace disputes do not go through formal procedures or reach formal settlement. We also suspect that this pattern is one part of the larger puzzle of aggregate patterns of employment inequality.

Workplace dispute resolution is a largely neglected topic within the context of research on gender, race, and employment inequality. Moreover, gender and race are largely neglected topics in research on workplace dispute resolution. The case of Anita Hill and Clarence Thomas, so vividly reported in the media in the fall of 1991, stimulates thinking on these issues. We believe that this nonpecuniary aspect of employment—race and gender patterns of workplace dispute resolution—has consequences for employment inequality more generally. This subject is inherently interdisciplinary and likely to have research and policy consequences in several disciplines. Although we have undoubtedly left unexamined many ideas potentially related to the general area, this essay opens the door for further investigation.

REFERENCES

Abel, E. K. *Who Cares for the Elderly? Public Policy and the Experiences of Adult Daughters.* Philadelphia: Temple University Press, 1991.

Barringer, F. "Psychologists Try to Explain Reason for Opposing Views." *New York Times*, Oct. 14, 1991, p. A11.

Berk, S. F. *The Gender Factory: The Apportionment of Work in American Households.* New York: Plenum, 1985.

Bielby, W. T., and Baron, J. N. "A Woman's Place is with Other Women: Sex Segregation Within Organizations." In B. F. Reskin (ed.), *Sex Segregation in the Workplace: Trends, Explanations, Remedies*. Washington, D.C.: National Academy Press, 1984.

Clark, P. F. "The Role of the Steward in Shaping Union Member Attitudes Toward the Grievance Procedure." *Labor Studies Journal*, 1988, 13, 3–17.

Costello, C. B. "WEA're Worth It! Work Culture and Conflict at the Wisconsin Education Association Insurance Trust." *Feminist Studies*, 1985, 11, 497–518.

Equal Employment Opportunity Commission. *Sex Discrimination Guidelines*. 29 Code of Federal Regulations 1604.11(a)(3). Washington, D.C.: U.S. Government Printing Office, 1980.

Gannage, C. *Double Day, Double Bind: Women Garment Workers*. Toronto: Women's Press, 1986.

Gwartney-Gibbs, P. A., and Lach, D. H. "Gender and Workplace Jurisprudence." University of Oregon, Center for the Study of Women in Society. Working Paper no. 35, 1990.

Gwartney-Gibbs, P. A., and Lach, D. H. "Workplace Dispute Resolution and Gender Inequality." *Negotiation Journal*, 1991, 7 (2), 187–200.

Gwartney-Gibbs, P. A., and Lach, D. H. "Gender Differences in Grievance Processing and Its Implications for Re-thinking Shopfloor Practices." In S. Cobble (ed.), *Women Workers and the Labor Movement: Forging a New Partnership*. II.R Press, forthcoming.

Hoyman, M., and Stallworth, I. "Suit Filing by Women: An Empirical Analysis." *N.O. Law Review*. 1986, 62, 61–82.

Jacobs, J. A. *Revolving Doors: Sex Segregation and Women's Careers*. Palo Alto, Calif.: Stanford University Press, 1989.

Kanter, R. M. *Men and Women of the Corporation*. New York: Basic Books, 1977a.

Kanter, R. M. "Some Effects of Proportions on Group Life: Skewed Sex Ratios and Responses to Token Women." *American Journal of Sociology*, 1977b, 82, 965–990.

Lewin, D. "Dispute Resolution in the Nonunion Firm." *Journal of Conflict Resolution*, 1987, 31, 465–502.

Lewin, D., and Peterson, R. *The Modern Grievance Procedure in the United States*. New York: Quorem, 1988.

MacKinnon, C. A. *Sexual Harassment of Working Women: A Case of Sex Discrimination*. New Haven, Conn.: Yale University Press, 1979.

Meritor Savings Bank v. Vinson, 54 U.S.L.W. 4703, 1986.

Nieva, V., and Gutek, B. *Women and Work: A Psychological Perspective*. New York: Praeger, 1981.

Reskin, B. F., and Padavic, I. "Supervisors as Gatekeepers: Male Supervisors' Response to Women's Integration in Plant Jobs." *Social Problems*, 1988, 35, 536–550.

Reskin, B. F., and Roos, P. A. *Job Queues, Gender Queues: Explaining Women's Inroads Into Male Occupations*. Philadelphia: Temple University Press, 1990.

Roos, P. A., and Reskin, B. F. "Institutional Factors Contributing to Sex Segregation in the Workplace." In B. F. Reskin (ed.), *Sex Segregation in the Workplace: Trends, Explanations, Remedies*. Washington, D.C.: National Academy Press, 1984.

Segura, D. A. "Conflict in Social Relations at Work: A Chicana Perspective." In M. Romero and C. Candelaria (eds.), *Studios Chicanos and the Politics of Community*. Boulder, Colo.: National Association for Chicano Studies, 1989.

Stanko, E. A. *Intimate Intrusions: Women's Experience of Male Violence*. New York: Routledge & Kegan Paul, 1985.

Stockard, J., and Johnson, M. M. *Sex and Gender in Society.* (2nd ed.) Englewood Cliffs, N.J.: Prentice Hall, 1992.

Swerdlow, M. "Men's Accommodations to Women Entering a Nontraditional Occupation: A Case of Rapid Transit Operatives," *Gender & Society*, 1989, 3 (3), 373–387.

PART II

The Individual and Society

8
The West's Debt to China

Robert Temple

One reason societies change is because cultural forms (for example, inventions, religion, language) are adopted from other societies. That was certainly the case where European power and culture brought changes in Africa, Latin America, the Indian subcontinent, and Southeast Asia. Less well recognized is the way Europe itself changed as a result of contact with China.

One of the greatest untold secrets of history is that the "modern world" in which we live is a unique synthesis of Chinese and Western ingredients. Possibly more than half of the basic inventions and discoveries upon which the "modern world" rests come from China. And yet few people know this. Why?

The Chinese themselves are as ignorant of this fact as Westerners. From the seventeenth century onwards, the Chinese became increasingly dazzled by European technological expertise, having experienced a period of amnesia regarding their own achievements. When the Chinese were shown a mechanical clock by Jesuit missionaries, they were awestruck. They had forgotten that it was they who had invented mechanical clocks in the first place!

It is just as much a surprise for the Chinese as for Westerners to realize that *modern* agriculture, *modern* shipping, the *modern* oil industry, *modern* astronomical observatories, *modern* music, decimal mathematics, paper money, umbrellas, fishing reels, wheelbarrows, multi-stage rockets, guns, underwater mines, poison gas, parachutes, hot-air balloons, manned flight, brandy, whisky, the game of chess, printing, and even the essential design of the steam engine, all came from China.

Without the importation from China of nautical and navigational improvements such as ships' rudders, the compass and multiple masts, the great European Voyages of Discovery could never have been undertaken, Columbus would not have sailed to America, and Europeans would never have established colonial empires.

Without the importation from China of the stirrup, to enable them to stay on horseback, knights of old would never have ridden in their shining armor to aid damsels in distress; there would have been no Age of Chivalry. And without the importation from China of guns and gunpowder, the knights would not have been knocked from their horses by bullets which pierced the armor, bringing the Age of Chivalry to an end.

Without the importation from China of paper and printing, Europe would have continued for much longer to copy books by hand. Literacy would not have become so widespread.

Johann Gutenberg did *not* invent movable type. It was invented in China. William Harvey did *not* discover the circulation of the blood in the body. It was discovered—or rather, always assumed—in China. Isaac Newton was *not* the first to discover his First Law of Motion. It was discovered in China.

These myths and many others are shattered by our discovery of the true Chinese origins of many of the things, all around us, which we take for granted. Some of our greatest achievements turn out to have been not achievements at all, but simple borrowings. Yet there is no reason for us to feel inferior or downcast at the realization that much of the genius of mankind's advance was Chinese rather than European. For it is exciting to realize that the East and the West are not as far apart in spirit or in fact as most of us have been led, by appearances, to believe, and that the East and the West *are already combined* in a synthesis so powerful and so profound that it is all-pervading. Within this synthesis we live our daily lives, and from it there is no escape. The modern world *is* a combination of Eastern and Western ingredients which are inextricably fused. The fact that we are largely unaware of it is perhaps one of the greatest cases of historical blindness in the existence of the human race.

Why are we ignorant of this gigantic, obvious truth? The main reason is surely that the Chinese themselves lost sight of it. If the very originators of the inventions and discoveries no longer claim them, and if even their memory of them has faded, why should their inheritors trouble to resurrect their lost claims? Until our own time, it is questionable whether many Westerners even wanted to know the truth. It is always more satisfying to the ego to think that we have reached our present position alone and unaided, that we are the proud masters of all abilities and all crafts. . . .

We need to set this matter right, from both ends. And I can think of no better single illustration of the folly of Western complacency and self-satisfaction than the lesson to be drawn from the history of agriculture. Today, a handful of Western nations have grain surpluses and feed the world. When Asia starves, the West sends grain. We assume that Western agriculture is the very pinnacle of what is possible in the productive use of soil for the growth of food. But we should take to heart the astonishing and disturbing fact that the European agricultural revolution, which laid the basis for the Industrial Revolution, came about only because of the importation of Chinese ideas and inventions. The growing of crops in rows, intensive hoeing of weeds, the "modern" seed drill, the iron plow, the moldboard to turn the plowed soil, and efficient harnesses were all imported from China. Before the arrival from China of the trace harness and collar harness, Westerners choked their horses with straps round their throats. Although ancient Italy could produce plenty of grain, it could not be transported overland to Rome for lack of satisfactory harnesses. Rome depended on shipments of grain by sea from places like Egypt. As for sowing methods—probably over half of Europe's seed was wasted every year before the Chinese idea of the seed drill came to the attention of Europeans. Countless millions of farmers throughout European history broke their backs and their spirits by plowing with ridiculously poor plows, while for two thousand years the Chinese were enjoying their relatively effortless method. Indeed, until two centuries ago, the West was so backward in agriculture compared to China, that the West was the Underdeveloped World in comparison to the Chinese Developed World. The tables have now turned. But for how long? And what an uncomfortable realization it is that the West owes its very ability to eat today to the adoption of Chinese inventions two centuries ago.

It would be better if the nations and the peoples of the world had a clearer understanding of each other, allowing the mental chasm between East and West to be bridged. After all they are, and have been for several centuries, intimate partners in the business of building a world civilization. The technological world of today is a product of both East and West to an extent which until recently no one had ever imagined. It is now time for the Chinese contribution to be recognized and acknowledged, by East and West alike. And, above all, let this be recognized by today's schoolchildren, who will be the generation to absorb it into their most fundamental conceptions about the world. When that happens, Chinese and Westerners will be able to look each other in the eye, knowing themselves to be true and full partners.

9
The Global Village Finally Arrives

Pico Iyer

The historic pattern for many immigrant groups has been to meld gradually into the dominant population and lose their ethnic identity within a couple of generations. Even with the influence of the media and the mass homogenization of habits and tastes, this may not be the pattern of the future. The richness of cultural diversity is described in this essay, where one city contains a mix of cultures from around the world.

This is the typical day of a relatively typical soul in today's diversified world. I wake up to the sound of my Japanese clock radio, put on a T shirt sent me by an uncle in Nigeria and walk out into the street, past German cars, to my office. Around me are English-language students from Korea, Switzerland and Argentina—all on this Spanish-named road in this Mediterranean-style town. On TV, I find, the news is in Mandarin; today's baseball game is being broadcast in Korean. For lunch I can walk to a sushi bar, a tandoori palace, a Thai café or the newest burrito joint (run by an old Japanese lady). Who am I, I sometimes wonder, the son of Indian parents and a British citizen who spends much of his time in Japan (and is therefore—what else?—an American permanent resident)? And where am I?

I am, as it happens, in Southern California, in a quiet, relatively un-international town, but I could as easily be in Vancouver or Sydney or London or Hong Kong. All the world's a rainbow coalition, more and more; the whole planet, you might say, is going global. When I fly to Toronto, or Paris, or Singapore, I disembark in a world as hyphenated as the one I left. More and more of the globe looks like America, but an America that is itself looking more and more like the rest of the globe. Los Angeles famously teaches 82 different languages in its schools. In this respect, the city seems only to bear out the old adage that what is in California today is in America tomorrow, and next week around the globe.

In ways that were hardly conceivable even a generation ago, the new world order is a version of the New World writ large: a wide-open frontier of polyglot terms and postnational trends. A common multiculturalism links us all—call it Planet Hollywood, Planet Reebok or the United Colors of Benetton. *Taxi* and *hotel* and *disco* are universal terms now, but so too are *karaoke* and *yoga* and *pizza*. For the gourmet alone, there is *tiramisù* at the Burger King in Kyoto, echt angel-hair pasta in Saigon and enchiladas on every menu in Nepal.

But deeper than mere goods, it is souls that are mingling. In Brussels, a center of the new "unified Europe," 1 new baby in every 4 is Arab. Whole parts of the Paraguayan capital of Asunción are largely Korean. And when the prostitutes of Melbourne distributed some pro-condom pamphlets, one of the languages they used was Macedonian. Even Japan, which prides itself on its centuries-old socially engineered uniculture, swarms with Iranian illegals, Western executives, Pakistani laborers and Filipina hostesses.

The global village is defined, as we know, by an international youth culture that takes its cues from American pop culture. Kids in Perth and Prague and New Delhi are all tuning in to *Santa Barbara* on TV, and wriggling into 501 jeans, while singing along to Madonna's latest in English. CNN (which has grown 70-fold in 13 years) now reaches more than 140 countries; an American football championship pits London against Barcelona. As fast as the world comes to America, America goes round the world—but it is an America that is itself multi-tongued and many hued, an America of Amy Tan and Janet Jackson and movies with dialogue in Lakota.

For far more than goods and artifacts, the one great influence being broadcast around the world in greater numbers and at greater speed than ever before is people. What were once clear divisions are now tangles of crossed lines: there are 40,000 "Canadians" resident in Hong Kong, many of whose first language is Cantonese. And with people come customs: while new immigrants from Taiwan and Vietnam and India—some of the so-called Asian Calvinists—import all-American values of hard work and family closeness and entrepreneurial energy to America, America is sending its values of upward mobility and individualism and melting-pot hopefulness to Taipei and Saigon and Bombay.

Values, in fact, travel at the speed of fax; by now, almost half the world's Mormons live outside the U.S. A diversity of one culture quickly becomes a diversity of many: the "typical American" who goes to Japan today may be a third-generation Japanese American, or the son of a Japanese woman married to a California serviceman, or the offspring of a Salvadoran father and an Italian mother from San Francisco. When he goes out with a Japanese woman, more than two cultures are brought into play.

None of this, of course, is new: Chinese silks were all the rage in Rome centuries ago, and Alexandria before the time of Christ was a paradigm of the modern universal city. Not even American eclecticism is new: many a small town has long known Chinese restaurants, Indian doctors and Lebanese grocers. But now all these cultures are crossing at the speed of light. And the rising diversity of the planet is something more than mere cosmopolitanism: it is a fundamental recoloring of the very complexion of societies. Cities like Paris, or Hong Kong, have always had a soigné, international air and served as magnets for exiles and émigrés, but now smaller places are multinational too. Marseilles speaks French with a distinctly North African twang. Islamic fundamentalism has one of its strongholds in Bradford, England. It is the sleepy coastal towns of Queensland, Australia, that print their menus in Japanese.

The dangers this internationalism presents are evident: not for nothing did the Tower of Babel collapse. As national borders fall, tribal alliances, and new manmade divisions, rise up, and the world learns every day terrible new meanings of the word Balkanization. And while some places are wired for international transmission, others (think of Iran or North Korea or Burma) remain as isolated as ever, widening the gap between the haves and the have-nots, or what Alvin Toffler has called the "fast" and the "slow" worlds. Tokyo has more telephones than the whole continent of Africa.

Nonetheless, whether we like it or not, the "transnational" future is upon us: as Kenichi Ohmae, the international economist, suggests with his talk of a "borderless economy," capitalism's allegiances are to products, not places. "Capital is now global," Robert Reich, the Secretary of Labor, has said, pointing out that when an Iowan buys a Pontiac from General Motors, 60% of his money goes to South Korea, Japan, West Germany, Taiwan, Singapore, Britain and Barbados. Culturally we are being re-formed daily by the cadences of world music and world fiction: where the great Canadian writers of an older generation had names like Frye and Davies and Laurence, now they are called Ondaatje and Mistry and Skvorecky.

As space shrinks, moreover, time accelerates. This hip-hop mishmash is spreading overnight. When my parents were in college, there were all of seven foreigners living in Tibet, a country the size of Western Europe, and in its entire history the country had seen fewer than 2,000 Westerners. Now a Danish student in Lhasa is scarcely more surprising than a Tibetan in Copenhagen. Already a city like Miami is beyond the wildest dreams of 1968; how much more so will its face in 2018 defy our predictions of today?

It would be easy, seeing all this, to say that the world is moving toward the *Raza Cósmica* (Cosmic Race), predicted by the Mexican thinker José Vasconcelos in the '20s—a glorious blend of mongrels and mestizos. It may be more relevant to suppose that more and more of the world may come to resemble Hong Kong, a stateless special economic zone full of expats and exiles linked by the lingua franca of English and the global marketplace. Some urbanists already see the world as a grid of 30 or so highly advanced city-regions, or technopoles, all plugged into the same international circuit.

The world will not become America. Anyone who has been to a baseball game in Osaka, or a Pizza Hut in Moscow, knows instantly that she is not in Kansas. But America may still, if only symbolically, be a model for the world. *E Pluribus Unum*, after all, is on the dollar bill. As Federico Mayor Zaragoza, the director-general of UNESCO, has said, "America's main role in the new world order is not as a military superpower, but as a multicultural superpower."

The traditional metaphor for this is that of a mosaic. But Richard Rodriguez, the Mexican-American essayist who is a psalmist for our new hybrid forms, points out that the interaction is more fluid than that, more human, subject to daily revision. "I am Chinese," he says, "because I live in San Francisco, a Chinese city. I became Irish in America. I became Portuguese in America." And even as he announces this new truth, Portuguese women are becoming American, and Irishmen are becoming Portuguese, and Sydney (or is it Toronto?) is thinking to compare itself with the "Chinese city" we know as San Francisco.

10
Amish Society

JOHN A. HOSTETLER

One of the most basic sociological truths is that people seek to organize their lives, families, and communities in order to become the kind of people they most admire. This is especially true for the Amish, who see their own beliefs as tied to the structure of their communities.

Small communities, with their distinctive character—where life is stable and intensely human—are disappearing. Some have vanished from the face of the earth, others are dying slowly, but all have undergone change as they have come into contact with an expanding machine civilization. The merging of diverse peoples into a common mass has produced tension among members of the minorities and the majority alike.

The Old Order Amish, who arrived on American shores in colonial times, have survived in the modern world in distinctive, viable, small communities. They have resisted the homogenization process more successfully than others. In planting and harvest time one can see their bearded men working the fields with horses and their women hanging out the laundry in neat rows to dry. Many American people have seen Amish families, with the men wearing broad-brimmed black hats and the women in bonnets and long dresses, in railway depots or bus terminals. Although the Amish have lived with industrialized America for over two and a half centuries, they have moderated its influence on their personal lives, their families, communities, and their values.

The Amish are often perceived by other Americans to be relics of the past who live an austere, inflexible life dedicated to inconvenient and archaic customs. They are seen as renouncing both modern conveniences and the American dream of success and progress. But most people have no quarrel with the Amish for doing things the old-fashioned way. Their conscientious objection was tolerated in wartime, for after all, they are meticulous farmers who practice the virtues of work and thrift.

In recent years the status of the Amish in the minds of most Americans has shifted toward a more favorable position. This change can scarcely be attributed to anything the Amish have done; rather, it is the result of changes in the way Americans perceive their minority groups. A century ago, hardly anyone knew the Amish existed. A half-century ago they were viewed as an obscure sect living by ridiculous customs, as stubborn people who resisted education and exploited the labor of their children. Today the Amish are the unwilling objects of a thriving tourist industry on the eastern seaboard. They are revered as hard-working, thrifty people with enormous agrarian stamina, and by some, as islands of sanity in a culture gripped by commercialism and technology run wild.

In the academic community several models have been advanced for understanding Amish society. Social scientists, like other Americans, have been influenced by the upward push of an advancing civilization and changes in the social discourse between the dominant society and its minorities. University teachers have traditionally taught their students to think of the Amish people as one of many old-world cultural islands left over in the modern world. The Amish have been considered "a sacred society," a "familistic society," as maintaining "organic solidarity," an "integrative social system," "primary" (face-to-face) rather than "secondary" relationships, and "Apollonian" instead of "Dionysian" orientations to life. They may be viewed from any one of these perspectives, but such objective models and abstractions leave out things that are important for understanding the whole perspective of Amish society.

The Amish are a church, a community, a spiritual union, a conservative branch of Christianity, a religion, a community whose members practice simple and austere living, a familistic entrepreneuring system, and an adaptive human community. In this chapter several models will be discussed in terms of their usefulness and limitations as avenues for understanding Amish society as a whole. By models I mean structured concepts currently used by anthropologists to characterize whole societies. The serious reader will want to transcend the scientific orientation and ask, What is the meaning of the Amish system? What, if anything, is it trying to say to us?

A COMMONWEALTH

The Amish are in some ways a little commonwealth, for their members claim to be ruled by the law of love and redemption. The bonds that unite them are many. Their beliefs, however, do not permit them solely to occupy and defend a particular territory. They are highly sensitive in caring for their own. They will move to other lands when circumstances force them to do so.

Commonwealth implies a place, a province, which means any part of a national domain that geographically and socially is sufficiently unified to have a true consciousness of its unity. Its inhabitants feel comfortable with their own ideas and customs, and the "place" possesses a sense of distinction from other parts of the country. Members of a commonwealth are not foot-loose. They have a sense of productivity and accountability in a province where "the general welfare" is accepted as a day-to-day reality. Commonwealth has come to have an archaic meaning in today's world, because when groups and institutions become too large, the sense of commonwealth or the common good is lost. Thus it is little wonder that the most recent dictionaries of the American English language render the meaning of commonwealth as "obsolescent." In reality, the Amish are in part a commonwealth. There is, however, no provision for outcasts.

It may be argued that the Amish have retained elements of wholesome provincialism, a saving power to which the world in the future will need more and more to appeal. Provincialism need not turn to ancient narrowness and ignorance, confines from which many have sought to escape. A sense of province or commonwealth, with its cherished love of people and self-conscious dignity, is a necessary basis for relating to the wider world community. Respect for locality, place, custom, and local idealism can go a long way toward checking the monstrous growth of consolidation in the nation and thus help to save human freedom and individual dignity.

A Sectarian Society

Sociologists tend to classify the Amish as a sectarian society. Several European scholars have compared the social structure of "sect" and "church" types of religious institutions. The established church was viewed as hierarchic and conservative. It appealed to the ruling classes, administered grace to all people in a territorial domain, and served as an agency of social control. The sect was egalitarian. Essentially a voluntary religious protest movement, its members separated themselves from others on the basis of beliefs, practices, and institutions. The sects rejected the authority of the established religious organizations and their leaders. The strains between sect and church were viewed as a dialectic principle at work within Christianity. The use of an ideal type helped to clarify particular characteristics of the sectarian groups. The Anabaptists, for example, were described as small, voluntary groupings attempting to model their lives after the spirit of the Sermon on the Mount (Matt. 5, 6, 7) while also exercising the power to exclude and discipline members. Absolute separation from all other religious loyalties was required. All members were considered equal, and none were to take oaths, participate in war, or take part in worldly government.

Sects have employed various techniques of isolation for maintaining separateness. Today the extreme mobility of modern life brings people together in multiple contexts. The spatial metaphors of separation (i.e., valley, region, sector, etc.) are fast becoming obsolete. Nevertheless, modern sectarians turn to psychic insularity and contexts that protect them from mainstream values and competing systems. Members of the sect remain segregated in various degrees, chiefly by finding a group whose philosophy of history contradicts the existing values so drastically that the group sustains itself for a generation or more. To the onlooker, sectarianism, like monasticism, may appear to serve as a shelter from the complications of an overly complex society. For its participants, it provides authentic ways of realizing new forms of service and humility as well as protection from mainstream culture.

Sectarians, it is claimed, put their faith first by ordering their lives in keeping with it. The established churches compromise their faith with other interests and with the demands of the surrounding environment. Sectarians are pervasively religious in that they practice their beliefs in everyday life. Sects are often considered marginal or odd groups of alienated people with fanatic ideas. Yet the sects have had an immense influence in shaping the course of history. The British sociologist Bryan Wilson has observed that sects are "self-conscious attempts by men to construct their own societies, not merely as political entities with constitutions, but as groups with a firm set of values and mores, of which they are conscious." The growth of religious toleration in America has resulted in the development of religious pluralism in a manner that has not been realized in Europe. Wilson, who has characterized modern Christian sects into several types, classes the Amish as *introversionist* rather than *conversionist* or *reformist*. "Salvation is to be found in the community of those who withdraw from involvement in the affairs of mankind." The Amish recognize the evil circumstance of man, attempt to moderate its influence upon them, and retreat into a community to experience, cultivate, and preserve the attributes of God in ethical relationships.

The sectarian model lends itself to a historical, religious context. As a model, it offers some insight into the proliferation of groups with a negative orientation during a specific time period. Today there are many types of movements that did not exist in the early stages of industrialization. Sects may lose their spontaneity in a variety of ways. While the model may teach us something of how sects originate and grow from a protest movement to a separate religious entity, it does not provide us with a knowledge of the dynamics of the group. The Amish, for example, are not sectarians in the sense that they demand that others conform to their practices. Nor do they claim to base all actions on holy writ. They are not in conflict with the dominant culture in the same way, or with the same intensity, as are a number of sects such as the "apocalyptic" or "manipulationist" types.

Many sectarian societies, including the Amish, make little or no attempt to communicate their message. They recognize instinctively that authentic communication would mean greater literacy, education, and sophistication, and this would mean the beginning of the end. "The contribution of the sect to the larger society is," according to Martin Marty, "made best through the sympathetic observer who carries with him a picture of the advantages or particularity and assertiveness back to the world of dialogical complexity." In the Amish case, the message of the sectarian society is exemplary. A way of living is more important than communicating it in words. The ultimate message is the life. An Amish person will have no doubt about his basic convictions, his view of the meaning and purpose of life, but he cannot explain it except through the conduct of his life.

A FOLK SOCIETY

Anthropologists, who have compared societies all over the world, have tended to call semiisolated peoples "folk societies," "primitives," or merely "simple societies." These societies constitute an altogether different type in contrast to the industrialized, or so-called civilized, societies. The "folk society," as conceptualized by Robert Redfield, is a small, isolated, traditional, simple, homogeneous society in which oral communication and conventionalized ways are important factors in integrating the whole of life. In such an ideal-type society, shared practical knowledge is more important than science, custom is valued more than critical knowledge, and associations are personal and emotional rather than abstract and categoric.

Folk societies are uncomfortable with the idea of change. Young people do what the old people did when they were young. Members communicate intimately with one another, not only by word of mouth but also through custom and symbols that reflect a strong sense of belonging to one another. A folk society is *Gemeinschaft*-like;[1] there is a strong sense of "we-ness." Leadership is personal rather than institutionalized. There are no gross economic inequalities. Mutual aid is characteristic of the society's members. The goals of life are never stated as matters of doctrine, but neither are they questioned. They are implied by the acts that constitute living in a small society. Custom tends to become sacred. Behavior is strongly patterned, and acts as well as cultural objects are given symbolic meaning that is often pervasively religious. Religion is diffuse and all-pervasive. In the typical folk society, planting and harvesting are as sacred in their own ways as singing and praying.

The significance of the Amish as an intimate, face-to-face primary group has long been recognized. Charles P. Loomis was the first to conceptualize the character of the Amish. In his construction of a scale he contrasted the Amish as a familistic *Gemeinschaft*-type system with highly rational social systems of the *Gesellschaft*-type in contemporary civilization.

The folk model lends itself well to understanding the tradition-directed character of Amish society. The heavy weight of tradition can scarcely be explained in any other way. The Amish, for example, have retained many of the customs and small-scale technologies that were common in rural society in the nineteenth century. Through a process of syncretism, Amish religious values have been fused with an earlier pe-

---

1. The German term, *Gemeinschaft*, is often translated as "community." Ferdenand Toennies classic work, *Gemeinschaft und Gesellschaft* provided sociology with this concept which is contrasted to urban, modern and industrialized society (*Gesellschaft*).

riod of simple country living when everyone farmed with horses and on a scale where family members could work together. The Amish exist as a folk or "little" community in a rural subculture within the modern state, as distinguished from the primitive or peasant types described in anthropological literature. Several aspects of Redfield's folk-society model and features of the Toennies-Loomis *Gemeinschaft* aid us in understanding the parameters of Amish society. They are *distinctiveness, smallness of scale, homogeneous culture patterns,* and the *strain toward self-sufficiency.*

Distinctiveness. The Amish people are highly visible. The outsider who drives through an Amish settlement cannot help but recognize them by their clothing, farm homes, furnishings, fields, and other material traits of culture. Although they speak perfect English with outsiders, they speak a dialect of German among themselves.

Amish life is distinctive in that religion and custom blend into a way of life. The two are inseparable. The core values of the community are religious beliefs. Not only do the members worship a deity they understand through the revelation of Jesus Christ and the Bible, but their patterned behavior has a religious dimension. A distinctive way of life permeates daily life, agriculture, and the application of energy to economic ends. Their beliefs determine their conceptions of the self, the universe, and man's place in it. The Amish world view recognizes a certain spiritual worth and dignity in the universe in its natural form. Religious considerations determine hours of work and the daily, weekly, seasonal, and yearly rituals associated with life experience. Occupation, the means and destinations of travel, and choice of friends and mate are determined by religious considerations. Religious and work attitudes are not far distant from each other. The universe includes the divine, and Amish society itself is considered divine insofar as the Amish recognize themselves as "a chosen people of God." The Amish do not seek to master nature or to work against the elements, but try to work with them. The affinity between Amish society and nature in the form of land, terrain, and vegetation is expressed in various degrees of intensity.

Religion is highly patterned, so one may properly speak of the Amish as a tradition-directed group. Though allusions to the Bible play an important role in determining their outlook on the world, and on life after death, these beliefs have been fused with several centuries of struggling to survive in community. Out of intense religious experience, societal conflict, and intimate agrarian experience, a mentality has developed that prefers the old rather than the new. While the principle seems to apply especially to religion, it has also become a charter for social behavior. "The old is the best, and the new is of the devil," has become a prevalent mode of thought. By living in closed communities where custom and a strong sense of togetherness prevail, the Amish have formed an integrated way of life and a folklike culture. Continuity of conformity and custom is assured and the needs of the individual from birth to death are met within an integrated and shared system of meanings. Oral tradition, custom, and conventionality play an important part in maintaining the group as a functioning whole. To the participant, religion and custom are inseparable. Commitment and culture are combined to produce a stable human existence.

These are some of the qualities of the little Amish community that make it distinctive. "Where the community begins and where it ends is apparent. The distinctiveness is apparent to the outside observer and is expressed in the group consciousness of the people of the community." The Amish community is in some aspects a functional part of modern society but is a distinctive subculture within it.

11
The Foundations of Third World Poverty

John Isbister

Prospects for positive change in the poorest countries of the world are not bright, at least in the immediate future. Much of the reason lies in the past relationship between poor and wealthy countries and the chain of events this relationship set in motion. Isbister's discussion encourages us to recognize that we are all tied into the global community, and that the benefit to each of us is dependent on a strategy of global change that benefits us all.

In the economic sphere, the legacy of imperialism is central. The dependency theorists are correct in insisting that imperialism formed the economic structures of the Third World, which even today leave the vast majority of the human race in desperately poor conditions. . . .

When we turn to . . . the effects of imperialism upon the economies and societies of Asia, the Middle East, Africa and Latin America, then the fact that the imperialists were capitalist is centrally important. The essence of capitalism is alienation. The factors of production—land, labor and capital—are treated in a capitalist system as commodities, to be bought or sold. They are not part of a person's birthright. In many peasant societies, in contrast, the factors of production are inherently connected as part of an integrated system. A person is born to a village society and automatically cultivates land passed down from one generation to the next, using the product to sustain the family. These peasants, although usually exploited by a landowning or ruling class, are nonetheless secure in knowing their place in the world. The advent of imperialism broke this world apart, creating labor forces that worked for wages on other people's projects, and land that could be bought and sold. Imperialism converted the peasants of the Third World into separate components of the capitalist system, components whose survival depended upon the vagaries of global markets over which they had no control.

Before the arrival of the imperialists, the majority of the people of the Third World were involved in producing food for their own use—as hunters and gatherers in some regions, but for the most part as cultivators of the soil. They typically produced some surplus food, over and above their own needs, which was used to support a ruling group, but this was usually a small portion of their production. For the most part, they produced what they needed to survive. Imperialism changed this picture. It did not totally displace subsistence production, of course, because people still had to eat; on top of subsistence production, however, the imperialists imposed the production of primary export commodities—agricultural goods and minerals from the colonies that were intended for use in the metropolitan centers. The colonies were turned into a vast production system for sugar, cacao, tobacco, wheat, cotton, meat, fish, jute, coffee, coconuts, rubber, wool, palm oil, rice, bananas, ground nuts, indigo, tin, gold, silver, bauxite, copper and many more products.

As Europe developed its manufacturing industries in the nineteenth century, and as its own peasants were drawn off the land and into its unspeakable cities, it required new sources of primary agricultural commodities—both to feed the urban labor force and to provide raw materials for the factories. It was no coincidence, then, that colonial export production intensified at the same time that capitalist industrial production was growing in Europe; the colonial exports were required for the growth of industry at the imperial centers.

Imperialism produced a world of economic specialization: manufacturing in the core of Europe and agricultural and mining production in the periphery of the Third World. The doctrines of free trade and comparative advantage . . . provided an intellectual justification for this specialization. . . .

The case against comparative advantage, and against the world division of production brought about by the imperialists, is not entirely easy to make, because there are obvious counterexamples. Canada is the best of the counterexamples. From the sixteenth century through to the twentieth, Canada fit precisely into the imperialist economic mode: it produced primary products for export to Europe, and it imported European manufactured goods. On the basis of those primary exports it was successful; it developed into one of the richest countries in the world, with a standard of living higher than most European countries. Canada developed its economy to a high level by exploiting a series of primary exports, or "staples." In the sixteenth century the French discovered the rich fisheries off the coast of Newfoundland. Their successors ventured inland, eventually across the entire continent, in search of beaver furs, which were processed into felt hats for European consumers. The fur trade was succeeded by timber, and then by the greatest staple export of all, wheat. In the twentieth century, wheat was supplemented by minerals. Immigrants flocked to the new land to develop each staple export as it came along. The income they generated was used both to raise their standard of living and to reinvest in productive activities designed for local use. In Canada, primary exports became the engine of sustained economic growth. A national manufacturing sector grew up behind the staples to meet the needs of the local settlers, and in this way Canada developed a technologically advanced, productive modern economy.

To cite the Canadian example is to show, however, how exceptional it was, for the export industries established in most of the rest of the colonial world did not lead automatically to self-sustaining economic growth for the local population. Far more often they led to poverty, to destitution on the land and to urbanization without hope. Even in Argentina, which for many decades resembled Canada, and by as late as the 1920's had a higher standard of living based upon its beef export industry, stagnation eventually set in.

The best answer to the question of why the concentration on colonial agricultural export production led to stagnation in the Third World instead of to prosperity as in Canada lies in the fact that the exports transformed the social structures of the Third World (but not of Canada) in such a way as to render genuine economic development less likely. The heart of social transformation in the Third World was the fact that the local labor force, or the land, or both, had to be wrested, often forcibly, from their existing uses. The problem of forcibly changing the use of local labor and land did not arise in Canada, because in that colony the native population was either exterminated or shunted off to reservations, leaving behind them lands that for the most part had never been tilled. But in the Third World, the local populations generally stayed and were in possession of the land.

The colonialists in the Third World often confronted intensive labor shortages. Frequently the local people did not constitute the sort of labor force that capitalist enterprises required; they were not willing to give up their subsistence pursuits and work for wages—at least not for the low wages normally offered by the white man. In some cases forced labor of the local people resulted in many deaths—for example, in the mines and plantations of the Spanish empire in Latin America. The slave trade was the first answer to this problem—millions of Africans were shipped to the western hemisphere—until it was effectively shut down towards the beginning of the nineteenth century. As the nineteenth century progressed, however, the need for colonial labor only increased, so other expedients were developed. Indentured service, or the labor contract, became common; it was a system by which a person made the commitment to work in a foreign land for a period of years in return for a guaranteed wage and a return passage home. Indentured Indians, Chinese and other Asians were shipped long distances to work in semifree conditions in the imperialist plantations. Many did not return to their homelands, and their descendants today create ethnic heterogeneity in many areas of the Third World.

In addition to importing labor, the Europeans devised ways of forcing the local people to work for them. In Indonesia the Dutch established the "culture system," a kind of throwback to European medieval feudalism, by which native people were required to devote a certain portion of their land and labor to the production of export products, these to take the place of taxes. A common technique in Africa and elsewhere was to impose a hut tax or a head tax. These were taxes that had to be paid in the imperialist's currency by each person. But the peasants did not earn or use this currency in their villages. So in order to pay the tax they had to earn the currency, and in order to earn the currency they had to work as laborers for the white man. The head tax led to the pernicious colonial theory of the "backward-bending supply curve of labor": the lower the wage rate the longer the natives would work, since their goal was to earn a certain fixed amount in order to be able to pay the hut tax. It was a system of forced labor, pure and simple. Frequently taxes did not induce sufficient work, however, and they were supplemented by more direct means: the compulsion of labor by military force. The use of armed force by King Leopold of Belgium in the Congo to create a labor force was particularly notorious. . . .

If the accumulation of a labor force was a problem, the amassing of land to be used by capitalist enterprises for export crops was often even more difficult. Most of the land was, of course, already occupied. The Europeans were faced with the need either to expel the local people from the most fertile land, or to persuade them to grow export crops in their villages. Expulsion was often the order of the day. . . . The land distribution in southern and East Africa became unbelievably skewed, with the Europeans, a small proportion of the population, owning the great majority of the land and the Africans crowded into small areas with inferior soil.

Far more common were the large plantations, in Africa and Asia owned and overseen by Europeans and worked exclusively by natives. . . . Landholding patterns became incredibly unequal; it was common in many areas of the Third World for a scant 1 or 2 percent of the landowners to control at least half of the arable land. The land available for peasant use was reduced proportionately and, of course, many of the peasants, having lost their land, had to work as wage laborers, usually for very low wages, on the great plantations. . . .

The imperialist world economy, and the insatiable demand of European industrialization for food and raw materials, therefore transformed the agricultural sectors of the Third World, where the great majority of the populations were located. Imperialism forced millions of people to migrate, it separated masses of people from the land and recreated them as wage laborers and it brought village-based, peasant agriculture into world markets.

In assessing this tremendous impact, it is helpful to return to the comparison of the Third World with Canada, since Canada parlayed a succession of primary exports into steady economic growth and one of the world's highest standards of living. Why did the concentration on primary exports not pay similar dividends in the Third World? It is a puzzle. Some of the answers that have been given to it over the years seem not very satisfying. Raúl Prebisch and some other Latin American economists argued that the problem was declining terms of trade—essentially that the prices of primary products were falling in world markets to such an extent that, even though Third World countries were selling more and more, they were earning less and less and could afford fewer imports of manufactured goods. The argument is valid for some primary exports and for some countries, over some time periods, but recent scholarship has shown conclusively that as a general explanation for the continuing poverty of the Third World it collapses. Certainly it cannot be a general explanation for the poverty of primary exporters, for if it were, Canada would be poverty stricken as well.

Another line of argument has been that the imperialists and their successors sent the profits that they earned back to their homelands, rather than reinvesting those profits in local enterprises. Modern imperialism and neocolonialism are seen through these lenses as a way of looting the Third World, just as surely as the sixteenth-century Spaniards looted the gold and silver of the Americas. This argument has more to it, since there certainly were enormous transfers of funds from the colonial areas back to Britain and the other colonial powers. It is not really satisfactory, though, as an explanation of continuing poverty, since profits were repatriated from Canada, too, and since even after subtracting the repatriated profits, considerable new wealth stayed in the colonies as a consequence of the export activities.

A more promising explanation is F. S. Weaver's, who argues that the export industries created new wealth and that the wealth reinforced whatever social structure was already existing in the colony. In Canada, the British settlers who populated most of the country outside the province of Quebec were entrepreneurial capitalists to begin with. There was no question of transforming them from feudal or subsistence peasants— they were capitalists from the day they entered the country, in the sense that they were committed to the market, to buying and selling, to producing for export and not for their own use. The income they earned was reinvested in the expansion of their small-scale enterprises, including family farms.

But in the colonies of what is now the Third World, conditions were very different. The relationship that the imperialists had to the natives, and that the *hacendados* had to the peons, was one of oppression. So, when the ruling classes in the Third World accumulated wealth through the export of primary products, they used that wealth and the power that went along with it to intensify the oppression of the local people and thereby to reinforce their own status. Imperialism reinforced the conditions that were already there. Profits were used to expand plantations, but for the local people this simply meant being part of a larger labor force, separate from their ancestral homes and working for minimal wages. Peasant-based export agriculture in theory might have been more beneficial to the local people, but in practice there were severe limits to the expansion of peasant agriculture, because the people stuck to their subsistence farming techniques; consequently, sufficient wealth seldom flowed to the villages to allow them really to escape from their poverty.

One could imagine conditions, therefore, under which agricultural and mineral exports could have led to the prosperity of the Third World—if the local people had not been oppressed, if they had been able to benefit from their own work, if they had been allowed the freedom to be creative and inventive. But these were not the conditions of the European empires.

An enormous system of worldwide trade in primary commodities grew up; it was a system that depended upon impoverished labor forces, in many cases pulled unceremoniously away from their villages and cultures. Income was earned in the colonies from these export industries, but it was not earned by the working people who might have been able to use it creatively to improve their lives. It was earned by upper and middle classes, who used it to increase their consumption and to secure their control over the poor.

By contrast, the primary export producers in Canada—the fur traders, the lumberjacks, the small farmers and the miners—slowly accumulated wealth and increased their demands for manufactured goods that could be produced locally. Over time an integrated economy was developed, with primary exports and manufacturing both growing and supporting each other. In the Third World, since most of the new income was kept from the workers, people could not afford manufactured products. The Latin American "structuralist" school has been particularly successful in showing how the local income generated by imperialist trade went into the hands of an increasingly well-off minority of the population, who turned to European imports to satisfy their demands for sophisticated consumer goods. No mass market for simple manufactured goods ever arose, and so local manufacturing could not get a start. . . .

If imperialism harmed the self-sufficiency of Third World agriculture, it absolutely devastated its manufacturing. Before the age of imperialism, the Third World had not enjoyed industrial production such as exists currently in the developed countries. Factory production is a result of the European industrial revolution. But most Third World areas did have thriving craft sectors, producing textiles, pottery, household utensils and the like. These were systematically destroyed by the imperialists, not at the muzzle of a gun but as a consequence of marketplace competition. The European industrial revolution spewed out manufactured goods that were much cheaper, and often of higher quality, than the colonies' crafts. The imperialists had no motive to protect the local crafts; on the contrary, they had every incentive to open up local markets to European exports. Imperialism led therefore to the collapse of manufacturing and craft production in the Third World. . . .

. . . [A]n entire class of independent craftspeople disappeared. They were for the most part people with highly developed skills who were used to making business decisions on their own, and many of them were to some extent entrepreneurial. They might very well have been able to adapt the new European technologies to their own needs, and as a consequence have led the way to the economic development of their societies. But they were wiped out. Almost the entire Indian textile industry was eliminated because of the import of cheap cotton goods from Britain.

The economic effects of European imperialism were therefore massive. Millions of people were pulled away from their accustomed pursuits to work in capitalist and export enterprises. Almost all were kept at low, subsistence incomes, without opportunity to share the benefits obtained from export production. Land that had been tilled for centuries for subsistence food crops was expropriated for the growth of export crops. In the countryside, single-crop agriculture brought with it ecological deterioration. Manufacturing and crafts disappeared, and as a consequence the economies of many Third World areas became much more specialized and concentrated. . . .

12

Queer Customs

CLYDE KLUCKHOLM

Culture provides "a storehouse of the pooled learning" of a group of people, according to the author. It provides meaning to the physical world and to our thoughts and emotions. Culture is a human construction and thus flexible and diverse. Yet to those who possess a particular culture, it is deadly serious. Culture is like a map—with it you can navigate a society; without it you will be barely human.

Why do the Chinese dislike milk and milk products? Why would the Japanese die willingly in a Banzai charge that seemed senseless to Americans? Why do some nations trace descent through the father, others through the mother, still others through both parents? Not because they were destined by God or Fate to different habits, not because the weather is different in China and Japan and the United States. Sometimes shrewd common sense has an answer that is close to that of the anthropologist: "because they were brought up that way." By "culture" anthropology means the total life way of a people, the social legacy the individual acquires from his group. Or culture can be regarded as that part of the environment that is the creation of man.

This technical term has a wider meaning than the "culture" of history and literature. A humble cooking pot is as much a cultural product as is a Beethoven sonata. In ordinary speech a man of culture is a man who can speak languages other than his own, who is familiar with history, literature, philosophy, or the fine arts. In some cliques that definition is still narrower. The cultured person is one who can talk about James Joyce, Scarlatti, and Picasso. To the anthropologist, however, to be human is to be cultured. There is culture in general, and then there are the specific cultures such as Russian, American, British, Hottentot, Inca. The general abstract notion serves to remind us that we cannot explain acts solely in terms of the biological properties of the people concerned, their individual past experience, and the immediate situation. The past experience of other men in the form of culture enters into almost every event. Each specific culture constitutes a kind of blueprint for all of life's activities.

One of the interesting things about human beings is that they try to understand themselves and their own behavior. While this has been particularly true of Europeans in recent times, there is no group which has not developed a scheme or schemes to explain man's actions. To the insistent human query "why?" the most exciting illumination anthropology has to offer is that of the concept of culture. Its explanatory importance is comparable to categories such as evolution in biology, gravity in physics, disease in medicine. A good deal of human behavior can be understood, and indeed predicted, if we know a people's design for living. Many acts are neither accidental nor due to personal peculiarities nor caused by supernatural forces nor simply mysterious. Even those of us who pride ourselves on our individualism follow most of the time a pattern not of our own making. We brush our teeth on arising. We put on pants—not a loincloth or a grass skirt. We eat three meals a day—not four or five or two. We sleep in a bed—not in a hammock or on a sheep pelt. I do not have to know the individual and his life history to be able to predict these and countless other regularities, including many in the thinking process, of all Americans who are not incarcerated in jails or hospitals for the insane.

To the American woman a system of plural wives seems "instinctively" abhorrent. She cannot understand how any woman can fail to be jealous and uncomfortable if she must share her husband with other women. She feels it "unnatural" to accept such a situation. On the other hand, a Koryak woman of Siberia, for example, would find it hard to understand how a woman could be so selfish and so undesirous of feminine companionship in the home as to wish to restrict her husband to one mate.

Some years ago I met in New York City a young man who did not speak a word of English and was obviously bewildered by American ways. By "blood" he was an American as you or I, for his parents had gone from Indiana to China as missionaries. Orphaned in infancy, he was reared by a Chinese family in a remote village. All who met him found him more Chinese than American. The facts of his blue eyes and light hair were less impressive than a Chinese style of gait, Chinese arm and hand movements, Chinese facial expression, and Chinese modes of thought. The biological heritage was American, but the cultural training had been Chinese. He returned to China.

Another example of another kind: I once knew a trader's wife in Arizona who took a somewhat devilish interest in producing a cultural reaction. Guests who came her way were often served delicious sandwiches filled with a meat that seemed to be neither chicken nor tuna fish yet was reminiscent of both. To queries she gave no reply until each had eaten his fill. She then explained that what they had eaten was not chicken, not tuna fish, but the rich, white flesh of freshly killed rattlesnakes. The response was instantaneous—vomiting, often violent vomiting. A biological process is caught in a cultural web.

A highly intelligent teacher with long and successful experience in the public schools of Chicago was finishing her first year in an Indian school. When asked how her Navaho pupils compared in intelligence with Chicago youngsters, she replied, "Well, I just don't know. Sometimes the Indians seem just as bright. At other times they just act like dumb animals. The other night we had a dance in the high school. I saw a boy who is one of the best students in my English class standing off by himself. So I took him over to a pretty girl and told them to dance. But they just stood there with their heads down. They wouldn't even say anything." I inquired if she knew whether or not they were members of the same clan. "What difference would that make?"

"How would you feel about getting into bed with your brother?" The teacher walked off in a huff, but, actually, the two cases were quite comparable in principle. To the Indian the type of bodily contact involved in our social dancing has a directly sexual connotation. The incest taboos between members of the same clan are as severe as between true brothers and sisters. The shame of the Indians at the suggestion that a clan brother and sister should dance and the indignation of the white teacher at the idea that she should share a bed with an adult brother represent equally nonrational responses, culturally standardized unreason.

All this does not mean that there is no such thing as raw human nature. The very fact that certain of the same institutions are found in all known societies indicates that at bottom all human beings are very much alike. The files of the Cross-Cultural Survey at Yale University are organized according to categories such as "marriage ceremonies," "life crisis rites," "incest taboos." At least seventy-five of these categories are represented in every single one of the hundreds of cultures analyzed. This is hardly surprising. The members of all human groups have about the same biological equipment. All men undergo the same poignant life experiences such as birth, helplessness, illness, old age, and death. The biological potentialities of the species are the blocks with which cultures are built. Some patterns of every culture crystallize around focuses provided by the inevitables of biology: the difference between the sexes, the presence of persons of different ages, the varying physical strength and skill of individuals. The facts of nature also limit culture forms. No culture provides patterns for jumping over trees or for eating iron ore.

There is thus no "either-or" between nature and that special form of nurture called culture. Culture determinism is as one-sided as biological determinism. The two factors are interdependent. Culture arises out of human nature, and its forms are restricted both by man's biology and by natural laws. It is equally true that culture channels biological processes—vomiting, weeping, fainting, sneezing, the daily habits of food intake and waste elimination. When a man eats, he is reacting to an internal "drive," namely, hunger contractions consequent upon the lowering of blood sugar, but his precise reaction to these internal stimuli cannot be predicted by physiological knowledge alone. Whether a healthy adult feels hungry twice, three times, or four times a day and the hours at which this feeling recurs is a question of culture. *What* he eats is of course limited by availability, but is also partly regulated by culture. It is a biological fact that some types of berries are poisonous; it is a cultural fact that, a few generations ago, most Americans considered tomatoes to be poisonous and refused to eat them. Such selective, discriminative use of the environment is characteristically cultural. In a still more general sense, too, the process of eating is channeled by culture. Whether a man eats to live, lives to eat, or merely eats and lives is only in part an individual matter, for there are also cultural trends. Emotions are physiological events. Certain situations will evoke fear in people from any culture. But sensations of pleasure, anger, and lust may be stimulated by cultural cues that would leave unmoved someone who has been reared in a different social tradition.

Except in the case of newborn babies and of individuals born with clear-cut structural or functional abnormalities we can observe innate endowments only as modified by cultural training. In a hospital in New Mexico where Zuñi Indian, Navaho Indian, and white American babies are born, it is possible to classify the newly arrived infants as unusually active, average, and quiet. Some babies from each "racial" group will fall into each category, though a higher proportion of the white babies will fall into the unusually active class. But if a Navaho baby, a Zuñi baby, and a white baby—all classified as unusually active at birth—are again observed at the age of two years, the Zuñi baby will no longer seem given to quick and restless activity—*as compared with the white child*—though he may seem so as compared with the other Zuñis of the same age. The Navaho child is likely to fall in between as contrasted with the Zuñi and the white, though he will probably still seem more active than the average Navaho youngster.

It was remarked by many observers in the Japanese relocation centers that Japanese who were born and brought up in this country, especially those who were reared apart from any large colony of Japanese, resemble in behavior their white neighbors much more closely than they do their own parents who were educated in Japan.

I have said "culture channels biological processes." It is more accurate to say "the biological functioning of individuals is modified if they have been trained in certain ways and not in others." Culture is not a disembodied force. It is created and transmitted by people. However, culture, like well-known concepts of the physical sciences, is a convenient abstraction. One never sees gravity. One sees bodies falling in regular ways. One never sees an electromagnetic field. Yet certain happenings that can be seen may be given a neat abstract formulation by assuming that the electromagnetic field exists. Similarly, one never sees culture as such. What is seen are regularities in the behavior or artifacts of a group that has adhered to a common tradition. The regularities in style and technique of ancient Inca tapestries or stone axes from Melanesian islands are due to the existence of mental blueprints for the group.

Culture is a *way* of thinking, feeling, believing. It is the group's knowledge stored up (in memories of men; in books and objects) for future use. We study the products of this "mental" activity: the overt behavior, the speech and gestures and activities of people, and the tangible results of these things such as tools, houses, cornfields, and what not. It has been customary in lists of "culture traits" to include such things as watches or lawbooks. This is a convenient way of thinking about them, but in the solution of any important problem we must remember that they, in themselves, are nothing but metals, paper, and ink. What is important is that some men know how to make them, others set a value on them, are unhappy without them, direct their activities in relation to them, or disregard them.

It is only a helpful shorthand when we say "The cultural patterns of the Zulu were resistant to Christianization." In the directly observable world of course, it was individual Zulus who resisted. Nevertheless, if we do not forget that we are speaking at a high level of abstraction, it is justifiable to speak of culture as a cause. One may compare the practice of saying "syphilis caused the extinction of the native population of the island." Was it "syphilis" or "syphilis germs" or "human beings who were carriers of syphilis?"

"Culture," then, is "a theory." But if a theory is not contradicted by any relevant fact and if it helps us to understand a mass of otherwise chaotic facts, it is useful. Darwin's contribution was much less the accumulation of new knowledge than the creation of a theory which put in order data already known. An accumulation of facts, however large, is no more a science than a pile of bricks is a house. Anthropology's demonstration that the most weird set of customs has a consistency and an order is comparable to modern psychiatry's showing that there is meaning and purpose in the apparently incoherent talk of the insane. In fact, the inability of the older psychologies and philosophies to account for the strange behavior of madmen and heathens was the principal factor that forced psychiatry and anthropology to develop theories of the unconscious and of culture.

Since culture is an abstraction, it is important not to confuse culture with society. A "society" refers to a group of people who interact more with each other than they do with other individuals—who cooperate with each other for the attainment of certain ends. You can see and indeed count the individuals who make up a society. A "culture" refers to the distinctive ways of life of such a group of people. Not all social events are culturally patterned. New types of circumstances arise frequently.

A culture constitutes a storehouse of the pooled learning of the group. A rabbit starts life with some innate responses. He can learn from his own experience and perhaps from observing other rabbits. A human infant is born with fewer instincts and greater plasticity. His main task is to learn the answers that persons he will never see, persons long dead, have worked out. Once he has learned the formulas supplied by the culture of his group, most of his behavior becomes almost as automatic and unthinking as if it were instinctive. There is a tremendous amount of intelligence behind the making of a radio, but not much is required to learn to turn it on.

The members of all human societies face some of the same unavoidable dilemmas, posed by biology and other facts of the human situation. This is why the basic categories of all cultures are so similar. Human culture without language is unthinkable. No culture fails to provide for aesthetic expression and aesthetic delight. Every culture supplies standardized orientations toward the deeper problems, such as death. Every culture is designed to perpetuate the group and its solidarity, to meet the demands of individuals for an orderly way of life and for satisfaction of biological needs.

However, the variations on these basic themes are numberless. Some languages are built up out of twenty basic sounds, others out of forty. Nose plugs were considered beautiful by the predynastic Egyptians but are not by the modern French. Puberty is a biological fact. But one culture ignores it, another prescribes informal instructions about sex but no ceremony, a third has impressive rites for girls only, a fourth for boys and girls. In this culture, the first menstruation is welcomed as a happy, natural event; in that culture the atmosphere is full of dread and supernatural threat. Each culture dissects nature according to its own system of categories. The Navaho Indians apply the same word to the color of a robin's egg and to that of grass. A psychologist once assumed that this meant a difference in the sense organs, that Navahos didn't have the physiological equipment to distinguish "green" from "blue." However, when he showed them objects of the two colors and asked them if they were exactly the same colors, they looked at him with astonishment. His dream of discovering a new type of color blindness was shattered.

Every culture must deal with the sexual instinct. Some, however, seek to deny all sexual expression before marriage, whereas a Polynesian adolescent who was not promiscuous would be distinctly abnormal. Some cultures enforce lifelong monogamy, others, like our own, tolerate serial monogamy; in still other cultures, two or more women may be joined to one man or several men to a single woman. Homosexuality has been a permitted pattern in the Greco-Roman world, in parts of Islam, and in various primitive tribes. Large portions of the population of Tibet, and of Christendom at some places and periods, have practiced complete celibacy. To us marriage is first and foremost an arrangement between two individuals. In many more societies marriage is merely one facet of a complicated set of reciprocities, economic and otherwise, between two families or two clans.

The essence of the cultural process is selectivity. The selection is only exceptionally conscious and rational. Cultures are like Topsy.[1] They just grew. Once, however, a way of handling a situation becomes institutionalized, there is ordinarily great resistance to change or deviation. When we speak of "our sacred beliefs," we mean of course that they are beyond criticism and that the person who suggests modification or abandonment must be punished. No person is emotionally indifferent to his culture. Certain cultural premises may become totally out of accord with a new factual situation. Leaders may recognize this and reject the old ways in theory. Yet their emotional loyalty continues in the face of reason because of the intimate conditionings of early childhood.

A culture is learned by individuals as the result of belonging to some particular group, and it constitutes that part of learned behavior which is shared with others. It is our social legacy, as contrasted with our organic heredity. It is one of the important factors which permits us to live together in an organized society, giving us ready-made solutions to our problems, helping us to predict the behavior of others, and permitting others to know what to expect of us.

Culture regulates our lives at every turn. From the moment we are born until we die there is, whether we are conscious of it or not, constant pressure upon us to follow certain types of behavior that other men have created for us. Some paths we follow willingly, others we follow because we know no other way, still others we deviate from or go back to most unwillingly. Mothers of small children know how unnaturally most of this comes to us—how little regard we have, until we are "culturalized," for the "proper" place, time, and manner for certain acts such as eating, excreting, sleeping, getting dirty, and making loud noises. But by more or less adhering to a system of related designs for carrying out all the acts of living, a group of men and women feel themselves linked together by a powerful chain of sentiments. Ruth Benedict gave an almost complete definition of the concept when she said, "Culture is that which binds men together."

It is true any culture is a set of techniques for adjusting both to the external environment and to other men. However, cultures create problems as well as solve them. If the lore of a people states that frogs are dangerous creatures, or that it is not safe to go about at night because of witches or ghosts, threats are posed which do not arise out of the inexorable facts of the external world. Cultures produce needs as well as provide a means of fulfilling them. There exists for every group culturally defined, acquired drives that may be more powerful in ordinary daily life than the biologically inborn drives. Many Americans, for example, will work harder for "success" than they will for sexual satisfaction.

1. Topsy is a young slave girl in Harriet Beecher Stowe's *Uncle Tom's Cabin* who explained to her new mistress, when asked if she know about God and her creator, "I spect I grow'd. Don't think nobody never made me." [Editor]

Most groups elaborate certain aspects of their culture far beyond maximum utility or survival value. In other words, not all culture promotes physical survival. At times, indeed, it does exactly the opposite. Aspects of culture which once were adaptive may persist long after they have ceased to be useful. An analysis of any culture will disclose many features which cannot possibly be construed as adaptations to the total environment in which the group now finds itself. However, it is altogether likely that these apparently useless features represent survivals, with modifications through time, of cultural forms once useful.

Any cultural practice must be functional or it will disappear before long. That is, it must somehow contribute to the survival of the society or to the adjustment of the individual. However, many cultural functions are not manifest but latent. A cowboy will walk three miles to catch a horse which he then rides one mile to the store. From the point of view of manifest function this is positively irrational. But the act has the latent function of maintaining the cowboy's prestige in the terms of his own subculture. One can instance the buttons on the sleeve of a man's coat, our absurd English spelling, the use of capital letters, and a host of other apparently nonfunctional customs. They serve mainly the latent function of assisting individuals to maintain their security by preserving continuity with the past and by making certain sectors of life familiar and predictable.

Every culture is a precipitate of history. In more than one sense history is a sieve. Each culture embraces those aspects of the past which, usually in altered form and with altered meanings, live on in the present. Discoveries and inventions, both material and ideological, are constantly being made available to a group through its historical contacts with other peoples or being created by its own members. However, only those that fit the total immediate situation in meeting the group's needs for survival or in promoting the psychological adjustment of individuals will become part of the culture. The process of culture building may be regarded as an addition to man's innate biological capacities, an addition providing instruments which enlarge, or may even substitute for, biological functions, and to a degree compensating for biological limitations—as in ensuring that death does not always result in the loss to humanity of what the deceased has learned.

Culture is like a map. Just as a map isn't the territory but an abstract representation of a particular area, so also a culture is an abstract description of trends toward uniformity in the words, deeds, and artifacts of a human group. If a map is accurate and you can read it, you won't get lost; if you know a culture you will know your way around in the life of a society.

13

Deep Play: Notes on the Balinese Cockfight

Clifford Geertz

Complexity, hidden meanings, doing one thing but saying another—these are the things that make for an interesting life. In this classic essay one of anthropology's great writers explores gender and images of the world in what might otherwise appear to be a rather brutal and pointless contest of dumb animals and their keepers.

Of Cocks and Men

Bali, mainly because it is Bali, is a well-studied place. Its mythology, art, ritual, social organization, patterns of child rearing, forms of law, even styles of trance, have all been microscopically examined for traces of that elusive substance Jane Belo called "The Balinese Temper." But, aside from a few passing remarks, the cockfight has barely been noticed, although as a popular obsession of consuming power it is at least as important a revelation of what being a Balinese "is really like" as these more celebrated phenomena. As much of America surfaces in a ball park, on a golf links, at a race track, or around a poker table, much of Bali surfaces in a cock ring. For it is only apparently cocks that are fighting there. Actually, it is men.

To anyone who has been in Bali any length of time, the deep psychological identification of Balinese men with their cocks is unmistakable. The double entendre here is deliberate. It works in exactly the same way in Balinese as it does in English, even to producing the same tired jokes, strained puns, and uninventive obscenities. Bateson and Mead have even suggested that, in line with the Balinese conception of the body as a set of separately animated parts, cocks are viewed as detachable, self-operating penises, ambulant genitals with a life of their own. And while I do not have the kind of unconscious material either to confirm or disconfirm this intriguing notion, the fact that they are masculine symbols *par excellence* is about as indubitable, and to the Balinese about as evident, as the fact that water runs downhill.

The language of everyday moralism is shot through, on the male side of it, with roosterish imagery. *Sabung*, the word for cock (and one which appears in inscriptions as early as A.D. 922), is used metaphorically to mean "hero," "warrior," "champion," "man of parts," "political candidate," "bachelor," "dandy," "lady-killer," or "tough guy." A pompous man whose behavior presumes above his station is compared to a tailless cock who struts about as though he had a large, spectacular one. A desperate man who makes a last, irrational effort to extricate himself from an impossible situation is likened to a dying cock who makes one final lunge at his tormentor to drag him along to a common destruction. A stingy man, who promises much, gives little, and begrudges that is compared to a cock which, held by the tail, leaps at another without in fact engaging him. A marriageable young man still shy with the opposite sex or someone in a new job anxious to make a good impression is called "a fighting cock caged for the first time." Court trials, wars, political contests, inheritance disputes, and street arguments are all compared to cockfights. Even the very island itself is perceived from its shape as a small, proud cock, poised, neck extended, back taut, tail raised, in eternal challenge to large, feckless, shapeless Java.

But the intimacy of men with their cocks is more than metaphorical. Balinese men, or anyway a large majority of Balinese men, spend an enormous amount of time with their favorites, grooming them, feeding them, discussing them, trying them out against one another, or just gazing at them with a mixture of rapt admiration and dreamy self-absorption. Whenever you see a group of Balinese men squatting idly in the council shed or along the road in their hips down, shoulders forward, knees up fashion, half or more of them will have a rooster in his hands, holding it between his thighs, bouncing it gently up and down to strengthen its legs, ruffling its feathers with abstract sensuality, pushing it out against a neighbor's rooster to rouse its spirit, withdrawing it toward his loins to calm it again. Now and then, to get a feel for another bird, a man will fiddle this way with someone else's cock for a while, but usually by moving around to squat in place behind it, rather than just having it passed across to him as though it were merely an animal.

In the houseyard, the high-walled enclosures where the people live, fighting cocks are kept in wicker cages, moved frequently about so as to maintain the optimum balance of sun and shade. They are fed a special diet, which varies somewhat according to individual theories but which is mostly maize, sifted for impurities with far more care than it is when mere humans are going to eat it and offered to the animal kernel by kernel. Red pepper is stuffed down their beaks and up their anuses to give them spirit. They are bathed in the same ceremonial preparation of tepid water, medicinal herbs, flowers, and onions in which infants are bathed, and for a prize cock just about as often. Their combs are cropped, their plumage dressed, their spurs trimmed, their legs massaged, and they are inspected for flaws with the squinted concentration of a diamond merchant. A man who has a passion for cocks, an enthusiast in the literal sense of the term, can spend most of his life with them, and even those, the overwhelming majority, whose passion though intense has not entirely run away with them, can and do spend what seems not only to an outsider, but also to themselves, an inordinate amount of time with them. "I am cock crazy," my landlord, a quite ordinary *afficionado* by Balinese standards, used to moan as he went to move another cage, give another bath, or conduct another feeding. "We're all cock crazy."

The madness has some less visible dimensions, however, because although it is true that cocks are symbolic expressions or magnifications of their owner's self, the narcissistic male ego writ out in Aesopian terms, they are also expressions—and rather more immediate ones—of what the Balinese regard as the direct inversion, aesthetically, morally, and metaphysically, of human status: animality.

The Balinese revulsion against any behavior regarded as animal-like can hardly be overstressed. Babies are not allowed to crawl for that reason. Incest, though hardly approved, is a much less horrifying crime than bestiality. (The appropriate punishment for the second is death by drowning, for the first being forced to live like an animal.) Most demons are represented—in sculpture, dance, ritual, myth—in some real or fantastic animal form. The main puberty rite consists in filing the child's teeth so they will not look like animal fangs. Not only defecation but eating is regarded as a disgusting, almost obscene activity, to be conducted hurriedly and privately, because of its association with animality. Even falling down or any form of clumsiness is considered to be bad for these reasons. Aside from cocks and a few domestic animals—oxen, ducks—of no emotional significance, the Balinese are aversive to animals and treat their large number of dogs not merely callously but with a phobic cruelty. In identifying with his cock, the Balinese man is identifying not just with his ideal self, or even his penis, but also, and at the same time, with what he most fears, hates, and, ambivalence being what it is, is fascinated by—The Powers of Darkness.

The connection of cocks and cockfighting with such Powers, with the animalistic demons that threaten constantly to invade the small, cleared off space in which the Balinese have so carefully built their lives and devour its inhabitants, is quite explicit. A cockfight, any cockfight, is in the first instance a blood sacrifice offered, with the appropriate chants and oblations, to the demons in order to pacify their ravenous, cannibal hunger. No temple festival should be conducted until one is made. (If it is omitted someone will inevitably fall into a trance and command with the voice of an angered spirit that the oversight be immediately corrected.) Collective responses to natural evils—illness, crop failure, volcanic eruptions—almost always involve them. And that famous holiday in Bali, The Day of Silence (Njepi), when everyone sits silent and immobile all day long in order to avoid contact with a sudden influx of demons chased momentarily out of hell, is preceded the previous day by large-scale cockfights (in this case legal) in almost every village on the island.

In the cockfight, man and beast, good and evil, ego and id, the creative power of aroused masculinity and the destructive power of loosened animality fuse in a bloody drama of hatred, cruelty, violence, and death. It is little wonder that when, as is the invariable rule, the owner of the winning cock takes the carcass of the loser—often torn limb from limb by its enraged owner—home to eat, he does so with a mixture of social embarrassment, moral satisfaction, aesthetic disgust, and cannibal joy. Or that a man who has lost an important fight is sometimes driven to wreck his family shrines and curse the gods, an act of metaphysical (and social) suicide. Or that in seeking earthly analogues for heaven and hell the Balinese compare the former to the mood of a man whose cock has just won, the latter to that of a man whose cock has just lost.

The Fight

Cockfights, *(tetadjen; sabungan)* are held in a ring about fifty feet square. Usually they begin toward late afternoon and run three or four hours until sunset. About nine or ten separate matches *(sehet)* comprise a program. Each match is precisely like the others in general pattern: there is no main match, no connection between individual matches, no variation in their format, and each is arranged on a completely ad hoc basis. After a fight has ended and the emotional debris is cleaned away—the bets paid, the curses cursed, the carcasses possessed—seven, eight, perhaps even a dozen men slip negligently into the ring with a cock and seek to find there a logical opponent for it. This process, which rarely takes less than ten minutes, and often a good deal longer, is conducted in a very subdued, oblique, even dissembling manner. Those not immediately involved give it at best but disguised, sidelong attention; those who, embarrassedly, are, attempt to pretend somehow that the whole thing is not really happening.

A match made, the other hopefuls retire with the same deliberate indifference, and the selected cocks have their spurs *(tadji)* affixed—razor sharp, pointed steel swords four or five inches long. This is a delicate job which only a small proportion of men, a half-dozen or so in most villages, know how to do properly. The man who attaches the spurs also provides them, and if the rooster he assists wins its owner awards him the spur-leg of the victim. The spurs are affixed by winding a long length of string around the foot of the spur and the leg of the cock. For reasons I shall come to presently, it is done somewhat differently from case to case, and is an obsessively deliberate affair. The lore about spurs is extensive—they are sharpened only at eclipses and the dark of the moon, should be kept out of the sight of women, and so forth. And they are handled, both in use and out, with the same curious combination of fussiness and sensuality the Balinese direct toward ritual objects generally.

The spurs affixed, the two cocks are placed by their handlers (who may or may not be their owners) facing one another in the center of the ring. A coconut pierced with a small hole is placed in a pail of water, in which it takes about twenty-one seconds to sink, a period known as a *tjeng* and marked at beginning and end by the beating of a slit gong.

During these twenty-one seconds the handlers *(pengangkeb)* are not permitted to touch their roosters. If, as sometimes happens, the animals have not fought during this time, they are picked up, fluffed, pulled, prodded, and otherwise insulted, and put back in the center of the ring and the process begins again. Sometimes they refuse to fight at all, or one keeps running away, in which case they are imprisoned together under a wicker cage, which usually gets them enraged.

Most of the time, in any case, the cocks fly almost immediately at one another in a wing-beating, head-thrusting, leg-kicking explosion of animal fury so pure, so absolute, and in its own way so beautiful, as to be almost abstract, a Platonic concept of hate. Within moments one or the other drives home a solid blow with his spur. The handler whose cock has delivered the blow immediately picks it up so that it will not get a return blow, for if he does not the match is likely to end in a mutually mortal tie as the two birds wildly hack each other to pieces. This is particularly true if, as often happens, the spur sticks in its victim's body, for then the aggressor is at the mercy of his wounded foe.

With the birds again in the hands of their handlers, the coconut is now sunk three times after which the cock which has landed the blow must be set down to show that he is firm, a fact he demonstrates by wandering idly around the rink for a coconut sink. The coconut is then sunk twice more and the fight must recommence.

During this interval, slightly over two minutes, the handler of the wounded cock has been working frantically over it, like a trainer patching a mauled boxer between rounds, to get it in shape for a last, desperate try for victory. He blows in its mouth, putting the whole chicken head in his own mouth and sucking and blowing, fluffs it, stuffs its wounds with various sorts of medicines, and generally tries anything he can think of to arouse the last ounce of spirit which may be hidden somewhere within it. By the time he is forced to put it back down he is usually drenched in chicken blood, but, as in prize fighting, a good handler is worth his weight in gold. Some of them can virtually make the dead walk, at least long enough for the second and final round.

In the climactic battle (if there is one; sometimes the wounded cock simply expires in the handler's hands or immediately as it is placed down again), the cock who landed the first blow usually proceeds to finish off his weakened opponent. But this is far from an inevitable outcome, for if a cock can walk he can fight, and if he can fight, he can kill, and what counts is which cock expires first. If the wounded one can get a stab in and stagger on until the other drops, he is the official winner, even if he himself topples over an instant later.

Surrounding all this melodrama—which the crowd packed tight around the ring follows in near silence, moving their bodies in kinesthetic sympathy with the movement of the animals, cheering their champions on with wordless hand motions, shiftings of the shoulders, turnings of the head, falling back *en masse* as the cock with the murderous spurs careens toward one side of the ring (it is said that spectators sometimes lose eyes and fingers from being too attentive), surging forward again as they glance off toward another—is a vast body of extraordinarily elaborate and precisely detailed rules.

These rules, together with the developed lore of cocks and cockfighting which accompanies them, are written down in palm leaf manuscripts (*lontar; rontal*) passed on from generation to generation as part of the general legal and cultural tradition of the villages. At a fight, the umpire (*saja komong; djuru kembar*)—the man who manages the coconut—is in charge of their application and his authority is absolute. I have never seen an umpire's judgment questioned on any subject, even by the more despondent losers, nor have I ever heard, even in private, a charge of unfairness directed against one, or, for that matter, complaints about umpires in general. Only exceptionally well-trusted, solid, and, given the complexity of the code, knowledgeable citizens perform this job, and in fact men will bring their cocks only to fights presided over by such men. It is also the umpire to whom accusations of cheating, which, though rare in the extreme, occasionally arise, are referred; and it is he who in the not infrequent cases where the cocks expire virtually together decides which (if either, for, though the Balinese do not care for such an outcome, there can be ties) went first. Likened to a judge, a king, a priest, and a policeman, he is all of these, and under his assured direction the animal passion of the fight proceeds within the civic certainty of the law. In the dozens of cockfights I saw in Bali, I never once saw an altercation about rules. Indeed, I never saw an open altercation, other than those between cocks, at all.

This crosswise doubleness of an event which, taken as a fact of nature, is rage untrammeled and, taken as a fact of culture, is form perfected, defines the cockfight as a sociological entity. A cockfight is what, searching for a name for something not vertebrate enough to be called a group and not structureless enough to be called a crowd, Erving Goffman has called a "focused gathering"—a set of persons engrossed in a common flow of activity and relating to one another in terms of that flow. Such gatherings meet and disperse; the participants in them fluctuate; the activity that focuses them is discrete—a particulate process that reoccurs rather than a continuous one that endures. They take their form from the situation that evokes them, the floor on which they are placed, as Goffman puts it; but it is a form, and an articulate one, nonetheless. For the situation, the floor is itself created, in jury deliberations, surgical operations, block meetings, sit-ins, cockfights, by the cultural preoccupations—here, as we shall see, the celebration of status rivalry —which not only specify the focus but, assembling actors and arranging scenery, bring it actually into being.

In classical times (that is to say, prior to the Dutch invasion of 1908), when there were no bureaucrats around to improve popular morality, the staging of a cockfight was an explicitly societal matter. Bringing a cock to an important fight was, for an adult male, a compulsory duty of citizenship; taxation of fights, which were usually held on market day, was a major source of public revenue; patronage of the art was a stated responsibility of princes; and the cock ring, or *wantilan*, stood in the center of the village near those other monuments of Balinese civility— the council house, the origin temple, the marketplace, the signal tower, and the banyan tree. Today, a few special occasions aside, the newer rectitude makes so open a statement of the connection between the ex- citements of collective life and those of blood sport impossible, but, less directly expressed, the connection itself remains intimate and intact.

14
Urban Legends

In nonliterate societies people rely on the spoken word to transmit culture and the lessons it contains. In societies pervaded by television, radio, and the Internet, one might think the spoken word would lose its place. Yet how many of you know the stories that Brunvand relates? How did you learn them? What lesson are you supposed to learn from them? How far removed are you from people in nonliterate societies?

THE PERFORMANCE OF LEGENDS

Whatever the origins of urban legends, their dissemination is no mystery. The tales have traveled far and wide, and have been told and retold from person to person in the same manner that myths, fairy tales, or ballads spread in earlier cultures, with the important difference that today's legends are also disseminated by the mass media. Groups of age-mates, especially adolescents, are one important American legend channel, but other paths of transmission are among office workers and club members, as well as among religious, recreational, and regional groups. Some individuals make a point of learning every recent rumor or tale, and they can enliven any coffee break, party, or trip with the latest supposed "news." The telling of one story inspires other people to share what they have read or heard, and in a short time a lively exchange of details occurs and perhaps new variants are created.

Tellers of these legends, of course, are seldom aware of their roles as "performers of folklore." The conscious purpose of this kind of storytelling is to convey a true event, and only incidentally to entertain an audience. Nevertheless, the speaker's demeanor is carefully orchestrated, and his or her delivery is low-key and soft-sell. With subtle gestures, eye movements, and vocal inflections the stories are made dramatic, pointed, and suspenseful. But, just as with jokes, some can tell them and some can't. Passive tellers of urban legends may just report them as odd rumors, but the more active legend tellers re-create them as dramatic stories of suspense and, perhaps, humor.

"THE BOYFRIEND'S DEATH"

With all these points in mind about folklore's subject-matter, style, and oral performance, consider this typical version of a well-known ur-

ban legend that folklorists have named "The Boyfriend's Death," collected in 1964 (the earliest documented instance of the story) by folklorist
Daniel R. Barnes from an eighteen-year-old freshman at the University
of Kansas. The usual tellers of the story are adolescents, and the normal
setting for the narration is a college dormitory room with fellow students
sprawled on the furniture and floors.

> This happened just a few years ago out on the road that turns off 59 highway
> by the Holiday Inn. This couple were parked under a tree out on this road.
> Well, it got to be time for the girl to be back at the dorm, so she told her
> boyfriend that they should start back. But the car wouldn't start, so he told
> her to lock herself in the car and he would go down to the Holiday Inn and
> call for help. Well, he didn't come back and he didn't come back, and pretty
> soon she started hearing a scratching noise on the roof of the car. "Scratch,
> scratch . . . scratch, scratch." She got scareder and scareder, but he didn't
> come back. Finally, when it was almost daylight, some people came along
> and stopped and helped her out of the car, and she looked up and there was
> her boyfriend hanging from the tree, and his feet were scraping against the
> roof of the car. This is why the road is called "Hangman's Road."

Here is a story that has traveled rapidly to reach nationwide oral
circulation, in the process becoming structured in the typical manner of
folk narratives. The traditional and fairly stable elements are the parked
couple, the abandoned girl, the mysterious scratching (sometimes joined
by a dripping sound and ghostly shadows on the windshield), the day-
break rescue, and the horrible climax. Variable traits are the precise location, the reason for her abandonment, the nature of the rescuers,
murder details, and the concluding placename explanation. While "The
Boyfriend's Death" seems to have captured teenagers' imaginations as a
separate legend only since the early 1960s, it is clearly related to at least
two older yarns, "The Hook" and "The Roommate's Death." . . .

"THE HOOK"

On Tuesday, November 8, 1960, the day when Americans went to the
polls to elect John F. Kennedy as their thirty-fifth president, thousands
of people must have read the following letter from a teenager in the
popular newspaper column written by Abigail Van Buren:

> DEAR ABBY: If you are interested in teenagers, you will print this story. I
> don't know whether it's true or not, but it doesn't matter because it served
> its purpose for me:
> A fellow and his date pulled into their favorite "lovers' lane" to listen to
> the radio and do a little necking. The music was interrupted by an announcer
> who said there was an escaped convict in the area who had served time for
> rape and robbery. He was described as having a hook instead of a right hand.
> The couple became frightened and drove away. When the boy took his girl
> home, he went around to open the car door for her. Then he saw—a hook
> on the door handle! I don't think I will ever park to make out as long as I
> live. I hope this does the same for other kids.
>
> JEANETTE

This juicy story seems to have emerged in the late 1950s, sharing some common themes with "The Death Car" and "The Vanishing Hitchhiker" and then . . . influencing "The Boyfriend's Death" as that legend developed in the early 1960s. The story of "The Hook" (or "The Hookman") really needed no national press report to give it life or credibility, because the teenage oral-tradition underground had done the job well enough long before the election day of 1960. Teenagers all over the country knew about "The Hook" by 1959, and like other modern legends the basic plot was elaborated with details and became highly localized.

One of my own students, originally from Kansas, provided this specific account of where the event supposedly occurred:

> Outside of "Mac" [McPherson, Kansas], about seven miles out towards Lindsborg, north on old highway 81 is an old road called "Hookman's Road." It's a curved road, a traditional parking spot for the kids. When I was growing up it [the legend] was popular, and that was back in the '60's, and it was old then.

Another student told a version of the story that she had heard from her baby-sitter in Albuquerque in 1960:

> . . . over the radio came an announcement that a crazed killer with a hook in place of a hand had escaped from the local insane asylum. The girl got scared and begged the boy to take her home. He got mad and stepped on the gas and roared off. When they got to her house, he got out and went around to the other side of the car to let her out. There on the door handle was a bloody hook.

But these two students were told, after arriving in Salt Lake City, that it had actually occurred *here* in Memory Grove, a well-wooded city park. "Oh, no," a local student in the class insisted, "This couple was parked outside of Salt Lake City *in a mountain canyon* one night, and . . ." It turned out that virtually every student in the class knew the story as adapted in some way to their hometowns.

Other folklorists have reported collecting "The Hook" in Maryland, Wisconsin, Indiana, Illinois, Kansas, Texas, Arkansas, Oregon, and Canada. Some of the informants' comments echo Dear Abby's correspondent in testifying to the story's effect (to discourage parking) even when its truth was suspect. The students said, "I believe that it *could* happen, and this makes it seem real," or "I don't really [believe it], but it's pretty scary; I sort of hope it didn't happen."

Part of the great appeal of "The Hook"—one of the most popular adolescent scare stories—must lie in the tidiness of the plot. Everything fits. On the other hand, the lack of loose ends would seem to be excellent testimony to the story's near impossibility. After all, what are the odds that a convicted criminal or crazed maniac would be fitted with a hook for a missing hand, that this same threatening figure would show up precisely when a radio warning had been broadcast of his escape, and that the couple would drive away rapidly just at the instant the hookman put his hook through the door handle? Besides, why wouldn't he try to open the door with his good hand, and how is it that the boy—furious at the interruption of their lovemaking—is still willing to go around politely to open the girl's door when they get home? Too much, too much—but it makes a great story. . . .

"THE ROOMMATE'S DEATH"

Another especially popular example of the American adolescent shocker story is the widely-known legend of "The Roommate's Death." It shares several themes with other urban legends. As in "The Killer in the Backseat" and "The Babysitter and the Man Upstairs," it is usually a lone woman in the story who is threatened—or thinks she is—by a strange man. As in "The Hook" and "The Boyfriend's Death," the assailant is often said to be an escaped criminal or a maniac. Finally, as in the latter legend, the actual commission of the crime is never described; only the resulting mutilated corpse is. The scratching sounds outside the girl's place of refuge are an additional element of suspense. Here is a version told by a University of Kansas student in 1965 set in Corbin Hall, a freshman women's dormitory there:

> These two girls in Corbin had stayed late over Christmas vacation. One of them had to wait for a later train, and the other wanted to go to a fraternity party given that night of vacation. The dorm assistant was in her room— sacked out. They waited and waited for the intercom, and then they heard this knocking and knocking outside in front of the dorm. So the girl thought it was her date and she went down. But she didn't come back and she didn't come back. So real late that night this other girl heard a scratching and gasping down the hall. She couldn't lock the door, so she locked herself in the closet. In the morning she let herself out and her roommate had had her throat cut, and if the other girl had opened the door earlier, she [the dead roommate] would have been saved.

At all the campuses where the story is told the reasons for the girls' remaining alone in the dorm vary, but they are always realistic and plausible. The girls' homes may be too far away for them to visit during vacation, such as in Hawaii or a foreign country. In some cases they wanted to avoid a campus meeting or other obligation. What separates the two roommates may be either that one goes out for food, or to answer the door, or to use the rest room. The girl who is left behind may hear the scratching noise either at her room door or at the closet door, if she hides there. Sometimes her hair turns white or grey overnight from the shock of the experience (an old folk motif). The implication in the story is that some maniac is after her (as is suspected about the pursuer in "The Killer in the Backseat"); but the truth is that her own roommate needs help, and she might have supplied it had she only acted more decisively when the noises were first heard. Usually some special emphasis is put on the victim's fingernails, scratched to bloody stumps by her desperate efforts to signal for help.

A story told by a California teenager, remembered from about 1964, seems to combine motifs of "The Baby-sitter and the Man Upstairs" with "The Roommate's Death." The text is unusually detailed with names and the circumstances of the crime:

> Linda accepted a baby-sitting job for a wealthy family who lived in a two-storey home up in the hills for whom she had never baby-sat for before. Linda was rather hesitant as the house was rather isolated and so she asked a girl-friend, Sharon, to go along with her, promising Sharon half of the baby-sitting fee she would earn. Sharon accepted Linda's offer and the two girls went up to the big two-storey house.
>
> The night was an especially dark and windy one and rain was threatening. All went well for the girls as they read stories aloud to the three little boys they were sitting for and they had no problem putting the boys to bed in the upstairs part of the house. When this was done, the girls settled down to watching television.
>
> It was not long before the telephone rang. Linda answered the telephone, only to hear the heavy breathing of the caller on the other end. She attempted to elicit a response from the caller but he merely hung up. Thinking little of it and not wanting to panic Sharon, Linda went back to watching her television program, remarking that the caller had dialed a wrong number. Upon receiving the second call at which time the caller first engaged in a bit of heavy breathing and then instructed them to check on the children, the two girls became frightened and decided to call the operator for assistance. The operator instructed the girls to keep the caller on the line as long as possible should he call again so that she might be able to trace the call. The operator would check back with them.
>
> The two girls then decided between themselves that one should stay downstairs to answer the phone. It was Sharon who volunteered to go upstairs. Shortly, the telephone rang again and Linda did as the operator had instructed her. Within a few minutes, the operator called back telling Linda to leave the house immediately with her friend because she had traced the calls to the upstairs phone.
>
> Linda immediately hung up the telephone and proceeded to run to the stairway to call Sharon. She then heard a thumping sound coming from the stairway and when she approached the stairs she saw her friend dragging herself down the stairs by her chin, all of her limbs severed from her body. The three boys also lay dead upstairs in their beds.

Once again, the Indiana University Folklore Archive has provided the best published report on variants of "The Roommate's Death," Linda Dégh's summary of thirty-one texts and several subtypes and related plots collected since 1961. The most significant feature, according to her report, is the frequent appearance of a male rescuer at the end of the story. In one version, for example, two girls are left behind alone in the dorm by their roommate when she goes downstairs for food; they hear noises, and so stay in their room all night without opening the door. Finally the mailman comes around the next morning, and they call him from the window:

> The mailman came in the front door and went up the stairs, and told the girls to stay in their room, that everything was all right but that they were to stay in their rooms [sic]. But the girls didn't listen to him 'cause he had said

it was all right, so they came out into the hall. When they opened the door, they saw their girlfriend on the floor with a hatchet in her head.

In other Indiana texts the helpful male is a handyman, a milkman, or the brother of one of the roommates.

According to folklorist Beverly Crane, the male-female characters are only one pair of a series of significant opposites, which also includes home and away, intellectual versus emotional behavior, life and death, and several others. A male is needed to resolve the female's uncertainty—motivated by her emotional fear—about how to act in a new situation. Another male has mutilated and killed her roommate with a blow to her head, "the one part of the body with which women are not supposed to compete." The girls, Crane suggested, are doubly out of place in the beginning, having left the haven of home to engage in intellectual pursuits, and having remained alone in the campus dormitory instead of rejoining the family on a holiday. Ironically, the injured girl must use her fingernails, intended to be long, lovely, feminine adornments, in order to scratch for help. But because her roommate fails to investigate the sound, the victim dies, her once pretty nails now bloody stumps. Crane concluded this ingenious interpretation with these generalizations:

> The points of value implicit in this narrative are then twofold. If women wish to depend on traditional attitudes and responses they had best stay in a place where these attitudes and responses are best able to protect them. If, however, women do choose to venture into the realm of equality with men, they must become less dependent, more self-sufficient, more confident in their own abilities, and, above all, more willing to assume responsibility for themselves and others.

One might not expect to find women's liberation messages embedded in the spooky stories told by teenagers, but Beverly Crane's case is plausible and well argued. Furthermore, it is not at all unusual to find up-to-date social commentary in other modern folklore—witness the many religious and sexual jokes and legends circulated by people who would not openly criticize a church or the traditional social mores. Folklore does not just purvey the old codes of morality and behavior; it can also absorb newer ideas. What needs to be done to analyze this is to collect what Alan Dundes calls "oral-literary criticism," the informants' own comments about their lore. How clearly would the girls who tell these stories perceive—or even accept—the messages extrapolated by scholars? And a related question: Have any stories with clear liberationist themes replaced older ones cautioning young women to stay home, be good, and—next best—be careful, and call a man if they need help?

15

Growing up as a Fore Is to Be "In Touch" and Free

E. Richard Sorenson

The author greatly admires the way these people of New Guinea traditionally imparted trust, independence, and the knowledge of Fore culture to their children. The Fore, however, are extremely open-minded and open to new cultural influences, and this brought radical change to their society. With the passing of the Fore way of life, the cultural diversity of the world was diminished, with the same loss of opportunity that accompanies the extinction of a species of plant or animal.

Untouched by the outside world, they had lived for thousands of years in isolated mountains and valleys deep in the interior of Papua New Guinea. They had no cloth, no metal, no money, no idea that their homeland was an island—or that what surrounded it was salt water. Yet the Fore *(for'ay)* people had developed remarkable and sophisticated approaches to human relations, and their child-rearing practices gave their young unusual freedom to explore. Successful as hunter-gatherers and as subsistence gardeners, they also had great adaptability, which brought rapid accommodation with the outside world after their lands were opened up.

It was alone that I first visited the Fore in 1963—a day's walk from a recently built airstrip. I stayed six months. Perplexed and fascinated, I returned six times in the next ten years, eventually spending a year and a half living with them in their hamlets.

Theirs was a way of life different from anything I had seen or heard about before. There were no chiefs, patriarchs, priests, medicine men or the like. A striking personal freedom was enjoyed even by the very young, who could move about at will and be where or with whom they liked. Infants rarely cried, and they played confidently with knives, axes and fire. Conflict between old and young did not arise; there was no "generation gap."

Older children enjoyed deferring to the interests and desires of the younger, and sibling rivalry was virtually undetectable. A responsive sixth sense seemed to attune the Fore hamlet mates to each other's interests and needs. They did not have to directly ask, inveigle, bargain or speak out for what they needed or wanted. Subtle, even fleeting expressions of interest, desire and discomfort were quickly read and helpfully acted on by one's associates. This spontaneous urge to share food, affection, work, trust, tools and pleasure was the social cement that held the Fore hamlets together. It was a pleasant way of life, for one could always be with those with whom one got along well.

Ranging and planting, sharing and living, the Fore diverged and expanded through high virgin lands in a pioneer region. They hunted out their gardens, tilled them while they lasted, then hunted again. Moving ever away from lands peopled and used, they had a self-contained life with its own special ways.

The underlying ecological conditions were like those that must have encompassed the world before agriculture set its imprint so broadly. Abutting the Fore was virtually unlimited virgin land, and they had food plants they could introduce into it. Like hunter-gatherers they sought their sources of sustenance first in one locale and then another, across an extended range, following opportunities provided by a providential nature. But like agriculturalists they concentrated their effort and attention more narrowly on selected sites of production, on their gardens. They were both seekers and producers. A pioneer people in a pioneer land, they ranged freely into a vast territory, but they planted to live.

Cooperative groups formed hamlets and gardened together. When the fertility of a garden declined, they abandoned it. Grass sprang up to cover these abandoned sites of earlier cultivation, and, as the Fore moved on to other parts of the forest, they left uninhabited grasslands to mark their passage.

The traditional hamlets were small, with a rather fluid system of social relations. A single large men's house provided shelter for 10 to 20 men and boys and their visiting friends. The several smaller women's houses each normally sheltered two married women, their unmarried daughters and their sons up to about six years of age. Formal kinship bonds were less important than friendship was. Fraternal "gangs" of youths formed the hamlets; their "clubhouses" were the men's houses.

During the day the gardens became the center of life. Hamlets were virtually deserted as friends, relatives and children went to one or more garden plots to mingle their social, economic and erotic pursuits in a pleasant and emotionally filled Gestalt of garden life. The boys and unmarried youths preferred to explore and hunt in the outlying lands, but they also passed through and tarried in the gardens.

Daily activities were not scheduled. No one made demands, and the land was bountiful. Not surprisingly the line between work and play was never clear.

The transmission of the Fore behavioral patterns to the young began in early infancy during a period of unceasing human physical contact. The effect of being constantly "in touch" with hamlet mates and their daily life seemed to start a process which proceeded by degrees: close rapport, involvement in regular activity, ability to handle seemingly dangerous implements safely, and responsible freedom to pursue individual interests at will without danger.

While very young, infants remained in almost continuous bodily contact with their mother, her house mates or her gardening associates. At first, mothers' laps were the center of activity, and infants occupied themselves there by nursing, sleeping and playing with their own bodies or those of their caretakers. They were not put aside for the sake of other activities, as when food was being prepared or heavy loads were being carried. Remaining in close, uninterrupted physical contact with those around them, their basic needs such as rest, nourishment, stimulation and security were continuously satisfied without obstacle.

By being physically in touch from their earliest days, Fore youngsters learned to communicate needs, desires and feelings through a body language of touch and response that developed before speech. This opened the door to a much closer rapport with those around them than otherwise would have been possible, and led ultimately to the Fore brand of social cement and the sixth sense that bound groups together through spontaneous, responsive sharing.

As the infant's awareness increased, his interests broadened to the things his mother and other caretakers did and to the objects and materials they used. Then these youngsters began crawling out to explore things that attracted their attention. By the time they were toddling, their interests continually took them on short sorties to nearby objects and persons. As soon as they could walk well, the excursions extended to the entire hamlet and its gardens, and then beyond with other children. Developing without interference or supervision, this personal exploratory learning quest freely touched on whatever was around, even axes, knives, machetes, fire, and the like. When I first went to the Fore, I was aghast.

Eventually I discovered that this capability emerged naturally from the Fore infant-handling practices in their milieu of close human physical proximity and tactile interaction. Because touch and bodily contact lend themselves naturally to satisfying the basic needs of young children, an early kind of communicative experience fostered cooperative interaction between infants and their caretakers, also kinesthetic contact with the activities at hand. This made it easy for them to learn the appropriate handling of the tools of life.

The early pattern of exploratory activity included frequent return to one of the "mothers." Serving as home base, the bastion of security, a woman might occasionally give the youngster a nod of encouragement, if he glanced in her direction with uncertainty. Yet rarely did the women attempt to control or direct, nor did they participate in the child's quests or jaunts.

As a result Fore children did not have to adjust to rule and schedule in order to find their place in life. They could pursue their interests and whims wherever they might lead and still be part of a richly responsive world of human touch which constantly provided sustenance, comfort, diversion and security.

Learning proceeded during the course of pursuing interests and exploring. Constantly "in touch" with people who were busy with daily activities, the Fore young quickly learned the skills of life from example. Muscle tone, movement and mood were components of this learning process; formal lessons and commands were not. Kinesthetic skills developed so quickly that infants were able to casually handle knives and similar objects before they could walk.

Even after several visits I continued to be surprised that the unsupervised Fore toddlers did not recklessly thrust themselves into unappreciated dangers, the way our own children tend to do. But then, why should they? From their earliest days, they enjoyed a benevolent sanctuary from which the world could be confidently viewed, tested and appreciated. This sanctuary remained ever available, but did not demand, restrain or impose. One could go and come at will.

In close harmony with their source of life, the Fore young were able confidently, not furtively, to extend their inquiry. They could widen their understanding as they chose. There was no need to play tricks or deceive in order to pursue life.

Emerging from this early childhood was a freely ranging young child rather in tune with his older and younger hamlet mates, disinclined to act out impulsively, and with a capable appreciation of the properties of potentially dangerous objects. Such children could be permitted to move out on their own, unsupervised and unrestricted. They were safe.

Such a pattern could persist indefinitely, re-creating itself in each new generation. However, hidden within the receptive character it produced was an Achilles heel: it also permitted adoption of new practices, including child-handling practices, which did *not* act to perpetuate the pattern. In only one generation after Western contact, the cycle of Fore life was broken.

Attuned as they were to individual pursuit of economic and social good, it did not take the Fore long to recognize the value of the new materials, practices and ideas that began to flow in. Indeed, change began almost immediately with efforts to obtain steel axes, salt, medicine and cloth. The Fore were quick to shed indigenous practices in favor of the Western example. They rapidly altered their ways to adapt to Western law, government, religion, materials and trade.

Sometimes change was so rapid that many people seemed to be afflicted by a kind of cultural shock. An anomie, even cultural amnesia, seemed to pervade some hamlets for a time. There were individuals who appeared temporarily to have lost memory of recent past events. Some Fore even forgot what type and style of traditional garments they had worn only a few years earlier, or that they had used stone axes and had eaten their dead close relatives.

Remarkably open-minded, the Fore so readily accepted reformulation of identity and practice that suggestion or example by the new government officers, missionaries and scientists could alter tribal affiliation, place names, conduct and hamlet style. When the first Australian patrol officer began to map the region in 1957, an error in communication led him to refer to these people as the "Fore." Actually they had had no name for themselves and the word, Fore, was their name for a quite different group, the Awa, who spoke another language and lived in another valley. They did not correct the patrol officer but adopted his usage. They all now refer to themselves as the Fore. Regional and even personal names changed just as readily.

More than anything else, it was the completion of a steep, rough, always muddy Jeep road into the Fore lands that undermined the traditional life. Almost overnight their isolated region was opened. Hamlets began to move down from their ridgetop sites in order to be nearer the road, consolidating with others.

The power of the road is hard to overestimate. It was a great artery where only restricted capillaries had existed before. And down this artery came a flood of new goods, new ideas and new people. This new road, often impassable even with four-wheel-drive vehicles, was perhaps the single most dramatic stroke wrought by the government. It was to the Fore an opening to a new world. As they began to use the road, they started to shed traditions evolved in the protective insularity of their mountain fastness, to adopt in their stead an emerging market culture.

THE COMING OF THE COFFEE ECONOMY

"Walkabout," nonexistent as an institution before contact, quickly became an accepted way of life. Fore boys began to roam hundreds of miles from their homeland in the quest for new experience, trade goods, jobs and money. Like the classic practice of the Australian aborigine, this "walkabout" took one away from his home for periods of varying length. But unlike the Australian practice, it usually took the boys to jobs and schools rather than to a solitary life in traditional lands. Obviously it sprang from the earlier pattern of individual freedom to pursue personal interests and opportunity wherever it might lead. It was a new expression of the old Fore exploratory pattern.

Some boys did not roam far, whereas others found ways to go to distant cities. The roaming boys often sought places where they might be welcomed as visitors, workers or students for a while. Mission stations and schools, plantation work camps, and the servants' quarters of the European population became way stations in the lives of the modernizing Fore boys.

Some took jobs on coffee plantations. Impressed by the care and attention lavished on coffee by European planters and by the money they saw paid to coffee growers, these young Fore workers returned home with coffee beans to plant.

Coffee grew well on the Fore hillsides, and in the mid-1960s, when the first sizable crop matured, Fore who previously had felt lucky to earn a few dollars found themselves able to earn a few hundred dollars. A rush to coffee ensued, and when the new gardens became productive a few years later, the Fore income from coffee jumped to a quarter of a million dollars a year. The coffee revolution was established.

At first the coffee was carried on the backs of its growers (sometimes for several days) over steep, rough mountain trails to a place where it could be sold to a buyer with a Jeep. However, as more and more coffee was produced, the villagers began to turn their efforts to planning and constructing roads in association with neighboring villages. The newly built roads, in turn, stimulated further economic development and the opening of new trade stores throughout the region.

Following European example, the segregated collective men's and women's houses were abandoned. Family houses were adopted. This changed the social and territorial arena for all the young children, who hitherto had been accustomed to living equally with many members of their hamlet. It gave them a narrower place to belong, and it made them more distinctly someone's children. Uncomfortable in the family houses, boys who had grown up in a freer territory began to gather in "boys' houses," away from the adult men who were now beginning to live in family houses with their wives. Mothers began to wear blouses, altering the early freer access to the breast. Episodes of infant and child frustration, not seen in traditional Fore hamlets, began to take place along with repeated incidents of anger, withdrawal, aggressiveness and stinginess.

So Western technology worked its magic on the Fore, its powerful materials and practices quickly shattering their isolated autonomy and life-style. It took only a few years from the time Western intruders built their first grass-thatched patrol station before the Fore way of life they found was gone.

Fortunately, enough of the Fore traditional ways were systematically documented on film to reveal how unique a flower of human creation they were. Like nothing else, film made it possible to see the behavioral patterns of this way of life. The visual record once made, captured data which was unnoticed and unanticipated at the time of filming and which was simply impossible to study without such records. Difficult-to-spot subtle patterns and fleeting nuances of manner, mood and human relations emerged by use of repeated reexamination of related incidents, some times by slow motion and stopped frame. Eventually the characteristic behavioral patterns of Fore life became clear, and an important aspect of human adaptive creation was revealed.

The Fore way of life was only one of the many natural experiments in living that have come into being through thousands of years of independent development in the world. The Fore way is now gone—those which remain are threatened. Under the impact of modern technology and commerce, the entire world is now rapidly becoming one system.

By the year 2000 all the independent natural experiments that have come into being during the world's history will be merging into a single world system.

One of the great tragedies of our modern time may be that most of these independent experiments in living are disappearing before we can discover the implications of their special expressions of human possibility. Ironically, the same technology responsible for the worldwide cultural convergence has also provided the means by which we may capture detailed visual records of the yet remaining independent cultures. The question is whether we will be able to seize this never-to-be repeated opportunity. Soon it will be too late. Yet, obviously, increasing our understanding of the behavioral repertoire of humankind would strengthen our ability to improve life in the world.

16
Role Distance in Surgery

ERVING GOFFMAN

Erving Goffman's genius was to see that the most seemingly insignificant events in everyday life follow many complex rules, rules that we follow but do not recognize. Similarly, who we purport to be is expressed both by our actions and others' acceptance of our claims. This is a dangerous activity when we claim one identity but don't behave according to the expected "script." Some people, like surgeons, can get away with this confusing role enactment to everyone's advantage.

A merry-go-round horse is a thing of some size, some height, and some movement; and while the track is never wet, it can be very noisy. American middle-class two-year-olds often find the prospect too much for them. They fight their parents at the last moment to avoid being strapped into a context in which it had been hoped they would prove to be little men. Sometimes they become frantic half-way through the ride, and the machine must be stopped so that they can be removed.

Here we have one of the classic possibilities of life. Participation in any circuit of face-to-face activity requires the participant to keep command of himself, both as a person capable of executing physical movements and as one capable of receiving and transmitting communications. A flustered failure to maintain either kind of role poise makes the system as a whole suffer. Every participant, therefore, has the function of maintaining his own poise, and one or more participants are likely to have the specialized function of modulating activity so as to safeguard the poise of the others. In many situated systems, of course, all contingencies are managed without such threats arising. However, there is no such system in which these troubles might not occur, and some systems, such as those in a surgery ward, presumably provide an especially good opportunity to study these contingencies.

Just as a rider may be disqualified during the ride because he proves to be unable to handle riding, so a rider will be removed from his saddle at the very beginning of the ride because he does not have a ticket or because, in the absence of his parents, he makes management fear for his safety. There is an obvious distinction, then, between qualifications required for permission to attempt a role and attributes required for performing suitable once the role has been acquired.

At three and four, the task of riding a wooden horse is still a challenge, but apparently a manageable one, inflating the rider to his full extent with demonstrations of capacity. Parents need no longer ride alongside to protect their youngsters. The rider throws himself into the role in a serious way, playing it with verve and an admitted engagement of all his faculties. Passing his parents at each turn, the rider carefully lets go one of his hands and grimly waves a smile of a kiss—this, incidentally, being an example of an act that is a typical part of the role but hardly an obligatory feature of it. Here, then, doing is being, and what was designated as a "playing at" is stamped with serious realization.

Just as "flustering" is a classic possibility in all situated systems, so also is the earnest way these youngsters of three or four ride their horses. Three matters seem to be involved: an admitted or expressed attachment to the role; a demonstration of qualifications and capacities for performing it; and active *engagement* or spontaneous involvement in the role activity at hand, that is, a visible investment of attention and muscular effort. Where these three features are present, I will use the term *embracement*. To embrace a role is to disappear completely into the virtual self available in the situation, to be fully seen in terms of the image, and to confirm expressively one's acceptance of it. To embrace a role is to be embraced by it. Particularly good illustrations of full embracement can be seen in persons in certain occupations: team managers during baseball games; traffic policemen at intersections during rush hours; landing signal officers who wave in planes landing on the decks of aircraft carriers; in fact, any one occupying a directing role where the performer must guide others by means of gestural signs.

An individual may affect the embracing of a role in order to conceal a lack of attachment to it, just as he may affect a visible disdain for a role, thrice refusing the kingly crown, in order to defend himself against the psychological dangers of his actual attachment to it. Certainly an individual may be attached to a role and fail to be able to embrace it, as when a child proves to have no ticket or to be unable to hang on.

Returning to the merry-go-round, we see that at five years of age the situation is transformed, especially for boys. To be a merry-go-round horse rider is now apparently not enough, and this fact must be demonstrated out of dutiful regard for one's own character. Parents are not likely to be allowed to ride along, and the strap for preventing falls is often disdained. One rider may keep time to the music by clapping his feet or a hand against the horse, an early sign of utter control. Another may make a wary stab at standing on the saddle or changing horses without touching the platform. Still another may hold on to the post with one hand and lean back as far as possible while looking up to the sky in a challenge to dizziness. Irreverence begins, and the horse may be held on to by his wooden ear or his tail. The child says by his actions: "Whatever I am, I'm not just someone who can barely manage to stay on a wooden horse." Note that what the rider is apologizing for is not some minor untoward event that has cropped up during the interaction, but the whole role. The image of him that is generated for him by the routine entailed in his mere participation—his virtual self in the context—is an image from which he apparently withdraws by *actively* manipulating the situation. Whether this skittish behavior is intentional or unintentional, sincere or affected, correctly appreciated by others present or not, it does constitute a wedge between the individual and his role, between doing and being. This "effectively" expressed pointed separateness between the individual and his putative role I shall call *role distance*. A shorthand is involved here: the individual is actually denying not the role but the virtual self that is implied in the role for all accepting performers.

In any case, the term role distance is not meant to refer to all behavior that does not directly contribute to the task core of a given role but only to those behaviors that are seen by someone present as relevant to assessing the actor's attachment to his particular role and relevant in such a way as to suggest that the actor possibly has some measure of disaffection from, and resistance against, the role. Thus, for example, a four-year-old halfway through a triumphant performance as a merry-go-round rider may sometimes go out of play, dropping from his face and manner any confirmation of his virtual self, yet may indulge in this break in role without apparent intent, the lapse reflecting more on his capacity to sustain any role than on his feelings about the present one. Nor can it be called role distance if the child rebels and totally rejects the role, stomping off in a huff, for the special facts about self that can be conveyed by holding a role off a little are precisely the ones that cannot be conveyed by throwing the role over.

At seven and eight, the child not only dissociates himself self-consciously from the kind of horseman a merry-go-round allows him to be but also finds that many of the devices that younger people use for this are now beneath him. He rides no-hands, gleefully chooses a tiger or a frog for a steed, clasps hands with a mounted friend across the aisle. He tests limits, and his antics may bring negative sanction from the adult in charge of the machine. And he is still young enough to show distance by handling the task with bored, nonchalant competence, a candy bar languidly held in one hand.

At eleven and twelve, maleness for boys has become a real responsibility, and no easy means of role distance seems to be available on merry-go-rounds. It is necessary to stay away or to exert creative acts of distancy, as when a boy jokingly treats his wooden horse as if it were a racing one: he jogs himself up and down, leans far over the neck of the horse, drives his heels mercilessly into its flanks, and uses the reins for a lash to get more speed, brutally reining in the horse when the ride is over. He is just old enough to achieve role distance by defining the whole undertaking as a lark, a situation for mockery.

Adults who choose to ride a merry-go-round display adult techniques of role distance. One adult rider makes a joke of tightening the safety belt around him; another crosses his arms, giving popcorn with his left hand to the person on his right and a coke with his right hand to the person on his left. A young lady riding sidesaddle tinkles out, "It's cold," and calls to her watching boy friend's boy friend, "Come on, don't be chicken." A dating couple riding adjacent horses hold hands to bring sentiment, not daring, to the situation. Two double-dating couples employ their own techniques: the male in front sits backwards and takes a picture of the other male rider taking a picture of him. And, of course, some adults, riding close by their threatened two-and-a-half-year-old, wear a face that carefully demonstrates that they do not perceive the ride as an event in itself, their only present interest being their child.

And finally there is the adult who runs the machine and takes the tickets. Here, often, can be found a fine flowering of role distance. Not only does he show that the ride itself is not—as a ride—an event to him, but he also gets off and on and around the moving platform with a grace and ease that can only be displayed by safely taking what for children and even adults would be chances.

Some general points can be made about merry-go-round role distance. First, while the management of a merry-go-round horse in our culture soon ceases to be a challenging "developmental task," the task of expressing that it is not continues for a long time to be a challenge and remains a felt necessity. A full twist must be made in the iron law of etiquette: the act through which one can afford to try to fit into the situation is an act that can be styled to show that one is somewhat out of place. One enters the situation to the degree that one can demonstrate that one does not belong.

A second general point about role distance is that immediate audiences figure very directly in the display of role distance. Merry-go-round horsemen are very ingenuous and may frankly wait for each time they pass their waiting friends before playing through their gestures of role distance. Moreover, if persons above the age of twelve or so are to trust themselves to making a lark of it, they almost need to have a friend along on the next horse, since persons who are "together" seem to be able to hold off the socially defining force of the environment much more than a person alone.

A final point: two different means of establishing role distance seem to be found. In one case the individual tries to isolate himself as much as possible from the contamination of the situation, as when an adult riding along to guard his child makes an effort to be completely stiff, affectless, and preoccupied. In the other case the individual cooperatively projects a childish self, meeting the situation more than halfway, but then withdraws from this castoff self by a little gesture signifying that the joking has gone far enough. In either case the individual can slip the skin the situation would clothe him in.

A summary of concepts is now in order. I have tried to distinguish among three easily confused ideas: *commitment*, *attachment*, and *embrace-*

ment. It is to be noted that these sociological terms are of a different order from that of *engagement*, a psychobiological process that a cat or a dog can display more beautifully than man. Finally, the term *role distance* was introduced to refer to actions which effectively convey some disdainful detachment of the performer from a role he is performing.

ROLE DISTANCE AND SERIOUS ACTIVITY

The role of merry-go-round rider can be regular at any amusement park but hardly by a regular performer. After a few years each of us "outgrows" the role and can only perform it as an occasional thing and as an occasion for the display of much role distance. As an example, then, merry-go-round riding is not a very serious one; furthermore, it is somewhat misleading, since it implies that role distance is displayed in connection with roles no adult can take seriously.

Actually, we deal with a more general phenomenon with roles that categories of individuals find it unwise to embrace. Even a short step away from merry-go-rounds shows this. Take, for example, six lower-middle-class high-school girls, not of the horsy set, taking a vacation in a national park and deciding to "do" horseback riding on one of their mornings. As long as they come to the riding stable in self-supporting numbers, they can nicely illustrate distance from a role that persons of another social class and region might take seriously all their lives. The six I observed came in clothing patently not designed as a consolidation of the horsewoman role: pedal pushers, cotton leotards, ballet-type flats, frilly blouses. One girl, having been allotted the tallest horse, made a mock scene of declining to get on because of the height, demanding to be allowed to go home. When she did get on, she called her horse "Daddy-O," diverting her conversation from her friends to her horse. During the ride, one girl pretended to post while the horse walked, partly in mockery of a person not in their party who was posting. Another girl leaned over the neck of her horse and shouted racing cries, again while the horse was locked in a walking file of other horses. She also slipped her right foot out of the stirrup and brought it over the saddle, making a joke of her affectation of riding sidesaddle and expressing that both positions were much alike to her—both equally unfamiliar and uncongenial; at the same time she tested the limits of the wrangler's permissiveness. Passing under low branches, the girls made a point of making a point of this by pulling off branches, waving them like flags, then feeding them to their horses. Evidences of the excretory capacities of the steeds were greeted with merriment and loud respect. During the latter part of the two-hour ride, two of the girls became visibly bored, dropped the reins over the saddlehorn, let their hands fall limply to their sides, and gave up all pretense at being in role.

Again we can detect some general facts about role distance. We can see that a role that some persons take seriously most of their lives may be one that others will never take seriously at any age. We see that participation with a group of one's similars can lend strength to the show of role distance and to one's willingness to express it. In the presence of age-peers elegantly attired for riding and skilled at it, the girls I observed might falter in displaying role distance, feeling hostile, resentful, and unconfident. Presumably, if one of these girls were alone with thorough-going horsewomen she would be even less prone to flourish this kind of distance. We can suspect, then, that role distance will have defensive functions. By manifesting role distance, the girls give themselves some elbow room in which to maneuver. "We are not to be judged by this incompetence," they say. Should they make a bad showing, they are in a position to dodge the reflection it could cast on them. Whatever their showing, they avoid having to be humbled before those who are socially placed to make a much better showing. By exposing themselves in a guise to which they have no serious claim, they leave themselves in full control of shortcomings they take seriously.

While horse trails and children's playgrounds provide fine places for studying repertoires of role distance, we need not look to situations that are so close to being unserious, situations where it is difficult to distinguish role playing from playing at. We know, for example, that tasks that might be embraced by a housewife or maid may be tackled by the man of the house with carefully expressed clumsiness and with self-mockery. Perhaps it should be noted that similar out-of-character situations can easily be created experimentally by asking subjects to perform tasks that are inappropriate to persons of their kind.

The published literature on some of our occupational byways provides serious material on role distance. Psychoanalysts, for example, who have told us so much about the contingencies of a particular trade (even when not telling us all we might want to know about their patients), provide interesting data on role distance in connection with "resistance" on the part of the patient. Resistance here takes the form of the patient refusing to provide relevant associations or refusing to allow the therapist to function solely as a "therapist." From the therapist's view of the patient's motivation, then, resistance expresses some rejection of the constraints of one's role as patient:

> Up to this point I found myself, as the doctor, comfortably installed in my explicit instrumental role; the role assignment given me by the patient appeared to be concerned with her "problem." The system of roles was complementary and apparently well integrated. The next moment, however, the patient initiated a new role assignment. She asked me if I had seen a recent performance of "Don Juan in Hell" from *Man and Superman*. The question seemed a simple enough request for information regarding my playgoing habits. But since I did not know what role I was being invited to take, and because I suspected that behind whatever explicit role this might turn out to be there lurked a more important implicit one, I did not answer the question. The patient paused for a moment, and then, perceiving that I would not answer the question, she continued. . . .

In continuing after the pause, the patient delivered a highly perceptive account of Shaw's intention in the Don Juan interlude, of the actors' interpretations, and of her reactions. The account was so long that I finally interrupted to ask if she knew why she wanted to tell all this. At the point of interruption I had become aware that my new role was an expressive one—to play the appreciative audience to her role as a gifted art and drama critic.

The therapist then goes on to explain that had he merely fallen in with the patient's maneuver to keep herself at a distance from the role of patient he would have had to pass up "the opportunity to get more information regarding the hidden, implicit role buried in this transaction and thus to learn more about her motivation for shifting out of her initial instrumental role in which she had started the interview." The therapist could have added that to ask the patient why she felt it necessary to run on so is a classic therapist's ploy to put the patient in her place, back in role.

Situated roles that place an individual in an occupational setting he feels is beneath him are bound to give rise to much role distance. A good example is provided by Isaac Rosenfeld in a reminiscence about a summer job as a barker at Coney Island. The writer begins his description by telling of his return after many years, seeing someone else handling his old job:

He was sneering, just as I used to do in the old days, and no doubt for the same reason: because the summer was hot, and the work hard, sweaty and irritating, stretching over long hours for poor pay. It was absolutely indispensable, now as it was then, to separate oneself from the job—one had to have a little ledge to stand on all to himself; otherwise perish. I used to pitch this ledge very high. The higher I stood, the greater my contempt, and the more precious the moments of freedom I won for myself by this trick of balancing above the crowd. I remembered how I used to mix T.S. Eliot with my spiel (in those days there was hardly anyone in Freshman English who did not know a good deal of *The Waste Land* by heart): "Step right up ladies and gentlemen mingling memory with desire for the greatest thrill show on earth only a dime the tenth part of a dollar will bring you to Carthage then I come burning burning burning O Lord thou pluckest me out ten cents!"

Some of the most appealing data on role distance come from situations where a subordinate must take orders or suggestions and must go along with the situation as defined by superordinates. At such times, we often find that although the subordinate is careful not to threaten those who are, in a sense, in charge of the situation, he may be just as careful to inject some expression to show, for any who care to see, that he is not capitulating completely to the work arrangement in which he finds himself. Sullenness, muttering, irony, joking, and sarcasm may all allow one to show that something of oneself lies outside the constraints of the moment and outside the role within whose jurisdiction the moment occurs.

Given these various examples of role distance, I want to go on to argue that this conduct is something that falls between role obligations on one hand and actual role performance on the other. This gap has always caused trouble for sociologists. Often, they try to ignore it. Faced with it, they sometimes despair and turn from their own direction of analysis; they look to the biography of the performer and try to find in his history some particularistic explanation of events, or they rely on psychology, alluding to the fact that in addition to playing the formal themes of his role, the individual always behaves personally and spontaneously, phrasing the standard obligations in a way that has a special psychological fit for him.

The concept of role distance provides a *sociological* means of dealing with one type of divergence between obligation and actual performance. First, we know that often distance is not introduced on an individual basis but can be predicted on the grounds of the performers' gross age-sex characteristics. Role distance is a part (but, of course, only one part) of *typical* role, and this routinized sociological feature should not escape us merely because role distance is not part of the normative framework of role. Secondly, that which one is careful to point out one is not, or not merely, necessarily has a directing and intimate influence on one's conduct, especially since the means for expressing this disaffection must be carved out of the standard materials available in the situation.

We arrive, then, at a broadened sociological way of looking at the trappings of a social role. A set of visible qualifications and known certifications, along with a social setting well designed as a showplace, provides the individual with something more than an opportunity to play his role self to the hilt, for this scene is just what he needs to create a clear impression of what he chooses not to lay claim to. The more extensive the trappings of a role, the more opportunity to display role distance. Personal front and social setting provide precisely the field an individual needs to cut a figure in—a figure that romps, sulks, glides, or is indifferent. Later in this paper, some additional social determinants of role distance will be considered.

Surgery as an Activity System

I have suggested some cases where the scene of activity generates for the individual a self which he is apparently loath to accept openly for himself, since his conduct suggests that some disaffiliation exists between himself and his role. But a peek into some odd corners of social life provides no basis, perhaps, for generalizing about social life. As a test, then, of the notion of role distance (and role), let us take a scene in which activity generates a self for the individual that appears to be a most likely one for self-attachment. Let us take, for example, the activity system sustained during a surgical operation. The components consist of verbal and physical acts and the changing state of the organism undergoing the operation. Here, if anywhere in our society, we should find performers flushed with a feeling of the weight and dignity of their action. A Hollywood ideal is involved: the white-coated chief surgeon strides into the operating theater after the patient has been anesthetized and opened by assistants. A place is automatically made for him. He grunts a few abbreviated preliminaries, then deftly, almost silently, gets to work, serious, grim, competently living up to the image he and his team have of him, yet in a context where momentary failure to exhibit competence might permanently jeopardize the relation he is allowed to have to his role. Once the critical phase of the operation is quite over, he steps back and, with a special compound of tiredness, strength, and disdain, rips off his gloves; he thus contaminates himself and abdicates his role, but at a time when his own labors put the others in a position to "close up." While he may be a father, a husband, or a baseball fan at home, he is here one and only one thing, a surgeon, and being a surgeon provides a fully rounded impression of the man. If the role perspective works, then, surely it works here, for in our society the surgeon, if anyone, is allowed and obliged to put himself into his work and get a self out of it.

As a contrast, then, to the insubstantial life of horses-for-ride, I want to report briefly on some observations of activity in surgery wards.

If we start with the situation of the lesser medical personnel, the intern and the junior resident, the test will not be fair, for here, apparently, is a situation much like the ones previously mentioned. The tasks these juniors are given to do—such as passing hemostats, holding retractors, cutting small tied-off veins, swabbing the operating area before the operation, and perhaps suturing or closing at the end—are not large enough to support much of a surgical role. Furthermore, the junior person may find that he performs even these lowly tasks inadequately, and that the scrub nurse as well as the chief surgeon tells him so. And when the drama is over and the star performer has dropped his gloves and gown and walked out, the nurses may underline the intern's marginal position by lightly demanding his help in moving the body from the fixed table to the movable one, while automatically granting him a taste of the atmosphere they maintain when real doctors are absent. As for the intern himself, surgery is very likely *not* to be his chosen specialty; the three-month internship is a course requirement and he will shortly see the last of it. The intern may confirm all this ambivalence to his work on occasions away from the surgery floor, when he scathingly describes surgery as a plumber's craft exercised by mechanics who are told what to look for by internists.

The surgical junior, especially the intern, has, then, a humbling position during surgery. Whether as a protection against this condition or not, the medical juniors I observed, like over-age merry-go-round riders, analysands, and carnival pitchmen, were not prepared to embrace their role fully; elaborate displays of role distance occurred. A careful, bemused look on the face is sometimes found, implying, "This is not the real me." Sometimes the individual will allow himself to go "away," dropping off into a brown study that removes him from the continuity of events, increases the likelihood that his next contributory act will not quite fit into the flow of action, and effectively gives the appearance of occupational disaffection; brought back into play, he may be careful to evince little sign of chagrin. He may rest himself by leaning on the patient or by putting a foot on an inverted bucket but in a manner too contrived to allow the others to feel it is a matter of mere resting. Interestingly enough, he sometimes takes on the function of the jester, endangering his reputation with antics that temporarily place him in a doubtful and special position, yet through this providing the others present with a reminder of less exalted worlds:

> CHIEF SURGEON JONES (*in this case a senior resident*): A small Richardson please.
> SCRUB NURSE: Don't have one.
> DR. JONES: O.K., then give me an Army and Navy.
> SCRUB NURSE: It looks like we don't have one.
> DR. JONES (*lightly joking*): No Army or Navy man here.
> INTERN (*dryly*): No one in the armed forces, but Dr. Jones here is in the Boy Scouts.

> SCRUB NURSE: Will there be more than three [sutures] more? We're running out of sutures.
> CHIEF SURGEON: I don't know.
> INTERN: We can finish up with Scotch tape.

> INTERN (*looking for towel clamps around body*): Where in the world . . . ?
> SCRUB NURSE: Underneath the towel.
> (*Intern turns to the nurse and in slow measure makes a full cold bow to her.*)

> SCRUB NURSE (*to intern*): Watch it, you're close to my table! [*A Mayo stand containing instruments whose asepsis she must guard and guarantee.*]
> (*Intern performs a mock gasp and clownishly draws back.*)

As I have suggested, just as we cannot use a child over four riding a merry-go-round as an exhibition of how to embrace an activity role, so also we cannot use the junior medical people on a surgical team. But surely the chief surgeon, at least, will demonstrate the embracing of a role. What we find, of course, is that even this central figure expresses considerable role distance.

Some examples may be cited. One can be found in medical etiquette. This body of custom requires that the surgeon, on leaving the operation, turn and thank his assistant, his anesthetist, and ordinarily his nurses as well. Where a team has worked together for a long time and where the members are of the same age-grade, the surgeon may guy this act, issuing the thanks in what he expects will be taken as an ironical and farcical tone of voice: "Miss Westly, you've done a simply wonderful job here." Similarly, there is a formal rule that in preparing a requested injection the nurse show the shelved vial to the surgeon before its sealed top is cracked off so that he can check its named contents and thereby take the responsibility on himself. If the surgeons are very busy at the time, this checking may be requested but not given. At other times, how-ever, the checking may be guyed.

> CIRCULATING NURSE: Dr. James, would you check this?
>
> DR. JAMES (*in a loud ministerial voice, reading the label*): Three cubic centi-meters of heparin at ten-milligram strength, put up by Invenex and held by Nurse Jackson at a forty-five-degree angle. That is right, Nurse Jackson.

Instead of employing technical terms at all times, he may tease the nurses by using homey appellations: "Give me the small knife, we'll get in just below the belly button"; and he may call the electric cauterizer by the apt name of "sizzler," ordering the assistant surgeon to "sizzle here, and here." Similarly, when a nurse allows her nonsterile undergown to be exposed a little, a surgeon may say in a pontifical and formal tone, "Nurse Bevan, can I call your attention to the anterior portion of your gown. It is exposing you. I trust you will correct this condition," thereby instituting social control, reference to the nurse's non-nursing attributes, and satire of the profession, all with one stroke. So, too, a nurse, return-ing to the operating room with a question, "Dr. Williams?" may be an-swered by a phrase of self-satirization: "In person," or, "This is Dr. Williams." And a well-qualified surgeon, in taking the situated role of assistant surgeon for the duration of a particular operation, may tell the nurses, when they have been informed by the chief surgeon that two electric cauterizers will be employed, "I'm going to get one too, just like the big doctors, that's what I like to hear." A chief surgeon, then, may certainly express role distance. Why he does so, and with what effect, are clearly additional questions, and ought to be considered.

17
"Getting" and "Making" a Tip

Greta Foff Paule

Waitresses, like many people who provide a service, are highly vulnerable to the whim of the customers who decide their pay. That is why they structure their encounters with more care than most of us realize. For those of you who have never been a waiter or waitress, this participant observation study may change forever the way you think about being serviced.

> The waitress can't help feeling a sense of personal failure and public censure when she is "stiffed."
> —*William F. Whyte, "When Workers and Customers Meet"*

> They're rude, they're ignorant, they're obnoxious, they're inconsiderate. . . . Half these people don't deserve to come out and eat, let alone try and tip a waitress.
> —*Route waitress*

The financial and emotional hazards inherent in the tipping system have drawn attention from sociologists, and more recently anthropologists, concerned with the study of work. In general these researchers have concluded that workers who receive gratuities exercise little control over the material outcome of tipping and less over its symbolic implications. . . .

MAKING A TIP AT ROUTE

A common feature of past research is that the worker's control over the tipping system is evaluated in terms of her efforts to con, coerce, compel, or otherwise manipulate a customer into relinquishing a bigger tip. Because these efforts have for the most part proven futile, the worker has been seen as having little defense against the financial vicissitudes of the tipping system. What these studies have overlooked is that an employee can increase her tip income by controlling the number as well as the size of tips she receives. This oversight has arisen from the tendency of researchers to concentrate narrowly on the relationship between server and served, while failing to take into account the broader organizational context in which this relationship takes place.

Like service workers observed in earlier studies, waitresses at Route strive to boost the amount of individual gratuities by rendering special services and being especially friendly. As one waitress put it, "I'll sell you the world if you're in my station." In general though, waitresses at Route Restaurant seek to boost their tip income, not by increasing the amount of individual gratuities, but by increasing the number of customers they serve. They accomplish this (a) by securing the largest or busiest stations and working the most lucrative shifts; (b) by "turning" their tables quickly; and (c) by controlling the flow of customers within the restaurant.

Technically, stations at Route are assigned on a rotating basis so that all waitresses, including rookies, work fast and slow stations equally. Station assignments are listed on the work schedule that is posted in the office window where it can be examined by all workers on all shifts, precluding the possibility of blatant favoritism or discrimination. Yet a number of methods exist whereby experienced waitresses are able to circumvent the formal rotation system and secure the more lucrative stations for themselves. A waitress can trade assignments with a rookie who is uncertain of her ability to handle a fast station; she can volunteer to take over a large station when a *call-out* necessitates reorganization of station assignments; or she can establish herself as the only waitress capable of handling a particularly large or chaotic station. Changes in station assignments tend not to be formally recorded, so inconsistencies in the rotation system often do not show up on the schedule. Waitresses on the same shift may notice of course that a co-worker has managed to avoid an especially slow station for many days, or has somehow ended up in the busiest station two weekends in a row, but the waitresses' code of noninterference . . . inhibits them from openly objecting to such irregularities.

A waitress can also increase her tip income by working the more lucrative shifts. Because day is the busiest and therefore most profitable shift at Route, it attracts experienced, professional waitresses who are most concerned and best able to maximize their tip earnings. There are exceptions: some competent, senior-ranking waitresses are unable to work during the day due to time constraints of family or second jobs. Others choose not to work during the day despite the potential monetary rewards, because they are unwilling to endure the intensely competitive atmosphere for which day shift is infamous.

The acutely competitive environment that characterizes day shift arises from the aggregate striving of each waitress to maximize her tip income by serving the greatest possible number of customers. Two strategies are enlisted to this end. First, each waitress attempts to *turn* her tables as quickly as possible. Briefly stated, this means she takes the order, delivers the food, clears and resets a table, and begins serving the next party as rapidly as customer lingering and the speed of the kitchen allow. A seven-year veteran of Route describes the strategy and its rewards:

What I do is I prebus my tables. When the people get up and go all I got is glasses and cups, pull off, wipe, set, and I do the table turnover. But see that's from day shift. See the girls on graveyard . . . don't understand the more times you turn that table the more money you make. You could have three tables and still make a hundred dollars. If you turn them tables.

As the waitress indicates, a large part of turning tables involves getting the table cleared and set for the next customer. During a rush, swing and grave waitresses tend to leave dirty tables standing, partly because they are less experienced and therefore less efficient, partly to avoid being given parties, or *sat*, when they are already behind. In contrast, day waitresses assign high priority to keeping their tables cleared and ready for customers. The difference in method reflects increased skill and growing awareness of and concern with money-making strategies.

A waitress can further increase her customer count by controlling the flow of customers within the restaurant. Ideally the hostess or manager running the front house rotates customers among stations, just as stations are rotated among waitresses. Each waitress is given, or *sat*, one party at a time in turn so that all waitresses have comparable customer counts at the close of a shift. When no hostess is on duty, or both she and the manager are detained and customers are waiting to be seated, waitresses will typically seat incoming parties.

Whether or not a formal hostess is on duty, day waitresses are notorious for bypassing the rotation system by racing to the door and directing incoming customers to their own tables. A sense of the urgency with which this strategy is pursued is conveyed in the comment of one five-year veteran, "They'll run you down to get that person at the door, to seat them in their station." The competition for customers is so intense during the day that some waitresses claim they cannot afford to leave the floor (even to use the restroom) lest they return to find a co-worker's station filled at their expense. "In the daytime, honey," remarks an eight-year Route waitress, "in the daytime it's like pulling teeth. You got to stay on the floor to survive. To survive." It is in part because they do not want to lose customers and tips to their co-workers that waitresses do not take formal breaks. Instead, they rest and eat between waiting tables or during lulls in business, returning to the floor intermittently to check on parties in progress and seat customers in their stations.

The fast pace and chaotic nature of restaurant work provide a cover for the waitress's aggressive pursuit of customers, since it is difficult for other servers to monitor closely the allocation of parties in the bustle and confusion of a rush. Still, it is not uncommon for waitresses to grumble to management and co-workers if they notice an obvious imbalance in customer distribution. Here again, the waitress refrains from directly criticizing her fellow servers, voicing her displeasure by commenting on the paucity of customers in her own station, rather than the overabundance of customers in the stations of certain co-waitresses. In response to these grumblings, other waitresses may moderate somewhat their efforts to appropriate new parties, and management may make a special effort to seat the disgruntled server favorably.

A waitress can also exert pressure on the manager or hostess to keep her station filled. She may, for instance, threaten to leave if she is not seated enough customers.

> I said, "Innes [a manager], I'm in [station] one and two. If one and two is not filled at all times from now until three, I'm getting my coat, my pocketbook, and I'm leaving." And one and two was filled, and I made ninety-five dollars.

Alternatively, she can make it more convenient for the manager or hostess to seat her rather than her co-workers, either by keeping her tables open (as described), or by taking extra tables. If customers are waiting to be seated, a waitress may offer to pick up parties in a station that is closed or, occasionally, to pick up parties in another waitress's station. In attempting either strategy, but especially the latter, the waitress must be adept not only at waiting tables, but in interpersonal restaurant politics. Autonomy and possession are of central concern to waitresses, and a waitress who offers to pick up tables outside her station must select her words carefully if she is to avoid being accused of invading her co-workers' territory. Accordingly, she may choose to present her bid for extra parties as an offer to help—the manager, another waitress, the restaurant, customers—rather than as a request.

The waitress who seeks to increase her tip income by maximizing the number of customers she serves may endeavor to cut her losses by refusing to serve parties that have stiffed her in the past. If she is a low-ranking waitress, her refusal is likely to be overturned by the manager. If she is an experienced and valuable waitress, the manager may ask someone else to take the party, assure the waitress he will take care of her (that is, pad the bill and give her the difference), or even pick up the party himself. Though the practice is far from common, a waitress may go so far as to demand a tip from a customer who has been known to stiff in the past.

> This party of two guys come in and they order thirty to forty dollars worth of food . . . and they stiff us. Every time. So Kaddie told them, "If you don't tip us, we're not going to wait on you." They said, "We'll tip you." So Kaddie waited on them, and they tipped her. The next night they came in, I waited on them and they didn't tip me. The third time they came in [the manager] put them in my station and I told [the manager] straight up, "I'm not waiting on them. . . ." So he made Hailey pick them up. And they stiffed Hailey. So when they came in the next night . . . [they] said, "Are you going to give us a table?" I said, "You going to tip me? I'm not going to wait on you. You got all that money, you sell all that crack on the streets and you come here and you can't even leave me a couple bucks?" . . . So they left me a dollar. So when they come in Tuesday night, I'm telling them a dollar ain't enough.

The tactics employed by waitresses, and particularly day-shift waitresses, to increase their customer count and thereby boost their tip earnings have earned them a resounding notoriety among their less competitive co-workers. Day (and some swing) waitresses are described as "money hungry," "sneaky little bitches," "self-centered," "aggressive," "backstabbing bitches," and "cutthroats over tables." The following remarks of two Route waitresses, however, indicate that those who employ these tactics see them as defensive, not aggressive measures. A sense of the waitress's preoccupation with autonomy and with protecting what is hers also emerges from these comments.

> You have to be like that. Because if you don't be like that, people step on you. You know, like as far as getting customers. I mean, you know, I'm sorry everybody says I'm greedy. I guess that's why I've survived this long at Route. Cause I am greedy. . . . *I want what's mine,* and if it comes down to me cleaning your table or my table, I'm going to clean my table. Because see I went through all that stage where I would do your table. To be fair. And you would walk home with seventy dollars, and I'd have twenty-five, cause I was being fair all night. (emphasis added)

> If the customer comes in the door and I'm there getting that door, don't expect me to cover your backside while you in the back smoking a cigarette and I'm here working for myself. You not out there working for me. . . . When I go to the door and get the customers, when I keep my tables clean and your tables are dirty, and you wonder why you only got one person . . . then that's just tough shit. . . . You're damn right my station is filled. *I'm not here for you.* (emphasis added)

Whether the waitress who keeps her station filled with customers is acting aggressively or defensively, her tactics are effective. It is commonly accepted that determined day waitresses make better money than less competitive co-workers even when working swing or grave. Moreover Nera, the waitress most infamous for her relentless use of "money-hungry" tactics, is at the same time most famous for her consistently high daily takes. While other waitresses jingle change in their aprons, Nera is forced to store wads of bills in her shoes and in paper bags to prevent tips from overflowing her pockets. She claims to make a minimum of five hundred dollars a week in tip earnings; her record for one day's work exceeds two hundred dollars and is undoubtedly the record for the restaurant.

Inverting the Symbolism of Tipping

It may already be apparent that the waitress views the customer—not as a master to pamper and appease—but as substance to be processed as quickly and in as large a quantity as possible. The difference in perspective is expressed in the objectifying terminology of waitresses: a customer or party is referred to as a *table*, or by table number, as *table five* or simply *five*; serving successive parties at a table is referred to as *turning the table*; taking an order is also known as *picking up a table*; and to serve water, coffee, or other beverages is to *water, coffee,* or *beverage* a table, number, or customer. Even personal acquaintances assume the status of inanimate matter, or tip-bearing plants, in the language of the server:

> I got my fifth-grade teacher [as a customer] one time. . . . I kept her coffeed. I kept her boyfriend coked all night. Sodaed. . . . And I kept them filled up.

If the customer is perceived as material that is processed, the goal of this processing is the production or extraction of a finished product: the tip. This image too is conveyed in the language of the floor. A waitress may comment that she "got a good tip" or "gets good tips," but she is more likely to say that she "made" or "makes good tips." She may also say that she "got five bucks out of" a customer, or complain that some customers "don't want to give up on" their money. She may accuse a waitress who stays over into her shift of "tapping on" her money, or warn an aspiring waitress against family restaurants on the grounds that "there's no money in there." In all these comments (and all are actual), the waitress might as easily be talking about mining for coal or drilling for oil as serving customers.

Predictably, the waitress's view of the customer as substance to be processed influences her perception of the meaning of tips, and especially substandard tips. At Route, low tips and stiffs are not interpreted as a negative reflection on the waitress's personal qualities or social status. Rather, they are felt to reveal the refractory nature or poor quality of the raw material from which the tip is extracted, produced, or fashioned. In less metaphorical terms, a low tip or stiff is thought to reflect the negative qualities and low status of the customer who is too cheap, too poor, too ignorant, or too coarse to leave an appropriate gratuity. In this context, it is interesting to note that *stiff*, the term used in restaurants to refer to incidents of nontipping or to someone who does not tip, has also been used to refer to a wastrel or penniless man . . . , a hobo, tramp, vagabond, deadbeat, and a moocher. . . .

Evidence that waitresses assign blame for poor tips to the tipper is found in their reaction to being undertipped or stiffed. Rather than breaking down in tears and lamenting her "personal failure," the Route waitress responds to a stiff by announcing the event to her co-workers and managers in a tone of angry disbelief. Co-workers and managers echo the waitress's indignation and typically ask her to identify the party (by table number and physical description), or if she has already done so, to be more specific. This identification is crucial for it allows sympathizers to join the waitress in analyzing the cause of the stiff, which is assumed a priori to arise from some shortcoming of the party, not the waitress. The waitress and her co-workers may conclude that the customers in question were rude, troublemakers, or bums, or they may explain their behavior by identifying them as members of a particular category of customers. It might be revealed for instance, that the offending party was a church group: church groups are invariably tightfisted.

It might be resolved that the offenders were senior citizens, Southerners, or businesspeople: all well-known cheapskates. If the customers were European, the stiff will be attributed to ignorance of the American tipping system; if they were young, to immaturity; if they had children, to lack of funds.

These classifications and their attendant explanations are neither fixed nor trustworthy. New categories are invented to explain otherwise puzzling incidents, and all categories are subject to exception. Though undependable as predictive devices, customer typologies serve a crucial function: they divert blame for stiffs and low tips from the waitress to the characteristics of the customer. It is for this reason that it is "important" for workers to distinguish between different categories of customers, despite the fact that such distinctions are based on "unreliable verbal and appearance clues." In fact, it is precisely the unreliability, or more appropriately the flexibility, of customer typologies that makes them valuable to waitresses. When categories can be constructed and dissolved on demand, there is no danger that an incident will fall outside the existing system of classification and hence be inexplicable.

While waitresses view the customer as something to be processed and the tip as the product of this processing, they are aware that the public does not share their understanding of the waitress-diner-tip relationship. Waitresses at Route recognize that many customers perceive them as needy creatures willing to commit great feats of service and absorb high doses of abuse in their anxiety to secure a favorable gratuity or protect their jobs. They are also aware that some customers leave small tips with the intent to insult the server and that others undertip on the assumption that for a Route waitress even fifty cents will be appreciated. One waitress indicated that prior to being employed in a restaurant, she herself subscribed to the stereotype of the down-and-out waitress "because you see stuff on television, you see these wives or single ladies who waitress and they live in slummy apartments or slummy houses and they dress in rags." It is these images of neediness and desperation, which run so strongly against the waitress's perception of herself and her position, that she attacks when strained relations erupt into open conflict.

> Five rowdy black guys walked in the door and they went to seat themselves at table seven. I said, "Excuse me. You all got to wait to be seated." "We ain't got to do *shit*. We here to eat. . . ." So they went and sat down. And I turned around and just looked at them. And they said, "Well, I hope you ain't our waitress, cause you blew your tip. Cause you ain't getting nothing from us." And I turned around and I said, "You need it more than I do, baby."

This waitress's desire to confront the customer's assumption of her destitution is widely shared among service workers whose status as tipped employees marks them as needy in the eyes of their customers. Davis . . . reports that among cabdrivers "a forever repeated story is of the annoyed driver, who, after a grueling trip with a Lady Shopper, hands the coin back, telling her, 'Lady, keep your lousy dime. You need it more than I do.' " Mars and Nicod . . . report a hotel waitress's claim that "if she had served a large family with children for one or two weeks, and then was given a 10p piece, she would give the money back, saying, 'It's all right, thank you, I've got enough change for my bus fare home.' " In an incident I observed (not at Route), a waitress followed two male customers out of a restaurant calling, "Excuse me! You forgot this!" and holding up the coins they had left as a tip. The customers appeared embarrassed, motioned for her to keep the money, and continued down the sidewalk. The waitress, now standing in the outdoor seating area of the restaurant and observed by curious diners, threw the money after the retreating men and returned to her work. Episodes such as these allow the worker to repudiate openly the evaluation of her financial status that is implied in an offensively small gratuity, and permit her to articulate her own understanding of what a small tip says and about whom. If customers can only afford to leave a dime, or feel a 10p piece is adequate compensation for two weeks' service, they must be very hard up or very ignorant indeed.

In the following incident the waitress interjects a denial of her neediness into an altercation that is not related to tipping, demonstrating that the customer's perception of her financial status is a prominent and persistent concern for her.

> She [a customer] wanted a California Burger with mayonnaise. And when I got the mayonnaise, the mayonnaise had a little brown on it. . . . So this girl said to me, she said, "What the fuck is this you giving me?" And I turned around, I thought, "Maybe she's talking to somebody else in the booth with her." And I turned around and I said, "Excuse me?" She said, "You hear what I said. I said, 'What the fuck are you giving me?' " And I turned around, I said, "I don't know if you're referring your information to *me*," I said, "but if you're referring your information to *me*," I said, "I don't *need* your bullshit." I said, "I'm not going to even take it. . . . Furthermore, I could care less if you eat or *don't* eat. . . . And you see this?" And I took her check and I ripped it apart. . . . And I took the California Burger and I says, "You don't have a problem anymore now, right?" She went up to the manager. And she says, "That black waitress"—I says, "Oh. By the way, what is my name? I don't have a name, [using the words] 'that black waitress.' . . . My name happens to be Nera. . . . That's N-E-R-A. . . . And I don't need your bullshit, sweetheart. . . . People like you I can walk on, because you don't know how to talk to human beings." And I said, "I don't need you. I don't need your quarters. I don't need your nickels. I don't need your dimes. So if you want service, be my guest. Don't you *ever* sit in my station, cause I won't wait on you." The manager said, "Nera, please. Would you wait in the back?" I said, "No. I don't take back seats no more for nobody."

In each of these cases, the waitress challenges the customer's definition of the relationship in which tipping occurs. By speaking out, by confronting the customer, she demonstrates that she is not subservient or in fear of losing her job; that she is not compelled by financial need or a sense of social hierarchy to accept abuse from customers; that she does not, in Nera's words, "take back seats no more for nobody." At the same time, she reverses the symbolic force of the low tip, converting a statement on her social status or work skills into a statement on the tipper's cheapness or lack of savoir faire.

18
A Look behind the Veil

Elizabeth W. Fernea and Robert A. Fernea

The social structure of North African and Middle Eastern societies both dictates and is reflected in the wearing of the veil. Gender relations, especially, are expressed in the veiling of women. Only as these change will the veil come down. Or will it?

What objects do we notice in societies other than our own? Ishi, the last of a "lost" tribe of North American Indians who stumbled into 20th Century California in 1911, is reported to have said that the truly interesting objects in the white man's culture were pockets and matches. Rifa'ah Tahtawi, one of the first young Egyptians to be sent to Europe to study in 1826, wrote an account of French society in which he noted that Parisians used many unusual articles of dress, among them something called a belt. Women wore belts, he said, apparently to keep their bosoms erect, and to show off the slimness of their waists and the fullness of their hips. Europeans are still fascinated by the Stetson hats worn by American cowboys; an elderly Dutch lady of our acquaintance recently carried six enormous Stetsons back to The Hague as presents for the male members of her family.

Many objects signify values in society and become charged with meaning, a meaning that may be different for members of the society and for observers of that society. The veil is one object used in Middle Eastern societies that stirs strong emotions in the West. "The feminine veil has become a symbol: that of the slavery of one portion of humanity," wrote French ethnologist Germaine Tillion in 1966. A hundred years earlier, Sir Richard Burton, British traveler, explorer, and translator of the *Arabian Nights*, recorded a different view. "Europeans inveigh against this article [the face veil] . . . for its hideousness and jealous concealment of charms made to be admired," he wrote in 1855. "It is, on the contrary, the most coquettish article of woman's attire . . . it conceals coarse skins, fleshy noses, wide mouths and vanishing chins, whilst it sets off to best advantage what in these lands is most lustrous and liquid—the eye. Who has not remarked this at a masquerade ball?"

In the present generation, the veil and purdah, or seclusion, have become a focus of attention for Western writers, both popular and academic, who take a measure of Burton's irony and Tillion's anger to equate modernization of the Middle East with the discarding of the veil.

"Iranian women return to veil in a resurgence of spirituality," headlines one newspaper; another writes, "Iran's 16 million women have come a long way since their floor-length cotton veil officially was abolished in 1935." The thousands of words written about the appearance and disappearance of the veil and of purdah do little to help us understand the Middle East or the cultures that grew out of the same Judeo-Christian roots as our own. The veil and the all-enveloping garments that inevitably accompany it (the *milayah* in Egypt, the *abbayah* in Iraq, the *chadoor* in Iran, the *yashmak* in Turkey, the *burga'* in Afghanistan, and the *djellabah* and the *haik* in North Africa) are only the outward manifestations of a cultural pattern and idea that is rooted deep in Mediterranean society.

"Purdah" is a Persian word meaning curtain or barrier. The Arabic word for veiling and secluding comes from the root *hajaba.* a *hijab* is an amulet worn to keep away the evil eye; it also means a diaphragm used to prevent conception. The gatekeeper or doorkeeper who guards the entrance to a government minister's office is a *hajib*, and in casual conversation a person might say, "I want to be more informal with my friend so-and-so, but she always puts a *hijab* (barrier) between us."

In Islam, the Koranic verse that sanctions the barrier between men and women is called the Sura of the *hijab* (curtain): "Prophet, enjoin your wives, your daughters and the wives of true believers to draw their veils close round them. That is more proper, so that they may be recognized and not molested. Allah is forgiving and merciful."

Certainly seclusion and some forms of veiling had been practiced before the time of Muhammad, at least among the upper classes, but it was his followers who apparently felt that his women should be placed in a special category. According to history, the *hijab* was established after a number of occasions on which Muhammad's wives were insulted by people who were coming to the mosque in search of the prophet. When chided for their behavior, they said they had mistaken Muhammad's wives for slaves. The *hijab* was established, and in the words of the historian Nabia Abbott, "Muhammad's women found themselves, on the one hand, deprived of personal liberty, and on the other hand, raised to a position of honor and dignity."

The veil bears many messages and tells us many things about men and women in Middle Eastern society, but as an object in and of itself it is far less important to members of the society than the values it represents. Nouha al Hejailan, wife of the Saudi Arabian ambassador to London, told Sally Quinn of *The Washington Post*, "If I wanted to take it all off (her *abbayah* and veil), I would have long ago. It wouldn't mean as much to me as it does to you." Early Middle Eastern feminists felt differently. Huda Sh'arawi, an early Egyptian activist who formed the first Women's Union, made a dramatic gesture of removing her veil in public to demonstrate her dislike of society's attitudes toward women and her defiance of the system. But Basima Bezirgan, a contemporary Iraqi feminist, says, "Compared to the real issues that are involved between men and women in the Middle East today, the veil is unimportant." A Moroccan linguist who buys her clothes in Paris laughs when asked about the veil. "My mother wears a *djellabah* and a veil. I have never worn them. But so what? I still cannot get divorced as easily as a man, and I am still a member of my family group and responsible to them for everything I do. What is the veil? A piece of cloth."

"The seclusion of women has many purposes," states Egyptian anthropologist Nadia Abu Zahra. "It expresses men's status, power, wealth, and manliness. It also helps preserve men's image of virility and masculinity, but men do not admit this; on the contrary they claim that one of the purposes of the veil is to guard women's honor." The veil and purdah are symbols of restriction, to men as well as to women. A respectable woman wearing a veil on a public street is signaling, "Hands off. Don't touch me or you'll be sorry." Cowboy Jim Sayre of Deadwood, South Dakota, says, "If you deform a cowboy's hat, he'll likely deform you." In the same way, a man who approaches a veiled woman is asking for trouble; not only the woman but also her family is shamed, and serious problems may result. "It is clear," says Egyptian anthropologist Ahmed Abou Zeid, "that honor and shame which are usually attributed to a certain individual or a certain kinship group have in fact a bearing on the total social structure, since most acts involving honor or shame are likely to affect the existing social equilibrium."

Veiling and seclusion almost always can be related to the maintenance of social status. Historically, only the very rich could afford to seclude their women, and the extreme example of this practice was found among the sultans of prerevolutionary Turkey. Stories of these secluded women, kept in harems and guarded by eunuchs, formed the basis for much of the Western folklore concerning the nature of male-female relationships in Middle Eastern society. The stereotype is of course contradictory; Western writers have never found it necessary to reconcile the erotic fantasies of the seraglio with the sexual puritanism attributed to the same society.

Poor men could not always afford to seclude or veil their women, because the women were needed as productive members of the family economic unit, to work in the fields and in cottage industries. Delta village women in Egypt have never been veiled, nor have the Berber women of North Africa. But this lack of veiling placed poor women in ambiguous situations in relation to strange men.

"In the village, no one veils, because everyone is considered a member of the same large family," explained Aisha bint Mohammed, a working-class wife of Marrakech. "But in the city, veiling is *sunnah*, required by our religion." Veiling is generally found in towns and cities, among all classes, where families feel that it is necessary to distinguish themselves from other strangers in the city.

Veiling and purdah not only indicate status and wealth, they also have some religious sanction and protect women from the world outside the home. Purdah delineates private space, distinguishes between the public and private sectors of society, as does the traditional architecture of the area. Older Middle Eastern houses do not have picture windows facing on the street, nor walks leading invitingly to front doors. Family life is hidden from strangers; behind blank walls may lie courtyards and gardens, refuges from the heat, the cold, the bustle of the outside world, the world of non-kin that is not to be trusted. Outsiders are pointedly excluded.

Even within the household, among her close relatives, a traditional Muslim woman veils before those kinsmen whom she could legally marry. If her maternal or paternal male cousins, her brothers-in-law, or sons-in-law come to call, she covers her head, or perhaps her whole face. To do otherwise would be shameless.

The veil does more than protect its wearers from known and unknown intruders; it can also be used to conceal identity. Behind the anonymity of the veil, women can go about a city unrecognized and uncriticized. Nadia Abu Zahra reports anecdotes of men donning women's veils in order to visit their lovers undetected; women may do the same. The veil is such an effective disguise that Nouri Al-Said, the late prime minister of Iraq, attempted to escape death by wearing the *abbayah* and veil of a woman; only his shoes gave him away.

Political dissidents in many countries have used the veil for their own ends. The women who marched, veiled, through Cairo during the Nationalist demonstrations against the British after World War I were counting on the strength of Western respect for the veil to protect them against British gunfire. At first they were right. Algerian women also used the protection of the veil to carry bombs through French army checkpoints during the Algerian revolution. But when the French discovered the ruse, Algerian women discarded the veil and dressed like Europeans to move about freely.

The multiple meanings and uses of purdah and the veil do not explain how the pattern came to be so deeply embedded in Mediterranean society. Its origins lie somewhere in the basic Muslim attitudes about men's roles and women's roles. Women, according to Fatima Mernissi, a Moroccan sociologist, are seen by men in Islamic societies as in need of protection because they are unable to control their sexuality, are tempting to men, and hence are a danger to the social order. In other words, they need to be restrained and controlled so that society may function in an orderly way.

The notion that women present a danger to the social order is scarcely limited to Muslim society. Anthropologist Julian Pitt-Rivers has pointed out that the supervision and seclusion of women is also to be found in Christian Europe, even though veiling was not usually practiced there. "The idea that women not subjected to male authority are a danger is a fundamental one in the writings of the moralists from the Archpriest of Talavera to Padre Haro, and it is echoed in the modern Andalusian *pueblo*. It is bound up with the fear of ungoverned female sexuality which had been an integral element of European folklore ever since prudent Odysseus lashed himself to the mast to escape the sirens."

Pitt-Rivers is writing about Mediterranean society, which, like all Middle Eastern societies, is greatly concerned with honor and shame rather than with individual guilt. The honor of the Middle Eastern extended family, its ancestors and its descendants, is the highest social value. The misdeeds of the grandparents are indeed visited on the children. Men and women always remain members of their natal families. Marriage is a legal contract but a fragile one that is often broken; the ties between brother and sister, mother and child, father and child are lifelong and enduring. The larger family is the group to which the individual belongs and to which the individual owes responsibility in exchange for the social and economic security that the family group provides. It is the group, not the individual, that is socially shamed or socially honored.

Male honor and female honor are both involved in the honor of the family, but each is expressed differently. The honor of a man, *sharaf*, is a public matter, involving bravery, hospitality, piety. It may be lost, but it may also be regained. The honor of a woman, *'ard*, is a private matter involving only one thing, her sexual chastity. Once lost, it cannot be regained. If the loss of female honor remains only privately known, a rebuke—and perhaps a reveiling—may be all that takes place. But if the loss of female honor becomes public knowledge, the other members of the family may feel bound to cleanse the family name. In extreme cases, the cleansing may require the death of the offending female member. Although such killings are now criminal offenses in the Middle East, suspended sentences are often given, and the newspapers in Cairo and Baghdad frequently carry sad stories of runaway sisters "gone bad" in the city and revenge taken upon them in the name of family honor by their brothers or cousins.

This emphasis on female chastity, many say, originated in the patrilineal society's concern with the paternity of the child and the inheritance that follows the male line. How does a man know that the child in his wife's womb is his own, and not that of another man? Obviously he cannot know unless his wife is a virgin at marriage. From this consideration may have developed the protective institutions called variously purdah, seclusion, or veiling.

Middle Eastern women also look upon seclusion as practical protection. In the Iraqi village where we lived from 1956 to 1958, one of us (Elizabeth) wore the *abbayah* and found that it provided a great sense of protection from prying eyes, dust, heat, flies. Parisian ladies visiting Istanbul in the 16th Century were so impressed by the ability of the all-enveloping garment to keep dresses clean of mud and manure and to keep women from being attacked by importuning men that they tried to introduce it into French fashion.

Perhaps of greater importance for many women reared in traditional cultures is the degree to which their sense of personal identity is tied to the use of the veil. Many women have told us that they felt self-conscious, vulnerable, and even naked when they first walked on a public street without the veil and *abbayah*—as if they were making a display of themselves.

The resurgence of the veil in countries like Morocco, Libya, and Algeria, which have recently established their independence from colonial dominance, is seen by some Middle Eastern and Western scholars as an attempt by men to reassert their Muslim identity and to reestablish their roles as heads of families. The presence of the veil is a sign that the males of the household are once more able to assume the responsibilities that were disturbed or usurped by foreign colonial powers.

But a veiled woman is seldom seen in Egypt or in many parts of Lebanon, Syria, Iran, Tunisia, Turkey, or the Sudan. And as respectable housewives have abandoned the veil, in some of these Middle Eastern countries prostitutes have put it on. They indicate their availability by manipulating the veil in flirtatious ways, but as Burton pointed out more than a century ago, prostitutes are not the first to discover the veil's seductiveness. Like women's garments in the West, the veil can be sturdy, utilitarian, and forbidding—or it can be filmy and decorative, hinting at the charms beneath it.

The veil is the outward sign of a complex reality. Observers are often deceived by the absence of that sign, and fail to see that in most Middle Eastern societies (and in many parts of Europe) basic attitudes are unchanged. Women who have taken off the veil continue to play the old roles within the family, and their chastity remains crucial. A woman's behavior is still the key to the honor and the reputation of her family.

In Middle Eastern societies, feminine and masculine continue to be strong polarities of identification. This is in marked contrast to Western society, where for more than a generation social critics have been striving to blur distinctions in dress, in status, and in type of labor. Almost all Middle Eastern reformers (most of whom are middle and upper class) are still arguing from the assumption of a fundamental difference between men and women. They do not demand an end to the veil (which is passing out of use anyway) but an end to the old principles, which the veil symbolizes, that govern patrilineal society. Middle Eastern reformers are calling for equal access to divorce, child custody, and inheritance; equal opportunities for education and employment; abolition of female circumcision and "crimes of honor"; and a law regulating the age of marriage.

An English woman film director, after several months in Morocco, said in an interview, "This business about the veil is nonsense. We all have our veils, between ourselves and other people. That's not what the Middle East is about. The question is what veils are used for, and by whom." The veil triggers Western reactions simply because it is the dramatic, visible sign of vexing questions, questions that are still being debated, problems that have still not been solved, in the Middle East or in Western societies.

Given the biological differences between men and women, how are the sexes to be treated equitably? Men and women are supposed to share the labor of society and yet provide for the reproduction and nurture of the next generation. If male fear and awe of woman's sexuality provokes them to control and seclude women, can they be assuaged? Rebecca West said long ago that "the difference between men and women is the rock on which civilization will split before it can reach any goal that could justify its expenditure of effort." Until human beings come to terms with this basic issue, purdah and the veil, in some form, will continue to exist in both the East and the West.

19

The Saints and the Roughnecks

WILLIAM J. CHAMBLISS

Almost every student can identify the "Saints" and "Roughnecks" in their high school, but it requires an astute observer like Richard Chambliss to show us how endemic this dichotomy is to a class-structured society. What are the long-term effects of being labeled a "Roughneck"? What are the consequences for those who enter our courts and prisons?

Eight promising young men—children of good, stable, white upper-middle-class families, active in school affairs, good pre-college students—were some of the most delinquent boys at Hanibal High School. While community residents knew that these boys occasionally sowed a few wild oats, they were totally unaware that sowing wild oats completely occupied the daily routine of these young men. The Saints were constantly occupied with truancy, drinking, wild driving, petty theft, and vandalism. Yet no one was officially arrested for any misdeed during the two years I observed them.

This record was particularly surprising in light of my observations during the same two years of another gang of Hanibal High School students, six lower-class white boys known as the Roughnecks. The Roughnecks were constantly in trouble with police and community even though their rate of delinquency was about equal with that of the Saints. What was the cause of this disparity? the result? The following consideration of the activities, social class, and community perceptions of both gangs may provide some answers.

THE SAINTS FROM MONDAY TO FRIDAY

The Saints' principal daily concern was with getting out of school as early as possible. The boys managed to get out of school with minimum danger that they would be accused of playing hookey through an elaborate procedure for obtaining "legitimate" release from class. The most common procedure was for one boy to obtain the release of another by fabricating a meeting of some committee, program, or recognized club. Charles might raise his hand in his 9:00 chemistry class and ask to be excused—a euphemism for going to the bathroom. Charles would go to Ed's math class and inform the teacher that Ed was needed for a 9:30 rehearsal of the drama club play. The math teacher would recognize Ed and Charles as "good students" involved in numerous school activities and would permit Ed to leave at 9:30. Charles would return to his class, and Ed would go to Tom's English class to obtain his release. Tom would engineer Charles's escape. The strategy would continue until as many of the Saints as possible were freed. After a stealthy trip to the car (which had been parked in a strategic spot), the boys were off for a day of fun.

Over the two years I observed the Saints, this pattern was repeated nearly every day. There were variations on the theme, but in one form or another, the boys used this procedure for getting out of class and then off the school grounds. Rarely did all eight of the Saints manage to leave school at the same time. The average number avoiding school on the days I observed them was five.

Having escaped from the concrete corridors the boys usually went either to a pool hall on the other (lower-class) side of town or to a café in the suburbs. Both places were out of the way of people the boys were likely to know (family or school officials), and both provided a source of entertainment. The pool hall entertainment was the generally rough atmosphere, the occasional hustler, the sometimes drunk proprietor and, of course, the game of pool. The café's entertainment was provided by the owner. The boys would "accidentally" knock a glass on the floor or spill cola on the counter—not all the time, but enough to be sporting. They would also bend spoons, put salt in sugar bowls and generally tease whoever was working in the café. The owner had opened the café recently and was dependent on the boys' business which was, in fact, substantial since between the horsing around and the teasing they bought food and drinks.

The Saints on Weekends

On weekends the automobile was even more critical than during the week, for on weekends the Saints went to Big Town—a large city with a population of over a million 25 miles from Hanibal. Every Friday and Saturday night most of the Saints would meet between 8:00 and 8:30 and would go into Big Town. Big Town activities included drinking heavily in taverns or nightclubs, driving drunkenly through the streets, and committing acts of vandalism and playing pranks.

By midnight on Fridays and Saturdays the Saints were usually thoroughly high, and one or two of them were often so drunk they had to be carried to the cars. Then the boys drove around town, calling obscenities to women and girls; occasionally trying (unsuccessfully so far as I could tell) to pick girls up; and driving recklessly through red lights and at high speeds with their lights out. Occasionally they played "chicken." One boy would climb out the back window of the car and across the roof to the driver's side of the car while the car was moving at high speed (between 40 and 50 miles an hour); then the driver would move over and the boy who had just crawled across the car roof would take the driver's seat.

Searching for "fair game" for a prank was the boys' principal activity after they left the tavern. The boys would drive alongside a foot patrolman and ask directions to some street. If the policeman leaned on the car in the course of answering the question, the driver would speed away, causing him to lose his balance. The Saints were careful to play this prank only in an area where they were not going to spend much time and where they could quickly disappear around a corner to avoid having their license plate number taken.

Construction sites and road repair areas were the special province of the Saints' mischief. A soon-to-be-repaired hole in the road inevitably invited the Saints to remove lanterns and wooden barricades and put them in the car, leaving the hole unprotected. The boys would find a safe vantage point and wait for an unsuspecting motorist to drive into the hole. Often, though not always, the boys would go up to the motorist and commiserate with him about the dreadful way the city protected its citizenry.

Leaving the scene of the open hole and the motorist, the boys would then go searching for an appropriate place to erect the stolen barricade. An "appropriate place" was often a spot on a highway near a curve in the road where the barricade would not be seen by an oncoming motorist. The boys would wait to watch an unsuspecting motorist attempt to stop and (usually) crash into the wooden barricade. With saintly bearing the boys might offer help and understanding.

A stolen lantern might well find its way onto the back of a police car or hang from a street lamp. Once a lantern served as a prop for a reenactment of the "midnight ride of Paul Revere" until the "play," which was taking place at 2:00 A.M. in the center of a main street of Big Town, was interrupted by a police car several blocks away. The boys ran, leaving the lanterns on the street, and managed to avoid being apprehended.

Abandoned houses, especially if they were located in out-of-the-way places, were fair game for destruction and spontaneous vandalism. The boys would break windows, remove furniture to the yard and tear it apart, urinate on the walls, and scrawl obscenities inside.

Through all the pranks, drinking, and reckless driving the boys managed miraculously to avoid being stopped by police. Only twice in two years was I aware that they had been stopped by a Big Town policeman. Once was for speeding (which they did every time they drove whether they were drunk or sober), and the driver managed to convince the policeman that it was simply an error. The second time they were stopped they had just left a nightclub and were walking through an alley. Aaron stopped to urinate and the boys began making obscene remarks. A foot patrolman came into the alley, lectured the boys and sent them home. Before the boys got to the car one began talking in a loud voice again. The policeman, who had followed them down the alley, arrested this boy for disturbing the peace and took him to the police station where the other Saints gathered. After paying a $5.00 fine, and with the assurance that there would be no permanent record of the arrest, the boy was released.

The boys had a spirit of frivolity and fun about their escapades. They did not view what they were engaged in as "delinquency," though it surely was by any reasonable definition of that word. They simply viewed themselves as having a little fun and who, they would ask, was really hurt by it? The answer had to be no one, although this fact remains one of the most difficult things to explain about the gang's behavior. Unlikely though it seems, in two years of drinking, driving, carousing, and vandalism no one was seriously injured as a result of the Saints' activities.

THE SAINTS IN SCHOOL

The Saints were highly successful in school. The average grade for the group was "B," with two of the boys having close to a straight "A" average. Almost all of the boys were popular and many of them held offices in the school. One of the boys was vice president of the student body one year. Six of the boys played on athletic teams.

At the end of their senior year, the student body selected ten seniors for special recognition as the "school wheels"; four of the ten were Saints. Teachers and school officials saw no problem with any of these boys and anticipated that they would all "make something of themselves."

How the boys managed to maintain this impression is surprising in view of their actual behavior in school. Their technique for covering truancy was so successful that teachers did not even realize that the boys were absent from school much of the time. Occasionally, of course, the system would backfire and then the boy was on his own. A boy who was caught would be most contrite, would plead guilty and ask for mercy. He inevitably got the mercy he sought.

Cheating on examinations was rampant, even to the point of orally communicating answers to exams as well as looking at one another's papers. Since none of the group studied, and since they were primarily dependent on one another for help, it is surprising that grades were so high. Teachers contributed to the deception in their admitted inclination to give these boys (and presumably others like them) the benefit of the doubt. When asked how the boys did in school, and when pressed on specific examinations, teachers might admit that they were disappointed in John's performance, but would quickly add that they "knew that he was capable of doing better," so John was given a higher grade than he had actually earned. How often this happened is impossible to know. During the time that I observed the group, I never saw any of the boys take homework home. Teachers may have been "understanding" very regularly.

One exception to the gang's generally good performance was Jerry, who had a "C" average in his junior year, experienced disaster the next year, and failed to graduate. Jerry had always been a little more nonchalant than the others about the liberties he took in school. Rather than wait for someone to come get him from class, he would offer his own excuse and leave. Although he probably did not miss any more class than most of the others in the group, he did not take the requisite pains to cover his absences. Jerry was the only Saint whom I ever heard talk back to a teacher. Although teachers often called him a "cut up" or a "smart kid," they never referred to him as a troublemaker or as a kid headed for trouble. It seems likely, then, that Jerry's failure his senior year and his mediocre performance his junior year were consequences of his not playing the game the proper way (possibly because he was disturbed by his parents' divorce). His teachers regarded him as "immature" and not quite ready to get out of high school.

The Police and the Saints

The local police saw the Saints as good boys who were among the leaders of the youth in the community. Rarely, the boys might be stopped in town for speeding or for running a stop sign. When this happened the boys were always polite, contrite and pled for mercy. As in school, they received the mercy they asked for. None ever received a ticket or was taken into the precinct by the local police.

The situation in Big Town, where the boys engaged in most of their delinquency, was only slightly different. The police there did not know the boys at all, although occasionally the boys were stopped by a patrolman. Once they were caught taking a lantern from a construction site. Another time they were stopped for running a stop sign, and on several occasions they were stopped for speeding. Their behavior was as before: contrite, polite and penitent. The urban police, like the local police, accepted their demeanor as sincere. More important, the urban police were convinced that these were good boys just out for a lark.

The Roughnecks

Hanibal townspeople never perceived the Saints' high level of delinquency. The Saints were good boys who just went in for an occasional prank. After all, they were well dressed, well mannered and had nice cars. The Roughnecks were a different story. Although the two gangs of boys were the same age, and both groups engaged in an equal amount of wild-oat sowing, everyone agreed that the not-so-well-dressed, not-so-well-mannered, not-so-rich boys were heading for trouble. Townspeople would say, "You can see the gang members at the drugstore, night after night, leaning against the storefront (sometimes drunk) or slouching around inside buying cokes, reading magazines, and probably stealing old Mr. Wall blind. When they are outside and girls walk by, even respectable girls, these boys make suggestive remarks. Sometimes their remarks are downright lewd."

From the community's viewpoint, the real indication that these kids were in trouble was that they were constantly involved with the police. Some of them had been picked up for stealing, mostly small stuff, of course, "but still it's stealing small stuff that leads to big time crimes." "Too bad," people said. "Too bad that these boys couldn't behave like the other kids in town; stay out of trouble, be polite to adults, and look to their future."

The community's impression of the degrees to which this group of six boys (ranging in age from 16 to 19) engaged in delinquency was somewhat distorted. In some ways the gang was more delinquent than the community thought; in other ways they were less.

The fighting activities of the group were fairly readily and accurately perceived by almost everyone. At least once a month, the boys would get into some sort of fight, although most fights were scraps between members of the group or involved only one member of the group and some peripheral hanger-on. Only three times in the period of observation did the group fight together: once against a gang from across town, once against two blacks, and once against a group of boys from another school. For the first two fights the group went out "looking for trouble"—and they found it both times. The third fight followed a football game and began spontaneously with an argument on the football field between one of the Roughnecks and a member of the opposition's football team.

Jack has a particular propensity for fighting and was involved in most of the brawls. He was a prime mover of the escalation of arguments into fights.

More serious than fighting, had the community been aware of it, was theft. Although almost everyone was aware that the boys occasionally stole things, they did not realize the extent of the activity. Petty stealing was a frequent event for the Roughnecks. Sometimes they stole as a group and coordinated their efforts; other things they stole in pairs. Rarely did they steal alone.

The thefts ranged from very small things like paperback books, comics, and ballpoint pens to expensive items like watches. The nature of the thefts varied from time to time. The gang would go through a period of systematically lifting items from automobiles or school lockers. Types of thievery varied with the whim of the gang. Some forms of thievery were more profitable than others, but all thefts were for profit, not just thrills.

Roughnecks siphoned gasoline from cars as often as they had access to an automobile, which was not very often. Unlike the Saints, who owned their own cars, the Roughnecks would have to borrow their parents' cars, an event which occurred only eight or nine times a year. The boys claimed to have stolen cars for joy rides from time to time.

Ron committed the most serious of the group's offenses. With an un-identified associate the boy attempted to burglarize a gasoline station. Although this station had been robbed twice previously in the same month, Ron denied any involvement in either of the other thefts. When Ron and his accomplice approached the station, the owner was hiding in the bushes beside the station. He fired both barrels of a double-barreled shotgun at the boys. Ron was severely injured; the other boy ran away and was never caught. Though he remained in critical condi-tion for several months, Ron finally recovered and served six months of the following year in reform school. Upon release from reform school, Ron was put back a grade in school, and began running around with a different gang of boys. The Roughnecks considered the new gang less delinquent than themselves, and during the following year Ron had no more trouble with the police.

The Roughnecks, then, engaged mainly in three types of delinquency: theft, drinking, and fighting. Although community members perceived that this gang of kids was delinquent, they mistakenly believed that their illegal activities were primarily drinking, fighting, and being a nuisance to passersby. Drinking was limited among the gang members, although it did occur, and theft was much more prevalent than anyone realized.

Drinking would doubtless have been more prevalent had the boys had ready access to liquor. Since they rarely had automobiles at their dis-posal, they could not travel very far, and the bars in town would not serve them. Most of the boys had little money, and this, too, inhibited their purchase of alcohol. Their major source of liquor was a local drunk who would buy them a fifth if they would give him enough extra to buy himself a pint of whiskey or a bottle of wine.

The community's perception of drinking as prevalent stemmed from the fact that it was the most obvious delinquency the boys engaged in. When one of the boys had been drinking, even a casual observer seeing him on the corner would suspect that he was high.

There was a high level of mutual distrust and dislike between the Roughnecks and the police. The boys felt very strongly that the police were unfair and corrupt. Some evidence existed that the boys were cor-rect in their perception.

The main source of the boys' dislike for the police undoubtedly stemmed from the fact that the police would sporadically harass the group. From the standpoint of the boys, these acts of occasional enforce-ment of the law were whimsical and uncalled for. It made no sense to them, for example, that the police would come to the corner occasionally and threaten them with arrest for loitering when the night before the boys had been out siphoning gasoline from cars and the police had been nowhere in sight. To the boys, the police were stupid on the one hand, for not being where they should have been and catching the boys in a serious offense, and unfair on the other hand, for trumping up "loiter-ing" charges against them.

From the viewpoint of the police, the situation was quite different. They knew, with all the confidence necessary to be a policeman, that these boys were engaged in criminal activities. They knew this partly from occasionally catching them, mostly from circumstantial evidence ("the boys were around when those tires were slashed"), and partly because the police shared the view of the community in general that this was a bad bunch of boys. The best the police could hope to do was to be sensitive to the fact that these boys were engaged in illegal acts and arrest them whenever there was some evidence that they had been involved. Whether or not the boys had in fact committed a particular act in a particular way was not especially important. The police had a broader view: their job was to stamp out these kids' crimes; the tactics were not as important as the end result.

Over the period that the group was under observation, each member was arrested at least once. Several of the boys were arrested a number of times and spent at least one night in jail. While most were never taken to court, two of the boys were sentenced to six months' incarceration in boys' schools.

The Roughnecks in School

The Roughnecks' behavior in school was not particularly disruptive. During school hours they did not all hang around together, but tended instead to spend most of their time with one or two other members of the gang who were their special buddies. Although every member of the gang attempted to avoid school as much as possible, they were not particularly successful and most of them attended school with surprising regularity. They considered school a burden—something to be gotten through with a minimum of conflict. If they were "bugged" by a particular teacher, it could lead to trouble. One of the boys, Al, once threatened to beat up a teacher and, according to the other boys, the teacher hid under a desk to escape him.

Teachers saw the boys the way the general community did, as heading for trouble, as being uninterested in making something of themselves. Some were also seen as being incapable of meeting the academic standards of the school. Most of the teachers expressed concern for this group of boys and were willing to pass them despite poor performance, in the belief that failing them would only aggravate the problem.

The group of boys had a grade point average just slightly above "C." No one in the group failed either grade, and no one had better than a "C" average. They were very consistent in their achievement or, at least, the teachers were consistent in their perception of the boys' achievement.

Two of the boys were good football players. Herb was acknowledged to be the best player in the school and Jack was almost as good. Both boys were criticized for their failure to abide by training rules, for refusing to come to practice as often as they should, and for not playing their best during practice. What they lacked in sportsmanship they made up for in skill, apparently, and played every game no matter how poorly they had performed in practice or how many practice sessions they had missed.

Two Questions

Why did the community, the school, and the police react to the Saints as though they were good, upstanding, nondelinquent youths with bright futures but to the Roughnecks as though they were tough, young criminals who were headed for trouble? Why did the Roughnecks and the Saints in fact have quite different careers after high school—careers which, by and large, lived up to the expectations of the community?

The most obvious explanation for the differences in the community's and law enforcement agencies' reactions to the two gangs is that one group of boys was "more delinquent" than the other. Which group was more delinquent? The answer to this question will determine in part how we explain the differential responses to these groups by the members of the community and, particularly, by law enforcement and school officials.

In sheer number of illegal acts, the Saints were the more delinquent. They were truant from school for at least part of the day almost every day of the week. In addition, their drinking and vandalism occurred with surprising regularity. The Roughnecks, in contrast, engaged sporadically in delinquent episodes. While these episodes were frequent, they certainly did not occur on a daily or even a weekly basis.

The difference in frequency of offenses was probably caused by the Roughnecks' inability to obtain liquor and to manipulate legitimate excuses from school. Since the Roughnecks had less money than the Saints, and teachers carefully supervised their school activities, the Roughnecks' hearts may have been as black as the Saints', but their misdeeds were not nearly as frequent.

There are really no clear-cut criteria by which to measure qualitative differences in antisocial behavior. The most important dimension is generally referred to as the "seriousness" of the offenses.

If seriousness encompasses the relative economic costs of delinquent acts, then some assessment can be made. The Roughnecks probably stole an average of about $5.00 worth of goods a week. Some weeks the figure was considerably higher, but these times must be balanced against long periods when almost nothing was stolen.

The Saints were more continuously engaged in delinquency but their acts were not for the most part costly to property. Only their vandalism and occasional theft of gasoline would so qualify. Perhaps once or twice a month they would siphon a tankful of gas. The other costly items were street signs, construction lanterns, and the like. All of these acts combined probably did not quite average $5.00 a week, partly because much

of the stolen equipment was abandoned and presumably could be recovered. The difference in cost of stolen property between the two
groups was trivial, but the Roughnecks probably had a slightly more
expensive set of activities than did the Saints.

Another meaning of seriousness is the potential threat of physical
harm to members of the community and to the boys themselves. The
Roughnecks were more prone to physical violence; they not only welcomed an opportunity to fight; they went seeking it. In addition, they
fought among themselves frequently. Although the fighting never included deadly weapons, it was still a menace, however minor, to the
physical safety of those involved.

The Saints never fought. They avoided physical conflict both inside
and outside the group. At the same time, though, the Saints frequently
endangered their own and other people's lives. They did so almost every
time they drove a car, especially if they had been drinking. Sober, their
driving was risky; under the influence of alcohol it was horrendous. In
addition, the Saints endangered the lives of others with their pranks.
Street excavations left unmarked were a very serious hazard.

Evaluating the relative seriousness of the two gangs' activities is difficult. The community reacted as though the behavior of the Roughnecks
was a problem, and they reacted as though the behavior of the Saints
was not. But the members of the community were ignorant of the array
of delinquent acts that characterized the Saints' behavior. Although concerned citizens were unaware of much of the Roughnecks' behavior as
well, they were much better informed about the Roughnecks' involvement in delinquency than they were about the Saints'.

VISIBILITY

Differential treatment of the two gangs resulted in part because one
gang was infinitely more visible than the other. This differential visibility
was a direct function of the economic standing of the families. The Saints
had access to automobiles and were able to remove themselves from the
sight of the community. In as routine a decision as to where to go to
have a milkshake after school, the Saints stayed away from the mainstream of community life. Lacking transportation, the Roughnecks could
not make it to the edge of town. The center of town was the only practical
place for them to meet since their homes were scattered throughout the
town and any noncentral meeting place put an undue hardship on some
members. Through necessity the Roughnecks congregated in a crowded
area where everyone in the community passed frequently, including
teachers and law enforcement officers. They could easily see the Roughnecks hanging around the drugstore.

The Roughnecks, of course, made themselves even more visible by
making remarks to passersby and by occasionally getting into fights on
the corner. Meanwhile, just as regularly, the Saints were either at the café

on one edge of town or in the pool hall at the other edge of town. Without any particular realization that they were making themselves inconspicuous, the Saints were able to hide their time-wasting. Not only were they removed from the mainstream of traffic, but they were almost always inside a building.

On their escapades the Saints were also relatively invisible, since they left Hanibal and traveled to Big Town. Here, too, they were mobile, roaming the city, rarely going to the same area twice.

DEMEANOR

To the notion of visibility must be added the difference in the responses of group members to outside intervention with their activities. If one of the Saints was confronted with an accusing policeman, even if he felt he was truly innocent of a wrongdoing, his demeanor was apologetic and penitent. A Roughneck's attitude was almost the polar opposite. When confronted with a threatening adult authority, even one who tried to be pleasant, the Roughneck's hostility and disdain were clearly observable. Sometimes he might attempt to put up a veneer of respect, but it was thin and was not accepted as sincere by the authority.

School was no different from the community at large. The Saints could manipulate the system by feigning compliance with the school norms. The availability of cars at school meant that once free from the immediate sight of the teacher, the boys could disappear rapidly. And this escape was well enough planned that no administrator or teacher was nearby when the boys left. A Roughneck who wished to escape for a few hours was in a bind. If it were possible to get free from class, downtown was still a mile away, and even if he arrived there, he was still very visible. Truancy for the Roughnecks meant almost certain detection, while the Saints enjoyed almost complete immunity from sanctions.

BIAS

Community members were not aware of the transgressions of the Saints. Even if the Saints had been less discreet, their favorite delinquencies would have been perceived as less serious than those of the Roughnecks.

In the eyes of the police and school officials, a boy who drinks in an alley and stands intoxicated on the street corner is committing a more serious offense than is a boy who drinks to inebriation in a nightclub or a tavern and drives around afterwards in a car. Similarly, a boy who steals a wallet from a store will be viewed as having committed a more serious offense than a boy who steals a lantern from a construction site.

Perceptual bias also operates with respect to the demeanor of the boys in the two groups when they are confronted by adults. It is not simply that adults dislike the posture affected by boys of the Roughneck ilk; more important is the conviction that the posture adopted by the Roughnecks is an indication of their devotion and commitment to deviance as a way of life. The posture becomes a cue, just as the type of the offense is a cue, to the degree to which the known transgressions are indicators of the youths' potential for other problems.

Visibility, demeanor, and bias are surface variables which explain the day-to-day operations of the police. Why do these surface variables operate as they do? Why did the police choose to disregard the Saints' delinquencies while breathing down the backs of the Roughnecks?

The answer lies in the class structure of American society and the control of legal institutions by those at the top of the class structure. Obviously, no representative of the upper class drew up the operational chart for the police which led them to look in the ghettos and on streetcorners—which led them to see the demeanor of lower-class youth as troublesome and that of upper-middle-class youth as tolerable. Rather, the procedures simply developed from experience—experience with irate and influential upper-middle-class parents insisting that their son's vandalism was simply a prank and his drunkenness only a momentary "sowing of wild oats"—experience with cooperative or indifferent, powerless, lower-class parents who acquiesced to the law's definition of their son's behavior.

Adult Careers of the Saints and the Roughnecks

The community's confidence in the potential of the Saints and the Roughnecks apparently was justified. If anything, the community members underestimated the degree to which these youngsters would turn out "good" or "bad."

Seven of the eight members of the Saints went on to college immediately after high school. Five of the boys graduated from college in four years. The sixth one finished college after two years in the army, and the seventh spent four years in the air force before returning to college and receiving a B.A. degree. Of these seven college graduates, three went on for advanced degrees. One finished law school and is now active in state politics, one finished medical school and is practicing near Hanibal, and one boy is now working for a Ph.D. The other four college graduates entered submanagerial, managerial, or executive training positions with larger firms.

The only Saint who did not complete college was Jerry. Jerry had failed to graduate from high school with the other Saints. During his second senior year, after the other Saints had gone on to college, Jerry began to hang around with what several teachers described as a "rough crowd"—the gang that was heir apparent to the Roughnecks. At the end of his second senior year, when he did graduate from high school, Jerry took a job as a used-car salesman, got married, and quickly had a child. Although he made several abortive attempts to go to college by attending night school, when I last saw him (ten years after high school) Jerry was unemployed and had been living on unemployment for almost a year. His wife worked as a waitress.

Some of the Roughnecks have lived up to community expectations. A number of them were headed for trouble. A few were not.

Jack and Herb were the athletes among the Roughnecks and their athletic prowess paid off handsomely. Both boys received unsolicited athletic scholarships to college. After Herb received his scholarship (near the end of his senior year), he apparently did an about-face. His demeanor became very similar to that of the Saints. Although he remained a member in good standing of the Roughnecks, he stopped participating in most activities and did not hang on the corner as often.

Jack did not change. If anything, he became more prone to fighting. He even made excuses for accepting the scholarship. He told the other gang members that the school had guaranteed him a "C" average if he would come to play football—an idea that seems far-fetched, even in this day of highly competitive recruiting.

During the summer after graduation from high school, Jack attempted suicide by jumping from a tall building. The jump would certainly have killed most people trying it, but Jack survived. He entered college in the fall and played four years of football. He and Herb graduated in four years, and both are teaching and coaching in high schools. They are married and have stable families. If anything, Jack appears to have a more prestigious position in the community than does Herb, though both are well respected and secure in their positions.

Two of the boys never finished high school. Tommy left at the end of his junior year and went to another state. That summer he was arrested and placed on probation on a manslaughter charge. Three years later he was arrested for murder; he pleaded guilty to second degree murder and is serving a 30-year sentence in the state penitentiary.

Al, the other boy who did not finish high school, also left the state in his senior year. He is serving a life sentence in a state penitentiary for first degree murder.

Wes is a small-time gambler. He finished high school and "bummed around." After several years he made contact with a bookmaker who employed him as a runner. Later he acquired his own area and has been working it ever since. His position among the bookmakers is almost identical to the position he had in the gang; he is always around but no one is really aware of him. He makes no trouble and he does not get into any. Steady, reliable, capable of keeping his mouth closed, he plays the game by the rules, even though the game is an illegal one.

That leaves only Ron. Some of his former friends reported that they had heard he was "driving a truck up north," but no one could provide any concrete information.

Reinforcement

The community responded to the Roughnecks as boys in trouble, and the boys agreed with that perception. Their pattern of deviancy was reinforced, and breaking away from it became increasingly unlikely. Once the boys acquired an image of themselves as deviants, they selected new friends who affirmed that self-image. As that self-conception became more firmly entrenched, they also became willing to try new and more extreme deviances. With their growing alienation came freer expression of disrespect and hostility for representatives of the legitimate society. This disrespect increased the community's negativism, perpetuating the entire process of commitment to deviance. Lack of a commitment to deviance works the same way. In either case, the process will perpetuate itself unless some event (like a scholarship to college or a sudden failure) external to the established relationship intervenes. For two of the Roughnecks (Herb and Jack), receiving college athletic scholarships created new relations and culminated in a break with the established pattern of deviance. In the case of one of the Saints (Jerry), his parents' divorce and his failing to graduate from high school changed some of his other relations. Being held back in school for a year and losing his place among the Saints had sufficient impact on Jerry to alter his self-image and virtually to assure that he would not go on to college as his peers did. Although the experiments of life can rarely be reversed, it seems likely in view of the behavior of the other boys who did not enjoy this special treatment by the school that Jerry, too, would have "become something" had he graduated as anticipated. For Herb and Jack outside intervention worked to their advantage; for Jerry it was his undoing.

Selective perception and labeling—finding, processing, and punishing some kinds of criminality and not others—means that visible, poor, non-mobile, outspoken, undiplomatic "tough" kids will be noticed, whether their actions are seriously delinquent or not. Other kids, who have established a reputation for being bright (even though underachieving), disciplined, and involved in respectable activities, who are mobile and monied, will be invisible when they deviate from sanctioned activities. They'll sow their wild oats—perhaps even wider and thicker than their lower-class cohorts—but they won't be noticed. When it's time to leave adolescence most will follow the expected path, settling into the ways of the middle class, remembering fondly the delinquent but unnoticed fling of their youth. The Roughnecks and others like them may turn around, too. It is more likely that their noticeable deviance will have been so reinforced by police and community that their lives will be effectively channeled into careers consistent with their adolescent background.

20
Recreating Motherhood

Barbara Katz Rothman

In the search for solutions to social problems, Americans often resort to the language of individual rights. These have guided the women's movement for more than a century but may be inadequate for the task ahead, according to Barbara Katz Rothman. What is required is not only a new way of defining "mothering." We must also think anew about the changes in social structure needed to support both the rights and the needs of mothering.

The ideology of capitalism, that goods are produced for profit, is clear to us; we know that some societies avoid the profit motive, and that most societies feel there should be some limit on the extent to which human life is viewed as a commodity. It may seem farfetched to apply this ideology to motherhood and to children. But the family has always been an economic unit as well as a social and psychological unit. What is new, perhaps, is the shift from children as workers to children as commodities, accompanying the change in the family as a unit of production to its new role as a unit of consumption.

For the most part, children aren't workers in the family anymore. The farm family in rural, traditional American society is mostly a thing of the past. Because children don't become real partners in work, they become, in a sense, luxury items. We talk about children in very much the same way we talk about other luxuries: Can we afford a second car? Can we afford a third child? Accompanying this change in the way we see children is a change in our view of motherhood. No longer an event shaped by religion and family, having a baby has become part of a high-tech medical world. There is artificial insemination, amniocentesis, contract surrogacy; during labor, a doctor manages the process, making it more efficient, predictable, rational. Likewise, when mothers and fathers push their babies onto a schedule, so that feeding the baby meshes into the nine-to-five day, parenting becomes an exercise in the rational and efficient use of time.

And this, I fear, is where it is all heading: the commodification of children and the proletarianization of motherhood. We are no longer talking about mothers and babies at all—we are talking about laborers and their products.

Mind-Body Dualism

Ours is a liberal philosophic tradition which holds that what is especially valuable about human beings is the capacity for rationality. But hand in hand with the valuing of rationality is a theoretical disdain for the significance of the body, and a disdain for physical work in preference for "mental" work. The latter, dividing the physical from the mental work, and then using machines and people interchangeably to do the menial physical work, is the essence of technological organization.

Blue-collar work is less valued than managerial work. The "white collar" is a status symbol for having risen above the work of the body. This division of labor is a particular problem for women as mothers: mothers *do* the physical work of the body, women *do* the menial work of body maintenance. Thus women become identified with the physical, the body, and men with the higher, the rational.

This mind-body dualism has deeper consequences as well: by viewing the body as a mechanism of production, we are encouraged to see it as a resource to be used. If the mind and rationality are held "above" the body, it becomes relatively easy to see the body as a resource for the use of the mind, and, specifically, women's reproductive bodies as "societal" resources. And it is here—between the body as "private property" and the body as "resource"—that we encounter the ubiquitous problem of reconciling individual freedom and social order.

The Body as Private Property

In the US, legal recognition of the body goes only to the view of it as individually owned. That is an idea deeply rooted in our liberal political system and our economic system, which is based on private ownership and free enterprise. And it is not a bad way of *legally* viewing the body: as property, privately and individually owned. Such a view protects each of us from all of us; protects us as individuals from potential abuses of power by the government.

In fact, intelligent feminist use of this individualist ethos has been invaluable in assuring women's rights in procreation. Once women are recognized as full citizens, then individual women must be accorded the same rights of bodily autonomy and integrity afforded men. For women, that means sexual and procreative autonomy. Because it is her body, she cannot be raped. Because it is her body, she cannot be forced to bear pregnancies she does not want. Because it is her body, she cannot be forced to abort pregnancies she does want.

Due in part to our current battles over the right to abortion, we tend to think that the three branches of government "permit" women to have abortions; as if the drive for continuing pregnancies came from the government, and the drive for abortions from women. In fact, the legal protection works also to permit women not to have abortions. When women's ownership rights over their bodies are lost, the rights to have and the rights *not* to have abortions are likewise lost.

In American society, when we bring it back to the simple legal questions—who can force an abortion or forcibly prevent one—we wisely retreat to safety, calling forth our most sacred value: the power of ownership.

This then is the way women have successfully been able to combine America's liberal philosophy with its economic ideology. Women have made use of the mind-body dualism, to allow a view of the body as owned, like a shelter which houses the more important mind. If one claims rationality for women—the essential liberal claim for all people —then simple fairness gives women the same rights of bodily ownership that men have, and the very high value of ownership, of property rights, is then turned to the advantage of women who can claim exclusive rights to their own bodies. In the name of ownership, women have demanded access to contraception, sterilization, and abortion.

Yet, while the "owned-body" principle has worked for women in avoiding motherhood, it is less clear how it can be made to work to empower women as mothers. A woman's body may be her own, but the bodies of mothers are not highly valued. In fact, in pregnancy women may simply be seen to own the space in which the fetuses are housed. This is the argument on which attempts to control women's behavior during pregnancy are based: owning her own body is not enough to assure her civil liberties if her body is believed to contain potential wards of the state. The anti-drug, anti-drinking "behave yourself" campaigns aimed increasingly at pregnant women, along with the judicial trend toward prosecuting drug-abusing mothers for "transporting illegal drugs to a minor" through her umbilical cord, are the most blatant examples of this trend toward separating the rights of the woman from the rights of the fetus growing in her womb.

Is it possible to make the legal concept of the owned body work in the interest of mothers? Women could take advantage of mechanistic thinking, and claim "sweat equity" in their babies: they are ours because we have done the work to make them. Women would then have made the connection between the owned body and the owned child. But the "sweat equity" idea will work only if women's labor, the "sweat," is valued.

THE LIMITATIONS OF LIBERAL FEMINISM

Though a great deal of progress has been made by the women's movement, as it stands, a generation of women have grown up to be exactly the kinds of parents they wanted their children's fathers to be. Women earn good money at secure, responsible, interesting jobs. Women take their work seriously—but they balance it against the needs of family.

With a few glorious exceptions, men have not taken up the slack.

While women have added full-time employment to the traditional mother role, men have mostly just added a few hours, at best, of "quality" time to traditional fathering.

The feminism that spread with the Industrial Revolution and that wanted to give women "equality with men" was liberal feminism, the feminist thinking that dominated the first, and probably the current, wave of the women's movement.

The simplest and least threatening version of feminism is to ask for what is seen in America as simple fairness. Demands for fairness consist largely of the insistence that prevailing liberal ideals be applied to women: equal pay for equal work, the same rights for women as for men, etc. Since in America we are living in a society founded on liberal principles, liberal feminism comes closest to mainstream values.

Liberal feminism has its roots deep in American culture; feminists as far back as Abigail Adams requested that the framers of the Constitution "remember the ladies." Liberal feminists, in asking that the ladies be remembered, were not so much offering a critique of American life and values as they were seeking full access.

Liberal feminism works best to defend women's rights to be like men, to enter into men's worlds, to work at men's jobs for men's pay, to have the rights and privileges of men. But what of our rights to be women? The liberal argument, the fairness argument, the equal rights argument, these all begin to break down when we look at women who are, or are becoming, mothers. Pregnancy is like nothing else, so how can uniqueness be made to fit into an equality model?

Liberal feminists, seeking equality and recognition of women's rationality, but discounting the value of the woman's body, claim equality of parenthood between men and women. It is, after all, only women's bodily experience that is different from men's. . . .

"Equal rights" sound good. But a focus on rights ignores *needs*. Giving women all the rights of men will not accomplish a whole lot for women facing the demands of pregnancy, birth, and lactation. Because of the focus on formal equality, because of the value of mind over body, and because of the manner in which our technologically-oriented society seeks efficiency through the separation of work and home, physical and mental, etc., liberal thinking tends to diminish the significance of the physical parts of motherhood.

As individuals, separation and compartmentalization form a central theme of liberal society. We "change hats"; "shift gears"; we carry our separate selves around, experiencing not only the compartmentalization between people, but within ourselves as well. We have "work lives" and "home lives." We change clothing in our different roles, we change style, we change tone.

Yet against this, we have motherhood, the physical embodiment of connectedness. We have in every pregnant woman the living proof that individuals do not enter the world as autonomous, atomistic, isolated beings, but begin socially, begin connected. And we have in every pregnant woman a walking contradiction of the segmentation of our lives: pregnancy does not permit it. In pregnancy the private self, the sexual, familial self, announces itself wherever the woman goes.

Motherhood is the embodied challenge to a liberal philosophy which serves to articulate the values and themes of technological society: order, predictability, rationality, control, rationalization of life, the systematizing and control of things and people as things, the reduction of all to component parts, and ultimately the vision of everything, including ourselves, as resources.

For those people who want to see women—their bodies, sexuality, motherhood—treated with respect, liberal feminism fails.

THE ATOMIZATION OF LIFE

Though liberal feminism has fallen short in many respects, the idea that "the personal is political" was an early insight, a shining, glorious insight of the women's movement. These women understood that the celebration of the individual's power to create, to overcome, etc. fell very hard on the people who were structurally placed so as not to be able to achieve.

Individualism is a deep-rooted theme in American society. Yet, because we as a society have conceptualized everything in terms of the individual—that it just takes gumption, strength, initiative—we must continually deal with the failure of the individual. We have obscured the structural barriers to success behind infinite examples of individual failures.

As long as we keep asking how working mothers can resolve their problems, the terms "working" and "mother" will remain an inherent contradiction.

The question should be: What is wrong with the way we have organized family and work so that they don't fit together? Certainly, two major social institutions should match. If they don't, there is a problem. And if we have created a notion of "work" in occupation and profession that precludes women from living full lives, there is something wrong with the social and economic organization of "livelihood."

First and foremost, we must rethink the nature of the family, and gender relations within the family. At the absolute height of the feminine mystique, for instance—when every mother was supposed to be in her home, in her own kitchen, with her own children—breast feeding in America was at its absolute low point. Regardless of biology, American women were standing over the stove sterilizing formula for their babies. So, one could not even claim that the mother needed to be at home to breast feed her baby.

Pregnancy, on the other hand, is certainly biological. But the issue of pregnancy, and the six-week maternity leave, has never really occupied the center of the family/work debate. The issue does not revolve around the physical experiences of pregnancy or birth. Rather, the issue centers on the care of children and the organization of family.

The nucleus of the debate is the three-month old that cannot be abandoned on a hook; it is the three-year old that needs attention; it is the six-year old that comes home from school at 3:30, though work ends for his parents at 5:30.

Women may not need fathers to share the mothering with, but they certainly need someone. Women cannot do it all. The problem of the double day for women, the unending circuit of paid work and then work in the household, not enough sleep, and back to work, inevitably takes its toll.

The fact is that the social relationship of parenting, of nurturing and of caring, needs a social base, not a genetic one. Through their pregnancies, women begin to establish that base. But if women are not to drop from exhaustion and lose all pleasure in life, someone is going to have to help with the kids.

Mothers are working in the nexus between the child and society. Children need their lives preserved and their growth fostered. The social group needs that growth shaped in ways appropriate and acceptable to it, for its own continuation, preservation and growth.

Maternal practice must meet three interests then; those of preservation, growth, and acceptability. The initial and most powerful demand is preservation: simply keeping the child alive, especially through its vulnerable early months and years, beginning, for birth mothers, with conception. But the mother must do more than keep this heart beating: she must foster the child's physical, emotional, and intellectual growth. And she must do that in such a way that her child becomes an acceptable adult. Both for the sake of the child and for the sake of the society of which the mother, too, is a member, the child must fit in, must grow to meet the needs of the society.

Looking at motherhood this way, as a discipline, a way of thinking, a response to the needs and demands that exist outside of the mother, shifts our focus from who the mother is to what she is doing. Who she is, who she feels herself to be, is deeply gender based: she is a woman, a mother. What she is doing is not gender based: the similarities in behavior of mothers has more to do with the similarities in their situations, in the demands they face from their children and from their societies, than it has to do with similarities in the women. And so the person engaged in this discipline of motherhood need not be a mother, need not be a woman, in order to engage in these activities, this way of thought and practice that is mothering.

Perhaps this is one of those moments of crisis a society faces, where there are two paths that can be taken. We can focus on nurturance, caring, human relations. We can come to accept and to respect a wider variety of family relationships and arrangements. Those qualities we have come to think of as maternal could become more widely shared, by both men and women. We could direct this nurturance, this maternal caring, not just to children, but to each other. The values and the experience of motherhood could come to shape the way we live in the world. This is, I suppose, the fantasy, the truly revolutionary potential of a recreated motherhood.

Or we can recreate motherhood to reflect the commodification of children and the degradation of the mothering project. That, I am afraid, is the direction we have been heading in for a long time, and what we are faced with now is the *reductio ad absurdum* of this process.

A society that creates a decent environment for motherhood is a civil society. It is a world that is supportive of nurturance, of caring, of involvement with one another.

21
Mixed Messages

RUTH SIDEL

The human body is a marvelous thing. So why do so many young women seem to hate their bodies and long for a physique seen only in the airbrushed advertisements of the most fashionable magazines? Does the body have anything to do with success, freedom, independence, or self-worth? Young women are told it does, but the author of this essay strongly questions this.

In an effort to understand the messages young women are receiving, fourteen women's magazines for March 1988 were systematically examined for content, for the ways in which women were portrayed, and for the values and norms that were both subtly and directly communicated. The magazines, chosen for their appeal to a broad spectrum of women by age, class, and interest, were *Seventeen, Mademoiselle, Glamour, Cosmopolitan, Harper's Bazaar, Vogue, Ladies' Home Journal, Working Mother, New Women, Self, Working Woman, Savvy, Ms.,* and *Essence.* All of the magazines focused, in varying degrees, on beauty tips, hair, fashion, fitness, health, food (both nutrition and recipes), and work. Virtually everyone pictured is clearly middle class; several magazines (*Vogue, Savvy,* and *Harper's Bazaar*) are upper middle class in tone, with an emphasis on upper-class life-style. A few of the magazines openly disparage the lower middle and working classes: a comic strip in *Seventeen* indicates that any high-school student foolish enough to invite a guy who works in an auto muffler shop to the school prom will find that he is no better than a prehuman ape, and *Mademoiselle* cautions women who want to move up the career ladder not to "leave the ratty little sweater on the chair just like the secretary does." Among the hundreds of features, viewpoints, articles, occasional fiction, advice, and how-to columns, there was not one instance of members of the working class being depicted in a positive light.

The overall message, transmitted both explicitly and implicitly, is "You can be all you want to be." You can be fit, thin, and trim; you can have a good job, be upwardly mobile, and invest your money wisely; you can wear stunning suits in your march toward success or slinky, sexy, almost childlike clothes, if you prefer; you can have an attractive, no-fuss hairstyle and blend just the right, ever-flattering makeup; you can have great (albeit safe) sex and know just what to do when *he* cannot perform; and, above all, you really *can* have it all—a warm, close family life and lucrative, pleasurable work. You really *can* have both love and success. It may mean starting your own business at home, but there are all those success stories to serve as models: Mrs. Fields, who has made millions on her chocolate-chip cookies and looks gorgeous too; the woman from Virginia who does $1 million worth of business annually making flags and is about to license national franchises; or the woman from Scottsdale, Arizona, who delivers teddy bears as special-occasion gifts the way FTD sells flowers and currently owns two stores, twenty-three franchises, and has annual sales of $1.5 million. What could be easier? And all that is involved are skills that women already have! Women are being told that they can use traditional female skills and make a fortune without ever leaving the kitchen or the sewing machine. The implication is that the fulfillment of the American Dream can be simply one clever idea or marketing strategy away.

Different magazines appeal, of course, to different constituencies: in March 1988, *Seventeen* features prom gowns and many advertisements for sanitary products; *Working Mother* had numerous articles on parenting and homemaking; *Vogue* and *Harper's Bazaar* showed the trendiest and most expensive clothes; and *Essence* dealt, for the most part, with issues particularly relevant to black women. But the overall message is that "working women" are "on the way up," that "you're headed for the top," and that you can "be your own boss."

Not only can you remake your career but you can also remake your looks. The "makeover" (frequently called the "five-minute makeover") is ubiquitous and offers the promise of instant results. Often using "ordinary" people, neither models nor film stars, the makeover is meant to show us all how much more appealing and contemporary we can look by the ever-changing standards of beauty. Are we to have accented lips or accented eyes? Slightly unmanageable long hair or a trim, stylish short cut? Must we still diet until we are reed slim, or is it once again fashionable to look voluptuous? If you do not look like the models and celebrities smiling on every page, you are not exercising properly, eating the correct food, getting the right haircut, using the appropriate gel or mousse; or perhaps you need cosmetic surgery—liposuction, eyelid surgery, nose alteration, or breast enlargement or reduction. The magazines often feature pro and con articles about cosmetic surgery, but the bottom line is that it is yet another legitimate weapon, currently very much in vogue, in women's endless struggle toward a more attractive face and body.

"Older" women are frequently exhorted by women's magazines to be beautiful, fit, and above all, youthful. While the positive aspects of the emphasis on mid-life beauty and fitness are that women in their forties, fifties, sixties, and beyond often see themselves today as vibrant, sexually attractive and truly in the prime of life, there are negative aspects as well. Columnist Ellen Goodman points out that the women who are currently held up as paragons raise the threshold of self-hate faster than the age span. . . . Those of us who failed to look like Brooke Shields at seventeen can now fail to look like Victoria Principal at thirty-three and like Linda Evans at forty-one and like Sophia Loren at fifty. When Gloria Steinem turned fifty . . . she updated her famous line from forty. She said, "This is what fifty looks like." With due apologies to the cult of midlife beauty, allow me two words: "Not necessarily."

And what is so sad, and in some sense shameful, is that a broad spectrum of businesses and advertisers are playing on that self-hatred in their unending quest to sell products and services. It is the combination of self-hatred and "willful suspension of disbelief" that leads women, over and over, to those cosmetics counters, health spas, and plastic surgeons. Maybe we can come just a little closer to what they tell us we should look like. . . .

Even *Ms.* promised that "whatever it is we want, we can succeed." Despite the opening paragraph of the editor's essay, which suggests that all women might not choose the stressful life of a "corporate or government job," the ultimate message is that whatever we do choose, "we can succeed." The *Essence* editor's column gave the same message: that although there are powerful forces "arrayed against us—racism, sexism, poverty, homelessness, illiteracy, poor health"—black women must reach for the sky, saying "I can!" The message is that changing our lives is fundamentally within our control: "If you're living below your standard, get busy devising a plan to improve your life. If your work is a bore, renew your attitude. . . . Surround yourself with positive people who encourage you. . . . Each of us must become an active participant in empowering ourselves and our people. Only the single-minded succeed."

To their credit, *Essence* and *Ms.* were the only magazines that suggested that the well-being of the individual is at all connected with the well-being of the larger group and made a point of urging their readers to work toward "empowering ourselves and our people."

Are women's magazines the Horatio Alger novels of our time? Part of their mission is to help women cope with a rapidly changing society. From the "tips" on hair, fashion, and makeup to the reviews of books, films, and drama and the longer, often thoughtful, articles on health, sexual mores, or work options, they put women in touch with current attitudes, norms, and expectations. And at the same time they reaffirm the American Dream: by telling women repeatedly that they can, if they work hard enough, exercise long enough, eat correctly, and dress fashionably, achieve their dreams, these powerful agents of socialization are reinforcing the ideology that in America the individual can indeed make of herself whatever she chooses. Since there is rarely a suggestion that opportunity is related to economic, political, or social factors beyond the control of the individual, if a woman does not succeed after all these how-tos, perhaps she has no one to blame but herself. Moreover, the constant emphasis on celebrities, on stars, on those who have succeeded beyond most people's wildest dreams serves to reinforce the message.

Some of the magazines deal explicitly with the American Dream and extend it beyond the individual to the family unit. With the March 1988 issue, *Ms.* began a new series entitled "Tracking the Dream." In the series the magazine plans to explore "how families are faring in the late 1980s." For their first family they chose a young couple with two small children who live in a small town in Pennsylvania. In this era of divorce, single-parent families, stepfamilies, urban alienation, and the "new poor," *Ms.* chose a family straight out of Norman Rockwell's America. The husband works repairing furnaces; his wife is a full-time homemaker. They live in the same community in which they were raised, with their extended family all around, able and willing to help one another. Their two children are "blond, curly-haired, blue-eyed, and have the [family's] famous . . . dimples." They are a Shirley Temple, "Leave It to Beaver," "Father Knows Best" family come to life.

Although their 1987 income was $29,565, just the U.S. median family income, "they have acquired a home [traditional Dutch colonial] of which they are rightfully proud, they eat well, and they enjoy life." They have a swimming pool in the back and swings in the basement playroom. They don't buy on credit; nor, by the way, do they vote. The husband does not want his wife to work and expects his daughters to live the same life as their mother. *Ms.* admits that this family is representative of only 6 percent of all Americans—those who "still live in families with a working father, a homemaker mother, and dependent children." And if we factor in living in small-town America with a readily available family support system, they are typical of an even smaller percentage of the American population.

Why, then, would *Ms.* choose such an old-fashioned, atypical family for their first "documentary portrait of American families today" and then portray their life-style in such glowing terms? Do the *Ms.* editors think that we want to believe in this traditional image of the United States, where men are men and women are women and children have dimples and grandparents are there to help out? Do they think that reaffirming our image of an America straight out of the Frank Capra film *It's a Wonderful Life* will woo more traditional women to the *Ms.* readership? But of course in selling themselves they are selling an ideology; they are reinforcing a largely outdated image of America that has clear implications for the formulation of social policy. *Ms.* is clearly sending a message that self-reliance, mutual aid, the importance of the extended family and traditional family roles are alive and well in the United States in the late 1980s. With families like this, why would we need job training programs, day care, or a comprehensive family policy? Did they choose this particular family in order to reaffirm that old American Dream, to say to the faint of heart, the disbelievers, the urban cynics, "You see, it can still be done"? If it had been put onto videotape, the entire piece could have been a Ronald Reagan campaign commercial.

That same month, March 1988, *Ladies' Home Journal* also ran an article on the American Dream. The lives and finances of four families, each with two children, were described: a black family with an annual income of $28,600, and three white families, one with an income of $43,000, another with an income of $60,000, and the last with an income of $150,000. Each of the families has two parents, and in all but one both parents work. (In the remaining family, the wife plans to return to work within the year, when the younger child enters school full-time.) All of the families own their own homes and various luxury consumer goods—VCRs, stereos, a cabin cruiser, central air conditioning—and one has taken an anniversary trip to Hawaii. The family earning $28,600 says that life is a constant struggle but stresses that they have come a long way from the near-poverty days early in their marriage. The family earning $150,000 is striving for an income of $250,000; the husband states, "Success is being able to work a four-day week and still get what you want." The *Ladies' Home Journal* summarizes, "The American Dream of the good life for all is still very much with us."

In all these magazines, scattered among the hairstyles, the fashion layouts, and the endless advertisements is perhaps the central message: the American Dream is alive and well. If you work hard, believe in yourself, and consume relentlessly, you too can be a success in America.

One of the most appealing twists on the "having it all" theme was pictured on the cover and inside the December 1987 *Harper's Bazaar* in an extensive and lavish layout. Amid the holiday glitter, the "festive fantasy" of "blazing gold sequins," "paillettes," and "huge faux gems," actresses Shelley Long and Phylicia Rashad and model Christie Brinkley were pictured in sumptuous designer gowns and jewels while holding their own young children, also dressed in lavish outfits. *Bazaar's* Christmas issue is not only celebrating gorgeous women who are performers and mothers ("The most popular mom on television, 'The Cosby Show's' Phylicia Rashad does an equally good job of parenting in reality" and "Nothing expresses the true meaning of this season more clearly than the special glow between mother and child") but is also celebrating the family ("For even in this age of high-tech and high finance, the primal bonds of family—no matter how stretched or strained—remain squarely at the heart of Christmas"). Nothing is sacred in the selling of consumerism—especially at Christmas time. The message is clear: these women truly have it all—money, beauty, fabulous careers, husbands, and beautiful babies. Should the rest of us expect anything less?

Yet another example of the having-it-all-including-baby theme is a Donna Karan advertisement in the August 1988 issue of *Vogue*. The "mother" is lying half on the bed and half on the floor, dressed in a black, scoop-backed bodysuit. She is presumably a professional woman, since she is reading papers concerning shareholders. Strewn around the bedroom are clothes, pocketbooks, shoes, and scads of jewelry. A baby is sitting on the bed, presumably a girl, also "working" with pen and paper, an open notebook nearby. The child is wearing nothing more than a diaper and a necklace—a Donna Karan necklace, one assumes. The message again is clear: it *is* possible to have it all—and, by the way, it is never too early to teach a girl to want pretty things!

If the fashion world and women's magazines are giving us contradictory messages about women's roles and goals in the late 1980s—that women should achieve in the workplace and take greater control of their lives but that they should also look great, feel great, consume ceaselessly, and play the old roles of sex object, dependent woman, and devoted mom—what is television telling us? According to a recent study conducted by the National Commission on Working Women, nearly one million adolescent girls watch prime-time network television programs every night, and many of the programs they watch contain adolescent female characters. The study found that "viewers are likely to see girls with no visible skills, no favorite subjects in school, no discussions about college majors or vocational plans. . . . These images create the impression that one can magically jump from an adolescence of dating and shopping to a well-paid professional career." The report continues by pointing out that "on TV, girls' looks count for more than their brains." Plots focus on shopping, makeup, and dating—girls are often pictured as misfits if they do not have a date on Friday or Saturday night. Adolescent girls outnumber boys on prime time, but boys are usually the center of the action while girls play more passive, subsidiary roles. Furthermore, 94 percent of adolescent girls on TV are middle class or wealthy; very few are working class or poor. In reality, over one-third of teenage girls live in families with incomes under $20,000.

The study does find some positives—intelligent teenagers who are pictured as likable and successful—but they are relatively rare. Far more common are outmoded, insidious stereotypes that suggest that young women are shallow, vain, materialistic—and sometimes the traditional dumb, sexy blonde. On one episode of "Who's the Boss?" "a young practical nurse, depicted as a dim-witted buxom blonde, claims she entered nursing after failing beauty school, where she was undone by the pressure of remembering different shades of nail polish. Unable to wash a dish or run an appliance, she's eager to give Tony, her patient, a sponge bath. 'I'm Doreen the practical nurse,' she purrs. 'I do it all.' " . . .

What, then, is popular culture telling young women? The messages are clearly conflicting. The fundamental message seems to be that while women's lives have changed dramatically because so many of them are in the work force, supporting or at the very least helping to support themselves and their families, many other aspects of their lives have changed very little. The message is that women can be successful in the workplace and look the part as well but had better not forget how to be provocative, sexy, dependent; that women are to be in charge of their own lives yet "carried away" either by their own feelings or by men;

that women can be it all, have it all, and do it all, but while ability and hard work are important, looks are still crucial. With the right clothes and the right look—in other words, the right packaging—women can market themselves the way any other commodity is marketed and achieve their dreams in both the public and the private sphere.

The messages of television and films are more complex. On the one hand, women can be anything they wish, but on the other, their personal lives, not their work lives, are nearly always predominant. You may be a lawyer, but your private life is what is really important. In much of popular culture the women may wear suits and carry briefcases, but their new roles often seem grafted onto the traditional ones of the past—the sex object, the "caring" person more involved with private than with public concerns, or the individual in search of fulfillment through love. Because American society has not truly accepted the implications of women's new roles and therefore not adapted to those profound changes, most popular culture has not really integrated these changes, either. It is often as though a veneer of pseudofeminism is lightly brushed over the story line but underneath that veneer is the same old message. Issues such as dominance and subservience, autonomy and dependence, and how to truly, realistically mesh career and caring are rarely explored seriously. When they are, conflicts are often resolved through traditional solutions.

Moreover, television's need for a wrap-up of the problem each week (or occasionally after two or more episodes) requires simplistic solutions that are invariably within the control of the individual. Seldom are problems depicted as larger than the individual's or the family unit's capacity for coping; rarely are problems depicted as systemic, originating in the very structure of society. The individual generally finds a solution, a formula for working out the problem or conflict, thereby further strengthening the ideology of individualism, an ideology that states, week after week, that we are indeed in charge of our lives and can make of them what we wish. Women may find it harder to regulate their lives because of their presumed greater need for love and approval or because of their again presumed greater conflicts around doing and caring, but in the long run the illusion of self-determination is generally preserved.

But the message of popular culture is above all that everyone is middle and upper middle class. Women are portrayed as doctors, lawyers, and television stars, rarely as salespeople, secretaries, nurse's aides. And when they are playing working-class roles, they are nearly always objects of derision, of sympathy, or of humor. For young women growing up today, the options as reflected by much of popular culture are upper-middle-class options. You need to have a job with status, dress stunningly, and live well if not magnificently. Other measures of success are rarely portrayed. While little in popular culture tells you how to get there, the implication is that the American Dream is there for those who want to make it a reality.

This narrow definition of success and the media's emphasis on individualism have clearly had an impact on all three groups of young women whom I interviewed. The New American Dreamers have most clearly accepted the upper-middle-class model and adopted it as their own. They sometimes see conflicts down the road but assume, as though they were in a thirty-minute sitcom, that they will work out the problems. The Neotraditionalists have more problems with the "having it all" model. While they too hope for a comfortable life-style, they more clearly reflect the conflicts portrayed by the characters in "Thirtysomething." They want to do and to be, but they also want to care and to nurture; and while they accept the ideology that these issues are individual problems to be worked out on an individual basis, they can't quite figure out how to put it all together. The Outsiders are perhaps most poignantly affected by much of popular culture, because they do not see themselves anywhere (except in the occasional film and in much contemporary popular music). Where are the teenagers who have had a baby and now must go it alone? Where are the "burnouts" who feel they fit in nowhere—not at home, not at school, not in their communities? Where are the poor, the near-poor, and the working class struggling to pay the rent and feed their children? "The Cosby Show" may be an advance in a medium that often ignores or denigrates people of color, but what can this quintessentially "Father Knows Best" upper-middle-class family mean to a single woman with two children living in a welfare hotel? By excluding so many Americans from the images and content of popular culture, the society is clearly reinforcing their feelings of being outside the society while simultaneously holding out the promise of the American Dream. Are working-class blacks supposed to feel that "if Bill Cosby can live like that, so can I"? Does identification with the Huxtable family show the way to millions of low-income black Americans, or does it, rather, deflect the anger they might otherwise feel at being largely outside the system? Does it, in other words, promote an unrealistic identification with an improbable, if not impossible, dream?

By defining success almost solely in terms of status, wealth, and power, we are presenting few realistic options for the vast majority of American women and men. Popular culture, by focusing almost entirely on the lives of the top fifth of the population, reinforces the ideology of the American Dream but implicitly devalues all those who will never achieve it. And when young women describe their dreams for the future—their hopes of affluence, their images of themselves as successful professionals, their conflicts around doing and caring, their belief that they must be able to take care of themselves and solve their problems on an individual basis, or, in some cases, when they speak flatly of their inability to imagine a future at all—we know they have been listening to the mixed messages of much of American popular culture.

PART III

Structures of Power

22
Masculinities and Athletic Careers

Michael Messner

Sociologists of sport have been at the forefront in challenging our most deeply held convictions that sports is a critical testing ground for personal character and success. The data is on the side of the sociologists. Many people persist in raising their children, and especially their boys, in the belief that the rituals of sports are—when properly practiced—important in cultivating an appropriate gender identity.

The growth of women's studies and feminist gender studies has in recent years led to the emergence of a new men's studies (Brod 1987; Kimmel 1987). . . . Within the sociology of sport, gender as a process that interacts with race and class is usually ignored or taken for granted—except when it is *women* athletes who are being studied. Sociologists who are attempting to come to grips with the experiences of black men in general, and in organized sports in particular, have almost exclusively focused their analytic attention on the variable "black," while uncritically taking "men" as a given. Hare and Hare (1984), for example, view masculinity as a biologically determined tendency to act as a provider and protector that is thwarted for black men by socioeconomic and racist obstacles. Staples (1982) does view masculinity largely as a socially produced script, but he accepts this script as a given, preferring to focus on black men's blocked access to male role fulfillment. These perspectives on masculinity fail to show how the male role itself, as it interacts with a constricted structure of opportunity, can contribute to locking black men into destructive relationships and life-styles (Franklin 1984; Majors 1986).

This article will examine the relationships among male identity, race, and social class. . . . Organized sports, it will be suggested, is a practice through which men's separation from and power over women is embodied and naturalized at the same time that hegemonic (white, heterosexual, professional-class) masculinity is clearly differentiated from marginalized and subordinated masculinities. . . .

MALE IDENTITY AND ORGANIZED SPORTS

Earlier studies of masculinity and sport argued that sports socialize boys to be men (Lever 1976; Schafer 1975). Here, boys learn cultural values and behaviors, such as competition, toughness, and winning at all costs, that are culturally valued aspects of masculinity. While offering important insights, these early studies of masculinity and sports suffered from the limiting assumptions of a gender-role theory that seems to assume that boys come to their first athletic experience as blank slates onto which the values of masculinity are imprinted. This perspective oversimplifies a complex reality. In fact, young boys bring an already gendered identity to their first sports experiences, an identity that is struggling to work through the developmental task of individuation (Chodorow 1978; Gilligan 1982). Yet, as Benjamin (1988) has argued, individuation is accomplished, paradoxically, only through relationships with other people in the social world. So, although the major task of masculinity is the development of a "positional identity" that clarifies the boundaries between self and other, this separation must be accomplished through some form of connection with others. For the men in my study, the rule-bound structure of organized sports became a context in which they struggled to construct a masculine positional identity.

All of the men in this study described the emotional salience of their earliest experiences in sports in terms of relationships with other males. It was not winning and victories that seemed important at first; it was something "fun" to do with fathers, older brothers or uncles, and eventually with same-aged peers. As a man from a white, middle-class family said, "The most important thing was just being out there with the rest of the guys—being friends." A 32-year-old man from a poor Chicano family, whose mother had died when he was 9 years old, put it more succinctly:

> What I think sports did for me is it brought me into kind of an instant family. By being on a Little League team, or even just playing with kids in the neighborhood, it brought what I really wanted, which was some kind of closeness.

Though sports participation may have initially promised "some kind of closeness," by the ages of 9 or 10, the less skilled boys were already becoming alienated from—or weeded out of—the highly competitive and hierarchical system of organized sports. Those who did experience some early successes received recognition from adult males (especially fathers and older brothers) and held higher status among peers. As a result, they began to pour more and more of their energies into athletic participation. It was only after they learned that they would get recognition from other people for being a good athlete—indeed, that this attention was contingent upon *being a winner*—that performance and winning (the dominant values of organized sports) became extremely important. For some, this created pressures that served to lessen or eliminated the fun of athletic participation (Messner 1987a, 1987b). . . .

Men from Higher-Status Backgrounds

The boyhood dream of one day becoming a professional athlete—a dream shared by nearly all the men interviewed in this study—is rarely realized. The sports world is extremely hierarchical. The pyramid of sports careers narrows very rapidly as one climbs from high school, to college, to professional levels of competition (Edwards 1984; Harris and Eitzen 1978; Hill and Lowe 1978). In fact, the chances of attaining professional status in sports are approximately 4/100,000 for a white man, 2/100,000 for a black man, and 3/100,000 for a Hispanic man in the United States (Leonard and Reyman 1988). For many young athletes, their dream ends early when coaches inform them that they are not big enough, strong enough, fast enough, or skilled enough to compete at the higher levels. But six of the higher-status men I interviewed did not wait for coaches to weed them out. They made conscious decisions in high school or in college to shift their attentions elsewhere—usually toward educational and career goals. Their decision not to pursue an athletic career appeared to them in retrospect to be a rational decision based on the growing knowledge of how very slim their chances were to be successful in the sports world. For instance, a 28-year-old white graduate student said:

> By junior high I started to realize that I was a good player—maybe even one of the best in my community—but I realized that there were all these people all over the country and how few will get to play pro sports. By high school, I still dreamed of being a pro—I was a serious athlete, I played hard—but I knew it wasn't heading anywhere. I wasn't going to play pro ball.

A 32-year-old white athletic director at a small private college had been a successful college baseball player. Despite considerable attention from professional scouts, he had decided to forgo a shot at a baseball career and to enter graduate school to pursue a teaching credential. As he explained this decision:

> At the time I think I saw baseball as pissing in the wind, really. I was married, I was 22 years old with a kid. I didn't want to spend 4 or 5 years in the minors with a family. And I could see I wasn't a superstar; so it wasn't really worth it. So I went to grad school. I thought that would be better for me.

Perhaps most striking was the story of a high school student body president and top-notch student who was also "Mr. Everything" in sports. He was named captain of his basketball, baseball, and football teams and achieved All-League honors in each sport. This young white man from a middle-class family received attention from the press and praise from his community and peers for his athletic accomplishments, as well as several offers of athletic scholarships from universities. But by the time he completed high school, he had already decided to quit playing organized sports. As he said:

> I think in my own mind I kind of downgraded the stardom thing. I thought
> that was small potatoes. And sure, that's nice in high school and all that, but
> on a broad scale, I didn't think it amounted to all that much. So I decided
> that my goal's to be a dentist, as soon as I can.

In his sophomore year of college, the basketball coach nearly persuaded
him to go out for the team, but eventually he decided against it:

> I thought, so what if I can spend two years playing basketball? I'm not
> going to be a basketball player forever and I might jeopardize my chances of
> getting into dental school if I play.

He finished college in three years, completed dental school, and now, in
his mid-30s, is again the epitome of the successful American man: a
professional with a family, a home, and a membership in the local country club.

How and why do so many successful male athletes from higher-status
backgrounds come to view sports careers as "pissing in the wind," or
as "small potatoes"? How and why do they make this early assessment
and choice to shift from sports and toward educational and professional
goals? The white, middle-class institutional context, with its emphasis on
education and income, makes it clear to them that choices exist and that
the pursuit of an athletic career is not a particularly good choice to make.
Where the young male once found sports to be a convenient institution
within which to construct masculine status, the postadolescent and
young adult man from a higher-status background simply *transfers* these
same strivings to other institutional contexts: education and careers.

For the higher-status men who had chosen to shift from athletic careers, sports remained important on two levels. First, having been a successful high school or college athlete enhances one's adult status among
other men in the community—but only as a badge of masculinity that
is *added* to his professional status. In fact, several men in professions
chose to be interviewed in their offices, where they publicly displayed
the trophies and plaques that attested to their earlier athletic accomplishments. Their high school and college athletic careers may have appeared
to them as "small potatoes," but many successful men speak of their
earlier status as athletes as having "opened doors" for them in their
present professions and in community affairs. Similarly, Farr's (1988)
research on "Good Old Boys Sociability Groups" shows how sports, as
part of the glue of masculine culture, continues to facilitate "dominance
bonding" among privileged men long after active sports careers end. The
college-educated, career-successful men in Farr's study rarely express
overtly sexist, racist, or classist attitudes; in fact, in their relationships
with women, they "often engage in expressive intimacies" and "make
fun of exaggerated 'machismo'" (Farr 1988, p. 276). But though they
outwardly conform more to what Pleck (1982) calls "the modern male
role," their informal relationships within their sociability groups, in effect, affirm their own gender and class status by constructing and clari-

fying the boundaries between themselves and women and lower-status men. This dominance bonding is based largely upon ritual forms of sociability (camaraderie, competition), "the superiority of which was first affirmed in the exclusionary play activities of young boys in groups" (Farr 1988, p. 265).

In addition to contributing to dominance bonding among higher-status adult men, sports remains salient in terms of the ideology of gender relations. Most men continued to watch, talk about, and identify with sports long after their own disengagement from athletic careers. Sports as a mediated spectacle provides an important context in which traditional conceptions of masculine superiority—conceptions recently contested by women—are shored up. As a 32-year-old white professional-class man said of one of the most feared professional football players today:

> A woman can do the same job as I can do—maybe even be my boss. But I'll be *damned* if she can go out on the football field and take a hit from Ronnie Lott.

Violent sports as spectacle provide linkages among men in the project of the domination of women, while at the same time helping to construct and clarify differences among various masculinities. The statement above is a clear identification with Ronnie Lott *as a man*, and the basis of the identification is the violent male body. As Connell (1987, p. 85) argues, sports is an important organizing institution for the embodiment of masculinity. Here, men's power over women becomes naturalized and linked to the social distribution of violence. Sports, as a practice, suppresses natural (sex) similarities, constructs differences, and then, largely through the media, weaves a structure of symbol and interpretation around these differences that naturalizes them (Hargreaves 1986, p. 112). It is also significant that the man who made the above statement about Ronnie Lott was quite aware that he (and perhaps 99 percent of the rest of the U.S. male population) was probably as incapable as most women of taking a "hit" from someone like Lott and living to tell of it. For middle-class men, the "tough guys" of the culture industry—the Rambos, the Ronnie Lotts who are fearsome "hitters," who "play hurt"—are the heroes who "prove" that "we men" are superior to women. At the same time, they play the role of the "primitive other," against whom higher-status men define themselves as "modern" and "civilized."

Sports, then, is important from boyhood through adulthood for men from higher-status backgrounds. But it is significant that by adolescence and early adulthood, most of these young men have concluded that sports *careers* are not for them. Their middle-class cultural environment encourages them to decide to shift their masculine strivings in more "rational" directions: education and nonsports careers. Yet their previous sports participation continues to be very important to them in terms of constructing and validating their status within privileged male peer groups and within their chosen professional careers. And organized sports, as a public spectacle, is a crucial locus around which ideologies of male superiority over women, as well as higher-status men's superiority over lower-status men, are constructed and naturalized.

Men from Lower-Status Backgrounds

For the lower-status young men in this study, success in sports was not an added proof of masculinity; it was often their only hope of achieving public masculine status. A 34-year-old black bus driver who had been a star athlete in three sports in high school had neither the grades nor the money to attend college, so he accepted an offer from the U.S. Marine Corps to play on their baseball team. He ended up in Vietnam, where a grenade blew four fingers off his pitching hand. In retrospect, he believed that his youthful focus on sports stardom and his concomitant lack of effort in academics made sense:

> You can go anywhere with athletics—you don't have to have brains. I mean, I didn't feel like I was gonna go out there and be a computer expert, or something that was gonna make a lot of money. The only thing I could do and live comfortably would be to play sports—just to get a contract—doesn't matter if you play second or third team in the pros, you're gonna make big bucks. That's all I wanted, a confirmed livelihood at the end of my ventures, and the only way I could do it would be through sports. So I tried. It failed, but that's what I tried.

Similar, and even more tragic, is the story of a 34-year-old black man who is now serving a life term in prison. After a career-ending knee injury at the age of 20 abruptly ended what had appeared to be a certain road to professional football fame and fortune, he decided that he "could still be rich and famous" by robbing a bank. During his high school and college years, he said, he was nearly illiterate:

> I'd hardly ever go to classes and they'd give me Cs. My coaches taught some of the classes. And I felt, "So what? They *owe* me that! I'm an *athlete*! I thought that was what I was born to do—to play sports—and everybody understood that.

Are lower-status boys and young men simply duped into putting all their eggs into one basket? My research suggested that there was more than "hope for the future" operating here. There were also immediate psychological reasons that they chose to pursue athletic careers. By the high school years, class and ethnic inequalities had become glaringly obvious, especially for those who attended socioeconomically heterogeneous schools. Cars, nice clothes, and other signs of status were often unavailable to these young men, and this contributed to a situation in which sports took on an expanded importance for them in terms of constructing masculine identities and status. A white, 36-year-old man from a poor, single-parent family who later played professional baseball had been acutely aware of his low-class status in his high school:

I had one pair of jeans, and I wore them every day. I was always afraid of what people thought of me—that this guy doesn't have anything, that he's wearing the same Levi's all the time, he's having to work in the cafeteria for his lunch. What's going on? I think that's what made me so shy. . . . But boy, when I got into sports, I let it all hang out—[laughs]—and maybe that's why I became so good, because I was frustrated, and when I got into that element, they gave me my uniform in football, basketball, and baseball, and I didn't have to worry about how I looked, because then it was *me* who was coming out, and not my clothes or whatever. And I think that was the drive.

Similarly, a 41-year-old black man who had a 10-year professional football career described his insecurities as one of the few poor blacks in a mostly white, middle-class school and his belief that sports was the one arena in which he could be judged solely on his merit:

I came from a poor family, and I was very sensitive about that in those days. When people would say things like "Look at him—he has dirty pants on," I'd think about it for a week. [But] I'd put my pants on and I'd go out on the football field with the intention that I'm gonna do a job. And if that calls on me to hurt you, I'm gonna do it. It's as simple as that. I demand respect just like everybody else.

"Respect" was what I heard over and over when talking with the men from lower-status backgrounds, especially black men. I interpret this type of respect to be a crystallization of the masculine quest for recognition through public achievement, unfolding within a system of structured constraints due to class and race inequities. The institutional context of education (sometimes with the collusion of teachers and coaches) and the constricted structure of opportunity in the economy made the pursuit of athletic careers appear to be the most rational choice to these young men.

The same is not true of young lower-status women. Dunkle (1985) points out that from junior high school through adulthood, young black men are far more likely to place high value on sports than are young black women, who are more likely to value academic achievement. There appears to be a gender dynamic operating in adolescent male peer groups that contributes toward their valuing sports more highly than education. Franklin (1986, p. 161) has argued that many of the normative values of the black male peer group (little respect for nonaggressive solutions to disputes, contempt for nonmaterial culture) contribute to the constriction of black men's views of desirable social positions, especially through education. In my study, a 42-year-old black man who did succeed in beating the odds by using his athletic scholarship to get a college degree and eventually becoming a successful professional said:

By junior high, you either got identified as an athlete, a thug, or a bookworm. It's very important to be seen as somebody who's capable in some area. And you *don't* want to be identified as a bookworm. I was very good with books, but I was kind of covert about it. I was a closet bookworm. But with sports, I was *somebody*; so I worked very hard at it.

For most young men from lower-status backgrounds, the poor quality of their schools, the attitudes of teachers and coaches, as well as the antieducation environment within their own male peer groups, made it extremely unlikely that they would be able to succeed as students. Sports, therefore, became *the* arena in which they attempted to "show their stuff." For these lower-status men, as Baca Zinn (1982) and Majors (1986) argued in their respective studies of chicano men and black men, when institutional resources that signify masculine status and control are absent, physical presence, personal style, and expressiveness take on increased importance. What Majors (1986, p. 6) calls "cool pose" is black men's expressive, often aggressive, assertion of masculinity. This self-assertion often takes place within a social context in which the young man is quite aware of existing social inequities. As the black bus driver, referred to above, said of his high school years:

> See, the rich people use their money to do what they want to do. I use my ability. If you wanted to be around me, if you wanted to learn something about sports, I'd teach you. But you're gonna take me to lunch. You're gonna let me use your car. See what I'm saying? In high school I'd go where I wanted to go. I didn't have to be educated. I was well-respected. I'd go somewhere, and they'd say, "Hey, that's Mitch Harris, yeah, that's a bad son of a bitch!'

Majors (1986) argues that although "cool pose" represents a creative survival technique within a hostile environment, the most likely long-term effect of this masculine posturing is educational and occupational dead ends. As a result, we can conclude, lower-status men's personal and peer-group responses to a constricted structure of opportunity—responses that are rooted, in part, in the developmental insecurities and ambivalences of masculinity—serve to lock many of these young men into limiting activities such as sports.

SUMMARY AND CONCLUSIONS

This research has suggested that within a social context that is stratified by social class and by race, the choice to pursue—or not to pursue—an athletic career is explicable as an individual's rational assessment of the available means to achieve a respected masculine identity. For nearly all of the men from lower-status backgrounds, the status and respect that they received through sports was temporary—it did not translate into upward mobility. Nonetheless, a strategy of discouraging young black boys and men from involvement in sports is probably doomed to fail, since it ignores the continued existence of structural constraints. Despite the increased number of black role models in nonsports professions, employment opportunities for young black males have actually deteriorated in the 1980s (Wilson and Neckerman 1986), and nonathletic opportunities in higher education have also declined. While blacks constitute 14 percent of the college-aged (18–24 years) U.S.

population, as a proportion of students in four-year colleges and universities, they have dropped to 8 percent. In contrast, by 1985, black men constituted 49 percent of all college basketball players and 61 percent of basketball players in institutions that grant athletic scholarships (Berghorn et al., 1988). For young black men, then, organized sports appears to be more likely to get them to college than their own efforts in non-athletic activities.

But it would be a mistake to conclude that we simply need to breed socioeconomic conditions that make it possible for poor and minority men to mimic the "rational choices" of white, middle-class men. If we are to build an appropriate understanding of the lives of all men, we must critically analyze white middle-class masculinity, rather than uncritically taking it as a normative standard. To fail to do this would be to ignore the ways in which organized sports serves to construct and legitimate gender differences and inequalities among men and women.

Feminist scholars have demonstrated that organized sports gives men from all backgrounds a means of status enhancement that is not available to young women. Sports thus serve the interests of all men in helping to construct and legitimize their control of public life and their domination of women (Bryson 1987; Hall 1987; Theberge 1987). Yet concrete studies are suggesting that men's experiences within sports are not all of a piece. Brian Pronger's (1990) research suggests that gay men approach sports differently than straight men do, with a sense of "irony." And my research suggests that although sports are important for men from both higher- and lower-status backgrounds, there are crucial differences. In fact, it appears that the meaning that most men give to their athletic strivings has more to do with competing for status among men than it has to do with proving superiority over women. How can we explain this seeming contradiction between the feminist claim that sports links all men in the domination of women and the research findings that different groups of men relate to sports in very different ways?

The answer to this question lies in developing a means of conceptualizing the interrelationships between varying forms of domination and subordination. Marxist-scholars of sports often falsely collapse everything into a class analysis; radical feminists often see gender domination as universally fundamental. Concrete examinations of sports, however, reveal complex and multilayered systems of inequality: Racial, class, gender, sexual preference, and age dynamics are all salient features of the athletic context. In examining this reality, Connell's (1987) concept of the "gender order" is useful. The gender order is a dynamic process that is constantly in a state of play. Moving beyond static gender-role theory and reductionist concepts of patriarchy that view men as an undifferentiated group which oppresses women, Connell argues that at any given historical moment, there are competing masculinities—some hegemonic, some marginalized, some stigmatized. Hegemonic masculinity (that definition of masculinity which is culturally ascendant) is constructed in relation to various subordinated masculinities as well as in relation to femininities. The project of male domination of women may tie all men together, but men share very unequally in the fruits of this domination.

These are key insights in examining the contemporary meaning of sports. Utilizing the concept of the gender order, we can begin to conceptualize how hierarchies of race, class, age, and sexual preference among men help to construct and legitimize men's overall power and privilege over women. And how, for some black, working-class, or gay men, the false promise of sharing in the fruits of hegemonic masculinity often ties them into their marginalized and subordinate statuses within hierarchies of intermale dominance. For instance, black men's development of what Majors (1986) calls "cool pose" within sports can be interpreted as an example of creative resistance to one form of social domination (racism); yet it also demonstrates the limits of an agency that adopts other forms of social domination (masculinity) as its vehicle. . . .

REFERENCES

Benjamin, J. 1988. *The Bonds of Love: Psychoanalysis, Feminism, and the Problem of Domination*. New York: Pantheon.
Berghorn, F. J. et al. 1988. "Racial Participation in Men's and Women's Intercollegiate Basketball: Continuity and Change, 1958–1985." *Sociology of Sport Journal* 5:107–24.
Brod, H. 1983–84. "Work Clothes and Leisure Suits: The Class Basis and Bias of the Men's Movement." *M: Gentle Men for Gender Justice* 11:10–12, 38–40.
Brod, H. (ed.). 1987. *The Making of Masculinities: The New Men's Studies*. Winchester, MA: Allen & Unwin.
Bryson, L. 1987. "Sport and the Maintenance of Masculine Hegemony." *Women's Studies International Forum* 10:349–60.
Chodorow, N. 1978. *The Reproduction of Mothering*. Berkeley: University of California Press.
Connell, R. W. 1987. *Gender and Power*. Stanford, CA: Stanford University Press.
———. 1990. "An Iron Man: The Body and Some Contradictions of Hegemonic Masculinity." In *Sport, Men, and the Gender Order: Critical Feminist Perspectives*, edited by M. A. Messner and D. S. Sabo. Champaign, IL: Human Kinetics.
Dunkle, M. 1985. "Minority and Low-Income Girls and Young Women in Athletics." *Equal Play* 5(Spring-Summer):12–13.
Duquin, M. 1984 "Power and Authority: Moral Consensus and Conformity in Sport." *International Review for Sociology of Sport* 19:295–304.
Edwards, H. 1971. "The Myth of the Racially Superior Athlete." *The Black Scholar* 3(November).
———. 1973. *The Sociology of Sport*. Homewood, IL: Dorsey.
———. 1984. "The Collegiate Athletic Arms Race: Origins and Implications of the 'Rule 48' Controversy." *Journal of Sport and Social Issues* 8:4–22.
Eitzen, D. S. and D. A. Purdy, 1986. "The Academic Preparation and Achievement of Black and White College Athletes." *Journal of Sport and Social Issues* 10:15–29.

Eitzen, D. S. and N. B. Yetman. 1977. "Immune From Racism?" *Civil Rights Digest* 9:3–13.

Farr, K. A. 1988. "Dominance Bonding Through the Good Old Boys Sociability Group." *Sex Roles* 18:259–77.

Franklin, C. W. II. 1984. *The Changing Definition of Masculinity.* New York: Plenum.

———. 1986. "Surviving the Institutional Decimation of Black Males: Causes, Consequences, and Intervention." Pp. 155–70 in *The Making of Masculinities: The New Men's Studies,* edited by H. Brod. Winchester, MA: Allen & Unwin.

Gilligan, C. 1982. *In a Different Voice: Psychological Theory and Women's Development.* Cambridge, MA: Harvard University Press.

Gruneau, R. 1983. *Class, Sports, and Social Development.* Amherst: University of Massachusetts Press.

Hall, M. A. (ed.). 1987. "The Gendering of Sport, Leisure, and Physical Education." *Women's Studies International Forum* 10:361–474.

Hare, N. and J. Hare. 1984. *The Endangered Black Family: Coping With the Unisexualization and Coming Extinction of the Black Race.* San Francisco, CA: Black Think Tank.

Hargreaves, J. A. 1986. "Where's the Virtue? Where's the Grace? A Discussion of the Social Production of Gender Through Sport." *Theory, Culture and Society* 3:109–21.

Harris, D. S. and D. S. Eitzen. 1978. "The Consequences of Failure in Sport." *Urban Life* 7:177–88.

Hill, P. and B. Lowe. 1978. "The Inevitable Metathesis of the Retiring Athlete." *International Review of Sport Sociology* 9:5–29.

Hooks, B. 1984. *Feminist Theory: From Margin to Center.* Boston: South End Press.

Kimmel, M. S. (ed.). 1987. *Changing Men: New Directions in Research on Men and Masculinity.* Newbury Park, CA: Sage.

Leonard, W. M. II and J. M. Reyman. 1988. "The Odds of Attaining Professional Athlete Status: Refining the Computations." *Sociology of Sport Journal* 5:162–69.

Lever, J. 1976. "Sex Differences in the Games Children Play." *Social Problems* 23:478–87.

Levinson, D. J. 1978. *The Seasons of a Man's Life.* New York: Ballantine.

Majors, R. 1986. "Cool Pose: The Proud Signature of Black Survival." *Changing Men: Issues in Gender, Sex, and Politics* 17:5–6.

———. 1990. "Cool Pose: Black Masculinity in Sports." In *Sport, Men, and the Gender Order: Critical Feminist Perspectives,* edited by M. A. Messner and D. S. Sabo. Champaign, IL: Human Kinetics.

Messner, M. 1985. "The Changing Meaning of Male Identity in the Lifecourse of the Athlete." *Arena Review* 9:31–60.

———. 1987a. "The Meaning of Success: The Athletic Experience and the Development of Male Identity." Pp. 193–209 in *The Making of Masculinities: The New Men's Studies,* edited by H. Brod. Winchester, MA: Allen & Unwin.

———. 1987b. "The Life of a Man's Seasons: Male Identity in the Lifecourse of the Athlete." Pp. 53–67 in *Changing Men: New Directions in Research on Men and Masculinity,* edited by M. S. Kimmel. Newbury Park, CA: Sage.

Pleck, J. H. 1982. *The Myth of Masculinity.* Cambridge: MIT Press.

Pronger, B. 1990. "Gay Jocks: A Phenomenology of Gay Men in Athletics." In *Sport, Men, and the Gender Order: Critical Feminist Perspectives,* edited by M. A. Messner and D. S. Sabo. Champaign, IL: Human Kinetics.

Rubin, L. B. 1985. *Just Friends: The Role of Friendship in Our Lives.* New York: Harper & Row.

Rudman, W. J. 1986. "The Sport Mystique in Black Culture." *Sociology of Sport Journal* 3:305–19.

Sabo, D. 1985. "Sport, Patriarchy, and Male Identity: New Questions About Men and Sport." *Arena Review* 9:1–30.

Sabo, D. and R. Runfola (eds.). 1980. *Jocks: Sports and Male Identity.* Englewood Cliffs, NJ: Prentice-Hall.

Schafer, W. E. 1975. "Sport and Male Sex Role Socialization." *Sport Sociology Bulletin* 4:17–54.

23
Sexual Stereotypes as Political Ideology

Barbara S. Deckard

Gender not only classifies the population; it also stratifies by creating a hierarchy of power and privilege. This is done by arranging access to opportunities through the socialization process, by the use of language, and by the perpetuation of stereotypes.

What is woman? Writers, past and present, have asked and answered this question over and over again. On the nature of woman everyone seems to consider himself an expert ("himself" because most of the answers come from men).

According to these "experts," woman is emotional rather than logical. In fact, she is not very bright.

> We may thus conclude that it is a general law that there should be naturally ruling elements and elements naturally ruled . . . the rule of the freeman over the slave is one kind of rule; that of the male over the female another. . . . the slave is entirely without the faculty of deliberation; the female indeed possesses it, but in a form which remains inconclusive. . . . [Aristotle]
> Women, then, are only children of larger growth: they have an entertaining tattle, and sometimes wit; but for solid, reasoning good sense, I never knew in my life one that had it, or who reasoned or acted consequentially for four and twenty hours together. [Lord Chesterfield]
> [Woman is] in every respect backward, lacking in reason and true morality . . . a kind of middle step between the child and the man, who is the true human being. [Schopenhauer]
> The chief distinction in the intellectual powers of the two sexes is shown by man attaining to a higher eminence, in whatever he takes up, than woman can attain—whether requiring deep thought, reason, or imagination or merely the use of the senses and hands. [Darwin]
> Feelings, moods and attitudes . . . rule a woman, not facts, reason nor logic. By herself, woman is all mixed up, but superb as an auxiliary. . . . [G. C. Payetter]
> Everything relating to exploration and cognition, all the forms and kinds of human culture and aspiration that require a strictly objective approach, are with few exceptions, the domain of the masculine intellect, of man's spiritual power, against which women can rarely compete. [Helen Deutsch]

Man is active and independent; woman, passive and dependent. He does, she is.

> Women, in general, want to be loved for what they are and men for what they accomplish. The first for their looks and charm, the latter for their actions. [Theodor Reik]

Women are usually more patient in working at unexciting, repetitive tasks. . . . Women on the average have more passivity in the inborn core of their personality. . . . I believe women are designed in their deeper instincts to get more pleasure out of life—not only sexually but socially, occupationally, maternally—when they are not aggressive. To put it another way I think that when women are encouraged to be competitive too many of them become disagreeable. [Benjamin Spock]

Women must give and give and give again because it is their one and only way to obtain happiness for themselves. [well-known American gynecologist]

It is a hard and hateful thing to see proud men, not to speak of enduring them. But it is annoying and impossible to suffer proud women, because in general Nature has given men proud and high spirits, while it has made women humble in character and submissive, more apt for delicate things than for ruling. [Boccaccio]

Women are naturally mothers; their greatest desire and only true ful-fillment lies in maternity. In fact, this is one of the few things women are any good at.

. . . As much as women want to be good scientists and engineers, they want, first and foremost, to be womanly companions of men and to be mothers. [Bruno Bettelheim]

Biologically and temperamentally, I believe, women were made to be con-cerned first and foremost with child care, husband care and home care. [Benjamin Spock]

. . . Woman is nurturance; . . . anatomy decrees the life of a woman. When women grow up without dread of their biological functions and without the subversion of feminist doctrine and therefore enter upon motherhood with a sense of fulfillment and altruistic sentiment, we shall attain the goal of a good life and a secure world in which to live. [Joseph Rheingold]

If woman is naturally stupid, dependent, and passive, then, of course, she is naturally subordinate to the male.

Wives, submit yourselves unto your husbands . . . for the husband is the head of the wife, even as Christ is the head of the church. [hesians 5:22–23]

The whole education of women ought to be relative to men. To please them, to be useful to them, to make themselves loved and honored by them, to educate them when young, to care for them when grown, to counsel them, to console them, and to make life sweet and agreeable to them—these are the duties of women at all times and what should be taught them from their infancy. [Jean-Jacques Rousseau]

Nature intended women to be our slaves; . . . they are our property, we are not theirs. They belong to us, just as a tree that bears fruit belongs to a gar-dener. What a mad idea to demand equality for women! . . . Women are nothing but machines for producing children. [Napoleon Bonaparte]

Man for the field and woman for the hearth:
Man for the sword and for the needle she:
Man with the head and woman with the heart:
Man to command and woman to obey;
All else confusion. [Alfred, Lord Tennyson]

When woman steps out of her natural role, disaster results:

A woman who is guided by the head and not the heart is a social pestilence: she has all the defects of the passionate and affectionate woman, with none of her compensations; she is without pity, without love, without virtue, without sex. [Honoré de Balzac]

Frigidity, as we see it today, is an outgrowth of woman's running away from her biological destiny, which is to be wife, mother, and homemaker. [Dr. Arthur Mandy]

Women's intellectuality is to a large extent paid for by the loss of valuable feminine qualities; it feeds on the sap of the affective life and results in impoverishment of this life. . . . All observations point to the fact that the intellectual woman is masculinized; in her, warm intuitive knowledge has yielded to cold unproductive thinking. [Helen Deutsch]

Mom got herself out of the nursery and the kitchen. She then got out of the house. . . . She also got herself the vote, and, although politics never interested her (unless she was exceptionally naive, a hairy foghorn, or a size 40 scorpion) the damage she forthwith did to society was so enormous and so rapid that the best men lost track of things . . . political scurviness, hoodlumism, gangsterism, labor strife, monopolistic thuggery, moral degeneration, civil corruption, smuggling, bribery, theft, murder, homosexuality, drunkenness, financial depression, chaos, and war. [Philip Wylie]

Aside from their often virulent nastiness, the aspect of these quotations that is most striking is the underlying assumption on which they are based—that all women are alike. The image of women presented is a stereotype—a simple-minded, unexamined notion based on prejudice. Similar statements about blacks—that they all have natural rhythm, for example—are immediately recognized as racist stereotyping. In most circles, racist slurs are no longer socially acceptable. In contrast, sexism is the last socially acceptable prejudice. People still tell and laugh at wife, mother-in-law, and sex jokes that depict women as stupid and empty-headed, unconcerned with anything but their looks, and worse.

The ideology of sexism is so deeply embedded in our society that, to a considerable extent, most people are unaware that they are prejudiced. The notion that women are inferior to or at least extremely different from men is taken as a self-evident truth.

Sexism, then, is an "ideology" in the sense that

Its beliefs and postulates are well integrated, it functions to direct and guide social and political activity, and it rests on assumptions that are not reliably tested, but that to some degree are accepted on faith.

For example, most tennis pros assumed that Bobby Riggs would beat Billie Jean King just because he was a man. When she beat him, they dismissed it as an exception. When looking at someone, a prejudiced person will interpret whatever behavior occurs in such a way that it fits in with the stereotype. A sociologist points out:

Whatever the facts about sex differences, anti-feminism—like any other prejudice—distorts perception and experience. . . . Thus, an anti-Semite watching a Jew may see devious or sneaky behavior. But in a Christian he would regard such behavior only as quiet, reserved, or perhaps even shy.

Since prejudice distorts perception, no amount of evidence can change it.

As an example of how prejudiced stereotyping is much too stubborn for evidence, imagine an employer interviewing a series of people for an executive job. Suppose he believes in the usual stereotypes of women. Suppose the first woman is sophisticated and careful before speaking. He thinks: She is too passive and "feminine" for the job. Suppose the second woman objects to something he says. He thinks: She is an aggressive bitch. Suppose the third person is a man; he gets the job. Therefore prejudiced stereotypes are not harmless; they lead directly to discrimination.

Even in minor ways and unconsciously, most people believe the myths. For example, if a man and woman order tea and coffee in a restaurant, the man will always get the coffee and the woman the tea (sometimes even if you ask for it the other way around). Why? Apparently tea is perceived as a light and delicate and therefore feminine drink. In reality, of course, most American women drink coffee. In the same way, if a man and a woman order a soft drink and a cocktail, the waiter or waitress will always give the soft drink to the woman without asking. Another myth.

A more dangerous myth is that all women stay home in beautiful houses doing nothing all day. In September 1957 a poll asked people what would happen if all working wives quit. The answers showed that most people believed that few wives work. Yet . . . a majority of women of working age now work at two jobs: a paid job in the economy and their traditional job in the home.

Like most stereotypes, the sexist stereotype is internally inconsistent. Depending upon the purpose, two quite different sets of characteristics are attributed to women. Women cannot be statesmen, captains of industry, or even auto mechanics because they are irrational, flighty, overemotional, sentimental, and unmechanical. On the other hand, women cannot be great poets and painters because they are practical, unadventuresome, unspontaneous, and unimaginative. Unfortunately, inconsistency never destroyed a healthy stereotype and sexism is still all too robust.

Religion has had a particularly important role in advancing and perpetuating sexist notions. The great religions of the world have mostly been pervaded to the core by sexism. Examples:

> . . . And the rib, which the Lord God had taken from man, made he a woman, and brought her unto the man. . . . : And the Lord God said unto the woman, What is this that thou hast done? And the woman said, The serpent beguiled me, and I did eat. . . . Unto the woman he said, I will greatly multiply thy sorrow and thy conception; in sorrow thou shalt bring forth children; and thy desire shall be to thy husband, and he shall rule over thee. [Genesis 2–3]

The Christian Saint Paul wrote:

> Let the woman learn in silence with all subjection. But I suffer not a woman to teach, nor to usurp authority over the man, but to be in silence. For Adam was first formed, then Eve. And Adam was not deceived, but the woman,

being deceived, was in the transgression. Notwithstanding she shall be saved in childbearing, if they continue in faith and charity and holiness with sobriety. [1 Tim. 2:11–15]

The Christian Bible also declares:

... how can he be clean that is born of a woman? [Job 25:4]

And the Pope says:

Woman as a person enjoys a dignity equal with men, but she was given different tasks by God and by Nature which perfect and complete the work entrusted to men. [Pope John XXIII]

Christianity is equaled, if not surpassed, by other religions. The male Orthodox Jew recites every morning:

Blessed art Thou, oh Lord our God, King of the Universe, that I was not born a woman.

The Koran, the Mohammedan sacred text, says:

Men are superior to women on account of the qualities in which God has given them pre-eminence.

The Hindu Code of Manu declared:

In childhood a woman must be subject to her father; In youth to her husband; when her husband is dead, to her sons. A woman must never be free of subjugation.

Finally, there are the profound sayings of Confucius:

The five worst infirmities that afflict the female are indocility, discontent, slander, jealousy, and silliness. . . . Such is the stupidity of woman's character, that it is incumbent upon her, in every particular, to distrust herself and to obey her husband.

The new high priests of Western society—the psychiatrists—are not much subtler in their sexism. . . .

Sexism in Language

Sexist thinking is so pervasive that it is deeply embedded in the English language. Anthropologists have discovered that many basic mores —often unconscious—are clearly revealed in the language of a people. We can thus see many reflections of sexist thinking in our own language.

A linguist writes: "The word *man* originally meant human being, but males appropriated it." This sexist usage, equating men with the human race, causes some confusion in very important texts as well as trivial ones. Does "foreman" or "handyman" or "freshman" mean that these positions cannot be filled by women? In fact, the earlier stereotypes implied just that—only men could be supervisory workers, only men are handy, only men should go to college. Or take the sentence, "All men are created equal." Many males have argued that this does not apply to women and thus would deny women their democratic rights. . . .

Many words with wicked or evil emotional connotations were sex-neutral in an earlier period. Eventually, however, the wickedness may come to be associated with women only. For example, *shrewish* first was applied to either male or female, then became associated with a stereotype of women. By contrast, some words gain a better emotional connotation when associated with men only. For example, *shrewd* (from the same root as *shrewish*) originally had an evil connotation; but when it became associated with powerful males, its emotional connotation became much more favorable.

The reason for all these developments is that language reflects the dominant ideology of the most powerful group in society; and sexism is the ideology of the male, who is dominant in Western society. More precisely, one linguist writes that "emotive words acquire their connotations by reflecting the sentiments of the dominant group in a society —in our case white Anglo-Saxon males (WASMs). . . ."

"But It's Natural"

The last refuge of people with no good argument is to say: "But it's natural." For example, it is "natural" for a woman to have the whole burden of household and child-rearing chores—even if she has an outside job in addition. It is "natural" for women to be passive and submissive; it is "natural" for men to command them and walk all over them. It is "natural" for women to be paid less than men. Before 1920, it was said to be "natural" for American men to vote but "unnatural" for women to vote.

What do people mean when they say, "It's natural"? Sometimes, *natural* is construed to mean "that which will happen if untouched by human invention." Thus, it is natural for a woman to get pregnant from sex, and unnatural for her to use any means of birth control. But then, isn't it natural for a man to grow a beard, and unnatural for him to shave? What about the use of small pox and polio vaccines? Are these to be considered unnatural? According to this definition, perpetual pregnancy, beards, and dying of smallpox are all natural. But, their being natural in this sense does not mean they are either unchangeable or desirable.

Another argument claims that male dominance is natural because it is based on "innate instincts" or "human nature." But, if women are prevented from doing some things by their nature, why must other barriers be erected? For example, if women's nature prevents them from being doctors, why must many medical schools prohibit the admission of all but a small quota from among all the qualified women applicants? If women's nature prevents them from being lawyers, why did many U.S. state laws have to prohibit qualified women law school graduates from practicing in the nineteenth century? . . .

As John Stuart Mill observed, "Everything which is usual appears natural. The subjection of women to men being a universal custom, any departure from it quite naturally appears unnatural." Usually when a person says that something is natural, he means that it is not just common but desirable. Such statements contain either a giant illogical leap or are simple assertions of preference. Male supremacy—and poverty, disease, and slavery—have been prevalent in many societies. That certainly does not make them desirable. Arguments based on the naturalness of male supremacy and female subordination should be attributed very little value.

SEXIST IDEOLOGY AND POWER

The sexist ideology is well integrated and elaborate. Its major premise is that woman is inferior to man. It is sufficiently flexible (inconsistent) so that any behavior a woman exhibits can be interpreted to conform with the major premise. The ideology is so pervasive that, until recently, few people were aware of its existence. Its tenets were simply accepted as self-evident truths.

Such an ideology neither develops nor survives without purpose. Its function is to justify and maintain a particular status quo—in this case the dominance of the male over the female. A ruling group always requires an ideology to justify its position of power. All slave societies, for example, developed a set of beliefs stating that slaves are innately inferior or even nonhuman. In essence, such beliefs put the onus for their condition on the slaves. Their status is decreed by their nature or by the gods; it is certainly not the fault of the slave owner.

The ideology is important as a self-justification for the ruling group. It is equally important in its effects on the subordinate group. Members of the subordinate group are inculcated with the ideology from early childhood. To a considerable extent they believe its claims—that they are, in fact, inferior and thus destined to play a subordinate role.

Sexual stereotyping thus is a *political* ideology. Its function is to maintain the power of the dominant group.

24
Private Lives

MERRILL GOOZNER

The sociology of sexual behavior barely exists in Japan. That does not keep sociologists and others from wondering about sexual practices in a modern industrial society that retains much of its rich traditional heritage. Recent polling data indicate that Japanese adults are more likely than Americans to approve of premarital and extramarital sexual activity. The gender split is very wide, however, and Japanese women are much less supportive of such behavior than Japanese men. The country remains a largely patriarchal society, as this essay shows.

Tokyo—On most weekday afternoons, businessmen in their trademark gray and blue suits can be seen climbing the curved, hilly streets of Tokyo's quiet Maruyama district that is famous for its many *rabu hoteru*, or love hotels. Their favorite female office clerk usually follows a discreet few steps behind.

Once inside the *rabu hoteru*, these temporary refugees from the office routine enter a world of heart-shaped beds, tawdry lighting, pornographic videos and, if they want to pay extra, sumptuous food. The cost for two hours is only 5,000 yen (about $60). For 20 percent extra, they can spend the whole day or night.

There are more than 20,000 love hotels in Japan, a thriving industry in nearly every town large enough to offer temporary anonymity. Their well-advertised presence offers incontrovertible evidence that extramarital affairs are commonplace in Japan.

But try to find out the prevalence of infidelity and you run into a stone wall. It isn't that people won't talk to the anonymous surveyor, it is simply that almost no one ever asks.

Unlike in the U.S., where a survey on the sex habits of Americans made front page news recently, the media, academics and government health service here seem oddly indifferent to the sexual activities of their compatriots.

Infidelity is not the only unexplored topic. The frequency and types of sex among married or unmarried partners also holds no fascination for most Japanese, who seem content to keep their private lives to themselves.

"There are fewer than five sexologists in Japan," said Naohide Yamamoto, director of the Japan Institute for Research on the Education and Culture of Human Sexuality. "There is no organization that takes leadership. There's no financial support."

Yamamoto, a free-lance researcher and writer on Japanese sexuality, has plied his lonely trade for more than three decades. But he soldiers on undeterred. His office is cluttered with artworks from all over the world celebrating human sexuality and fertility. His swept-back gray and black hair and smooth-skinned face makes him seem much younger than his 62 years.

When asked about infidelity, he reached into his bookshelf and pulled out a 13-year-old survey, the last time anyone took a scientific look at Japanese sexuality. The survey revealed that 22 percent of men either married or living with a woman had been unfaithful. The comparable figure for women was 8 percent.

When it was suggested that the figures didn't seem that high and wouldn't support the obviously thriving love hotel industry, Yamamoto said, "These figures are for one year. I think one in five married men having an affair each year is quite high."

Some have suggested that Japanese men's propensity for extramarital affairs stems from special cultural traits. "The Japanese believe we all have two co-existing souls," an Australian travel writer wrote recently. "One is spiritual, timeless and uplifting—this is the soul that works long, arduous hours and puts one's company and family obligations first.

"The other soul is earthbound and pleasure-seeking. The Japanese do not believe the pleasures of the flesh are evil. On the contrary, Japanese men believe it is their right to enjoy sex," he wrote.

STATE OF THEIR UNIONS

Yamamoto scoffed at such mystifications and launched into his favorite topic: the impoverished emotional state of most Japanese marriages.

"In Japan, the basis of marriage and the reason to stay together has nothing to do with love," he said. "You have to have a husband or wife to be socially credible. You need to raise children. And then there's economics.

"Instead of divorce, many men and more and more women have affairs. They don't have the courage to divorce, but they have the courage to have affairs."

Japan's divorce rate, while rising, remains low by Western standards. In 1993, marriages outnumbered the 188,000 divorces by more than 4-1.

Besides the social and financial pressures to stay together, the Japanese workplace encourages male infidelity. Men often spend their evening hours drinking and carousing with office compatriots, many of them young women who are known as office ladies.

Office lady is a distinct occupational category in Japan. Most companies employ small armies of young women, some even college-trained, for clerical tasks and to make the afternoon tea. These non-career-path women bore the brunt of dismissals and reduced hiring during the four-year economic slowdown, and they generally are expected to leave the workforce when they marry.

After these long nights out, men often arrive home too drunk or exhausted for sex with their wives, who probably don't want to have anything to do with them at that point in any case. They then wake up early the next morning to make the long commutes that begin the process all over again.

It is a pattern that many women, especially younger women who are more likely than their parents to have chosen their marriage partner, are less willing to accept. "Things are getting shaky. Even though they don't divorce, they have a *konnai rekkon*, or inside marriage divorce," Yamamoto said.

This emotional impoverishment leads directly to the high rate of infidelity, Yamamoto said. (The recent U.S. sex survey found that fewer than two in five American men had an affair over the course of their lifetime.) "It's as if the top half of their body and the lower half have nothing to do with each other," he said.

THE FEMALE SIDE

Meanwhile, female sexuality, a subject of endless fascination in the women's magazines in the U.S., gets plenty of space in the media here. But few devote the resources needed to conduct scientific surveys.

One exception was More, a fashion magazine, that asked more than 5,000 of its female readers about their sex lives in 1981 and again in 1987. The results were published in 1990.

Yamamoto said the results were similar to the Hite report in the U.S. However, while the report delved into numbers of partners (usually one to three before marriage), orgasms (54 percent have them) and infidelity, it skipped questions about what activities other than sexual intercourse go on behind closed doors.

"No one in Japan has ever asked a question about those things," said Yamamoto. "These practices were unthinkable before the war. For people in their 20s to 40s, it may have become common, but before that it was unthinkable."

One shouldn't get the idea from the undeveloped state of Japanese sexology that sex is somehow a forbidden topic in Japan. The video stores and magazine racks are filled with soft pornographic films and magazines, where the models' genitalia have been carefully eliminated by the censor's airbrush.

Photographs of naked women, a regular feature of most weekly men's magazines, in the past two years began including pubic hair, a radical departure from past practice.

CHANGING TIMES

Sexually explicit materials have a long history in Japan. Many colorful woodblock *ukiyo-e* prints from the isolationist Edo era (1600–1858) included detailed if exaggerated drawings of the genitalia of men and women enjoying sexual intercourse. Young women just before marriage would receive explicit comic books outlining in graphic detail what was expected from them in the marriage chamber.

But all that changed in the imperial era, when the new rulers imposed a Victorian morality on Japan to promote its efforts to catch up to the West. Little changed after the war. From 1947 to 1965, the government waged a "purity education" campaign in schools to stamp out the prostitution that had temporarily flourished amid the devastation of the immediate postwar years.

While the campaign didn't have much effect on adult sexuality, it does appear to have succeeded in dampening teenage sexual activity, at least compared to the U.S. In the only regular sex survey in Japan, the Japan Sex Education Association every three years asks nearly 5,000 junior and senior high school and college students about their sexual activity.

The survey is funded by comic-book publishers who include graphic sexual material in their magazines. They use the results to fend off criticism that their magazines encourage teenage sex.

According to the 1993 survey, 27 percent of 12th grade boys and 22 percent of 12th grade girls in Japan are sexually active. Rates among girls have been steadily rising, up from only 12 percent in 1984. The boys' rate had been 27 percent in 1987, but fell to 21 percent in 1990 before returning to the higher rate in the most recent survey.

But in the second year of college, all the rates soar, reaching 72 percent for men and 65 percent for women.

"Through high school, kids are under tremendous pressure from the exam system," said Hiroshi Masuyama, director of the association. "But once they're in college, the pressure is off and they're away from home. The taboos are gone."

25
Media Magic: Making Class Invisible

Gregory Mantsios

Most households in the United States have one or two workers who provide an annual income sufficient to meet the basic needs and wants of their household's members. Since the heads of U.S. households have to work to meet these needs but are fairly successful at fulfilling them, they pride themselves on being "middle class" and tend to reject labels such as "elite" and "poor." Still, class structure is very real and influences our lives in many critical ways. You would not know this, however, if your only source of information about the United States was the mass media.

Of the various social and cultural forces in our society, the mass media is arguably the most influential in molding public consciousness. Americans spend an average twenty-eight hours per week watching television. They also spend an undetermined number of hours reading periodicals, listening to the radio, and going to the movies. Unlike other cultural and socializing institutions, ownership and control of the mass media is highly concentrated. Twenty-three corporations own more than one-half of all the daily newspapers, magazines, movie studios, and radio and television outlets in the U.S. The number of media companies is shrinking and their control of the industry is expanding. And a relatively small number of media outlets is producing and packaging the majority of news and entertainment programs. For the most part, our media is national in nature and single-minded (profit-oriented) in purpose. This media plays a key role in defining our cultural tastes, helping us locate ourselves in history, establishing our national identity, and ascertaining the range of national and social possibilities. In this essay, we will examine the way the mass media shapes how people think about each other and about the nature of our society.

The United States is the most highly stratified society in the industrialized world. Class distinctions operate in virtually every aspect of our lives, determining the nature of our work, the quality of our schooling, and the health and safety of our loved ones. Yet remarkably, we, as a nation, retain illusions about living in an egalitarian society. We maintain these illusions, in large part, because the media hides gross inequities from public view. In those instances when inequities are revealed, we are provided with messages that obscure the nature of class realities and blame the victims of class-dominated society for their own plight. Let's briefly examine what the news media, in particular, tells us about class.

ABOUT THE POOR

The news media provides meager coverage of poor people and poverty. The coverage it does provide is often distorted and misleading.

The Poor Do Not Exist

For the most part, the news media ignore the poor. Unnoticed are forty million poor people in the nation—a number that equals the entire population of Maine, Vermont, New Hampshire, Connecticut, Rhode Island, New Jersey, and New York combined. Perhaps even more alarming is that the rate of poverty is increasing twice as fast as the population growth in the United States. Ordinarily, even a calamity of much smaller proportion (e.g., flooding in the Midwest) would garner a great deal of coverage and hype from a media usually eager to declare a crisis, yet less than one in five hundred articles in the *New York Times* and one in one thousand articles listed in the *Readers Guide to Periodic Literature* are on poverty. With remarkably little attention to them, the poor and their problems are hidden from most Americans.

When the media does turn its attention to the poor, it offers a series of contradictory messages and portrayals.

The Poor Are Faceless

Each year the Census Bureau releases a new report on poverty in our society and its results are duly reported in the media. At best, however, this coverage emphasizes annual fluctuations (showing how the numbers differ from previous years) and ongoing debates over the validity of the numbers (some argue the number should be lower, most that the number should be higher). Coverage like this desensitizes us to the poor by reducing poverty to a number. It ignores the human tragedy of poverty— the suffering, indignities, and misery endured by millions of children and adults. Instead, the poor become statistics rather than people.

The Poor Are Undeserving

When the media does put a face on the poor, it is not likely to be a pretty one. The media will provide us with sensational stories about welfare cheats, drug addicts, and greedy panhandlers (almost always urban and Black). Compare these images and the emotions evoked by them with the media's treatment of middle class (usually white) "tax evaders," celebrities who have a "chemical dependency," or wealthy businesspeople who use unscrupulous means to "make a profit." While the behavior of the more affluent offenders is considered an "impropriety" and a deviation from the norm, the behavior of the poor is considered repugnant, indicative of the poor in general, and worthy of our indignation and resentment.

The Poor Are an Eyesore

When the media does cover the poor, they are often presented through the eyes of the middle class. For example, sometimes the media includes a story about community resistance to a homeless shelter or storekeeper annoyance with panhandlers. Rather than focusing on the plight of the poor, these stories are about middle-class opposition to the poor. Such stories tell us that the poor are an inconvenience and an irritation.

The Poor Have Only Themselves to Blame

In another example of media coverage, we are told that the poor live in a personal and cultural cycle of poverty that hopelessly imprisons them. They routinely center on the Black urban population and focus on perceived personality or cultural traits that doom the poor. While the women in these stories typically exhibit an "attitude" that leads to trouble or a promiscuity that leads to single motherhood, the men possess a need for immediate gratification that leads to drug abuse or an unquenchable greed that leads to the pursuit of fast money. The images that are seared into our mind are sexist, racist, and classist. Census figures reveal that most of the poor are white not Black or hispanic, that they live in rural or suburban areas not urban centers, and hold jobs at least part of the year. Yet, in a fashion that is often framed in an understanding and sympathetic tone, we are told that the poor have inflicted poverty on themselves.

The Poor Are down on Their Luck

During the Christmas season, the news media sometimes provide us with accounts of poor individuals or families (usually white) who are down on their luck. These stories are often linked to stories about soup kitchens or other charitable activities and sometimes call for charitable contributions. These "Yule time" stories are as much about the affluent as they are about the poor: they tell us that the affluent in our society are a kind, understanding, giving people—which we are not.[1] The series

1. American households with incomes of less than $10,000 give an average of 5.5 percent of their earning to charity or to a religious organization, while those making more than $100,000 a year give only 2.9 percent. After changes in the 1986 tax code reduced the benefits of charitable giving, taxpayers earning $500,000 or more slashed their average donation by nearly one-third. Furthermore, many of these acts of benevolence do not help the needy. Rather than provide funding to social service agencies that aid the poor, the voluntary contributions of the wealthy go to places and institutions that entertain, inspire, cure, or educate wealthy Americans—art museums, opera houses, theaters, orchestras, ballet companies, private hospitals, and elite universities. (Robert Reich, "Secession of the Successful," *New York Times Magazine*, February 17, 1991 p. 43.)

of unfortunate circumstances that have led to impoverishment are presumed to be a temporary condition that will improve with time and a change in luck.

Despite appearances, the messages provided by the media are not entirely disparate. With each variation, the media informs us what poverty is not (i.e., systemic and indicative of American society) by informing us what it is. The media tells us that poverty is either an aberration of the American way of life (it doesn't exist, it's just another number, it's unfortunate but temporary) or an end product of the poor themselves (they are a nuisance, do not deserve better, and have brought their predicament upon themselves).

By suggesting that the poor have brought poverty upon themselves, the media is engaging in what William Ryan has called "blaming the victim." The media identify in what ways the poor are different as a consequence of deprivation, then define those differences as the cause of poverty itself. Whether blatantly hostile or cloaked in sympathy, the message is that there is something fundamentally wrong with the victims—their hormones, psychological makeup, family environment, community, race, or some combination of these—that accounts for their plight and their failure to lift themselves out of poverty.

But poverty in the United States is systemic. It is a direct result of economic and political policies that deprive people of jobs, adequate wages, or legitimate support. It is neither natural nor inevitable: there is enough wealth in our nation to eliminate poverty if we chose to redistribute existing wealth or income. The plight of the poor is reason enough to make the elimination of poverty the nation's first priority. But poverty also impacts dramatically on the nonpoor. It has a dampening effect on wages in general (by maintaining a reserve army of unemployed and underemployed anxious for any job at any wage) and breeds crime and violence (by maintaining conditions that invite private gain by illegal means and rebellion-like behavior, not entirely unlike the urban riots of the 1960s). Given the extent of poverty in the nation and the impact it has on us all, the media must spin considerable magic to keep the poor and the issue of poverty and its root causes out of the public consciousness.

About Everyone Else

Both the broadcast and the print news media strive to develop a strong sense of "we-ness" in their audience. They seek to speak to and for an audience that is both affluent and like-minded. The media's solidarity with affluence, that is, with the middle and upper class, varies little from one medium to another. Benjamin DeMott points out, for example, that the *New York Times* understands affluence to be intelligence, taste, public spirit, responsibility, and a readiness to rule and "conceives itself as spokesperson for a readership awash in these qualities." Of course, the flip side to creating a sense of "we" or "us," is establishing a perception of the "other." The other relates back to the faceless, amoral, undeserving, and inferior "underclass." Thus, the world according to the news media is divided between the "underclass" and everyone else. Again the messages are often contradictory.

The Wealthy Are Us

Much of the information provided to us by the news media focuses attention on the concerns of a very wealthy and privileged class of people. Although the concerns of a small fraction of the populace, they are presented as though they were the concerns of everyone. For example, while relatively few people actually own stock, the news media devotes an inordinate amount of broadcast time and print space to business news and stock market quotations. Not only do business reports cater to a particular narrow clientele, so do the fashion pages (with $2,000 dresses), wedding announcements, and the obituaries. Even weather and sports news often have a class bias. An all news radio station in New York City, for example, provides regular national ski reports. International news, trade agreements, and domestic policies issues are also reported in terms of their impact on business climate and the business community. Besides being of practical value to the wealthy, such coverage has considerable ideological value. Its message: the concerns of the wealthy are the concerns of us all.

The Wealthy (as a Class) Do Not Exist

While preoccupied with the concerns of the wealthy, the media fails to notice the way in which the rich as a class of people create and shape domestic and foreign policy. Presented as an aggregate of individuals, the wealthy appear without special interests, interconnections, or unity in purpose. Out of public view are the class interests of the wealthy, the interlocking business links, the concerted actions to preserve their class privileges and business interests (by running for public office, supporting political candidates, lobbying, etc.). Corporate lobbying is ignored, taken for granted, or assumed to be in the public interest. (Compare this with the media's portrayal of the "strong arm of labor" in attempting to defeat trade legislation that is harmful to the interests of working people.) It is estimated that two-thirds of the U.S. Senate is composed of millionaires. Having such a preponderance of millionaires in the Senate, however, is perceived to be neither unusual nor antidemocratic; these millionaire senators are assumed to be serving "our" collective interests in governing.

The Wealthy Are Fascinating and Benevolent

The broadcast and print media regularly provide hype for individuals who have achieved "super" success. These stories are usually about celebrities and superstars from the sports and entertainment world. Society pages and gossip columns serve to keep the social elite informed of each others doings, allow the rest of us to gawk at their excesses, and help to keep the American dream alive. The print media is also fond of feature stories on corporate empire builders. These stories provide an occasional "insiders" view of the private and corporate life of industrialists by suggesting a rags to riches account of corporate success. These stories tell us that corporate success is a series of smart moves, shrewd acquisitions, timely mergers, and well thought out executive suite shuffles. By painting the upper class in a positive light, innocent of any wrongdoing (labor leaders and union organizations usually get the opposite treatment), the media assure us that wealth and power are benevolent. One person's capital accumulation is presumed to be good for all. The elite, then, are portrayed as investment wizards, people of special talent and skill, who even their victims (workers and consumers) can admire.

The Wealthy Include a Few Bad Apples

On rare occasions, the media will mock selected individuals for their personality flaws. Real estate investor Donald Trump and New York Yankees owner George Steinbrenner, for example, are admonished by the media for deliberately seeking publicity (a very un-upper class thing to do); hotel owner Leona Hemsley was caricatured for her personal cruelties; and junk bond broker Michael Milkin was condemned because he had the audacity to rob the rich. Michael Parenti points out that by treating business wrongdoings as isolated deviations from the socially beneficial system of "responsible capitalism," the media overlook the features of the system that produce such abuses and the regularity with which they occur. Rather than portraying them as predictable and frequent outcomes of corporate power and the business system, the media treats abuses as if they were isolated and atypical. Presented as an occasional aberration, these incidents serve not to challenge, but to legitimate the system.

The Middle Class Is Us

By ignoring the poor and blurring the lines between the working people and the upper class, the news media create a universal middle class. From this perspective, the size of one's income becomes largely irrelevant: what matters is that most of "us" share an intellectual and moral superiority over the disadvantaged. As *Time* magazine once concluded, "Middle America is a state of mind." "We are all middle class," we are told, "and we all share the same concerns:" job security, inflation, tax burdens, world peace, the cost of food and housing, health care, clean air and water, and the safety of our streets. While the concerns of the wealthy are quite distinct from those of the middle class (e.g., the wealthy worry about investments, not jobs), the media convinces us that "we [the affluent] are all in this together."

The Middle Class Is a Victim

For the media, "we" the affluent not only stand apart from the "other"—the poor, the working class, the minorities, and their problems—"we" are also victimized by the poor (who drive up the costs of maintaining the welfare roles), minorities (who commit crimes against us), and by workers (who are greedy and drive companies out and prices up). Ignored are the subsidies to the rich, the crimes of corporate America, and the policies that wreak havoc on the economic well-being of middle America. Media magic convinces us to fear, more than anything else, being victimized by those less affluent than ourselves.

The Middle Class Is Not a Working Class

The news media clearly distinguish the middle class (employees) from the working class (i.e., blue collar workers) who are portrayed, at best, as irrelevant, outmoded, and a dying breed. Furthermore, the media will tell us that the hardships faced by blue collar workers are inevitable (due to progress), a result of bad luck (chance circumstances in a particular industry), or a product of their own doing (they priced themselves out of a job). Given the media's presentation of reality, it is hard to believe that manual, supervised, unskilled, and semiskilled workers actually represent more than 50 percent of the adult working population. The working class, instead, is relegated by the media to "the other."

In short, the news media either lionizes the wealthy or treats their interests and those of the middle class as one in the same. But the upper class and the middle class do not share the same interests or worries. Members of the upper class worry about stock dividends (not employment), they profit from inflation and global militarism, their children attend exclusive private schools, they eat and live in a royal fashion, they call on (or are called upon by) personal physicians, they have few consumer problems, they can escape whenever they want from environmental pollution, and they live on streets and travel to other areas under the protection of private police forces.[2]

The wealthy are not only a class with distinct life-styles and interests, they are a ruling class. They receive a disproportionate share of the country's yearly income, own a disproportionate amount of the country's wealth, and contribute a disproportionate number of their members to governmental bodies and decision-making groups—all traits that Wil-

2. The number of private security guards in the United States now exceeds the number of public police officers. (Robert Reich, "Secession of the Successful", *New York Times Magazine*, February 17, 1991, p. 42.)

liam Domhoff, in his classic work *Who Rules America*, defined as characteristic of a governing class.

This governing class maintains and manages our political and economic structures in such a way that these structures continue to yield an amazing proportion of our wealth to a minuscule upper class. While the media is not above referring to ruling classes in other countries (we hear, for example, references to Japan's ruling elite), their treatment of the news proceeds as though there were no such ruling class in the United States.

Furthermore, the news media inverts reality so that those who are working class and middle class learn to fear, resent, and blame those below, rather than those above them in the class structure. We learn to resent welfare, which accounts for only two cents out of every dollar in the federal budget (approximately $10 billion) and provides financial relief for the needy,[3] but learn little about the $11 billion the federal government spends on individuals with incomes in excess of $100,000 (not needy), or the $17 billion in farm subsidies, or the $214 billion (twenty times the cost of welfare) in interest payments to financial institutions.

Middle-class whites learn to fear African Americans and Latinos, but most violent crime occurs within poor and minority communities and is neither interracial[4] nor interclass. As horrid as such crime is, it should not mask the destruction and violence perpetrated by corporate America. In spite of the fact that 14,000 innocent people are killed on the job each year, 100,000 die prematurely, 400,000 become seriously ill, and 6 million are injured from work-related accidents and diseases, most Americans fear government regulation more than they do unsafe working conditions.

Through the media, middle class—and even working class—Americans learn to blame blue collar workers and their unions for declining purchasing power and economic security. But while workers who managed to keep their jobs and their unions struggled to keep up with inflation, the top 1 percent of American families saw their average incomes soar 80 percent in the last decade. Much of the wealth at the top was accumulated as stockholders and corporate executives moved their companies abroad to employ cheaper labor (56 cents per hour in El Salvador) and avoid paying taxes in the United States. Corporate America is a world made up of ruthless bosses, massive layoffs, favoritism and nepotism, health and safety violations, pension plan losses, union busting, tax evasions, unfair competition, and price gouging, as well as fast buck deals, financial speculation, and corporate wheeling and dealing that

3. A total of $20 billion is spent on welfare when you include all state funding. But the average state funding also comes to only two cents per state dollar.
4. In 92 percent of the murders nationwide the assailant and the victim are the same race (46 percent are white/white, 46 percent are black/black), 5.6 percent are black on white, and 2.4 percent are white on black. (FBI and Bureau of Justice Statistics, 1985–1986)

serve the interests of the corporate elite, but are generally wasteful and destructive to workers and the economy in general.

It is no wonder Americans cannot think straight about class. The mass media is neither objective, balanced, independent, nor neutral. Those who own and direct the mass media are themselves part of the upper class, and neither they nor the ruling class in general have to conspire to manipulate public opinion. Their interest is in preserving the status quo, and their view of society as fair and equitable comes naturally to them. But their ideology dominates our society and justifies what is in reality a perverse social order—one that perpetuates unprecedented elite privilege and power on the one hand and widespread deprivation on the other. A mass media that did not have its own class interests in preserving the status quo would acknowledge that inordinate wealth and power undermines democracy and that a "free market" economy can ravage a people and their communities.

26

As the World Turns

ROBERT B. REICH

With the expansion of global markets, global manufacturing and global services, there are winners and losers. A good job for your parents may not be a good one for you, for reasons largely beyond your control. New forms of inequality are emerging that threaten to make even wider the gulf between jobs that are valued and jobs that are not.

Between 1978 and 1987, the poorest fifth of American families became 8 percent poorer, and the richest fifth became 13 percent richer. That leaves the poorest fifth with less than 5 percent of the nation's income, and the richest fifth with more than 40 percent. This widening gap can't be blamed on the growth in single-parent lower-income families, which in fact slowed markedly after the late 1970s. Nor is it due mainly to the stingy social policy of the Reagan years. Granted, Food Stamp benefits have dropped in real terms by about 13 percent since 1981, and many states have failed to raise benefits for the poor and unemployed to keep up with inflation. But this doesn't come close to accounting for the growing inequality. Rather, the trend is connected to a profound change in the American economy as it merges with the global economy. And because the merging is far from complete, this trend will not stop of its own accord anytime soon.

It is significant that the growth of inequality shows up most strikingly among Americans who have jobs. Through most of the postwar era, the wages of Americans at different income levels rose at about the same pace. Although different workers occupied different steps on the escalator, everyone moved up together. In those days poverty was the condition of *jobless* Americans, and the major economic challenge was to create enough jobs for everyone. Once people were safely on the work force escalator, their problems were assumed to be over. Thus "full employment" became a liberal rallying cry, while conservatives fretted over the inflationary tendencies of a full-employment economy.

In recent years working Americans have been traveling on two escalators—one going up, the other going down. In 1987 the average hourly earnings of non-supervisory workers, adjusted for inflation, were lower than in any year since 1966. Middle-level managers fared much better, although their median real earnings were only slightly above the levels of the 1970s. Executives, however, did spectacularly well. In 1988 alone, CEOs of the hundred largest publicly held industrial corporations received raises averaging almost 12 percent. The remunerations of lesser executives rose almost as much, and executives of smaller companies followed close behind.

Between 1978 and 1987, as the real earnings of unskilled workers were declining, the real incomes of workers in the securities industry (investment bankers, arbitrageurs, and brokers) rose 21 percent. Few investment bankers pocket anything near the $50 million lavished yearly upon the partners of Kohlberg, Kravis, Roberts & Company, or the $550 million commandeered last year by Michael Milken, but it is not unusual for a run-of-the-mill investment banker to bring home comfortably over a million dollars. Partners in America's largest corporate law firms are comparatively deprived, enjoying average yearly earnings of only $400,000 to $1.2 million.

Meanwhile, the number of impoverished *working* Americans climbed by nearly two million, or 23 percent, between 1978 and 1987. The number who worked full time and year round but were poor climbed faster, by 43 percent. Nearly 60 percent of the 20 million people who now fall below the Census Bureau's poverty line are from families with at least one member in full-time or part-time work.

The American economy, in short, is creating a wider range of earnings than at any other time in the postwar era. The most basic reason, put simply, is that America itself is ceasing to exist as a system of production and exchange separate from the rest of the world. One can no more meaningfully speak of an "American economy" than of a "Delaware economy." We are becoming but a region—albeit still a relatively wealthy region—of a global economy, whose technologies, savings, and investments move effortlessly across borders, making it harder for individual nations to control their economic destinies.

By now Washington officials well understand that the nation's fiscal and monetary policies cannot be set without taking account of the savings that will slosh in or slosh out of the nation in consequence. Less understood is the speed and ease with which new technologies now spread across the globe, from computers in, say, San Jose, to satellite, and then back down to computers in Taiwan. (America's efforts to stop the Japanese from copying our commercial designs and the Soviets from copying our military designs are about equally doomed.) And we have yet to come to terms with the rise of the global corporation, whose managers, shareholders, and employees span the world. Our debates over the future of American jobs still focus on topics like the competitiveness of the American automobile industry or the future of American manufacturing. But these categories are increasingly irrelevant. They assume the existence of a separate American economy in which all the jobs associated with a particular industry, or even more generally with a particular sector, are bound together, facing a common fate.

New technologies of worldwide communication and transportation have redrawn the playing field. American industries no longer compete against Japanese or European industries. Rather, a company with headquarters in the United States, production facilities in Taiwan, and a marketing force spread across many nations competes with another, similarly ecumenical company. So when General Motors, say, is doing well, that probably is good news for a lot of executives in Detroit, and for GM shareholders across the globe, but it isn't necessarily good news for a lot of assembly-line workers in Detroit, because there may, in fact, be very few GM assembly-line workers in Detroit, or anywhere else in America. The welfare of assembly-line workers in Detroit may depend, instead, on the health of corporations based in Japan or Canada.

More to the point, even if those Canadian and Japanese corporations are doing well, these workers may be in trouble. For they are increasingly part of an international labor market, encompassing Asia, Africa, Western Europe—and perhaps, before long, Eastern Europe. Corporations can with relative ease relocate their production centers, and alter their international lines of communication and transportation accordingly, to take advantage of low wages. So American workers find themselves settling for low wages in order to hold on to their jobs. More and more, your "competitiveness" as a worker depends not on the fortunes of any American corporation, or of any American industry, but on what function you serve within the global economy. GM executives are becoming more "competitive" even as GM production workers become less so, because the functions that GM executives perform are more highly valued in the world market than the functions that GM production workers perform.

In order to see in greater detail what is happening to American jobs, it helps to view the work Americans do in terms of functional categories that reflect the real competitive positions of workers in the global economy. Essentially, three broad categories are emerging. Call them symbolic-analytic services, routine production services, and routine personal services.

(1) *Symbolic-analytic services* are based on the manipulation of information: data, words, and oral and visual symbols. Symbolic analysis comprises some (but by no means all) of the work undertaken by people who call themselves lawyers, investment bankers, commercial bankers, management consultants, research scientists, academics, public-relations executives, real estate developers, and even a few creative accountants. Also: advertising and marketing specialists, art directors, design engineers, architects, writers and editors, musicians, and television and film producers. Some of the manipulations performed by symbolic analysts reveal ways of more efficiently deploying resources or shifting financial assets, or of otherwise saving time and energy. Other manipulations grab money from people who are too slow or naive to protect themselves by manipulation in response. Still others serve to entertain the recipients.

Most symbolic analysts work alone or in small teams. If they work with others, they often have partners rather than bosses or supervisors, and their yearly income is variable, depending on how much value they add to the business. Their work environments tend to be quiet and tastefully decorated, often within tall steel-and-glass buildings. They rarely come in direct contact with the ultimate beneficiaries of their work. When they are not analyzing, designing, or strategizing, they are in meetings or on the telephone—giving advice or making deals. Many of them spend inordinate time in jet planes and hotels. They are articulate and well groomed. The vast majority are white males.

Symbolic analysis now accounts for more than 40 percent of America's gross national product, and almost 20 percent of our jobs. Within what we still term our "manufacturing sector," symbolic-analytic jobs have been increasing at a rate almost three times that of total manufacturing employment in the United States, as routine manufacturing jobs have drifted overseas or been mastered by machines.

The services performed by America's symbolic analysts are in high demand around the world, regardless of whether the symbolic analysts provide them in person or transmit them via satellite and fiber-optic cable. The Japanese are buying up the insights and inventions of America's scientists and engineers (who are only too happy to sell them at a fat profit). The Europeans, meanwhile, are hiring our management consultants, business strategists, and investment bankers. Developing nations are hiring our civil and design engineers; and almost everyone is buying the output of our pop musicians, television stars, and film producers.

It is the same with the global corporation. The central offices of these sprawling entities, headquartered in America, are filled with symbolic analysts who manipulate information and then export their insights via the corporation's far-flung enterprise. IBM doesn't export machines from the United States; it makes machines all over the globe, and services them on the spot. IBM world headquarters, in Armonk, New York, just exports strategic planning and related management services.

Thus has the standard of living of America's symbolic analysts risen. They increasingly find themselves part of a global labor market, not a national one. And because the United States has a highly developed economy, and an excellent university system, they find that the services they have to offer are quite scarce in the context of the whole world. So elementary laws of supply and demand ensure that their salaries are quite high.

These salaries are likely to go even higher in the years ahead, as the world market for symbolic analysis continues to grow. Foreigners are trying to learn these skills and techniques, to be sure, but they still have a long way to go. No other country does a better job of preparing its most fortunate citizens for symbolic analysis than does the United States. None has surpassed America in providing experience and training, often with entire regions specializing in one or another kind of symbolic analysis (New York and Chicago for finance, Los Angeles for music and film, the San Francisco Bay area and greater Boston for science and engineering). In this we can take pride. But for the second major category of American workers—the providers of routine production services—the laws of supply and demand don't bode well.

(2) *Routine production services* involve tasks that are repeated over and over, as one step in a sequence of steps for producing a finished product. Although we tend to associate these jobs with manufacturing, they are becoming common in the storage and retrieval of information. Banking, insurance, wholesaling, retailing, health care—all employ hordes of people who spend their days processing data, often putting information into computers or taking it out.

Most providers of routine production services work with many other people who do similar work within large, centralized facilities. They are overseen by supervisors, who in turn are monitored by more senior supervisors. They are usually paid an hourly wage. Their jobs are monotonous. Most of these people do not have a college education; they need only be able to take directions and, occasionally, undertake simple computations. Those who deal with metal are mostly white males; those who deal with fabrics or information tend to be female and/or minorities.

Decades ago, jobs like these were relatively well paid. Henry Ford gave his early production workers five dollars a day, a remarkable sum for the time, in the (correct) belief that they and their neighbors would be among the major buyers of Fords. But in recent years America's providers of routine production services have found themselves in direct competition with millions of foreign workers, most of whom are eager to work for a fraction of the pay of American workers. Through the miracle of satellite transmission, even routine data-processing can now be undertaken in relatively poor nations, thousands of miles away from the skyscrapers where the data are finally used. This fact has given management-level symbolic analysts ever greater bargaining leverage. If routine producers living in America don't agree to reduce their wages, then the work will go abroad.

And it has. In 1950 routine production services constituted about 30 percent of our national product and well over half of American jobs. Today such services represent about 20 percent of national product and one-fourth of jobs. And the scattering of foreign-owned factories placed here to circumvent American protectionism isn't going to reverse the trend. So the standard of living of America's routine production workers will likely keep declining. The dynamics behind the wage concessions, plant closings, and union-busting that have become commonplace are not likely to change.

(3) *Routine personal services* also entail simple, repetitive work, but, unlike routine production services, they are provided in person. Their immediate objects are specific customers rather than streams of metal, fabric, or data. Included in this employment category are restaurant and

hotel workers, barbers and beauticians, retail sales personnel, cabdrivers, household cleaners, day-care workers, hospital attendants and orderlies, truck drivers, and—among the fastest-growing of all—custodians and security guards.

Like production workers, providers of personal services are usually paid by the hour, are carefully supervised, and rarely have more than a high school education. But unlike people in the other two categories of work, these people are in direct contact with the ultimate beneficiaries of what they do. And the companies they work for are often small. In fact, some routine personal-service workers turn entrepreneurial. (Most new businesses and new jobs in America come from this sector—now constituting about 20 percent of GNP and 30 percent of jobs.) Women and minorities make up the bulk of routine personal-service workers.

Apart from the small number who strike out on their own, these workers are paid poorly. They are sheltered from the direct effects of global competition, but not the indirect effects. They often compete with illegal aliens willing to work for low wages, or with former or would-be production workers who can't find well-paying production jobs, or with labor-saving machinery (automated tellers, self-service gas pumps, computerized cashiers) dreamed up by symbolic analysts in America and manufactured in Asia. And because they tend to be unskilled and dispersed among small businesses, personal-service workers rarely hire a union or a powerful lobby group to stand up for their interests. When the economy turns sour, they are among the first to feel the effects. These workers will continue to have jobs in the years ahead and may experience some small increase in real wages. They will have demographics on their side, as the American work force shrinks. But for all the foregoing reasons, the gap between their earnings and those of the symbolic analysts will continue to grow.

These three functional categories—symbolic analysis, routine production, and routine personal service—cover at least three out of four American jobs. The rest of the nation's work force consists mainly of government employees (including public school teachers), employees in regulated industries (like utility workers), and government-financed workers (engineers working on defense weapons systems), many of whom are sheltered from global competition. One further clarification: Some traditional job categories overlap with several functional categories. People called "secretaries," for example, include those who actually spend their time doing symbolic-analytic work closely allied to what their bosses do; those who do routine data entry or retrieval of a sort that will eventually be automated or done overseas; and those who provide routine personal services.

The important point is that workers in these three functional categories are coming to have a different competitive position in the world economy. Symbolic analysts hold a commanding position in an increasingly global labor market. Routine production workers hold a relatively weak position in an increasingly global labor market. Personal-service workers still find themselves in a national labor market, but for various reasons they suffer the indirect effects of competition from workers abroad.

How should we respond to these trends? One response is to accept them as inevitable consequences of change, but try to offset their polarizing effects through a truly progressive income tax, coupled with more generous income assistance—including health insurance—for poor working Americans. (For a start, we might reverse the extraordinarily regressive Social Security amendments of 1983, through which poor working Americans are now financing the federal budget deficit, often paying more in payroll taxes than in income taxes.)

A more ambitious response would be to guard against class rigidities by ensuring that any talented American kid can become a symbolic analyst—regardless of family income or race. Here we see the upside of a globalized economy. Unlike America's old vertically integrated economy, whose white-collar jobs were necessarily limited in proportion to the number of blue-collar jobs beneath them, the global economy imposes no particular limit upon the number of Americans who can sell symbolic-analytic services. In principle, all of America's routine production workers could become symbolic analysts and let their old jobs drift overseas. In practice, of course, we can't even inch toward such a state anytime soon. Not even America's gifted but poor children can aspire to such jobs until the government spends substantially more than it does now to ensure excellent public schools in every city and region to which talented children can go, and ample financial help when they are ready to attend college.

Of course, it isn't clear that even under those circumstances there would be radical growth in the number of Americans who became research scientists, design engineers, musicians, management consultants, or (even if the world needed them) investment bankers and lawyers. So other responses are also needed. Perhaps the most ambitious would be to increase the numbers of Americans who could apply symbolic analysis to production and to personal services.

There is ample evidence, for example, that access to computerized information can enrich production jobs by enabling workers to alter the flow of materials and components in ways that generate new efficiencies. (Shoshana Zuboff's recent book *In the Age of the Smart Machine* carefully documents these possibilities.) Production workers who thus have broader responsibilities and more control over how production is organized cease to be "routine" workers—becoming, in effect, symbolic analysts at a level very close to the production process. The same transformation can occur in personal-service jobs. Consider, for example, the checkout clerk whose computer enables her to control inventory and decide when to reorder items from the factory.

The number of such technologically empowered jobs, of course, is limited by the ability of workers to learn on the job. That means a far greater number of Americans will need good health care (including prenatal and postnatal) and also a good grounding in mathematics, basic science, and reading and communicating. So once again, comfortably integrating the American work force into the new world economy turns out to rest heavily on education.

Education and health care for poor children are apt to be costly. Since poorer working Americans, already under a heavy tax load, can't afford it, the cost would have to be borne by wealthier Americans—who also would have to bear the cost of any income redistribution plans designed to neutralize the polarizing domestic effects of a globalized economy. Thus a central question is the willingness of the more fortunate American citizens—especially symbolic analysts, who constitute the most fortunate fifth, with 40 percent of the nation's income—to bear the burden. But here lies a Catch-22. For as our economic fates diverge, the top fifth may be losing the sense of connectedness with the bottom fifth, or even the bottom half, that would elicit such generosity.

The conservative tide that has swept the land during the last decade surely has many causes, but these economic fundamentals should not be discounted. It is now possible for the most fortunate fifth to sell their expertise directly in the global market, and thus maintain and enhance their standard of living and that of their children, even as that of other Americans declines. There is less and less basis for a strong sense of interclass interdependence. Meanwhile, the fortunate fifth have also been able to insulate themselves from the less fortunate, by living in suburban enclaves far removed from the effects of poverty. Neither patriotism nor altruism may be sufficient to overcome these realities. Yet without the active support of the fortunate fifth, it will be difficult to muster the political will necessary for change.

On withdrawing from the presidential race of 1988, Paul Simon of Illinois said, "Americans instinctively know that we are one nation, one family, and when anyone in that family hurts, all of us hurt." Sadly, that is coming to be less and less the case.

27

Imagine a Country

HOLLY SKLAR

Most of us grow up with a sense of pride in our country; we like to compare it favorably to other countries. Holly Sklar jolts us with her list of unfavorable statistical observations, tempting us to attribute them to another country. It is not a pretty exercise, but it is one that reminds us of the pervasive and deep inequality in the United States.

Imagine a country where one out of four children is born into poverty while the top 1 percent of families have a net worth greater than that of the bottom 90 percent. The top one half of the 1 percent hold over one-fourth of the nation's total private wealth. Imagine a country where budget deficits go hand in hand with greed surpluses. Where the poor and middle class are told to tighten their belts to pay off the debts, high salaries and tax breaks of the rich.

It's not Mexico.

Imagine a country whose economy, says a leading business magazine, grew enough from 1977 to 1989 to "have lifted everybody's real income by 10 percent if the gains had been distributed evenly. Instead, the top 1 percent of families—about 1 million in 1989—saw their average incomes soar by 80 percent, while the living standards of most" of their countrypeople stagnated or fell. The top 4 percent of wage earners are paid as much as the lower 51 percent.

Imagine a country where the average chief executive officer (CEO) of a large corporation earned as much as 42 factory workers in 1980, 93 factory workers in 1988 and 104 factory workers in 1991.

It's not Japan. There, CEOs earn about as much as 18 factory workers.

From 1980 to 1991, CEO compensation leaped 138 percent, after inflation. CEO greed raised enough of an outcry to cause an apparent 1991 cut of 7 percent in average salary and bonuses to $1.1 million. But when less visible longterm compensation such as stock options are counted, the average CEO's total pay jumped by 26 percent to $2.5 million (nearly 5 times the Japanese average), not counting the tax-deductible perks unavailable to workers.

Imagine a country where average workers' wages have crashed 19 percent, after inflation, since 1973. In 1973, before two-income families were the majority, median household income was $30,944. In 1991, adjusting for inflation, it was $30,126. Most children can't expect to equal their parents' living standards. Many can expect less.

Imagine a country where, according to a leading news magazine, "Unemployment stands at 7.6 percent . . . but more people are experiencing distress. A comprehensive tally would include workers who are employed well below their skill level, those who cannot find more than a part-time job, people earning poverty-level wages, workers who have been jobless for more than four weeks at a time and all those who have grown discouraged and quit looking. Last year those distressed workers totaled 36 million, or 40 percent of the . . . labor force. . . . The much touted job gains of the 1980s were, for the most part, low-wage positions earning $250 a week or less. More than 25 percent of the . . . work force now toils in this class of job, up from less than 19 percent in 1979. Laid-off workers who return to the market often must take huge pay cuts."

It's not Britain.

Imagine a country where people are working more for less. According to a leading business journal, the average work year for all people holding jobs is 1,890 hours (1,938 for manufacturing), the second highest among industrial nations and 15 percent higher than it was in the 1950s. The average worker has less than 11 paid vacation days (most European countries provide 4 to 6 weeks). The average worker has no right to leave, paid or unpaid, in the case of the illness, birth or adoption of a child. Less than 16 percent of workers are unionized.

Imagine a country where, as the rich got richer, they got even stingier. In the 1980s, for all wage groups who itemized deductions on their tax returns, the average charitable contributions increased by over 9 percent; average contributions by those with pretax incomes above $1 million decreased by nearly 39 percent.

In 1968, the country had a progressive tax with a bottom tax rate of 14 percent and a top rate of 75 percent. In 1992, it has three rates: 15, 28 and 31. Whether you are middle class or a billionaire, you pay almost the same rate. And then the rich get more of it back in the form of tax-free interest on the national debt—debt incurred, in part, to pay for the tax breaks of the rich. The richest 1 percent will owe $43 billion less in federal taxes in 1993 than they would have paying at the 1977 rates.

How much is $43 billion? More than the total budgets for AFDC (Aid to Families with Dependent Children), Food Stamps and Head Start plus most of the budget for employment and jobs training. The way the budget cutters throw women and children overboard, you'd think they were sinking the boat. In fact, AFDC accounted for less than 1 percent of federal outlays in 1991 and 2 percent of spending by states.

Imagine a country with the world's richest economy that has more children die before their first birthday than 23 other nations. The people of 14 countries have longer life expectancies. It is one of only two industrialized countries without national health insurance. Studies estimating the number of hungry people in the country range from a low of 20.4 million to a high of 42.8 million. A three-year study in a major city showed that the number of emergency room visits by underweight children increased by 30 percent after the coldest months of the year when poor parents face the cruel dilemma of "heat or eat."

Imagine a country which is first in military spending among 19 industrialized countries, but last in spending on housing, social security and welfare.

Imagine a country where one out of every seven people are poor. Many of them work. Between 1979 and 1990 the proportion of full-time, year-round workers paid low wages (below $12,195 in 1990) increased by half—to nearly one in every five full-time workers overall, one out of four women workers, one out of four Black workers, and one out of three Hispanic workers. Three of every four low-wage workers were high school graduates. Among young full-time workers (18–24), the percent earning low wages jumped from 23 percent in 1979 to over 43 percent in 1990. Among young women workers, the figure was nearly one in two workers.

People are encouraged to see unemployment and poverty as personal failures though jobs are so scarce that when one company announced 100 jobs at its new television assembly plant some 20,000 people responded. The purchasing power of the federal minimum wage, now $4.25 an hour, is 23 percent below its average value during the 1970s. Federal funding of employment and training programs has been cut by more than half since 1981, after adjusting for inflation.

Imagine a country where corrupt banks are bailed out while farmers and unemployed homeowners are foreclosed. Homeownership is increasingly out of reach for all but the richest. Mortgages are tax-deductible, not rent. In fiscal year 1990, direct spending on federal low income housing assistance programs totaled $18.3 billion. More than four times as much was spent through the tax code in the form of homeowner deductions amounting to some $78.4 billion. In 1991, about 81 percent of the $37 billion in tax benefits from deductible mortgage interest went to the top 20 percent of households with incomes above $50,000.

Imagine a country where corporations are rewarded with government subsidies to move abroad to "free trade zones" where they are free to pay workers much less and repress them much more. Where they are free of taxes and environmental regulation. One ad financed by the country's agency for international development shows a Salvadoran woman in front of a sewing machine. It tells corporations, "You can hire her for 33 cents an hour."

Imagine a country where nearly two out of three women with children under six work outside the home, but there is no national day care (in 1960, 20 percent of women with children under six were in the labor force). Most working mothers work full time. Women earn 74 cents for every dollar men earn; 66 cents if part-time work is included. Women don't pay three-fourths what men pay for their college degrees or three-fourths as much to feed their children.

Sixty-two countries have more women legislators. In the early 1970s, 99 percent of corporate senior management was male. Now, 97 percent of senior management is male. And, in the words of a leading business magazine, "at the same level of management, the typical woman's pay is lower than her male colleague's—even when she has the exact same qualifications, works just as many years, relocates just as often, provides the main financial support for her family, takes no time off for personal reasons, and wins the same number of promotions to comparable jobs."

Imagine a country which leads the world in rape and where violence against women is so epidemic it is their number one health risk. Much of the violence, from beatings to murder, is so-called "domestic violence," a term as inadequate as the response. The country has no equal rights amendment.

It's not Saudi Arabia.

Imagine a country where descendants of its first inhabitants live on reservations stripmined of resources and opportunity. There life expectancy averages in the 40s—not the 70s. Infant mortality is seven times higher than the national average and a higher proportion of people live in poverty than any other ethnic group.

Imagine a country where Indian names are used as labels for sports teams, cars and beer. Where a popular children's toy catalog advertises cowboy and Indian gear with lines like "It's heap big fun to wear this Indian Brave costume" and "Hunt for game and defend your homestead with these Wild West toy firearms." Where 500 years of plunder and lies are masked in expressions like "Indian giver." Where the military still dubs enemy territory, "Indian country."

Imagine a country where one out of two Black children are poor. Black infant mortality is twice that of whites. Black life expectancy is five years less. Blacks are turned down for mortgages at twice the rate of whites with similar incomes. Blacks are rejected more often than whites when they apply for benefits under social security disability programs. Black unemployment is three times that of whites. One out of two Black young adults are unemployed. The proportion of Black males ages 25–34 who were either unemployed or earned below the poverty threshold rose from 36.5 percent in 1979 to 45.3 percent in 1989.

Imagine a country that subsidized decades of segregated suburbanization for whites while the inner cities left to Blacks became outsider cities—with underclass housing, underclass schools, underclass street repair, underclass trash removal, underclass job opportunities. "Separate and unequal" is present, not past.

Imagine a country that imprisons more Black men than any other. One out of four Black men between 20 and 29 are either in jail, on probation or on parole. How many of them are there because of trumped up charges by racist cops whose mission apparently is not to stop crime but make sure every young Black man, guilty or innocent, has a record? A recent newspaper article is titled, "GUILTY . . . of being black: Black men say success doesn't save them from being suspected, harassed and detained." A bank CEO says he has had trouble cashing checks and hesitates to shop in neighboring suburbs where suspicious shopkeepers don't know him. A prominent law professor says he has "encounters with police almost annually, and they never cease to amaze me. They frequently happen when I am out of uniform—that is, not wearing my suit and tie. They are as innocuous as being pulled over because my car looks suspicious, or being stopped and frisked because I fit the description of someone who is wanted by police." A professional basketball player was forced to the pavement by police with drawn guns who mistook him for a bank robber; never mind that he didn't fit the description. In another state, a university recently helped a local police dragnet by providing a list of all Black male students.

It's not South Africa.

Imagine a country where public school budgets are determined largely by private property taxes. In one large state spending per pupil ranges from $3,190 in the poorest schools to $11,801 in the richest. In the rich schools, kids take well-stocked libraries and computers for granted. In the poor schools, they are rationing textbooks and toilet paper. The rich schools look like country clubs—with manicured sports fields, swimming pools and tennis courts. The poor schools look like jails—with concrete, metal detectors and grated windows.

Imagine a country where corporations serve students fast food in their school lunchrooms and fast news laced with advertising in their classrooms. The country ranks 18th in school-age population per teacher.

Imagine a country which has the world's leading homicide rate and you can buy a gun in many states more easily than you can register to vote. One out of two homes have guns. More teenage boys die from gunshots than from all natural causes combined. Homicide is the second-largest killer of young people ages 15 to 24, after accidents; AIDS is third.

Imagine a country where children are taught violence through entertainment. Where television is becoming increasingly violent and the most violent programs on television are children's cartoons. Toy commercials and music videos ranked fourth and fifth. Numerous private and government studies have shown that television violence leads to more aggressive behavior by those who watch and contributes to crime and violence in society. Many urban parents keep children indoors as much as possible to protect them—indoors where they watch the violence that passes for children's programs on TV.

It's not Nazi Germany.

Imagine a country where the new Supreme Court motto for those on death row is "Better 10 guilty prisoners are executed quickly than 1 innocent prisoner goes free."

Imagine a country that puts a far higher portion of its people behind bars than any other.

It's not China.

The prison population has more than doubled since 1980, a time of heavy cutbacks in education, job programs, housing and wages. Half the prisoners are drug offenders, many of them small-time dealers trying to feed their own habits. They can't check in to the clinics treating the elite. They can't exchange the $25,000 or $30,000 it costs the state to keep them in prison for a high school or college degree. Their neighborhoods don't get to use it for economic revitalization.

Imagine a country where first-time cocaine dealers can get mandatory-minimum sentences of life without parole. With jails overflowing, officials sometimes let violent criminals out to make room for nonviolent prisoners with mandatory minimums.

It's not Turkey.

The same country is number 4 in alcohol consumption and number 1 in drunk-driving fatalities per capita. And it is the number 1 exporter of weapons and addictive, cancer-causing tobacco.

Imagine a country that has only 5 percent of the world's population, but uses 25 percent of the world's oil resources. Only 3 percent of the public's trips is made by public transportation. It has no national conservation policy. It is the number 1 contributor to global warming. It has felled more trees since 1978 than any other country.

It's not Brazil.

Imagine a country spending almost $300 billion a year on the military even though the enemy long used to justify it no longer exists. It has no national plan for military-civilian conversion though its people need jobs and homes, its schools are in crisis and its public works infrastructure is crumbling.

Imagine a country whose congressional representatives earn more at $125,100 than 95 percent of their constituents (senators make $135,100). Among their many perks and benefits is free health care.

The country is 51 percent female and 49 percent male. It is 75 percent non-Hispanic white, 12 percent Black, 9 percent Hispanic, 3 percent Asian and Pacific Islander (the fastest growing group), and 1 percent Indian, Eskimo or Aluet (more if Hispanic Indians are included). In the nation's 102nd Congress, women hold 2 seats in the 100-member Senate and 6 percent in the 435-member House. Blacks hold no seats in the Senate and 6 percent in the House. Hispanics hold no seats in the Senate and 3 percent in the House. Asian and Pacific Islanders have two seats in the Senate and 1 percent in the House. There is one Indian member of Congress.

Imagine a country where people stand tall on the backs of others, and encourage those they are standing on to look down in anger, not up. The anger is directed into punishing those even worse off—taking food from the mouths of poor babies, not higher taxes from the bulging wallets of the rich.

Imagine a country where at the national convention renominating the President for reelection a White House communications director-turned TV-commentator-turned presidential candidate declares that another party's candidates "would impose . . . abortion on demand, a litmus test for the Supreme Court, homosexual rights, discrimination against religious schools, women in combat units. . . . It is not the kind of change we can abide in a nation we still call God's country. . . . There is a religious war going on in this country. It is a cultural war." Delegates wave signs saying "Gay Rights Never"—the 1990s version of segregation forever. The speaker's concluding words turn to recent rioting in a major city. He says, "I met the troopers of the 18th Cavalry, who had come to save the city . . . And as those boys took back the streets of [that city], block by block, my friends, we must take back our cities and take back our culture and take back our country."

It's not Iran.

Imagine a country where the President's[1] sons repeatedly cash in on their family value at taxpayer expense. They've enriched themselves and cost taxpayers hundreds of millions of dollars in banking scandals, Medicare fraud and assorted overt and covert scandals.

Imagine a country where numerous officials from the last Administration were convicted of crimes and misdemeanors including a national security adviser, assistant secretary of state and CIA officers. The secretary of defense and two high level CIA officials are still under indictment. The then President and Vice President were never held accountable and the Congress let expire the independent counsel legislation which makes such prosecutions possible.

It's not Greece.

Imagine a country where the President's press secretary told reporters after a 1984 debate with his then-vice presidential opponent: "You can say anything you want in a debate, and 80 million people hear it. If reporters then document that a candidate spoke untruthfully, so what? Maybe 200 people read it, or 2,000 or 20,000."

Imagine a country where only half the eligible voters cast ballots in the 1988 presidential election.

Sound familiar? It's the disUnited States.

---

1. Here Sklar refers to George Bush, and in the next paragraph to Ronald Reagan (president) and George Bush (vice president). [Editor]

28

Men and Jobs

ELLIOT LIEBOW

This excerpt from the author's well-known ethnography, Tally's Corner, *tells part of the story of the working poor. With few job skills or in jobs that offer only seasonal employment, these African-American men are unable to provide a steady income for a family. Because of their "failure" in their desired role as provider, many come to see themselves as human failures.*

Both getting the construction job and getting to it are . . . relatively more difficult than is the case for the menial jobs in retailing and the service trades. Job competition is always fierce. In the city, the large construction projects are unionized. One has to have ready cash to get into the union to become eligible to work on these projects and, being eligible, one has to find an opening. Unless one "knows somebody," say a foreman or a laborer who knows the day before that they are going to take on new men in the morning, this can be a difficult and disheartening search.

Many of the nonunion jobs are in suburban Maryland or Virginia. The newspaper ads say, "Report ready to work to the trailer at the intersection of Rte. 11 and Old Bridge Rd., Bunston, Virginia (or Maryland)," but this location may be ten, fifteen, or even twenty-five miles from the Carry-out.[1] Public transportation would require two or more hours to get there, if it services the area at all. Without access to a car or to a car-pool arrangement, it is not worthwhile reading the ad. So the men do not. Jobs such as these are usually filled by word of mouth information, beginning with someone who knows someone or who is himself working there and looking for a paying rider. Furthermore, nonunion jobs in out-lying areas tend to be smaller projects of relatively short duration and to pay somewhat less than scale.

Still another objective factor is the work itself. For some men, whether the job be digging, mixing mortar, pushing a wheelbarrow, unloading materials, carrying and placing steel rods for reinforcing concrete, or building or laying concrete forms, the work is simply too hard. Men such as Tally and Wee Tom can make such work look like child's play; some of the older work-hardened men, such as Budder and Stanton, can do it

---

1. The New Deal Carry-out is a food take-out establishment located near the White House in downtown Washington, D.C., in a working- to lower-class African-American neighbor-hood of apartments and businesses. [Editor]

too, although not without showing unmistakable signs of strain and weariness at the end of the workday. But those who lack the robustness of a Tally or the time-inured immunity of a Budder must either forego jobs such as these or pay a heavy toll to keep them. For Leroy, in his early twenties, almost six feet tall but weighing under 140 pounds, it would be as difficult to push a loaded wheelbarrow, or to unload and stack 96-pound bags of cement all day long, as it would be for Stoopy with his withered leg.

Heavy, backbreaking labor of the kind that used to be regularly associated with bull gangs or concrete gangs is no longer characteristic of laboring jobs, especially those with the larger, well-equipped construction companies. Brute strength is still required from time to time, as on smaller jobs where it is not economical to bring in heavy equipment or where the small, undercapitalized contractor has none to bring in. In many cases, however, the conveyor belt has replaced the wheelbarrow or the Georgia buggy, mechanized forklifts have eliminated heavy, manual lifting, and a variety of digging machines have replaced the pick and shovel. The result is fewer jobs for unskilled laborers and, in many cases, a work speed-up for those who do have jobs. Machines now set the pace formerly set by men. Formerly, a laborer pushed a wheelbarrow of wet cement to a particular spot, dumped it, and returned for another load. Another laborer, in hip boots, pushed the wet concrete around with a shovel or a hoe, getting it roughly level in preparation for the skilled finishers. He had relatively small loads to contend with and had only to keep up with the men pushing the wheelbarrows. Now, the job for the man pushing the wheelbarrow is gone and the wet concrete comes rushing down a chute at the man in the hip boots who must "spread it quick or drown."

Men who have been running an elevator, washing dishes, or "pulling trash" cannot easily move into laboring jobs. They lack the basic skills for "unskilled" construction labor, familiarity with tools and materials, and tricks of the trade without which hard jobs are made harder. Previously unused or untrained muscles rebel in pain against the new and insistent demands made upon them, seriously compromising the man's performance and testing his willingness to see the job through.

A healthy, sturdy, active man of good intelligence requires from two to four weeks to break in on a construction job. Even if he is willing somehow to bull his way through the first few weeks, it frequently happens that his foreman or the craftsman he services with materials and general assistance is not willing to wait that long for him to get into condition or to learn at a glance the difference in size between a rough 2" × 8" and a finished 2" × 10". The foreman and the craftsman are themselves "under the gun" and cannot "carry" the man when other men, who are already used to the work and who know the tools and materials, are lined up to take the job. . . .

Sometimes, the strain and effort is greater than the man is willing to admit, even to himself. In the early summer of 1963, Richard was rooming at Nancy's place. His wife and children were "in the country" (his grandmother's home in Carolina), waiting for him to save up enough money so that he could bring them back to Washington and start over again after a disastrous attempt to "make it" in Philadelphia. Richard had gotten a job with a fence company in Virginia. It paid $1.60 an hour. The first few evenings, when he came home from work, he looked ill from exhaustion and the heat. Stanton said Richard would have to quit, "he's too small [thin] for that kind of work." Richard said he was doing O.K. and would stick with the job. . . .

Richard stayed on the job two more weeks, then suddenly quit, ostensibly because his pay check was three dollars less than what he thought it should have been.

In summary of objective job considerations, then, the most important fact is that a man who is able and willing to work cannot earn enough money to support himself, his wife, and one or more children. A man's chances for working regularly are good only if he is willing to work for less than he can live on, and sometimes not even then. On some jobs, the wage rate is deceptively higher than on others, but the higher the wage rate, the more difficult it is to get the job, and the less the job security. Higher-paying construction work tends to be seasonal and, during the season, the amount of work available is highly sensitive to business and weather conditions and to the changing requirements of individual projects. Moreover, high-paying construction jobs are frequently beyond the physical capacity of some of the men, and some of the low-paying jobs are scaled down even lower in accordance with the self-fulfilling assumption that the man will steal part of his wages on the job.

Bernard assesses the objective job situation dispassionately over a cup of coffee, sometimes poking at the coffee with his spoon, sometimes staring at it as if, like a crystal ball, it holds tomorrow's secrets. He is twenty-seven years old. He and the woman with whom he lives have a baby son, and she has another child by another man. Bernard does odd jobs —mostly painting—but here it is the end of January, and his last job was with the Post Office during the Christmas mail rush. He would like postal work as a steady job, he says. It pays well (about $2.00 an hour) but he has twice failed the Post Office examination (he graduated from a Washington high school) and has given up the idea as an impractical one. He is supposed to see a man tonight about a job as a parking attendant for a large apartment house. The man told him to bring his birth certificate and driver's license, but his license was suspended because of a backlog of unpaid traffic fines. A friend promised to lend him some money this evening. If he gets it, he will pay the fines tomorrow morning and have his license reinstated. He hopes the man with the job will wait till tomorrow night. . . .

When we look at what the men bring to the job rather than at what the job offers the men, it is essential to keep in mind that we are not looking at men who come to the job fresh, just out of school perhaps, and newly prepared to undertake the task of making a living, or from another job where they earned a living and are prepared to do the same on this job. Each man comes to the job with a long job history characterized by his not being able to support himself and his family. Each man carries this knowledge, born of his experience, with him. He comes to the job flat and stale, wearied by the sameness of it all, convinced of his own incompetence, terrified of responsibility—of being tested still again and found wanting. Possible exceptions are the younger men not yet, or just, married. They suspect all this but have yet to have it confirmed by repeated personal experience over time. But those who are or have been married know it well. It is the experience of the individual and the group; of their fathers and probably their sons. Convinced of their inadequacies, not only do they not seek out those few better-paying jobs which test their resources, but they actively avoid them, gravitating in a mass to the menial, routine jobs which offer no challenge—and therefore pose no threat—to the already diminished images they have of themselves.

Thus Richard does not follow through on the real estate agent's offer. He is afraid to do on his own—minor plastering, replacing broken windows, other minor repairs and painting—exactly what he had been doing for months on a piecework basis under someone else (and which provided him with a solid base from which to derive a cost estimate). . . .

. . . [A] man's low self-esteem generates a fear of being tested and prevents him from accepting a job with responsibilities or, once on a job, from staying with it if responsibilities are thrust on him, even if the wages are commensurately higher. Richard refuses such a job, Leroy leaves one, and another man, given more responsibility and more pay, knows he will fail and proceeds to do so, proving he was right about himself all along. The self-fulfilling prophecy is everywhere at work. In a hallway, Stanton, Tonk and Boley are passing a bottle around. Stanton recalls the time he was in the service. Everything was fine until he attained the rank of corporal. He worried about everything he did then. Was he doing the right thing? Was he doing it well? When would they discover their mistake and take his stripes (and extra pay) away? When he finally lost his stripes, everything was all right again. . . .

A crucial factor in the streetcorner man's lack of job commitment is the overall value he places on the job. *For his part, the streetcorner man puts no lower value on the job than does the larger society around him.* He knows the social value of the job by the amount of money the employer is willing to pay him for doing it. In a real sense, every pay day, he counts in dollars and cents the value placed on the job by society at large. He is no more (and frequently less) ready to quit and look for another job than his employer is ready to fire him and look for another man. Neither the streetcorner man who performs these jobs nor the society which requires him to perform them assesses the job as one "worth doing and worth doing well." Both employee and employer are contemptuous of the job. The employee shows his contempt by his reluctance to accept it or keep it, the employer by paying less than is required to support a family. Nor does the low-wage job offer prestige, respect, interesting work, opportunity for learning or advancement, or any other compensation. With few exceptions, jobs filled by the streetcorner men are at the bottom of the employment ladder in every respect, from wage level to prestige. Typically, they are hard, dirty, uninteresting and underpaid. The rest of society (whatever its ideal values regarding the dignity of labor) holds the job of the dishwasher or janitor or unskilled laborer in low esteem if not outright contempt. So does the streetcorner man. He cannot do otherwise. He cannot draw from a job those social values which other people do not put into it. . . .

One reason for the relative absence of talk about one's job is, as suggested earlier, that the sameness of job experiences does not bear reiteration. Another and more important reason is the emptiness of the job experience itself. The man sees middle-class occupations as a primary source of prestige, pride and self-respect; his own job affords him none of these. To think about his job is to see himself as others see him, to remind him of just where he stands in this society.[2] And because society's criteria for placement are generally the same as his own, to talk about his job can trigger a flush of shame and a deep, almost physical ache to change places with someone, almost anyone, else.[3] The desire to be a person in his own right, to be noticed by the world he lives in, is shared by each of the men on the streetcorner. Whether they articulate this desire (as Tally does below) or not, one can see them position themselves to catch the attention of their fellows in much the same way that plants bend or stretch to catch the sunlight.

Tally and I were in the Carry-out. It was summer, Tally's peak earning season as a cement finisher, a semiskilled job a cut or so above that of the unskilled laborer. His take-home pay during these weeks was well over a hundred dollars—"a lot of bread." But for Tally, who no longer had a family to support, bread was not enough.

> "You know that boy came in last night? That Black Moozlem? That's what I ought to be doing. I ought to be in his place."
> "What do you mean?"

2. "[In our society] a man's work is one of the things by which he is judged, and certainly one of the more significant things by which he judges himself. . . . A man's work is one of the more important parts of his social identity, of his self; indeed, of his fate in the one life he has to live." Everett C. Hughes, *Men and Their Work*, pp. 42–43.
3. Noting that lower-class persons "are constantly exposed to evidence of their own irrelevance," Lee Rainwater spells out still another way in which the poor are poor: "The identity problems of lower class persons make the soul-searching of middle class adolescents and adults seem rather like a kind of conspicuous consumption of psychic riches" ("Work and Identity in the Lower Class," p. 3).

"Dressed nice, going to [night] school, got a good job."

"He's no better off than you, Tally. You make more than he does."

"It's not the money. [Pause] It's position, I guess. He's got position. When he finish school he gonna be a supervisor. People respect him. . . . Thinking about people with position and education gives me a feeling right here [pressing his fingers into the pit of his stomach]."

"You're educated, too. You have a skill, a trade. You're a cement finisher. You can make a building, pour a sidewalk."

"That's different. Look, can anybody do what you're doing? Can anybody just come up and do your job? Well, in one week I can teach you cement finishing. You won't be as good as me 'cause you won't have the experience but you'll be a cement finisher. That's what I mean. Anybody can do what I'm doing and that's what gives me this feeling. [Long pause] Suppose I like this girl. I go over to her house and I meet her father. He starts talking about what he done today. He talks about operating on somebody and sewing them up and about surgery. I know he's a doctor 'cause of the way he talks. Then she starts talking about what she did. Maybe she's a boss or a supervisor. Maybe she's a lawyer and her father says to me, 'And what do you do, Mr. Jackson?' [Pause] You remember at the courthouse, Lonny's trial? You and the lawyer was talking in the hall? You remember? I just stood there listening. I didn't say a word. You know why? 'Cause I didn't even know what you was talking about. That's happened to me a lot."

"Hell, you're nothing special. That happens to everybody. Nobody knows everything. One man is a doctor, so he talks about surgery. Another man is a teacher, so he talks about books. But doctors and teachers don't know anything about concrete. You're a cement finisher and that's your specialty."

"Maybe so, but when was the last time you saw anybody standing around talking about concrete?"

The streetcorner man wants to be a person in his own right, to be noticed, to be taken account of, but in this respect, as well as in meeting his money needs, his job fails him. The job and the man are even. The job fails the man and the man fails the job.

Furthermore, the man does not have any reasonable expectation that, however bad it is, his job will lead to better things. Menial jobs are not, by and large, the starting point of a track system which leads to even better jobs for those who are able and willing to do them. The busboy or dishwasher in a restaurant is not on a job track which, if negotiated skillfully, leads to chef or manager of the restaurant. The busboy or dishwasher who works hard becomes, simply, a hard-working busboy or dishwasher. Neither hard work nor perseverance can conceivably carry the janitor to a sitdown job in the office building he cleans up. And it is the apprentice who becomes the journeyman electrician, plumber, steam fitter or bricklayer, not the common unskilled Negro laborer.

Thus, the job is not a stepping stone to something better. It is a dead end. It promises to deliver no more tomorrow, next month or next year than it does today.

Delivering little, and promising no more, the job is "no big thing." The man appears to treat the job in a cavalier fashion, working and not working as the spirit moves him, as if all that matters is the immediate satisfaction of his present appetites, the surrender to present moods, and the indulgence of whims with no thought for the cost, the consequences, the future. To the middle-class observer, this behavior reflects a "present-time orientation"—an "inability to defer gratification." It is this "present-time" orientation—as against the "future orientation" of the middle-class person—that "explains" to the outsider why Leroy chooses to spend the day at the Carry-out rather than report to work; why Richard, who was paid Friday, was drunk Saturday and Sunday and penniless Monday; why Sweets quit his job today because the boss looked at him "funny" yesterday.

But from the inside looking out, what appears as a "present-time" orientation to the outside observer is, to the man experiencing it, as much a future orientation as that of his middle-class counterpart. The difference between the two men lies not so much in their different orientations to time as in their different orientations to future time or, more specifically, to their different futures.

The future orientation of the middle-class person presumes, among other things, a surplus of resources to be invested in the future and a belief that the future will be sufficiently stable both to justify his investment (money in a bank, time and effort in a job, investment of himself in marriage and family, etc.) and to permit the consumption of his investment at a time, place and manner of his own choosing and to his greater satisfaction. But the streetcorner man lives in a sea of want. He does not, as a rule, have a surplus of resources, either economic or psychological. Gratification of hunger and the desire for simple creature comforts cannot be long deferred. Neither can support for one's flagging self-esteem. Living on the edge of both economic and psychological subsistence, the streetcorner man is obliged to expend all his resources on maintaining himself from moment to moment.

As for the future, the young streetcorner man has a fairly good picture of it. In Richard or Sea Cat or Arthur he can see himself in his middle twenties; he can look at Tally to see himself at thirty, at Wee Tom to see himself in his middle thirties, and at Budder and Stanton to see himself in his forties. It is a future in which everything is uncertain except the ultimate destruction of his hopes and the eventual realization of his fears. The most he can reasonably look forward to is that these things do not come too soon. Thus, when Richard squanders a week's pay in two days it is not because, like an animal or a child, he is "present-time oriented," unaware of or unconcerned with his future. He does so precisely because he is aware of the future and the hopelessness of it all. . . .

29
Manifesto of the Communist Party

Karl Marx and Friedrich Engels

Europe in the eighteenth and nineteenth centuries changed dramatically with the onset of industrialization and the phenomenal growth of cities. While some writers saw great promise of abundance and freedom in these changes, the reality for millions of people was increased labor and grinding poverty. Marx and Engels were among the most articulate critics of this disparity between possibility and reality, and they sought to explain the reasons for this in a pamphlet written for Belgian workers from which the following excerpt comes.

I. Bourgeois and Proletarians[1]

The history of all hitherto existing society[2] is the history of class struggles.

Freeman and slave, patrician and plebeian, lord and serf, guild-master[3] and journeyman, in a word, oppressor and oppressed, stood in constant opposition to one another, carried on an uninterrupted, now hidden, now open fight, a fight that each time ended, either in a revolutionary re-constitution of society at large, or in the common ruin of the contending classes.

In the earlier epochs of history, we find almost everywhere a complicated arrangement of society into various orders, a manifold gradation of social rank. In ancient Rome we have patricians, knights, plebeians, slaves; in the Middle Ages, feudal lords, vassals, guild-masters, journey-

---

1. By bourgeoisie is meant the class of modern Capitalists, owners of the means of social production and employers of wage-labour. By proletariat, the class of modern wage-labourers who, having no means of production of their own, are reduced to selling their labour-power in order to live. [*Engels, English edition of 1888*]

2. That is, all *written* history. In 1847, the pre-history of society, the social organisation existing previous to recorded history, was all but unknown. Since then, Haxthausen discovered common ownership of land in Russia, Maurer proved it to be the social foundation from which all Teutonic races started in history, and by and by village communities were found to be, or to have been the primitive form of society everywhere from India to Ireland. The inner organisation of this primitive Communistic society was laid bare, in its typical form, by Morgan's crowning discovery of the true nature of the *gens* and its relation to the *tribe*. With the dissolution of these primaeval communities society begins to be differentiated into separate and finally antagonistic classes. I have attempted to retrace this process of dissolution in: "Der Ursprung der Familie, des Privateigenthums und des Staats" [*The Origin of the Family, Private Property and the State*], 2nd edition, Stuttgart 1886. [*Engels, English edition of 1888*]

3. Guild-master, that is, a full member of a guild, a master within, not a head of a guild. [*Engels, English edition of 1888*]

men, apprentices, serfs; in almost all of these classes, again, subordinate gradations.

The modern bourgeois society that has sprouted from the ruins of feudal society has not done away with class antagonisms. It has but established new classes, new conditions of oppression, new forms of struggle in place of the old ones.

Our epoch, the epoch of the bourgeoisie, possesses, however, this distinctive feature: it has simplified the class antagonisms: Society as a whole is more and more splitting up into two great hostile camps, into two great classes directly facing each other: Bourgeoisie and Proletariat.

From the serfs of the Middle Ages sprang the chartered burghers of the earliest towns. From these burgesses the first elements of the bourgeoisie were developed.

The discovery of America, the rounding of the Cape, opened up fresh ground for the rising bourgeoisie. The East-Indian and Chinese markets, the colonisation of America, trade with the colonies, the increase in the means of exchange and in commodities generally, gave to commerce, to navigation, to industry, an impulse never before known, and thereby, to the revolutionary element in the tottering feudal society, a rapid development.

The feudal system of industry, under which industrial production was monopolised by closed guilds, now no longer sufficed for the growing wants of the new markets. The manufacturing system took its place. The guild-masters were pushed on one side by the manufacturing middle class; division of labour between the different corporate guilds vanished in the face of division of labour in each single workshop.

Meantime the markets kept ever growing, the demand ever rising. Even manufacture no longer sufficed. Thereupon, steam and machinery revolutionised industrial production. The place of manufacture was taken by the giant, Modern Industry, the place of the industrial middle class, by industrial millionaires, the leaders of whole industrial armies, the modern bourgeois.

Modern industry has established the world-market, for which the discovery of America paved the way. This market has given an immense development to commerce, to navigation, to communication by land. This development has, in its turn, reacted on the extension of industry; and in proportion as industry, commerce, navigation, railways extended, in the same proportion the bourgeoisie developed, increased its capital, and pushed into the background every class handed down from the Middle Ages.

We see, therefore, how the modern bourgeoisie is itself the product of a long course of development, of a series of revolutions in the modes of production and of exchange.

Each step in the development of the bourgeoisie was accompanied by a corresponding political advance of that class. An oppressed class under the sway of the feudal nobility, an armed and self-governing association in the mediaeval commune;[4] here independent urban republic (as in Italy and Germany), there taxable "third estate" of the monarchy (as in France), afterwards, in the period of manufacture proper, serving either the semi-feudal or the absolute monarchy as a counterpoise against the nobility, and, in fact, corner-stone of the great monarchies in general, the bourgeoisie has at last, since the establishment of Modern Industry and of the world-market, conquered for itself, in the modern representative State, exclusive political sway. The executive of the modern State is but a committee for managing the common affairs of the whole bourgeoisie.

The bourgeoisie, historically, has played a most revolutionary part.

The bourgeoisie, wherever it has got the upper hand, has put an end to all feudal, patriarchal, idyllic relations. It has pitilessly torn asunder the motley feudal ties that bound man to his "natural superiors," and has left remaining no other nexus between man and man than naked self-interest, than callous "cash payment." It has drowned the most heavenly ecstasies of religious fervour, of chivalrous enthusiasm, of philistine sentimentalism, in the icy water of egotistical calculation. It has resolved personal worth into exchange value, and in place of the numberless indefeasible chartered freedoms, has set up that single, unconscionable freedom—Free Trade. In one word, for exploitation, veiled by religious and political illusions, it has substituted naked, shameless, direct, brutal exploitation.

The bourgeoisie has stripped of its halo every occupation hitherto honoured and looked up to with reverent awe. It has converted the physician, the lawyer, the priest, the poet, the man of science, into its paid wage-labourers.

The bourgeoisie has torn away from the family its sentimental veil, and has reduced the family relation to a mere money relation.

The bourgeoisie has disclosed how it came to pass that the brutal display of vigour in the Middle Ages, which Reactionists so much admire, found its fitting complement in the most slothful indolence. It has been the first to show what man's activity can bring about. It has accomplished wonders far surpassing Egyptian pyramids, Roman aqueducts, and Gothic cathedrals; it has conducted expeditions that put in the shade all former Exoduses of nations and crusades.

The bourgeoisie cannot exist without constantly revolutionising the instruments of production, and thereby the relations of production, and with them the whole relations of society. Conservation of the old modes of production in unaltered form, was, on the contrary, the first condition

---

4. "Commune" was the name taken, in France, by the nascent towns even before they had conquered from their feudal lords and masters local self-government and political rights as the "Third Estate." Generally speaking, for the economical development of the bourgeoisie, England is here taken as the typical country; for its political development, France. [*Engels, English edition of 1888*]

This was the name given their urban communities by the townsmen of Italy and France, after they had purchased or wrested their initial rights of self-government from their feudal lords. [*Engels, German edition of 1890*]

of existence for all earlier industrial classes. Constant revolutionising of production, uninterrupted disturbance of all social conditions, everlasting uncertainty and agitation distinguish the bourgeois epoch from all earlier ones. All fixed, fast-frozen relations, with their train of ancient and venerable prejudices and opinions, are swept away, all new-formed ones become antiquated before they can ossify. All that is solid melts into air, all that is holy is profaned, and man is at last compelled to face with sober senses, his real conditions of life, and his relations with his kind.

The need of a constantly expanding market for its products chases the bourgeoisie over the whole surface of the globe. It must nestle everywhere, settle everywhere, establish connexions everywhere.

The bourgeoisie has through its exploitation of the world-market given a cosmopolitan character to production and consumption in every country. To the great chagrin of Reactionists, it has drawn from under the feet of industry the national ground on which it stood. All old-established national industries have been destroyed or are daily being destroyed. They are dislodged by new industries, whose introduction becomes a life and death question for all civilised nations, by industries that no longer work up indigenous raw material, but raw material drawn from the remotest zones; industries whose products are consumed, not only at home, but in every quarter of the globe. In place of the old wants, satisfied by the productions of the country, we find new wants, requiring for their satisfaction the products of distant lands and climes. In place of the old local and national seclusion and self-sufficiency, we have intercourse in every direction, universal inter-dependence of nations. And as in material, so also in intellectual production. The intellectual creations of individual nations become common property. National one-sidedness and narrow-mindedness become more and more impossible, and from the numerous national and local literatures, there arises a world literature.

The bourgeoisie, by the rapid improvement of all instruments of production, by the immensely facilitated means of communication, draws all, even the most barbarian, nations into civilisation. The cheap prices of its commodities are the heavy artillery with which it batters down all Chinese walls, with which it forces the barbarians' intensely obstinate hatred of foreigners to capitulate. It compels all nations, on pain of extinction, to adopt the bourgeois mode of production; it compels them to introduce what it calls civilisation into their midst, *i.e.*, to become bourgeois themselves. In one word, it creates a world after its own image.

The bourgeoisie has subjected the country to the rule of the towns. It has created enormous cities, has greatly increased the urban population as compared with the rural, and has thus rescued a considerable part of the population from the idiocy of rural life. Just as it has made the country dependent on the towns, so it has made barbarian and semi-barbarian countries dependent on the civilised ones, nations of peasants on nations of bourgeois, the East on the West.

The bourgeoisie keeps more and more doing away with the scattered state of the population, of the means of production, and of property. It has agglomerated population, centralised means of production, and has concentrated property in a few hands. The necessary consequence of this was political centralisation. Independent, or but loosely connected provinces, with separate interests, laws, governments and systems of taxation, became lumped together into one nation, with one government, one code of laws, one national class-interest, one frontier and one customs-tariff.

The bourgeoisie, during its rule of scarce one hundred years, has created more massive and more colossal productive forces than have all preceding generations together. Subjection of Nature's forces to man, machinery, application of chemistry to industry and agriculture, steam-navigation, railways, electric telegraphs, clearing of whole continents for cultivation, canalisation of rivers, whole populations conjured out of the ground—what earlier century had even a presentiment that such productive forces slumbered in the lap of social labour?

We see then: the means of production and of exchange, on whose foundation the bourgeoisie built itself up, were generated in feudal society. At a certain stage in the development of these means of production and of exchange, the conditions under which feudal society produced and exchanged, the feudal organisation of agriculture and manufacturing industry, in one word, the feudal relations of property became no longer compatible with the already developed productive forces; they became so many fetters. They had to be burst asunder; they were burst asunder.

Into their place stepped free competition, accompanied by a social and political constitution adapted to it, and by the economical and political sway of the bourgeois class.

A similar movement is going on before our own eyes. Modern bourgeois society with its relations of production, of exchange and of property, a society that has conjured up such gigantic means of production and of exchange, is like the sorcerer, who is no longer able to control the powers of the nether world whom he has called up by his spells. For many a decade past the history of industry and commerce is but the history of the revolt of modern productive forces against modern conditions of production, against the property relations that are the conditions for the existence of the bourgeoisie and of its rule. It is enough to mention the commercial crises that by their periodical return put on its trial, each time more threateningly, the existence of the entire bourgeois society. In these crises a great part not only of the existing products, but also of the previously created productive forces, are periodically destroyed. In these crises there breaks out an epidemic that, in all earlier epochs, would have seemed an absurdity—the epidemic of over-production. Society suddenly finds itself put back into a state of momentary barbarism; it appears as if a famine, a universal war of devastation had cut off the supply of every means of subsistence; industry and commerce seem to be destroyed; and why? Because there is too much civilisation, too much means of subsistence, too much industry, too much commerce. The productive forces at the disposal of society no longer tend to further the development of the conditions of bourgeois property; on the contrary, they have become too powerful for these conditions, by which they are fettered, and so soon as they overcome these fetters, they bring disorder into the whole of bourgeois society, endanger the existence of bourgeois property. The conditions of bourgeois society are too narrow to comprise the wealth created by them. And how does the bourgeoisie get over these crises? On the one hand by enforced destruction of a mass of productive forces; on the other, by the conquest of new markets, and by the more thorough exploitation of the old ones. That is to say, by paving the way for more extensive and more destructive crises, and by diminishing the means whereby crises are prevented.

The weapons with which the bourgeoisie felled feudalism to the ground are now turned against the bourgeoisie itself.

But not only has the bourgeoisie forged the weapons that bring death to itself; it has also called into existence the men who are to wield those weapons—the modern working class—the proletarians.

In proportion as the bourgeoisie, *i.e.*, capital, is developed, in the same proportion is the proletariat, the modern working class, developed—a class of labourers, who live only so long as they find work, and who find work only so long as their labour increases capital. These labourers, who must sell themselves piece-meal, are a commodity, like every other article of commerce, and are consequently exposed to all the vicissitudes of competition, to all the fluctuations of the market.

Owing to the extensive use of machinery and to division of labour, the work of the proletarians has lost all individual character, and consequently, all charm for the workman. He becomes an appendage of the machine, and it is only the most simple, most monotonous, and most easily acquired knack, that is required of him. Hence, the cost of production of a workman is restricted, almost entirely, to the means of subsistence that he requires for his maintenance, and for the propagation of his race. But the price of a commodity, and therefore also of labour,[5] is equal to its cost of production. In proportion, therefore, as the repulsiveness of the work increases, the wage decreases. Nay more, in proportion as the use of machinery and division of labour increases, in the same proportion the burden of toil also increases, whether by prolon-

5. Subsequently Marx pointed out that the worker sells not his labour but his labour power.

gation of the working hours, by increase of the work exacted in a given time or by increased speed of the machinery, etc.

Modern industry has converted the little workshop of the patriarchal master into the great factory of the industrial capitalist. Masses of labourers, crowded into the factory, are organised like soldiers. As privates of the industrial army they are placed under the command of a perfect hierarchy of officers and sergeants. Not only are they slaves of the bourgeois class, and of the bourgeois State; they are daily and hourly enslaved by the machine, by the over-looker, and, above all, by the individual bourgeois manufacturer himself. The more openly this despotism proclaims gain to be its end and aim, the more petty, the more hateful and the more embittering it is.

The less the skill and exertion of strength implied in manual labour, in other words, the more modern industry becomes developed, the more is the labour of men superseded by that of women. Differences of age and sex have no longer any distinctive social validity for the working class. All are instruments of labour, more or less expensive to use, according to their age and sex.

No sooner is the exploitation of the labourer by the manufacturer, so far, at an end, that he receives his wages in cash, than he is set upon by the other portions of the bourgeoisie, the landlord, the shopkeeper, the pawnbroker, etc.

The lower strata of the middle class—the small tradespeople, shopkeepers, and retired tradesmen generally, the handicraftsmen and peasants—all these sink gradually into the proletariat, partly because their diminutive capital does not suffice for the scale on which Modern Industry is carried on, and is swamped in the competition with the large capitalists, partly because their specialised skill is rendered worthless by new methods of production. Thus the proletariat is recruited from all classes of the population.

The proletariat goes through various stages of development. With its birth begins its struggle with the bourgeoisie. At first the contest is carried on by individual labourers, then by the workpeople of a factory, then by the operatives of one trade, in one locality, against the individual bourgeois who directly exploits them. They direct their attacks not against the bourgeois conditions of production, but against the instruments of production themselves; they destroy imported wares that compete with their labour, they smash to pieces machinery, they set factories ablaze, they seek to restore by force the vanished status of the workman of the Middle Ages.

At this stage the labourers still form an incoherent mass scattered over the whole country, and broken up by their mutual competition. If anywhere they unite to form more compact bodies, this is not yet the consequence of their own active union, but of the union of the bourgeoisie, which class, in order to attain its own political ends, is compelled to set the whole proletariat in motion, and is moreover yet, for a time, able to do so. At this stage, therefore, the proletarians do not fight their enemies, but the enemies of their enemies, the remnants of absolute monarchy, the landowners, the non-industrial bourgeois, the petty bourgeoisie. Thus the whole historical movement is concentrated in the hands of the bourgeoisie; every victory so obtained is a victory for the bourgeoisie.

But with the development of industry the proletariat not only increases in number; it becomes concentrated in greater masses, its strength grows, and it feels that strength more. The various interests and conditions of life within the ranks of the proletariat are more and more equalised, in proportion as machinery obliterates all distinctions of labour, and nearly everywhere reduces wages to the same low level. The growing competition among the bourgeois, and the resulting commercial crises, make the wages of the workers ever more fluctuating. The unceasing improvement of machinery, ever more rapidly developing, makes their livelihood more and more precarious; the collisions between individual workmen and individual bourgeois take more and more the character of collisions between two classes. Thereupon the workers begin to form combinations (Trades Unions) against the bourgeois; they club together in order to keep up the rate of wages; they found permanent associations in order to make provision beforehand for these occasional revolts. Here and there the contest breaks out into riots.

Now and then the workers are victorious, but only for a time. The real fruit of their battles lies, not in the immediate result, but in the ever-expanding union of the workers. This union is helped on by the improved means of communication that are created by modern industry and that place the workers of different localities in contact with one another. It was just this contact that was needed to centralise the numerous local struggles, all of the same character, into one national struggle between classes. But every class struggle is a political struggle. And that union, to attain which the burghers of the Middle Ages, with their miserable highways, required centuries, the modern proletarians, thanks to railways, achieve in a few years.

This organisation of the proletarians into a class, and consequently into a political party, is continually being upset again by the competition between the workers themselves. But it ever rises up again, stronger, firmer, mightier. It compels legislative recognition of particular interests of the workers, by taking advantage of the divisions among the bourgeoisie itself. Thus the ten-hours' bill in England was carried.

Altogether collisions between the classes of the old society further, in many ways, the course of development of the proletariat. The bourgeoisie finds itself involved in a constant battle. At first with the aristocracy; later on, with those portions of the bourgeoisie itself, whose interests have become antagonistic to the progress of industry; at all times, with the bourgeoisie of foreign countries. In all these battles it sees itself compelled to appeal to the proletariat, to ask for its help, and thus, to drag it into the political arena. The bourgeoisie itself, therefore, supplies the proletariat with its own elements of political and general education, in other words, it furnishes the proletariat with weapons for fighting the bourgeoisie.

Further, as we have already seen, entire sections of the ruling classes are, by the advance of industry, precipitated into the proletariat, or are at least threatened in their conditions of existence. These also supply the proletariat with fresh elements of enlightenment and progress.

Finally, in times when the class struggle nears the decisive hour, the process of dissolution going on within the ruling class, in fact within the whole range of society, assumes such a violent, glaring character, that a small section of the ruling class cuts itself adrift, and joins the revolutionary class, the class that holds the future in its hands. Just as, therefore, at an earlier period, a section of the nobility went over to the bourgeoisie, so now a portion of the bourgeoisie goes over to the proletariat, and in particular, a portion of the bourgeois ideologists, who have raised themselves to the level of comprehending theoretically the historical movement as a whole.

Of all the classes that stand face to face with the bourgeoisie today, the proletariat alone is a really revolutionary class. The other classes decay and finally disappear in the face of Modern Industry; the proletariat is its special and essential product.

The lower middle class, the small manufacturer, the shopkeeper, the artisan, the peasant, all these fight against the bourgeoisie, to save from extinction their existence as fractions of the middle class. They are therefore not revolutionary, but conservative. Nay more, they are reactionary, for they try to roll back the wheel of history. If by chance they are revolutionary, they are so only in view of their impending transfer into the proletariat, they thus defend not their present, but their future interests, they desert their own standpoint to place themselves at that of the proletariat.

The "dangerous class," the social scum, that passively rotting mass thrown off by the lowest layers of old society, may, here and there, be swept into the movement by a proletarian revolution; its conditions of life, however, prepare it far more for the part of a bribed tool of reactionary intrigue.

In the conditions of the proletariat, those of old society at large are already virtually swamped. The proletarian is without property; his relation to his wife and children has no longer anything in common with the bourgeois family-relations; modern industrial labour, modern subjection to capital, the same in England as in France, in America as in Germany, has stripped him of every trace of national character. Law, morality, religion, are to him so many bourgeois prejudices, behind which lurk in ambush just as many bourgeois interests.

All the preceding classes that got the upper hand, sought to fortify their already acquired status by subjecting society at large to their conditions of appropriation. The proletarians cannot become masters of the productive forces of society, except by abolishing their own previous mode of appropriation, and thereby also every other previous mode of appropriation. They have nothing of their own to secure and to fortify; their mission is to destroy all previous securities for, and insurances of, individual property.

All previous historical movements were movements of minorities, or in the interests of minorities. The proletarian movement is the self-conscious, independent movement of the immense majority, in the interests of the immense majority. The proletariat, the lowest stratum of our present society, cannot stir, cannot raise itself up, without the whole super-incumbent strata of official society being sprung into the air.

Though not in substance, yet in form, the struggle of the proletariat with the bourgeoisie is at first a national struggle. The proletariat of each country must, of course, first of all settle matters with its own bourgeoisie.

In depicting the most general phases of the development of the proletariat, we traced the more or less veiled civil war, raging within existing society, up to the point where that war breaks out into open revolution, and where the violent overthrow of the bourgeoisie lays the foundation for the sway of the proletariat.

Hitherto, every form of society has been based, as we have already seen, on the antagonism of oppressing and oppressed classes. But in order to oppress a class, certain conditions must be assured to it under which it can, at least, continue its slavish existence. The serf, in the period of serfdom, raised himself to membership in the commune, just as the petty bourgeois, under the yoke of feudal absolutism, managed to develop into a bourgeois. The modern labourer, on the contrary, instead of rising with the progress of industry, sinks deeper and deeper below the conditions of existence of his own class. He becomes a pauper, and pauperism develops more rapidly than population and wealth. And here it becomes evident, that the bourgeoisie is unfit any longer to be the ruling class in society, and to impose its conditions of existence upon society as an over-riding law. It is unfit to rule because it is incompetent to assure an existence to its slave within his slavery, because it cannot help letting him sink into such a state, that it has to feed him, instead of being fed by him. Society can no longer live under this bourgeoisie, in other words, its existence is no longer compatible with society.

The essential condition for the existence, and for the sway of the bourgeois class, is the formation and augmentation of capital; the condition for capital is wage-labour. Wage-labour rests exclusively on competition between the labourers. The advance of industry, whose involuntary promoter is the bourgeoisie, replaces the isolation of the labourers, due to competition, by their revolutionary combination, due to association. The development of Modern Industry, therefore, cuts from under its feet the very foundation on which the bourgeoisie produces and appropriates products. What the bourgeoisie, therefore, produces, above all, is its own grave-diggers. Its fall and the victory of the proletariat are equally inevitable.

30
On Becoming a Chicano

RICHARD RODRIGUEZ

It is sometimes hard for members of a society's dominant group to understand the feelings of minority persons who say that they have faced discrimination and prejudice. While it might be easier to disclaim one's "differences" and seek acceptance through conformity, the author describes how he took another path.

Today I am only technically the person I once felt myself to be—a Mexican-American, a Chicano. Partly because I had no way of comprehending my racial identity except in this technical sense, I gave up long ago the cultural consequences of being a Chicano.

The change came gradually but early. When I was beginning grade school, I noted to myself the fact that the classroom environment was so different in its styles and assumptions from my own family environment that survival would essentially entail a choice between both worlds. When I became a student, I was literally "remade"; neither I nor my teachers considered anything I had known before as relevant. I had to forget most of what my culture had provided, because to remember it was a disadvantage. The past and its cultural values became detachable, like a piece of clothing grown heavy on a warm day and finally put away.

Strangely, the discovery that I have been inattentive to my cultural past has arisen because others—students, colleagues and faculty members—have started to assume that I am a Chicano. The ease with which the assumption is made forces me to suspect that the label is not meant to suggest cultural, but racial, identity. Nonetheless, as a graduate student and a prospective university faculty member, I am routinely expected to assume intellectual leadership *as a member of a racial minority*. Recently, for example, I heard the moderator of a panel discussion introduce me as "Richard Rodriguez, a Chicano intellectual." I wanted to correct the speaker—because I felt guilty representing a nonacademic cultural tradition that I had willingly abandoned. So I can only guess what it would have meant to have retained my culture as I entered the classroom, what it would mean for me to be today a *Chicano intellectual*. (The two words juxtaposed excite me; for years I thought a Chicano had to decide between being one or the other.)

Does the fact that I barely spoke any English until I was nine, or that as a child I felt a surge of *self*-hatred whenever a passing teenager would yell a racial slur, or that I saw my skin darken each summer—do any of these facts shape the ideas which I have or am capable of having? Today, I suspect they do—in ways I doubt the moderator who referred to me as a "Chicano intellectual" intended. The peculiar status of being a "Chicano intellectual" makes me grow restless at the thought that I have lost at least as much as I have gained through education.

I remember when, 20 years ago, two grammar-school nuns visited my childhood home. They had come to suggest—with more tact than was necessary, because my parents accepted without question the church's authority—that we make a greater effort to speak as much English around the house as possible. The nuns realized that my brothers and I led solitary lives largely because we were barely able to comprehend English in a school where we were the only Spanish-speaking students. My mother and father complied as best they could. Heroically, they gave up speaking to us in Spanish—the language that formed so much of the family's sense of intimacy in an alien world—and began to speak a broken English. Instead of Spanish sounds, I began hearing sounds that were new, harder, less friendly. More important, I was encouraged to respond in English.

The change in language was the most dramatic and obvious indication that I would become very much like the "gringo"—a term which was used descriptively rather than pejoratively in my home—and unlike the Spanish-speaking relatives who largely constituted my preschool world. Gradually, Spanish became a sound freighted with only a kind of sentimental significance, like the sound of the bedroom clock I listened to in my aunt's house when I spent the night. Just as gradually, English became the language I came not to *hear* because it was the language I used every day, as I gained access to a new, larger society. But the memory of Spanish persisted as a reminder of the society I had left. I can remember occasions when I entered a room and my parents were speaking to one another in Spanish, seeing me, they shifted into their more formalized English. Hearing them speak to me in English troubled me. The bonds their voices once secured were loosened by the new tongue.

This is not to suggest that I was being *forced* to give up my Chicano past. After the initial awkwardness of transition, I committed myself, fully and freely, to the culture of the classroom. Soon what I was learning in school was so antithetical to what my parents knew and did that I was careful about the way I talked about myself at the evening dinner table. Occasionally, there were moments of childish cruelty: a son's condescending to instruct either one of his parents about a "simple" point of English pronunciation or grammar.

Social scientists often remark, about situations such as mine, that children feel a sense of loss as they move away from their working-class identifications and models. Certainly, what I experienced, others have also—whatever their race. Like other generations of, say, Polish-American or Irish-American children coming home from college, I was to know the silence that ensues so quickly after the quick exchange of news and the dwindling of common interests.

In addition, however, education seemed to mean not only a gradual dissolving of familial and class ties but also a change of racial identity. The new language I spoke was only the most obvious reason for my associating the classroom with "gringo" society. The society I knew as Chicano was barely literate—in English *or* Spanish—and so impatient with either prolonged reflection or abstraction that I found the academic environment a sharp contrast. Sharpening the contrast was the stereotype of the Mexican as a mental inferior. (The fear of this stereotype has been so deep that only recently have I been willing to listen to those, like D. H. Lawrence, who celebrate the "noncerebral" Mexican as an alternative to the rational and scientific European man.) Because I did not know how to distinguish the healthy nonrationality of Chicano culture from the mental incompetency of which Chicanos were unjustly accused, I was willing to abandon my nonmental skills in order to disprove the racist's stereotype.

I was wise enough not to feel proud of the person education had helped me to become. I knew that education had led me to repudiate my race. I was frequently labeled a *pocho*, a Mexican with gringo pretensions, not only because I could not speak Spanish but also because I would respond in English with precise and careful sentences. Uncles would laugh good-naturedly, but I detected scorn in their voices. For my grandmother, the least assimilated of my relations, the changes in her grandson since entering school were especially troubling. She remains today a dark and silently critical figure in my memory, a reminder of the Mexican-Indian ancestry that somehow my educational success has violated.

Nonetheless, I became more comfortable reading or writing careful prose than talking to a kitchen filled with listeners, withdrawing from situations to reflect on their significance rather than grasping for meaning at the scene. I remember, one August evening, slipping away from a gathering of aunts and uncles in the backyard, going into a bedroom tenderly lighted by a late sun, and opening a novel about life in nineteenth-century England. There, by an open window, reading, I was barely conscious of the sounds of laughter outside.

With so few fellow Chicanos in the university, I had no chance to develop an alternative consciousness. When I spent occasional weekends tutoring lower-class Chicano teenagers or when I talked with Mexican-American janitors and maids around the campus, there was a kind of sympathy—a sense, however privately held—that we knew something about one another. But I regarded them all primarily as people from my past. The maids reminded me of my aunts (similarly employed); the students I tutored reminded me of my cousins (who also spoke English with barrio accents).

When I was young, I was taught to refer to my ancestry as Mexican-American. *Chicano* was a word used among friends or relatives. It implied a familiarity based on shared experience. Spoken casually, the term easily became an insult. In 1968 the word *Chicano* was about to become a political term. I heard it shouted into microphones as Third World groups agitated for increased student and faculty representation in higher education. It was not long before I *became* a Chicano in the eyes of students and faculty members. My racial identity was assumed for only the simplest reasons: my skin color and last name.

On occasion I was asked to account for my interests in Renaissance English literature. When I explained them, declaring a need for cultural assimilation on the campus, my listener would disagree. I sensed suspicion on the part of a number of my fellow minority students. When I could not imitate Spanish pronunciations of the dialect of the barrio, when I was plainly uninterested in wearing ethnic costumes and could not master a special handshake the minority students often used with one another, they knew I was different. And I was. I was assimilated into the culture of a graduate department of English. As a result, I watched how in less than five years nearly every minority graduate student I knew dropped out of school, largely for cultural reasons. Often they didn't understand the value of analyzing literature in professional jargon, which others around them readily adopted. Nor did they move as readily to lofty heights of abstraction. They became easily depressed by the seeming uselessness of the talk they heard around them. "It's not for real," I still hear a minority student murmur to herself and perhaps to me, shaking her head slowly, as we sat together in a class listening to a discussion on punctuation in a Renaissance epic.

I survived—thanks to the accommodation I had made long before. In fact, I prospered, partly as a result of the political movement designed to increase the enrollment of minority students less assimilated than I in higher education. Suddenly grants, fellowships, and teaching offers became abundant.

In 1972 I went to England on a Fulbright scholarship. I hoped the months of brooding about racial identity were behind me. I wanted to concentrate on my dissertation, which the distractions of an American campus had not permitted. But the freedom I anticipated did not last for long. Barely a month after I had begun working regularly in the reading room of the British Museum, I was surprised, and even frightened, to have to acknowledge that I was not at ease living the rarefied life of the academic. With my pile of research file cards growing taller, the mass of secondary materials and opinions was making it harder for me to say anything original about my subject. Every sentence I wrote, every thought I had, became so loaded with qualifications and footnotes, that it said very little. My scholarship became little more than an exercise in caution. I had an accompanying suspicion that whatever I did manage to write and call my dissertation would be of little use. Opening books so dusty that they must not have been used in decades, I began to doubt the value of writing what only a few people would read.

Obviously, I was going through the fairly typical crisis of the American graduate student. But with one difference: After four years of involvement with questions of racial identity, I now saw my problems as a scholar in the context of the cultural issues that had been raised by my racial situation. So much of what my work in the British Museum lacked, my parents' culture possessed. They were people not afraid to generalize or to find insights in their generalities. More important, they had the capacity to make passionate statements, something I was beginning to doubt my dissertation would ever allow me to do. I needed to learn how to trust the use of "I" in my writing the way they trusted its use in their speech. Thus developed a persistent yearning for the very Chicano culture that I had abandoned as useless.

Feelings of depression came occasionally but forcefully. Some days I found my work so oppressive that I had to leave the reading room and stroll through the museum. One afternoon, appropriately enough, I found myself in an upstairs gallery containing Mayan and Aztec sculptures. Even there the sudden yearning for a Chicano past seemed available to me only as nostalgia. One morning, as I was reading a book about Puritan autobiography, I overhead two Spaniards whispering to one another. I did not hear what they said, but I did hear the sound of their Spanish—and it embraced me, filling my mind with swirling images of a past long abandoned.

I returned from England, disheartened, a few months later. My dissertation was coming along well, but I did not know whether I wanted to submit it. Worse, I did not know whether I wanted a career in higher education. I detested the prospect of spending the rest of my life in libraries and classrooms, in touch with my past only through the binoculars nostalgia makes available. I knew that I could not simply re-create a version of what I would have been like had I not become an academic. There was no possibility of going back. But if the culture of my birth was to survive, it would have to animate my academic work. That was the lesson of the British Museum.

I frankly do not know how my academic autobiography will end. Sometimes I think I will have to leave the campus, in order to reconcile my past and present. Other times, more optimistically, I think that a kind of negative reconciliation is already in progress, that I can make creative use of my sense of loss. For instance, with my sense of the cleavage between past and present, I can, as a literary critic, identify issues in Renaissance pastoral—a literature which records the feelings of the courtly when confronted by the alternatives of rural and rustic life. And perhaps I can speak with unusual feeling about the price we must pay, or have paid, as a rational society for confessing seventeenth-century Cartesian faiths. Likewise, because of my sense of cultural loss, I may be able to identify more readily than another the ways in which language has meaning simply as sound and what the printed word can and cannot give us. At the very least, I can point up the academy's tendency to ignore the cultures beyond its own horizons.

31
American Apartheid: Segregation and the Making of the Underclass

Douglas S. Massey and Nancy A. Denton

African-Americans experienced an escalation of racial intolerance and discriminatory practices in the latter half of the nineteenth century. The upsurge of Jim Crow (segregation and exclusion) legislation and the systematic use of violence after 1890 erected features of American society that ensured the denial of equal rights to African-Americans well into the twentieth century. The authors show how the forces of industrial expansion, antilabor strategies, violence, and institutional racism combined to create the racially segregated urban landscape that continues to exist today.

Creating the Ghetto, 1900–1940

The era of integrated living and widespread interracial contact was rapidly effaced in American cities after 1900 because of two developments: the industrialization of America and the concomitant movement of blacks from farms to cities. The pace of change was most rapid in the north, not only because industrialization was quicker and more complete there, but also because the south's Jim Crow system provided an effective alternative to the ghetto in bringing about the subjugation of blacks. Moreover, the interspersed pattern of black and white settlement in southern cities carried with it a physical inertia that retarded the construction of the ghetto.

Industrialization in the north unleashed a set of social, economic, and technological changes that dramatically altered the urban environment in ways that promoted segregation between social groups. Before industrialization, production occurred primarily in the home or small shop, but by the turn of the century manufacturing had shifted decisively to large factories that employed hundreds of laborers. Individual plants clustered in extensive manufacturing districts together demanded thousands of workers. Dense clusters of tenements and row houses were constructed near these districts to house the burgeoning work force.

The new demand for labor could not be met by native white urbanites alone, so employers turned to migrants of diverse origins. Before World War I, the demand for unskilled labor was met primarily by rural immigrants from southern and eastern Europe. Their migration was guided and structured by social networks that connected them to relatives and friends who had arrived earlier. Drawing upon the ties of kinship and common community origin, the new migrants obtained jobs and housing in U.S. cities, and in this way members of specific ethnic groups were channeled to particular neighborhoods and factories.

At the same time, the need to oversee industrial production—and to administer the wealth it created—brought about a new managerial class composed primarily of native white Americans. As their affluence increased, the retail sector also expanded dramatically. Both administration and retail sales depended on face-to-face interaction, which put a premium on spatial proximity and high population densities. The invention of structural steel and mechanical elevators allowed cities to expand upward in skyscrapers, which were grouped into central business districts that brought thousands of people into regular daily contact. The development of efficient urban rail systems permitted the city to expand outward, creating new residential districts in suburban areas to house the newly affluent class of middle-class managers and service workers.

These developments brought about an unprecedented increase in urban social segregation. Not only was class segregation heightened, but the "new" immigrant groups—Jews, Poles, Italians, Czechs—experienced far more segregation from native whites than did the "old" immigrant groups of Irish and Germans. Whereas European immigrant segregation, as measured by the index of dissimilarity, rarely exceeded 50 before 1870, after the turn of the century values in the range of 50 to 65 were common.

Southern blacks also formed part of the stream of migrants to American cities, but until 1890 the flow was relatively small; only 70,000 blacks left the south during the 1870s and 80,000 departed during the 1880s. In contrast, the number of European immigrants ran into the millions in both decades. Immigration, however, was cyclical and strongly affected by economic conditions abroad. When the demand for labor in European cities was strong, migration to the United States fell, and when European demand flagged, immigration to the United States rose.

This periodic ebb and flow of European immigration created serious structural problems for American employers, particularly when boom periods in Europe and America coincided. When this occurred, European migrants moved to their own industrial cities and U.S. factories had difficulty attracting new workers. Periodic labor shortages caused northern employers to turn to domestic sources of labor, especially migrants from American rural areas and particularly those in the south. Thus black migration to northern cities oscillated inversely with the ebb and flow of European immigration.

But northern employers also found another reason to employ southern blacks, for by the turn of the century, they had discovered their utility as strikebreakers. Blacks were repeatedly employed in this capacity in northern labor disputes between 1890 and 1930: black strikebreakers were used seven times in New York between 1895 and 1916, and were employed in Cleveland in 1896, in Detroit in 1919, in Milwaukee in 1922, and in Chicago in 1904 and 1905. Poor rural blacks with little understanding of industrial conditions and no experience with unions were recruited in the south and transported directly to northern factories, often on special trains arranged by factory owners.

The association of blacks with strikebreaking was bound to earn them the enmity of white workers, but discrimination against blacks by labor unions cannot be attributed to this animosity alone. European groups had also been used as strikebreakers, but labor leaders overcame these attempts at union-busting by incorporating each new wave of immigrants into the labor movement. Unions never employed this strategy with southern blacks, however. From the start, African Americans suffered unusually severe discrimination from white unions simply because they were black.

Most of the skilled crafts unions within the American Federation of Labor, for example, excluded blacks until the 1930s; and the Congress of Industrial Organizations accepted blacks only grudgingly, typically within segregated Jim Crow locals that received poorer contracts and lower priorities in job assignments. Being denied access to the benefits of white unions, blacks had little to lose from crossing picket lines, thereby setting off a cycle of ongoing mutual hostility and distrust between black and white workers.

Black out-migration from the south grew steadily from the end of the nineteenth century into the first decades of the new century. During the 1890s, some 174,000 blacks left the south, and this number rose to 197,000 between 1900 and 1910. The event that transformed the stream into a flood, however, was the outbreak of World War I in 1914. The war both increased the demand for U.S. industrial production and cut off the flow of European immigrants, northern factories' traditional source of labor. In response, employers began a spirited recruitment of blacks from the rural south.

The arrival of the recruiters in the south coincided with that of the Mexican boll weevil, which had devastated Louisiana's cotton crops in 1906 before moving on to Mississippi in 1913 and Alabama in 1916. The collapse of southern agriculture was aggravated by a series of disastrous floods in 1915 and 1916 and low cotton prices up to 1914. In response, southern planters shifted production from cotton to food crops and livestock, both of which required fewer workers. Thus the demand for black tenant farmers and day laborers fell just when the need for unskilled workers in northern cities skyrocketed.

This coincidence of push and pull factors increased the level of black out-migration to new heights and greatly augmented the black populations of Chicago, Detroit, Cleveland, Philadelphia, and New York. Between 1910 and 1920, some 525,000 African Americans left their traditional homes in the south and took up life in the north, and during the 1920s the outflow reached 877,000. This migration gradually acquired a dynamic of its own, as established migrants found jobs and housing for their friends and relatives back home. At the same time, northern black newspapers such as the *Chicago Defender*, which were widely read in the south, exhorted southern blacks to escape their oppression and move northward. As a result of this dynamic, black out-migration from the south continued at a substantial rate even during the Great Depression.

Northern whites viewed this rising tide of black migration with increasing hostility and considerable alarm. Middle-class whites were repelled by what they saw as the uncouth manners, unclean habits, slothful appearance, and illicit behavior of poorly educated, poverty-stricken migrants who had only recently been sharecroppers, and a resurgence of white racist ideology during the 1920s provided a theoretical, "scientific" justification for these feelings. Working-class whites, for their part, feared economic competition from the newcomers; and being first- or second-generation immigrants who were themselves scorned by native whites, they reaffirmed their own "whiteness" by oppressing a people that was even lower in the racial hierarchy. Blacks in the early twentieth century frequently said that the first English word an immigrant learned was "nigger."

As the size of the urban black population rose steadily after 1900, white racial views hardened and the relatively fluid and open period of race relations in the north drew to a close. Northern newspapers increasingly used terms such as "nigger" and "darkey" in print and carried unflattering stories about black crimes and vice. After decades of relatively integrated education, white parents increasingly refused to enroll their children in schools that included blacks. Doors that had permitted extensive interracial contact among the elite suddenly slammed shut as black professionals lost white clients, associates, and friends.

The most dramatic harbinger of the new regime in race relations was the upsurge in racial violence. In city after northern city, a series of communal riots broke out between 1900 and 1920 in the wake of massive black migration. Race riots struck New York City in 1900; Evansville, Indiana, in 1903; Springfield, Illinois, in 1908; East St. Louis, Illinois, in 1917; and Chicago in 1919. In each case, individual blacks were attacked because of the color of their skin. Those living away from recognized "black" neighborhoods had their houses ransacked or burned. Those unlucky or unwise enough to be caught trespassing in "white" neighborhoods were beaten, shot, or lynched. Blacks on their way to work were pulled from trolleys and pummeled. Rampaging bands of whites roamed the streets for days, attacking blacks at will. Although most of the rioters were white, most of the arrests, and nearly all of the victims, were black.

As the tide of violence rose in northern cities, blacks were increasingly divided from whites by a hardening color line in employment, education, and especially housing. Whites became increasingly intolerant of black neighbors and fear of racial turnover and black "invasion" spread. Those blacks living away from recognized Negro areas were forced to move into expanding "black belts," "darkytowns," "Bronzevilles," or "Niggertowns." Well-educated, middle-class blacks of the old elite found themselves increasingly lumped together with poorly educated, impoverished migrants from the rural south; and well-to-do African Americans were progressively less able to find housing commensurate with their social status. In white eyes, black people belonged in black neighborhoods no matter what their social or economic standing; the color line grew increasingly impermeable.

Thus levels of residential segregation between blacks and whites began a steady rise at the turn of the century that would last for sixty years. . . .

The progressive segregation of blacks continued in subsequent decades, and by World War II the foundations of the modern ghetto had been laid in virtually every northern city. . . .

With a rapidly growing black population being accommodated by an ever-smaller number of neighborhoods and an increasingly uneven residential configuration, the only possible outcome was an increase in the spatial isolation of blacks. . . . Chicago led the way. . . . As of 1930 the typical black Chicagoan lived in a neighborhood that was over two-thirds black. That the level of black racial isolation also rose in other cities indicated the growth of more incipient ghettos. . . .

The increasing ghettoization of blacks was not simply a result of their growing numbers. Stanley Lieberson has clearly demonstrated that the segregation of blacks in the urban north increased after 1900 not only because their share of the population grew but because the same racial composition led to more isolation than it had during earlier periods. As the new century wore on, areas of acceptable black residence became more and more narrowly circumscribed: the era of the ghetto had begun.

Migration and industrial development also segregated the "new" European immigrant groups, of course, but recent studies have made it clear that immigrant enclaves in the early twentieth century were in no way comparable to the black ghetto that formed in most northern cities by 1940. To be sure, certain neighborhoods could be identified as "Italian," "Polish," or "Jewish"; but these ethnic enclaves differed from black ghettos in three fundamental ways.

First, unlike black ghettos, immigrant enclaves were never homogeneous and always contained a wide variety of nationalities, even if they were publicly associated with a particular national origin group. In

Chicago's "Magyar district" of 1901, for example, twenty-two different ethnic groups were present and only 37% of all family heads were Magyar (26% were Polish). Similarly, an 1893 color-coded block map of Chicago's West Side prepared by the U.S. Department of Labor showed the location of European ethnic groups using eighteen separate colors. The result was a huge rainbow in which no block contained a single color. The average number of colors per block was eight, and four out of five *lots* within blocks were mixed. In none of the "Little Italys" identified on the map was there an all-Italian block.

The myth of the immigrant ghetto was perpetuated by Ernest Burgess, a founder of the "Chicago School" of urban sociology. In 1933 he published a well-known map showing the spatial location Chicago's various immigrant groups. On it, he identified specific German, Irish, Italian, Russian, Polish, Swedish, and Czech "ghettos." A closer examination of these data by Thomas Philpott, however, revealed that Burgess's immigrant "ghettos" were more fictive than real. The average number of nationalities per ghetto was twenty-two, ranging from twenty in ostensibly Italian and Czech neighborhoods to twenty-five in areas that were theoretically Irish, German, and Swedish. In none of these "ghettos" did the ghettoized group constitute even a bare majority of the population, with the sole exception of Poles, who comprised 54% of their enclave. In areas that Burgess identified as being part of the black ghetto, however, blacks comprised 82% of the population.

A second crucial distinction is that most European ethnics did not live in immigrant "ghettos," as ethnically diluted as they were. Burgess's Irish ghetto contained only 3% of Chicago's Irish population, and only 50% of the city's Italian lived in the "Little Italys" he identified. Only among Poles did a majority, 61%, live in neighborhoods that were identified as being part of the Polish enclave. In contrast, 93% of Chicago's black population lived within the black ghetto.

Thus even at the height of their segregation early in this century, European ethnic groups did not experience a particularly high degree of isolation from American society, even in 1910 at the end of the peak decade of European immigration. . . .

The last difference between immigrant enclaves and black ghettos is that whereas ghettos became a permanent feature of black residential life, ethnic enclaves proved to be a fleeting, transitory stage in the process of immigrant assimilation. The degree of segregation and spatial isolation among European ethnic groups fell steadily after 1910, as native-born children of immigrants experienced less segregation than their parents and as spatial isolation decreased progressively with socioeconomic advancement. For European immigrants, enclaves were places of absorption, adaptation, and adjustment to American society. They served as springboards for broader mobility in society, whereas blacks were trapped behind an increasingly impermeable color line.

The emergence of severe racial segregation in the north was not primarily a reflection of black housing preferences or a natural outcome of migration processes. On the contrary, as the ghetto walls grew thicker and higher, well-to-do class blacks complained bitterly and loudly about their increasing confinement within crowded, dilapidated neighborhoods inhabited by people well below their social and economic status. Although they fought the construction of the ghetto as best they could, the forces arrayed against them proved to be overwhelming.

Foremost among the tools that whites used to construct the ghetto was violence. The initial impetus for ghetto formation came from a wave of racial violence, already noted, that swept over northern cities in the period between 1900 and 1920. These disturbances were communal in nature, and victims were singled out strictly on the basis of skin color. As history has repeatedly shown, during periods of communal strife, the only safety is in numbers. Blacks living in integrated or predominantly white areas—or even simply traveling through white areas to their own homes—proved to be extremely vulnerable.

Blacks that survived these attacks were loath to return to their former dwellings where they feared (correctly) that they would be subject to further violence. Following the riots, there was an outflow of blacks from outlying neighborhoods into the emerging ghetto, as the old integrated elite resigned itself to the new realities of racial segregation. Blacks who had been contemplating a move to better housing in white areas before the riots thought better of the idea afterward.

Racial violence did not end when the riots ceased in 1920, however, it simply assumed new, more controlled forms. As the black settlement pattern imploded and scattered areas of black residence were eliminated or consolidated, a contiguous core of solidly black neighborhoods formed in most northern cities during the first decades of the century. By the time black migration quickened during the 1920s, new arrivals had to be accommodated within a very compact and spatially restricted area that was not open to easy expansion.

After 1920 the pattern of racial strife shifted from one of generalized communal violence aimed at driving blacks out of white neighborhoods to a new pattern of targeted violence concentrated along the periphery of an expanding ghetto. As migration continued and housing pressures within the ghetto became intolerable, and as health, sanitary, and social conditions deteriorated, middle-class black families were eventually driven across the color line into white neighborhoods adjacent to the ghetto. Their moves set off an escalating pattern of racial violence.

The pattern typically began with threatening letters, personal harassment, and warnings of dire consequences to follow. Sometimes whites, through their churches, realtors, or neighborhood organizations, would take up a collection and offer to buy the black homeowner out, hinting of less civilized inducements to follow if the offer was refused. If these entreaties failed to dislodge the resident, spontaneous mobs would often grow out of neighborhood meetings or barroom discussions, and a pack of agitated, angry whites would surround the house, hurling rocks and insults and at times storming the home and ransacking it. Periodic outbursts of mob violence would be interspersed with sporadic incidents of rock-throwing, gunshots, cross burnings, and physical attack.

If the escalating violence still failed to produce the desired result the last step was dramatic and guaranteed to attract the attention, not only of the homeowner, but of the entire black community: bombing. During and after World War I, a wave of bombings followed the expansion of black residential areas in cities throughout the north. In Chicago, fifty-eight black homes were bombed between 1917 and 1921, one every twenty days; and one black real estate agent, Jesse Binga, had his home and office bombed seven times in one year. In Cleveland, a wealthy black doctor who constructed a new home in an exclusive white suburb had his house surrounded by a violent mob, and when this attack failed to dislodge him, the home was dynamited twice. Bombings were also reported to be a common means of combating the expansion of Detroit's ghetto.

The wave of violence and bombings crested during the 1920s, although the sporadic use of these techniques has continued up to the present. Violence, however, has its problems as a strategy for maintaining the residential color line. Although it was employed by whites of all classes at first, those in the middle and upper classes eventually realized its limitations. Not only did violent actions often destroy property within neighborhoods being "defended," but injuries or death could bring legal charges as well as unfavorable publicity that decreased an area's stability. After the 1920s, middle-class whites increasingly turned to more civilized and institutionalized methods to build the ghetto.

A typical organizational solution to the threat of black residential expansion was the formation of neighborhood "improvement associations." Although ostensibly chartered for the purpose of promoting neighborhood security and property values, their principal raison d'être was the prevention of black entry and the maintenance of the color line. On Chicago's South Side, for example, the Hyde Park Improvement and Protective Club and the Woodlawn Society were formed implicitly to rid their neighborhoods of unwanted black settlers and to prevent future black entry. In New York, whites banded together in Harlem's Property Owners' Improvement Corporation and Brooklyn's Gates Avenue Association, again for the same reasons. In other cities, similar organizations dedicated themselves to checking the expansion of black settlement along the ghetto's frontier.

These voluntary associations employed a variety of tools in their efforts to preserve the racial homogeneity of threatened neighborhoods. They lobbied city councils for zoning restrictions and for the closing of hotels and rooming houses that attracted blacks; they threatened boycotts of real estate agents who sold homes to blacks; they withdrew their patronage from white businesses that catered to black clients; they agitated for public investments in the neighborhood in order to increase property values and keep blacks out by economic means; they collected money to create funds to buy property from black settlers or to purchase homes that remained vacant for too long; they offered cash bonuses to black renters who agreed to leave the neighborhood. In the exclusive Chicago suburb of Wilmette, a committee of citizens went so far as to ask wealthy homeowners to lodge all maids, servants, and gardeners on premises, or else to fire all Negroes in their employ.

One of the most important functions of the neighborhood associations, however, was to implement restrictive covenants. These documents were contractual agreements among property owners stating that they would not permit a black to own, occupy, or lease their property. Those signing the covenant bound themselves and their heirs to exclude blacks from the covered area for a specified period of time. In the event of the covenant's violation, any party to the agreement could call upon the courts for enforcement and could sue the transgressor for damages. As typically employed, covenants took effect when some fixed percentage of property owners in a given area had signed, whereupon the remaining nonsignatories were pressured to sign also. A typical covenant lasted twenty years and required the assent of 75% of the property owners to become enforceable.

Prior to 1900, such covenants did not exist. Legal restrictions on the transfer of property to blacks took the form of deed restrictions, which covered single parcels and did not solve the problem of massive black entry into white neighborhoods. Deed restrictions also did not lend themselves to forceful collective action. After 1910, the use of restrictive covenants spread widely throughout the United States, and they were employed frequently and with considerable effectiveness to maintain the color line until 1948, when the U.S. Supreme Court declared them unenforceable.

Local real estate boards often took the lead in establishing restrictive covenants and arranging for their widespread use. In 1927, for example, the Chicago Real Estate Board devised a model covenant that neighborhood organizations could adapt for their own use; the board then organized a special drive to ensure its adoption by all of the "better" neighborhoods in the city. Although Chicago's local board may have been unusually active in defending the color line, these actions were consistent with official policies of the National Association of Real Estate Brokers, which in 1924 adopted an article in its code of ethics stating that "a Realtor should never be instrumental in introducing into a neighborhood . . . members of any race or nationality . . . whose presence will clearly be detrimental to property values in that neighborhood," a provision that remained in effect until 1950.

The maintenance of a rigid color line in housing through violence and institutionalized discrimination paradoxically also created the conditions for ghetto expansion. Rapid black migration into a confined residential area created an intense demand for housing within the ghetto, which led to a marked inflation of rents and home prices. The racially segmented market generated real estate values in black areas that far exceeded anything in white neighborhoods, and this simple economic fact created a great potential for profits along the color line, guaranteeing that some real estate agent would specialize in opening up new areas to black settlement.

White real estate boards, of course, attempted to forestall such actions by threatening agents who violated the color line with expulsion, but because black agents were excluded from real estate boards anyway, this threat had little effect on them. Furthermore, the potential profits were great enough that many whites were willing to face public opprobrium for the sake of the money to be earned. In the end, the real estate industry settled on a practical compromise of keeping "blacks from moving into white residential areas haphazardly and to see to it that they filled a block solidly before being allowed to move into the next one." Essentially this strategy represented a policy of containment and tactical retreat before an advancing color line. For some, it proved to be a very profitable compromise.

The methods that realtors used to open up neighborhoods to black entry and to reap profits during the transition came to be known as "blockbusting." The expansion of the ghetto generally followed the path of least resistance, slowing or stopping at natural boundaries such as rivers, railroad tracks, or major thoroughfares, and moving toward low status rather than high status areas. Blockbusting agents would select a promising area for racial turnover, most often an area adjacent to the ghetto that contained older housing, poorer families, aging households, and some apartment buildings. Agents would then quietly acquire a few homes or apartments in the area, and rent or sell them to carefully chosen black families.

The inevitable reaction of white violence and resistance was countered with deliberate attempts to increase white fears and spur black demand. Agents would go door to door warning white residents of the impending "invasion" and offer to purchase or rent homes on generous terms. They often selected ostentatiously lower-class blacks to be the first settlers in the neighborhood in order to heighten fears and encourage panic; at times, these "settlers" were actually confederates of the realtor. In neighborhoods of family homes, a realtor might divide up the first black-occupied house into small units, which were intentionally rented to poor southern arrivals who were desperate for housing and willing to pay high rents for cramped rooms of low quality. While white panic was spreading, the realtors would advertise widely within the black community, pointing out the availability of good housing in a newly opened neighborhood, thereby augmenting black demand.

Given the intensity of black demand and the depths of white prejudice, the entry of a relatively small number of black settlers would
quickly surpass the threshold of white tolerance and set off a round of
racial turnover. No white renters or home buyers would enter the area
under the cloud of a black invasion, and as the rate of white departures
accelerated, each departing white family would be replaced with one or
more black families. As the threat of violence subsided and whites gave
up defending the neighborhood, black demand soared and agents reaped
substantial profits, because the new entrants were willing to pay prices
much higher than those previously paid by whites.

In neighborhoods of single-family homes, the initial black entrants
tended to be middle- and upper-class families seeking to escape the de-
plorable conditions of the ghetto. Like other middle-class people, they
sought more agreeable surroundings, higher-quality schools, lower crime
rates, bigger houses, larger properties, and a "better class of people."
Because white banks did not make loans to black applicants, realtors
were able to augment their profits by acting as bankers as well as sales
agents; and given the racially segmented credit market, they were able
to charge interest rates and demand down payments well above those
paid by whites.

The attempts of black middle-class families to escape the ghetto were
continually undermined, however, by real estate agents seeking quick
profits. Often they sold homes to black families who needed quality
housing but were in no position to pay for it. As both seller and lender,
the agent would collect a cash advance and several months of mortgage
payments before the buyer defaulted; then the family was evicted and
the house was resold to another family under similar terms. In this way,
agents could "sell" a home several times in the course of a year, generating extra profits. Frequently agents bought homes in single-family
neighborhoods, subdivided them into rooming houses, and then leased
the resulting "kitchenette" apartments at high rents to poor families.

The prevalence of these quick-profit schemes meant that the ghetto
constantly followed the black middle class as it sought to escape from
the poverty, blight, and misery of the black slum. Following resegrega-
tion, neighborhoods fell into progressive neglect and disrepair as owners
were shuffled in and out of homes, which sat vacant between sales. Nor
could owners who were paying rents and mortgages beyond their means
afford repairs and routine maintenance. In addition, the illegal subdivi-
sion of single-family homes brought the very poor into what were originally middle-class areas. Complaints to city inspectors by black
homeowners usually went unheard, because real estate agents were typically careful to pay off local officials; many were only too happy to turn
a blind eye to problems in the black community if there was money to
be made.

During the 1920s and 1930s, therefore, black ghettos expanded behind
a leading edge of middle-class pioneers who were subsequently

swamped by an influx of poor families, which caused the progressive deterioration of the neighborhood. As the decline accelerated, affluent families were prompted to seek new quarters in adjacent white neighborhoods, beginning a new round of neighborhood transition and decay. This process, when repeated across neighborhoods, yielded a distinct class gradient in the ghetto, with the poorest families being concentrated toward the center in the worst, most crowded, and least desirable housing, and the middle and upper classes progressively increasing their share of the population as one moved from the core toward the periphery of the ghetto.

As the black ghetto became more dense and spatially concentrated, a struggle for power, influence, and ideological control emerged within the black community between the old elite and the "New Negroes" of the 1920s and 1930s. The latter were politicians and, to a lesser extent, business owners who benefited from the spatial concentration of black demand within a racially segmented market. In ideological terms, the struggle was symbolized by the debate between the adherents of W. E. B. Du Bois and the followers of Booker T. Washington. The former argued that blacks should fight white injustice and demand their rightful share of the fruits of American society; the latter advocated accommodating white racism while building an independent black economic base.

The rise of the ghetto, more than anything else, brought about the eclipse of the old elite of integrationist blacks who dominated African American affairs in northern cities before 1910. These professionals and tradespeople who catered to white clients and aspired to full membership in American society were supplanted by a class of politicians and entrepreneurs whose source of power and wealth lay in the black community itself. Rather than being caterers, barbers, doctors, and lawyers who served a white or racially mixed clientele, the new elite were politicians and business owners with a self-interested stake in the ghetto. With their ascendancy, the ideal of an integrated society and the fight against racial segregation went into a long remission.

These "New Negroes" included real estate tycoons, such as Chicago's Jesse Binga and New York's Philip A. Payton, men who specialized in opening up new areas for black settlement and made millions in the process. Publishing newspapers for a black audience brought wealth and influence to Robert S. Abbott, who built the *Chicago Defender* into the most important black newspaper in the country, and Dr. P. M. H. Savory, who published the *Amsterdam News* from the 1920s until his death in the 1965. With the concentration of black population, moreover, came the concentration of black votes and buying power, and a new generation of politicians and business owners came to the fore—people such as Oscar DePriest, who became Chicago's first black alderman and the first African American elected to Congress from the north, and New York's Madame C. J. Walker, who made a fortune with a line of black cosmetics and hair-straightening products. The interests of these new economic and political leaders were tied to the ghetto and its concerns rather than to issues growing out of an attempt to pursue an integrated life within the mainstream of American society.

Meanwhile, in the south, conditions for urban blacks were considerably less tolerant than in the north. The Jim Crow system of race relations was in its heyday during the early years of the twentieth century, but its paternalistic system of race relations guaranteed the subordination of blacks and paradoxically lessened the need for a rigid system of housing segregation. Among older southern cities, in particular, the traditional grid pattern of white avenues and black alleys kept segregation levels relatively low. Although direct evidence on the degree of racial segregation in southern cities is limited, the few available studies suggest that it was less severe in the early twentieth century than in the emerging ghettos of the north. . . .

Southern whites were not completely immune to threats posed by black urbanization. After 1910 black populations also began to rise in southern cities, for essentially the same reasons as in the north, and whites similarly became alarmed at the influx of black migrants. In the context of Jim Crow, however, the reaction of southern whites never reached the extremes of panic and fear experienced in the north. Rather, given the tradition of legally enforced segregation in other spheres, southern whites turned to the law to promote greater separation between the races in housing.

The movement toward legally enforced residential segregation began in 1910, when Baltimore's city council passed an ordinance establishing separate white and black neighborhoods in the city. Additional laws to establish legal segregation in housing were passed in Virginia between 1911 and 1913, when Ashland, Norfolk, Portsmouth, Richmond, and Roanoke all adopted ordinances emulating Baltimore's. By 1913, the movement had spread southward to Winston-Salem and Greenville, North Carolina, and it reached Atlanta, Georgia, in the same year. By 1916, Louisville, St. Louis, Oklahoma City, and New Orleans all had passed laws establishing separate black and white districts in their cities. As the movement gathered steam, some northern cities began to consider the possibility of adopting similar ordinances to resolve their racial difficulties.

In 1916, however, the National Association for the Advancement of Colored People filed suit in federal court to block the implementation of Louisville's segregation law, and one year later the U.S. Supreme Court declared it unconstitutional. The movement toward legally sanctioned housing segregation ended, and thereafter racial segregation in southern cities was accomplished by the same means as in the north: through violence, collective antiblack action, racially restrictive covenants, and discriminatory real estate practices. Segregation, nonetheless, continued to develop at a slower pace than in northern cities owing to the slower pace of industrialization, the unique spatial organization of southern cities, and the greater social control of blacks afforded by Jim Crow. . . .

. . . Although the walls of the ghetto were rising in the south by 1940, they had not yet reached the height of those in the north, particularly in the older cities.

32
The McDonald's System

GEORGE RITZER

McDonald's has become a buzzword not only for fast food but for a way of organizing activities, calculated to maximize efficiency by minimizing opportunities for error. For some this is wonderful, but for others this is lifeless and without joy, despite the images that appear in McDonald's commercials. Ultimately, it may not be as efficient as it seems.

THE DIMENSIONS OF MCDONALDIZATION: FROM DRIVE-THROUGHS TO UNCOMFORTABLE SEATS

Even if some domains are able to resist McDonaldization, this book intends to demonstrate that many other aspects of society are being, or will be, McDonaldized. This raises the issue of why the McDonald's model has proven so irresistible. Four basic and alluring dimensions lie at the heart of the success of the McDonald's model and, more generally, of the process of McDonaldization.

First, McDonald's offers *efficiency*. That is, the McDonald's system offers us the optimum method for getting from one point to another. Most generally, this means that McDonald's proffers the best available means of getting us from a state of being hungry to a state of being full. . . . Other institutions, fashioned on the McDonald's model, offer us similar efficiency in losing weight, lubricating our cars, filling eyeglass prescriptions, or completing income tax forms. In a fast-paced society in which both parents are likely to work, or where there may be only a single parent, efficiently satisfying the hunger and many other needs of people is very attractive. In a highly mobile society in which people are rushing, usually by car, from one spot to another, the efficiency of a fast-food meal, perhaps without leaving one's car while passing by the drive-through window, often proves impossible to resist. The fast-food model offers us, or at least appears to offer us, an efficient method for satisfying many of our needs.

Second, McDonald's offers us food and service that can be easily *quantified* and *calculated*. In effect, McDonald's seems to offer us "more bang for the buck." (One of its recent innovations, in response to the growth of other fast-food franchises, is to proffer "value meals" at discounted prices.) We often feel that we are getting a *lot* of food for a modest amount of money. Quantity has become equivalent to quality; a lot of something means it must be good. As two observers of contemporary

American culture put it, "As a culture, we tend to believe—deeply—
that in general 'bigger is better.'" Thus, we order the *Quarter Pounder*,
the *Big* Mac, the *large* fries. We can quantify all of these things and feel
that we are getting a lot of food, and, in return, we appear to be shelling
out only a nominal sum of money. This calculus, of course, ignores an
important point: the mushrooming of fast-food outlets, and the spread
of the model to many other businesses, indicates that our calculation is
illusory and it is the owners who are getting the best of the deal.

There is another kind of calculation involved in the success of
McDonald's—a calculation involving time. People often, at least implicitly, calculate how much time it will take them to drive to McDonald's,
eat their food, and return home and then compare that interval to the
amount of time required to prepare the food at home. They often conclude, rightly or wrongly, that it will take less time to go and eat at the
fast-food restaurant than to eat at home. This time calculation is a key
factor in the success of Domino's and other home-delivery franchises,
because to patronize them people do not even need to leave their homes.
To take another notable example, Lens Crafters promises us "Glasses
fast, glasses in one hour." Some McDonaldized institutions have come
to combine the emphases on time and money. Domino's promises pizza
delivery in one-half hour, or the pizza is free. Pizza Hut will serve us a
personal pan pizza in five minutes, or it, too, will be free.

Third, McDonald's offers us predictability. We know that the Egg
McMuffin we eat in New York will be, for all intents and purposes,
identical to those we have eaten in Chicago and Los Angeles. We also
know that the one we order next week or next year will be identical to
the one we eat today. There is great comfort in knowing that McDonald's
offers no surprises, that the food we eat at one time or in one place will
be identical to the food we eat at another time or in another place. We
know that the next Egg McMuffin we eat will not be awful, but we also
know that it will not be exceptionally delicious. The success of the
McDonald's model indicates that many people have come to prefer a
world in which there are no surprises.

Fourth and finally, control especially through the substitution of nonhuman for human technology, is exerted over the human beings who enter
the world of McDonald's. The humans who work in fast-food restaurants
are trained to do a very limited number of things in precisely the way
they are told to do them. Managers and inspectors make sure that workers toe the line. The human beings who eat in fast-food restaurants are
also controlled, albeit (usually) more subtly and indirectly. Lines, limited
menus, few options, and uncomfortable seats all lead diners to do what
the management wishes them to do—eat quickly and leave. Further, the
drive-through (and in some cases walk-through) window leads diners to
first leave and then eat rapidly. This attribute has most recently been
extended by the Domino's model, according to which customers are expected to *never* come, yet still eat speedily.

McDonald's also controls people by using nonhuman technology to replace human workers. Human workers, no matter how well they are programmed and controlled, can foul up the operation of the system. A slow or indolent worker can make the preparation and delivery of a Big Mac inefficient. A worker who refuses to follow the rules can leave the pickles or special sauce off a hamburger, thereby making for unpredictability. And a distracted worker can put too few fries in the box, making an order of large fries seem awfully skimpy. For these and other reasons, McDonald's is compelled to steadily replace human beings with nonhuman technologies, such as the soft-drink dispenser that shuts itself off when the glass is full, the french-fry machine that rings when the fries are crisp, the preprogrammed cash register that eliminates the need for the cashier to calculate prices and amounts, and, perhaps at some future time, the robot capable of making hamburgers. (Experimental robots of this type already exist.) All of these technologies permit greater control over the human beings involved in the fast-food restaurant. The result is that McDonald's is able to reassure customers about the nature of the employee to be encountered and the nature of the service to be obtained.

In sum, McDonald's (and the McDonald's model) has succeeded because it offers the consumer efficiency and predictability, and because it seems to offer the diner a lot of food for little money and a slight expenditure of effort. It has also flourished because it has been able to exert greater control through nonhuman technologies over both employees and customers, leading them to behave the way the organization wishes them to. The substitution of nonhuman for human technologies has also allowed the fast-food restaurant to deliver its fare increasingly more efficiently and predictably. Thus, there are good, solid reasons why McDonald's has succeeded so phenomenally and why the process of McDonaldization continues unabated.

A Critique of McDonaldization: The Irrationality of Rationality

There is a downside to all of this. We can think of efficiency, predictability, calculability, and control through nonhuman technology as the basic components of a *rational* system. However, as we shall see in later chapters, rational systems often spawn irrationalities. The downside of McDonaldization will be dealt with most systematically under the heading of the *irrationality of rationality*. Another way of saying this is that rational systems serve to deny human reason; rational systems can be unreasonable.

For example, the fast-food restaurant is often a dehumanizing setting in which to eat or work. People lining up for a burger, or waiting in the drive-through line, often feel as if they are dining on an assembly line, and those who prepare the burgers often appear to be working on a burger assembly line. Assembly lines are hardly human settings in which to eat, and they have been shown to be inhuman settings in which to work. As we will see, dehumanization is only one of many ways in which the highly rationalized fast-food restaurant is extremely irrational.

Of course, the criticisms of the irrationality of the fast-food restaurant will be extended to all facets of our McDonaldizing world. This extension has recently been underscored and legitimated at the opening of Euro DisneyLand outside Paris. A French socialist politician acknowledged the link between Disney and McDonald's as well as their common negative effects when he said that Euro Disney will "bombard France with uprooted creations that are to culture what fast food is to gastronomy."

Such critiques lead to a question: Is the headlong rush toward McDonaldization around the world advantageous or not? There are great gains to be made from McDonaldization, some of which will be discussed below. But there are also great costs and enormous risks, which this book will focus on. Ultimately, we must ask whether the creation of these rationalized systems creates an even greater number of irrationalities. At the minimum, we need to be aware of the costs associated with McDonaldization. McDonald's and other purveyors of the fast-food model spend billions of dollars each year outlining the benefits to be derived from their system. However, the critics of the system have few outlets for their ideas. There are no commercials on Saturday morning between cartoons warning children of the dangers associated with fast-food restaurants. Although few children are likely to read this book, it is aimed, at least in part, at their parents (or parents-to-be) in the hope that it will serve as a caution that might be passed on to their children.

A legitimate question may be raised about this analysis: Is this critique of McDonaldization animated by a romanticization of the past and an impossible desire to return to a world that no longer exists? For some critics, this is certainly the case. They remember the time when life was slower, less efficient, had more surprises, when people were freer, and when one was more likely to deal with a human being than a robot or a computer. Although they have a point, these critics have undoubtedly exaggerated the positive aspects of a world before McDonald's, and they have certainly tended to forget the liabilities associated with such a world. More importantly, they do not seem to realize that we are *not* returning to such a world. The increase in the number of people, the acceleration in technological change, the increasing pace of life—all this and more make it impossible to go back to a nonrationalized world, if it ever existed, of home-cooked meals, traditional restaurant dinners, high-quality foods, meals loaded with surprises, and restaurants populated only by workers free to fully express their creativity.

While one basis for a critique of McDonaldization is the past, another is the future. The future in this sense is what people have the potential to be if they are unfettered by the constraints of rational systems. This critique holds that people have the potential to be far more thoughtful, skillful, creative, and well-rounded than they now are, yet they are unable to express this potential because of the constraints of a rationalized world. If the world were less rationalized, or even derationalized, people would be better able to live up to their human potential. This critique is based not on what people were like in the past, but on what they could be like in the future, if only the constraints of McDonaldized systems were eliminated, or at least eased substantially. The criticisms to be put forth in this book are animated by the latter, future-oriented perspective rather than by a romanticization of the past and a desire to return to it.

THE ADVANTAGES OF McDONALDIZATION: FROM THE CAJUN BAYOU TO SUBURBIA

Much of this book will focus on the negative side of McDonald's and McDonaldization. At this point it is important, however, to balance this view by mentioning some of the benefits of these systems and processes. The economic columnist, Robert Samuelson, for example, is a strong supporter of McDonald's and confesses to "openly worship McDonald's." He thinks of it as "the greatest restaurant chain in history." (However, Samuelson does recognize that there are those who "can't stand the food and regard McDonald's as the embodiment of all that is vulgar in American mass culture.")

Let me enumerate some of the advantages of the fast-food restaurant as well as other elements of our McDonaldized society:

- The fast-food restaurant has expanded the alternatives available to consumers. For example, more people now have ready access to Italian, Mexican, Chinese, and Cajun foods. A McDonaldized society is, in this sense, more egalitarian.
- The salad bar, which many fast-food restaurants and supermarkets now offer, enables people to make salads the way they want them.
- Microwave ovens and microwavable foods enable us to have dinner in minutes or even seconds.
- For those with a wide range of shopping needs, supermarkets and shopping malls are very efficient sites. Home shopping networks allow us to shop even more efficiently without ever leaving home.
- Today's high-tech, for-profit hospitals are likely to provide higher quality medical care than their predecessors.
- We can receive almost instantaneous medical attention at our local, drive-in "McDoctors."
- Computerized phone systems (and "voice mail") allow people to do things that were impossible before, such as obtain a bank balance in the middle of the night or hear a report on what went on in their child's class during the day and what home-work assignments were made. Similarly, automated bank teller machines allow people to obtain money any time of the day or night.
- Package tours permit large numbers of people to visit countries that they would otherwise not visit.

- Diet centers like Nutri/System allow people to lose weight in a carefully regulated and controlled system.
- The 24-second clock in professional basketball has enabled outstanding athletes such as Michael Jordan to more fully demonstrate their extraordinary talents.
- Recreational vehicles let the modern camper avoid excessive heat, rain, insects, and the like.
- Suburban tract houses have permitted large numbers of people to afford single-family homes.

CONCLUSION

The previous list gives the reader a sense not only of the advantages of McDonaldization but also of the range of phenomena that will be discussed under that heading throughout this book. In fact, such a wide range of phenomena will be discussed under the heading of McDonaldization that one is led to wonder: What isn't McDonaldized? Is McDonaldization the equivalent of modernity? Is everything contemporary McDonaldized?

While much of the world has been McDonaldized, it is possible to identify at least three aspects of contemporary society that have largely escaped McDonaldization. First, there are phenomena traceable to an earlier, "premodern" age that continue to exist within the modern world. A good example is the Mom and Pop grocery store. Second, there are recent creations that have come into existence, at least in part, as a reaction against McDonaldization. A good example is the boom in bed and breakfasts (B&Bs), which offer rooms in private homes with personalized attention and a homemade breakfast from the proprietor. People who are fed up with McDonaldized motel rooms in Holiday Inn or Motel 6 can instead stay in so-called B&Bs. Finally, some analysts believe that we have moved into a new, "postmodern" society and that aspects of that society are less rational than their predecessors. Thus, for example, in a postmodern society we witness the destruction of "modern" high-rise housing projects and their replacement with smaller, more livable communities. Thus, although it is ubiquitous, McDonaldization is *not* simply another term for contemporary society. There *is* more to the contemporary world than McDonaldization.

In discussing McDonaldization, we are *not* dealing with an all-or-nothing process. Things are not either McDonaldized or not McDonaldized. There are degrees of McDonaldization; it is a continuum. Some phenomena have been heavily McDonaldized, others moderately McDonaldized, and some only slightly McDonaldized. There are some phenomena that may have escaped McDonaldization completely. Fast-food restaurants, for example, have been heavily McDonaldized, universities moderately McDonaldized, and the Mom and Pop grocers mentioned earlier only slightly McDonaldized. It is difficult to think of social phenomena that

have escaped McDonaldization totally, but I suppose there is local enterprise in Fiji that has been untouched by this process. In this context,
McDonaldization thus represents a process—a process by which more
and more social phenomena are being McDonaldized to an increasing
degree.

Overall, the central thesis is that McDonald's represents a monumen-
tally important development and the process that it has helped spawn,
McDonaldization, is engulfing more and more sectors of society and areas of the world. It has yielded a number of benefits to society, but it
also entails a considerable number of costs and risks.

Although the focus is on McDonald's and McDonaldization, it is important to realize that this system has important precursors in our recent
history. . . . That is, McDonaldization is not something completely new,
but rather its success has been based on its ability to bring together a
series of earlier innovations. Among the most important precursors to
McDonaldization are bureaucracy, scientific management, the assembly
line, and the original McDonald brothers' hamburger stand. . . .

33
Japanese Etiquette and Ethics in Business

BOYE DE MENTE

Americans tend to be very direct. They like to "get down to business" and distrust people who won't say what is on their minds. This is a "queer custom" for many other people, however. In fact, if you want to close a deal in Japan, you had better learn that there are some disadvantages to doing business the American way.

SHU-SHIN KOYO (IT'S FOR LIFE)

Probably the most talked about and notorious facet of Japan's family-patterned company system is *shu-shin koyo* (shuu-sheen koe-yoe), or "lifetime employment," which applies, however, to only an elite minority of the nation's workers. Although a direct descendant of feudal Japan, when peasants and craftsmen were attached to a particular clan by birth, the lifetime employment system did not become characteristic of large-scale modern Japanese industry until the 1950s. In the immediate postwar period, losing one's job was tantamount to being sentenced to starvation. To prevent employees from being fired or arbitrarily laid off, national federation union leaders took advantage of their new freedom and the still weak position of industry to force adoption of the lifetime employment system by the country's major enterprises.

Under the lifetime employment system, all *permanent* employees of larger companies and government bureaus are, in practice, hired for life. These organizations generally hire only once a year, directly from schools. Well before the end of the school year, each company and government ministry or agency decides on how many new people it wants to bring in. The company or government bureau then invites students who are to graduate that year (in some cases only from certain universities) to take written and oral examinations for employment.

One company, for example, may plan on taking two hundred university graduates as administrative trainees, and five hundred junior and senior high school graduates for placement in blue-collar work. Since "permanent" employment is "for life," companies are careful to select candidates who have well-rounded personalities and are judged most likely to adjust to that particular company or agency's philosophy and "style."

This method of employee selection is known as *Shikaku Seido* or "Personal Qualifications System." This means that new employees are selected on the basis of their education, character, personality, and family backgrounds; as opposed to work experience or technological backgrounds.

A larger Japanese company hiring new employees, as well as firms entering into new business tie-ups, are sometimes compared to *miai kek-kon* or "arranged marriages." The analogy is a good one. Both employment and joint-venture affiliations are, in principle, for life. Therefore, both parties want to be sure not only of the short-term intentions of the potential partner but also of the character and personality—even if there are any "black sheep" in the family. Thus both prospective employee and potential business partner must undergo close scrutiny. When the Japanese commit themselves, the commitment is expected to be total.

Choosing employees on the basis of personal qualifications is especially important to Japanese supervisors and managers, because they personally cannot hire, fire, or hold back promotions. They must acquire and keep the trust, goodwill, and cooperation of their subordinates, and manage by example and tact.

Besides exercising control over employee candidates by allowing only students from certain universities to take their entrance examinations, many companies in Japan also depend upon well-known professors in specific universities to recommend choice candidates to them each year. The reputations of some professors, especially in the physical sciences, are often such that they can actually "parcel out" the best students from their graduating classes to top firms in their field.

NENKO JORETSU (THE "MERIT OF YEARS")

Once hired by a larger company, the permanent Japanese employee who is a university graduate is on the first rung of a pay/promotion escalator system that over the years will gradually and automatically take him to or near the upper management level. This is the famous (or infamous) *nenko joretsu* (nane-koe joe-ray-t'sue), "long-service rank" or seniority system, under which pay and promotions are primarily based on longevity.

Not surprisingly, the employee, at least in administrative areas, is considered more important than the job in the Japanese company system. As a result, job classifications on the administrative level may be clear enough, but specific duties of individuals tend to be ill-defined or not defined at all. Work is more or less assigned on a collective basis, and each employee tends to work according to his or her ability and inclinations. Those who are capable, diligent, and ambitious naturally do most of the work. Those who turn out to be lazy or incompetent are given tasks befitting their abilities and interests.

Young management trainees are switched from one job to another every two or three years, and in larger companies they are often transferred to other offices or plants. The reason for this is to expose them to a wide range of experiences so they will be more valuable to the company as they go up the promotion ladder. Individuals are "monitored" and informally rated, and eventually the more capable are promoted faster than the other members of their age group. The ones promoted the fastest usually become managing directors; and one of their number generally becomes president.

During the first twelve to fifteen years of employment, the most capable junior managers accrue status instead of more pay raises and faster promotions. If they prove to be equally capable in their personal relations with others, they are the ones who are eventually singled out to reach the upper levels of the managerial hierarchy.

The seniority system in Japanese companies takes ordinary, even incapable, people who have toed the company line and made no blunders, to the head of departments, and occasionally to the head of companies. But their limitations are recognized, and the department or company is run by competent people below them, with little or no damage to the egos of the less capable executives or to the overall harmony within the firm.

Each work-section of a Japanese company is three-layered, consisting of young, on-the-job trainees (a status that often lasts for several years); mature, experienced workers who carry most of the burden; and older employees whose productivity has fallen off due to their age.

Direct, specific orders do not set well with the members of these work-sections. Such orders leave them with the impression they are not trusted and that management has no respect for them. Even the lowest clerk or delivery boy in a company is very sensitive about being treated with respect. The Japanese say they prefer general "ambiguous" instructions. All that workgroups want from management "are goals and direction."

Because human relations are given precedence in the Japanese management system, great importance is attached to the "unity of employees" within each of these groups. The primary responsibility of the senior manager in a group is not to direct the people in their work but to make "adjustments" among them in order to maintain harmonious relations within the group.

"What is required of the ideal manager," say the Japanese, "is that he know how to adjust human relations rather than be knowledgeable about the operation of his department or the overall function of the company. In fact, the man who is competent and works hard is not likely to be popular with other members of his group and as a result does not make a good manager," they add.

Besides "appearing somewhat incompetent" as far as work is concerned while being skilled at preventing interemployee friction, the ideal Japanese manager has one other important trait. He is willing to shoulder all the responsibility for any mistakes or failings of his subordinates—hoping, of course, there will be no loss of face.

The efficient operation of this group system is naturally based on personal obligations and trust between the manager and his staff. The manager must make his staff obligated to him in order to keep their cooperation and in order to ensure that none of them will deliberately do anything or leave anything undone that would cause him embarrassment. Whatever knowledge and experience are required for the group to be productive is found among the manager's subordinates if he is weak in this area.

SEISHIN . . . (TRAINING IN SPIRIT)

The Japanese associate productivity with employees having *seishin* (say-e-sheen), or "spirit," and being imbued with "Japanese morality." Company training, therefore, covers not only technical areas but also moral, philosophical, aesthetic, and political factors. Each of the larger companies has its own particular company philosophy and image, which are incorporated into its training and indoctrination programs. This is one of the prime reasons . . . major Japanese companies prefer not to hire older, experienced "outsiders"; it is assumed that they could not wholly accept or fit into the company mold.

ONJO SHUGI ("MOTHERING" EMPLOYEES)

The amount of loyalty, devotion, and hard work displayed by most Japanese employees is in direct proportion to the paternalism, *onjo shugi* (own-joe shuu-ghee), of the company management system. The more paternalistic (maternalistic would seem to be a better word) the company, the harder working and the more devoted and loyal employees tend to be. Japanese-style paternalism includes the concept that the employer is totally responsible for the livelihood and well-being of all employees and must be willing to go all the way for an employee when the need arises.

The degree of paternalism in Japanese companies varies tremendously, with some of them literally practicing cradle-to-grave responsibility for employees and their families. Many managers thus spend a great deal of time participating in social events involving their staff members—births, weddings, funerals, and so on.

Fringe benefits make up a very important part of the income of most Japanese workers, and they include such things as housing or housing subsidies, transportation allowances, family allowances, child allowances, health services, free recreational facilities, educational opportunities, retirement funds, etc.

The wide range of fringe benefits received by Japanese employees is an outgrowth of spiraling inflation and an increasingly heavy income tax system during the years between 1945 and 1955. Companies first began serving employees free lunches. Then larger companies built dormitories, apartments, and houses. Eventually, recreational, educational, and medical facilities were added to employee benefits.

Japan's famous twice-a-year bonuses, *shoyo* (show-yoe), were originally regarded as a fringe benefit by employees and management, but workers and unions have long since considered them an integral part of wages. Unions prefer to call the bonuses *kimatsu teate* (kee-mot-sue tayah-tay), or "seasonal allowances." The bonuses, usually the equivalent of two to six or eight months of base wages, are paid in midsummer just before *Obon* (Oh-bone), a major Buddhist festival honoring the dead, and just before the end of the calendar year in December.

Rinji Saiyo (The Outsiders)

Not all employees of Japanese companies, including the larger ones, are hired for life or come under the *nenko joretsu* system of pay and promotion. There are two distinct categories of employees in most Japanese companies: those who are hired as permanent employees under the *shu-shin koyo* and *nenko joretsu* systems, and those hired under the *rinji saiyo* or "temporary appointment" system. The latter may be hired by the day or by the year, but they cannot be hired on contract for more than one year at a time. They are paid at a lower scale than permanent employees and may be laid off or fired at any time.

The *rinji saiyo* system of temporary employees is, of course, a direct outgrowth of the disadvantages of a permanent employment system, which at most is viable only in a booming, continuously growing economy.

The rapid internationalization of Japan's leading corporations is also having a profound effect on their policies regarding young Japanese who have graduated from foreign universities. Until the mid-1980s most Japanese companies simply would not consider hiring someone who had been partly or wholly educated abroad. Their rationale was that such people were no longer 100 percent Japanese and, therefore, would not fit into the training programs or the environment of Japanese companies.

Now a growing number of Japanese corporations with large international operations are looking for young people who have been educated abroad, speak a foreign language, and already have experience in living overseas. Ricoh, for example, now has a regular policy of hiring some of its annual crop of new employees from the group of Japanese students attending American universities.

Several Japanese employment agencies are now active among Japanese students in the U.S., providing them with information about job opportunities with Japanese companies overseas.

Jimusho No Hana ("Office Flowers")

Women, mostly young, make up a highly visible percentage of Japan's labor force, particularly in offices (where they are often referred to as *jimusho no hana* or "office flowers") and in light manufacturing industries requiring precision handwork. Most of these young women are expected to leave the work force when they get married, but increasing numbers of them are staying on after marriage, at least until they begin having children, and are returning to the labor force after their children are raised.

Equally significant is that, little by little, women are beginning to cross the barrier between staff and management, and participate in the heady world of planning and decision-making.

While female managers are still generally confined to such industries as public relations, advertising, publishing, and retailing, economic and social pressures are gradually forcing other industries as well to begin thinking about desegregating their male-only management systems.

Another highly conspicuous phenomenon in Japan today is the growing number of women who head up their own successful companies in such areas as real estate, cosmetics, apparel, and the food business.

The world of Japanese business is still very much a male preserve, however, with many of the relationships and rituals that make up a vital part of daily business activity still closed to women. There are virtually no women in the numerous power groups, factions, clubs, and associations that characterize big business in Japan.

Foreign women who choose to do business in or with Japan face most of the same barriers that handicap Japanese women. They are unable to participate in the ritualistic after-work drinking and partying that are a major part of developing and maintaining effective business relations within the Japanese system. They cannot transcend their sex and be accepted as business persons first and foremost. They are unable to deal with other women on a managerial level in other companies simply because there generally are none.

They must also face the fact that most Japanese executives have had no experience in dealing with female managers, have no protocol for doing so, and are inclined to believe that women are not meant to be business managers in the first place.

This does not mean that foreign women cannot successfully engage in business in Japan, but they must understand the barriers, be able to accept them for what they are, and work around them. If they come on strong, as women or as managers, to Japanese businessmen who are traditionally oriented, they will most likely fail. They must walk a much finer line than men.

At the same time, a foreign woman who is both attractive and really clever in knowing how to use her femininity to manipulate men can succeed in Japan where others fail. This approach can be especially effective if the woman concerned is taken under the wing of an older, powerful Japanese businessman who likes her and takes a personal interest in her success.

Perhaps the most important lesson the foreign businesswoman in Japan must learn is that the Japanese regard business as a personal matter, and believe that the personal element must be satisfied before any actual business transpires. This means she must go through the process of establishing emotional rapport with her male Japanese counterparts, and convince them that she is a knowledgeable, experienced, trustworthy, and dependable business person.

It is often difficult for foreign men to develop this kind of relationship with Japanese businessmen, particularly when language is a problem, so the challenge to foreign women who want to do business in Japan (unless they go just as buyers or artists, etc.) is formidable.

The type of foreign woman who is most likely to do well in the Japanese environment is one who has a genuine affinity for the language and the culture, and appreciates both the opportunities and challenges offered by the situation. She must also have an outstanding sense of humor, be patient, and be willing to suppress some of her rational, liberal feelings.

RINGI SEIDO (PUTTING IT IN WRITING)

In addition to the cooperative-work approach based on each employee contributing according to his or her ability and desire, many large Japanese companies divide and diversify management responsibility by a system known as *ringi seido* (reen-ghee say-ee-doe), which means, more or less, "written proposal system." This is a process by which management decisions are based on proposals made by lower level managers, and it is responsible for the "bottom-up" management associated with many Japanese companies.

Briefly, the *ringi* system consists of proposals written by the initiating section or department that are circulated horizontally and vertically to all layers of management for approval. Managers and executives who approve of the proposal stamp the document with their *hanko* (hahn-koe) name seals in the prescribed place. Anyone who disapproves either passes the document on without stamping it or puts his seal on it sideways or upside down to indicate conditional approval.

When approval is not unanimous, higher executives may send the document back with recommendations that more staff work be done on it or that the opinions of those who disapprove be taken into consideration. Managers may attach comments to the proposal if they wish.

In practice, the man who originates a *ringi-sho* (written proposal document) informally consults with other managers before submitting it for official scrutiny. He may work for weeks or months in his efforts to get the idea approved unofficially. If he runs into resistance, he will invariably seek help from colleagues who owe him favors. They in turn will approach others who are obligated to them.

The efficiency and effectiveness of the *ringi seido* varies with the company. In some it is little more than a formality, and there is pressure from the top to eliminate the system altogether. In other companies the system reigns supreme, and there is strong opposition to any talk of eliminating it. The system is so deeply entrenched in both the traditional management philosophy of the Japanese and the aspirations and ambitions of younger managers that it will no doubt be around for a long time.

The foreign businessman negotiating with a Japanese company should be aware that his proposals may be the subject of one or more *ringi-sho* which not only takes up a great deal of time (they must be circulated in the proper chain-of-status order), it also exposes them to the scrutiny of as many as a dozen or more individuals whose interests and attitudes may differ.

Whether or not a *ringi* proposal is approved by the president is primarily determined by who has approved it by the time it gets to him. If all or most of the more important managers concerned have stamped the *ringi-sho*, chances are the president will also approve it.

While this system is cumbersome and slow, generally speaking it helps build and maintain a cooperative spirit within companies. In addition, it assures that when a policy change or new program is initiated, it will have the support of the majority of managers.

As can be seen from the still widespread use of the *ringi seido*, top managers in many Japanese companies are not always planners and decision-makers. Their main function is to see that the company operates smoothly and efficiently as a team, to see that new managers are nurtured within the system, and to "pass judgment" on proposals made by junior managers.

Nemawashi (Behind the Scenes)

Just as the originator of a *ringi* proposal will generally not submit it until he is fairly sure it will be received favorably, Japanese managers in general do not, unlike their foreign counterparts, hold formal meetings to discuss subjects and make decisions. They meet to agree formally on what has already been decided in informal discussions behind the scenes.

These informal discussions are called *nemawashi* (nay-mah-wah-she) or "binding up the roots"—to make sure a plant's roots are protected when it is transplanted.

Nemawashi protocol does not require that all managers who might be concerned be consulted. But agreement must always be obtained from the "right" person—meaning the individual in the department, division, or upper echelon of the company management—who really exercises power . . .

Juyaku Ga Nai ("No Executives in Japan")

One authority on Japanese management makes the rather astounding observation that while there are "business managers" in Japan, there are no "business executives" in the Western sense. Masaaki Imai, managing director of Cambridge Research Institute-Japan, says that in a situation where employment is permanent and management is collective, there can be "no such thing" as an executive. Imai explains:

> In a way, every white collar employee in a company is an executive, and everyone is not. When a university graduate joins a company, he knows that some 13 to 15 years later he will be promoted to *kacho* (section chief), even if his first assignment is clipping newspapers. So do all of his colleagues who joined the company when he did.
>
> Thus from the standpoint of the individual, the transition from employee to "executive" is automatic. Until he is promoted to *kacho* level, he belongs to the union and makes such demands as pay raises to the management. One morning he wakes up to find he has become a *kacho*, and starts dealing with the union on behalf of the company . . .
>
> . . . Whether a Japanese is an executive or not is not so much derived from his own will and effort, but from the years he has spent in the company.

Imai adds that many companies often reserve important management positions for union leaders for the day when they stop being union leaders. (In Japan, most unions are "company unions" as opposed to craft or trade unions.)

The role of the *juyaku* (juu-yah-kuu) or "Big Executive" in typical, large Japanese companies is also quite different from that in comparable American companies. Most major Japanese firms select the members of their Board of Directors, *Tori Shimari Yakkai* (Toe-ree She-mah-ree Yaak-kie), from within their own company. The boards are generally made up of the president of the particular company and other line executives down to and including some *bu cho* (department chiefs). The function of the board is mostly ceremonial, and the title of "director" is primarily "social."

The board that really runs the large Japanese company—if one does —is the *Jomu Kai* (Joe-muu Kie) or "Managing Directors' Board." This board is made up of the heads of key departments, with the president as the chairman. Most *Jomu Kai* are little more than rubber-stamp boards, however, that are dominated by one man because the *sempai-kohai*, or senior-junior, system invariably prevails.

HANKO (CHOPPING PEOPLE DOWN)

The Japanese have traditionally used *hanko* (hahn-koe), name stamps, seals, or "chops," in lieu of written signatures when signing contracts and other types of formal or official documents. Especially where government bureaus and agencies are concerned, up to a dozen or more individuals in as many departments may be required to stamp a document, sometimes several times each in different places.

The mechanics of the practice by itself are irksome, often to an extreme degree, but it is usually something that time and great patience can surmount—if no hitches develop. Among the problems that can and do develop regularly: one (or more) of the people whose stamp is required is not available and following their hierarchical habit of grading everything, the name seals may have to go on in a prescribed order, causing long delays; someone decides he is not going to cooperate because he disapproves of the document, the person who originated it, or because he may be feuding with some of the other managers, etc.

Foreign businessmen living and working in Japan have the right to get a *hanko* stamp made and, if it is registered (*natsuin*) (not-sue-een), use it as their official signature. But few go to the trouble since the foreigner is allowed to write out his name—although in some cases the signing has to be certified before it is legal. Also, the *hanko* present a security problem since they can bind their owners to a contract even if affixed without their knowledge or authorization.

While written signatures are now the rule in international business in Japan, the *hanko* is still something to be reckoned with in dealings within the confines of Japanese companies and with government agencies, and it is likely to remain so for some time.

MIBUN (THE RIGHTS HAVE IT)

Everybody in Japan has his or her *mibun* (me-boon), "personal rights" or "station in life," and every *bun* has its special rights and responsibilities. There are special rights and special restrictions applying to managers only, to students only, to teachers only, to workers only, etc. The restrictions of a particular category are usually clear-cut and are intended to control the behavior of the people within these categories at all times—for example, the office employee even when he is not working or the student when he isn't in school.

The traditional purpose of the feudalistic *mibun* concept was to maintain harmony within and between different categories of people. A second purpose was to prevent anyone from bringing discredit or shame upon his category or his superiors.

A good example of the *mibun* system at work was once told by Konosuke Matsushita, founder of the huge Matsushita Electric Company (Panasonic, National, etc.). At the age of ten, Matsushita was apprenticed to a bicycle shop, which meant that he was practically a slave, forced to work from five in the morning until bedtime.

In addition to his regular duties, Matsushita had to run to a tobacco store several times a day for customers who came into the bicycle shop. Before he could go, however, he had to wash. After several months of this, he hit upon the idea of buying several packs of cigarettes at one time, with his own meager savings, so that when a customer asked for tobacco, he not only could hand it to him immediately but also profit a few *sen* on each pack, since he received a discount by buying twenty packs at a time.

This pleased not only the bicycle shop customers but also Matsushita's master, who complimented him highly on his ingenuity. A few days later, however, the master of the shop told him that all the other workers were complaining about his enterprise and that he would have to stop it and return to the old system.

It was not within the *bun* of a mere flunky to demonstrate such ability.

The aims of foreign businessmen are often thwarted because they attempt to get things done by Japanese whose *bun* does not allow them to do whatever is necessary to accomplish the desired task. Instead of telling the businessmen they cannot do it or passing the matter on to someone who can, there is a tendency for the individual to wait a certain period, or until they are approached again by the businessmen, then announce that it is impossible.

In any dealings with a Japanese company, it is especially important to know the *bun* of the people representing the firm. The Japanese businessman who does have individual authority is often buttressed behind subordinates whose *bun* are strictly limited. If the outsider isn't careful, a great deal of time can be wasted on the wrong person.

It is the special freedoms or "rights" of the *bun* system that cause the most trouble. As is natural everywhere, the Japanese minimize the responsibilities of their *bun* and emphasize the rights, with the result that there are detailed and well-known rules outlining the rights of each category, but few rules covering the responsibilities.

As one disillusioned bureaucrat-turned-critic put it, "The rights of government and company bureaucrats tend to be limitless, while responsibilities are ignored or passed on to underlings. The underlings in turn say they are powerless to act without orders from above—or that it isn't their responsibility." The same critic also said that the only ability necessary to become a bureaucrat was that of escaping responsibility without being criticized.

A story related by a former editor of one of Japan's better known intellectual magazines illustrates how the *mibun* system penetrates into private life. While still an editor with the magazine, Mr. S went out one night for a few drinks with a very close writer-friend. While they were drinking, another writer, the noted Mr. D, came into the bar and joined them.

Mr. S continues: "I was not 'in charge' of Mr. D in my publishing house and didn't know him very well, but according to Japanese etiquette I should have bowed to him, paid him all kinds of high compliments, and told him how much I was obligated to him. But it was long after my working hours and I was enjoying a drink with a friend who was also a writer, so I just bowed and paid little attention to him.

"At this, Mr. D became angry and commanded me in a loud voice to go home. I refused to move, and he began shouting curses at me. I shouted back at him that I was drinking with a friend and it was none of his business, but he continued to abuse me loudly until my friend finally managed to quiet him down. Of course, I would have been fired the next day except that my friend was able to keep Mr. D from telling the directors of my company."

In doing business with a Japanese firm, it is important to find out the rank of each individual you deal with so you can determine the extent of his *bun*. It is also vital that you know the status of his particular section or department, which has its own ranking within the company.

There are other management characteristics that make it especially difficult for the uninitiated foreigner to deal with Japanese companies, including barriers to fast, efficient communication between levels of management within the companies. Everything must go through the proper chain of command, in a carefully prescribed, ritualistic way. If any link in this vertical chain is missing—away on business or sick—routine communication usually stops there. The ranking system does not allow Japanese management to delegate authority or responsibility to any important extent. Generally, one person cannot speak for another.

In fact, some Japanese observers have begun criticizing the consensus system of business and political management, saying its absolute power represents a major threat to Japan in that it prevents rapid decision-making and often makes it impossible for the Japanese to react swiftly enough to either problems or opportunities.

HISHOKAN (WHERE ARE ALL THE SECRETARIES?)

As most Western businessmen would readily admit, they simply could not get along without their secretaries. In many ways, secretaries are as important, if not more so, than the executives themselves. In Japan only the rare businessman has a secretary whose role approximates the function of the Western secretary.

The reason for the scarcity of secretaries in Japan is many-fold. The style of Japanese management—the collective work-groups, decision-making by consensus, face-to-face communication, and the role of the manager as harmony-keeper instead of director—practically precludes the secretarial function. Another factor is the language itself, and the different language levels demanded by the subordinate-superior system. Japanese does not lend itself to clear, precise instructions because of the requirements of etiquette. It cannot be transcribed easily or quickly, either in shorthand or by typewriter—although the appearance of Japanese-language computers in the early 1980s [began] to change that.

As a result, the Japanese are not prepared psychologically or practically for doing business through or with secretaries. The closest the typical Japanese company comes to having secretaries in the American sense are receptionists—usually pretty, young girls who are stationed at desks in building lobbies and in central floor and hall areas. They announce visitors who arrive with appointments and try to direct people who come in on business without specific appointments to the right section or department. When a caller who has never had any business with the company, and has no appointment, appears at one of the reception desks, the girl usually tries to line him up with someone in the General Affairs (*Somu Bu*) Department.

Small Japanese companies and many departments in larger companies do not have receptionists. In such cases, no specific individual is responsible for greeting and taking care of callers. The desks nearest the door are usually occupied by the lowest ranking members in the department, and it is usually up to the caller to get the attention of one of them and make his business known.

SHIGOTO (IT'S NOT THE SLOT)

The importance of face-to-face meetings in the conduct of business in Japan has already been mentioned. Regular, personal contact is also essential in maintaining "established relations" (the ability to *amaeru*) with business contacts. The longer two people have known each other and the more often they personally meet, the firmer this relationship.

This points up a particular handicap many foreign companies operating in Japan inadvertently impose on themselves by switching their personnel every two, three, or four years. In the normal course of business in Japan, it takes at least two years and sometimes as many as five years before the Japanese begin to feel like they really know their foreign employer, supplier, client, or colleague.

It also generally takes the foreign businessman transferred to Japan anywhere from one to three years or so to learn enough to really become effective in his job. Shortly afterward, he is transferred, recalled to the head office, is fired, or quits, and is replaced by someone else.

American businessmen in particular tend to pay too little attention to the disruption caused by personnel turnover, apparently because they think more in terms of the "position" or "slot" being filled by a "body" that has whatever qualifications the job calls for. Generally speaking, they play down the personality and character of the person filling the position and often do not adequately concern themselves with the role of human relations in business.

This, of course, is just the opposite of the Japanese way of doing things, and it accounts for a great deal of the friction that develops between Japanese and Westerners in business matters. . . .

TSUSHIN (DON'T CALL ME . . .)

One of the most common complaints about Japanese companies is that they often fail to answer business inquiries or requests for information. There are, of course, two sides to the story. Many Japanese companies receive hundreds of letters every week from all over the world. Some of the inquiries are from large, reputable firms. Others are from small companies trying to get started in business—ranging from retail shops to private individuals. The letters from abroad come in many different languages, including such lesser known ones as Urdu, Swahili, Tagalog, and Tamil.

Imagine, if you will, how many American, British, or French companies that receive dozens of letters from unknown sources, frequently in rare languages, would bother to do anything with them. But over and above this consideration, there are several reasons why written inquiries to Japanese companies are often not answered.

The individual Japanese section or department manager does not have a secretary or even a "pool" typist to take care of correspondence. Inquiries coming from abroad, unless they are addressed to a specific individual in a section or department, most likely go to the General Affairs Department, where they tend to end up in the hands of young employees who are still undergoing on-the-job training. They generally do not read English very well, much less other foreign languages, and may or may not spend hours with a foreign-language dictionary trying to decipher what the letters say. Most letters to Japanese companies do not go beyond this point.

Besides this, it is not customary for Japanese companies to provide information about their products or services to unknown outsiders (except for the annual reports, catalogs, or flyers available on special occasions). The reaction tends to be, "Who wants to know, and why?"

SEKININ SHA (FINDING WHERE THE BUCK STOPS)

In Western countries there is almost always one person who has final authority and responsibility, and it is easy to identify this person. All you have to do is ask, "Who is in charge?" In Japanese companies, however, no one individual is in charge. Both authority and responsibility are dispersed among the managers as a group. The larger the company, the more people are involved. When there are mistakes or failures, Japanese management does not try to single out any individual to blame. They try to focus on the cause of the failing in an effort to find out why it happened. In this way, the employee who made the mistake (if one individual was involved) does not lose face, and all concerned have an opportunity to learn a lesson.

Ranking Japanese businessmen advise that it is difficult to determine who has real authority and who makes final decisions in a Japanese company. Said a Sony director: "Even a top executive must consult his colleagues before he 'makes' a decision because he has become a high executive more by his seniority than his leadership ability. To keep harmony in his company he must act as a member of a family." Sony's cofounder Akio Morita adds that because of this factor, the traditional concept of promotion by seniority may not have much of a future in Japan. He agrees, however, that it is not something that can be changed in a short period of time.

In approaching a Japanese company about a business matter, it is therefore almost always necessary to meet and talk with the heads of several sections and departments on different occasions. After having gone through this procedure, you may still not get a clear-cut response from anyone, particularly if the various managers you approached have not come to a favorable consensus among themselves. It is often left up to you to synthesize the individual responses you receive and draw your own conclusions.

It is always important and often absolutely essential that the outsider (foreign or Japanese) starting a new business relationship with a Japanese company establish good rapport with each level of management in the company. Only by doing so can the outsider be sure his side of the story, his needs and expectations, will get across to all the necessary management levels.

Earle Okumura, a Los Angeles-based consultant, and one of the few Americans who is bilingual and bicultural and has had extensive business experience in Japan, suggests the following approach to establishing "lines of communication" with a Japanese company when the project concerns the introductions of new technology to be used by the Japanese firm:

Step I. Ask a director or the head of the Research & Development Department to introduce you to the *kacho* (section chief) who is going to be directly in charge of your project within his department. Take the time to develop a personal relationship with the *kacho* (eating and drinking with him, etc.) then ask him to tell you exactly what you should do, and how you should go about trying to achieve and maintain the best possible working relationship with the company.

Step II. Ask the R&D *kacho*, with whom you now have at least the beginning of an *amae* relationship, to introduce you to his counterparts in the Production Department, Quality Control, and Sales Departments, etc., and go through the same get-acquainted process with each of them, telling them about yourself, your company, and your responsibilities. In all of these contacts, care must be taken not to pose any kind of threat or embarrassment to the different section managers.

Step III. After you have established a good, working relationship with the various *kacho* concerned, thoroughly explained your side of the project, and gained an understanding of their thinking, responsibilities, and capabilities, the third step is to get an appointment with the managing director or president of the company for a relaxed, casual conversation about policies, how much you appreciate being able to work with his company, and the advantages that should accrue to both parties as a result of the joint venture.

Do not, Okumura cautions, get involved in trying to pursue details of the project with the managing director or president. He will most likely not be familiar with them and, in any event, will be more concerned about your reliability, sincerity, and ability to deal with the company.

Before an American businessman commits himself to doing business with another company, he checks out the company's assets, technology, financial stability, etc. The Japanese businessman is first interested in the character and quality of the people in the other company and secondarily interested in its facilities and finances. The Japanese put more stock in goodwill and the quality of interpersonal relationships in their business dealings.

MIZU SHOBAI (THE "WATER BUSINESS")

Mizu shobai (Mee-zoo show-bye), literally "water business," is a euphemism for the so-called entertainment trade—which is another euphemism for the hundreds of thousands of bars, cabarets, night clubs, "soap houses" (formerly known as Turkish baths), hotspring spas, and geisha inns that flourish in Japan. The term *mizu* is applied to this area of Japanese life because, like pleasure, water sparkles and soothes, then goes down the drain or evaporates into the air (and the business of catering to fleshly pleasures was traditionally associated with hot baths). *Shobai* or "business" is a very appropriate word, because the *mizu shobai* is one of the biggest businesses in Japan, employing some 5 million men and women.

Drinking and enjoying the companionship of attractive young women in *mizu shobai* establishments is an important part of the lives of Japanese businessmen. There are basically two reasons for their regular drinking. First, ritualistic drinking developed into an integral part of religious life in ancient times, and from there it was carried over into social and business life.

Thus, for centuries, no formal function or business dealing of any kind has been complete without a drinking party (*uchiage*) (uu-chee-ah-gay) to mark the occasion. At such times, drinking is more of a duty than anything else. Only a person who cannot drink because of some physical condition or illness is normally excused.

The second reason for the volume of customary drinking that goes on in Japan is related to the distinctive subordinate-superior relationships between people and to the minutely prescribed etiquette that prevents the Japanese from being completely informal and frank with each other *except when drinking.*

Because the Japanese must be so circumspect in their behavior at all "normal" times, they believe it is impossible to really get to know a person without drinking with him. The sober person, they say, will always hold back and not reveal his true character. They feel ill at ease with anyone who refuses to drink with them at a party or outing. They feel that refusing to drink indicates a person is arrogant, excessively proud, and unfriendly. The ultimate expression of goodwill, trust, and humility is to drink to drunkenness with your coworkers and with close or important business associates in general. Those who choose for any reason not to go all the way must simulate drunkenness in order to fulfill the requirements of the custom.

Enjoying the companionship of pretty, young women has long been a universal prerogative of successful men everywhere. In Japan it often goes further than that. It has traditionally been used as an inducement to engage in business as well as to seal bargains, probably because it is regarded as the most intimate activity men can share.

When the Japanese businessman offers his Western guest or client intimate access to the charms of attractive and willing young women— something that still happens regularly—he is not "pandering" or engaging in any other "nasty" practice. He is merely offering the Western businessman a form of hospitality that has been popular in Japan since ancient times. In short, Japanese businessmen do openly and without guilt feelings, what many Western businessmen do furtively.

The foreign businessman who "passes" when offered the opportunity to indulge in this honorable Japanese custom, either before or after a bargain is struck, may be regarded as foolish or prudish for letting the opportunity go by, but he is no longer likely to be accused of insincerity.

Many Westerners find it difficult to join in wholeheartedly at the round of parties typically held for them by their Japanese hosts, especially if it is nothing more than a drinking party at a bar or cabaret. Westerners have been conditioned to intersperse their drinking with jokes, boasting, and long-winded opinions—supposedly rational—on religion, politics, business, or what-have-you.

Japanese businessmen, on the other hand, do not go to bars or clubs at night to have serious discussions. They go there to relax emotionally and physically—to let it all hang out. They joke, laugh, sing, dance, and make short, rapid-fire comments about work, their superiors, personal problems, and so on; but they do not have long, deep discussions.

When the otherwise reserved and carefully controlled Japanese businessman does relax in a bar, cabaret, or at a drinking party, he often acts—from a Western viewpoint—like a high school kid in his "cups" for the first time.

At a reception given by a group of American dignitaries at one of Tokyo's leading hotels, my table partner was the chief of the research division of the Japanese company being honored. The normally sober and distinguished scientist had had a few too many by the time the speeches began, and he was soon acting in the characteristic manner of the Japanese drunk. All during the speeches he giggled, sang, burped, and whooped it up, much to the embarrassment of both sides.

Most Japanese businessmen, particularly those in lower and middle management, drink regularly and have developed an extraordinary capacity to drink heavily night after night and keep up their day-to-day work. Since they drink to loosen up and enjoy themselves, to be hospitable and to get to know their drinking partners, they are suspicious of anyone who drinks and remains formal and sober. They call this "killing the *sake*," with the added connotation that it also kills the pleasure.

During a boisterous drinking bout in which they sing and dance and trade risqué banter with hostesses or geisha, Japanese businessmen often sober up just long enough to have an important business exchange with a guest or colleague and then go back to the fun and games.

Foreign businessmen should be very cautious about trying to keep up with their Japanese hosts at such drinking rituals. It is all too common to see visiting businessmen being returned to their hotels well after midnight, sodden drunk. The key to this important ceremony is to drink moderately and simulate drunkenness.

In recent years, inflation has dimmed some of the nightly glow from geisha houses, the great cabarets, the bars, and the "in" restaurants in Japan's major cities. The feeling is also growing that the several billion dollars spent each year in the *mizu shobai* is incompatible with Japan's present-day needs. But like so many other aspects of Japanese life, the *mizu shobai* is deeply embedded in the overall socioeconomic system, as well as in the national psyche. It is not about to disappear in the foreseeable future.

Most of the money spent in the *mizu shobai* comes from the so-called *Sha-Yo Zoku* (Shah-Yoe Zoe-kuu), "Expense-Account Tribe"—the large number of salesmen, managers, and executives who are authorized to entertain clients, prospects, and guests at company expense. Japanese companies are permitted a substantial tax write-off for entertainment expenses to begin with, and most go way beyond the legal limit (based on their capital), according to both official and unofficial sources.

34
Beyond Steve Canyon and Rambo: Feminist Histories of Militarized Masculinity

CYNTHIA ENLOE

The human construction of identities, roles, and institutions is well illustrated in this essay. Most importantly, the author shows how these constructions are related to one another, capturing the idea in her phrase, "the militarization of masculinity." Like other institutions today, the military is feeling strains and making changes in light of changing gender roles and relations in the society at large.

Militarization is a societal process, just as urbanization or industrialization are societal processes. Gendering, the masculinizing and feminizing of certain roles and symbols, has been as central to militarization as it has been to other social processes. Yet the relationship between gender and militarization remains obscure, in part because we assume that the military has always been men's business, always requiring a certain type of masculinity.

Now that large numbers of persons of the female sex are also in the armed forces, it would seem that gender would be a subject of considerable interest. However, recognition of gender is not just a matter of giving women a place in military history, for gender was there long before women were. Gender is what is understood as the differences between the sexes, what is ascribed to masculinity and femininity, what men and women are supposed to stand for, whatever they may actually be. The gendering of the military thus has a long history predating the modern female soldier; and the militarization of gender affects men and women who have nothing to do with the military as such. As societal processes, gendering and militarization are inseparable, though their relationship has varied widely over time and space and is never unproblematic or uncontested. The definition of sexual difference has been constantly changing in the present century. The idea of what militarized masculinity should be was not necessarily the same in the First and Second World Wars as it has been in the post-1960s wars. Nor does the militarization of either masculinity or femininity necessarily take the same form or depend on the same lures and sanctions to be sustained in Japan as it does in Britain or in Vietnam. How "motherhood," "sweetheart," "buddy," or "nerd" as proscriptive characterizations will support or undermine militarization has to be explored in the context of a given time and place. This essay will only suggest some of the dimensions of the gendering process on which the militarization process has depended in order to make it both more visible and more problematic.

I grew up with a blue-haired Superman fighting Nazi spies. Golden-haired Steve Canyon was my comic strip passport to wartime Asia. My father, serving as a physician with Wingate's commandos in Burma, was part of the group of British, American, and Australian soldiers who inspired Milton Caniff to write his famed Steve Canyon strip. In a process analogous to novelist Bobbie Ann Mason's teenage Kentucky girl making sense of her father's death in the Vietnam War by watching tv reruns of M*A*S*H, I began to formulate ideas about what it was like to be my father in World War II Burma by reading Steve Canyon comics. Perhaps even the men who were in those unconventional commando units mingle their own memories today with images from Steve Canyon and Terry and the Pirates. My mother, on the other hand, didn't inspire wartime comic book creators. She was neither the Dragon Lady nor Cheetah. And I don't remember her ever reading these strips. She took care of my brother David and me as essentially a single parent for months at a time. She cooked meals and provided a home-away-from-home for my father's army air corps friends when they and he were back in the United States between overseas duties.

Each of us in our own way took for granted a symmetry between masculinity and militarism, whether that was presented in popular culture or in the lives of family members. I didn't give any thought to whether the link between masculinity and militarism had to be forged. I didn't wonder about how that forging was done. I didn't imagine debates, obstacles, manipulative strategies, setbacks, or costs.

It is only now, forty years later, reading my mother's enticingly cryptic diaries from those years, listening to my father describe plans for commando reunions, comparing Steve Canyon reprints with the latest Rambo toy narratives that I have begun to ask questions. How have men from different cultures had their notions of manhood—and womanhood—shaped and reshaped by officials (largely male) so as to permit governments to wage the sorts of wars they have imagined to be necessary? What contradictions or failures have had to be camouflaged in order to allow the ideological symmetry between masculinity and militarism to appear unproblematic, "natural?"

In the late 1980s, Rambo has caught the imaginations of millions of people. For a time it was the top film in both the United States and Britain. It is being viewed on vcrs from the mountains of Luzon in the Philippines to downtown Helsinki by people as different as Filipino guerrillas and anti–Cold War Finns. Sylvester Stallone's character has gone on to inspire fashions, dolls, and television series. "Rambo" has slipped quickly into the global lingo of adults as well as children, of militarism's critics as well as its enthusiasts. For many of us, "Rambo" has become, I think, a handy shorthand for a complex package of ideas and processes that we believe are dangerous to all women and many men. Rambo's brand of militarized masculinity is being compared and contrasted by students of popular culture with those of World War II movie idol John Wayne and contemporary National Security Council bureaucratic entrepreneur Lt. Col. Oliver North.

One of the most important contributions feminists have made to the analysis of war and peace—and militarized peace—is their descriptions of how notions about masculinity and femininity have helped to promote and sustain the military. While other critical analysts have given economic, racist, and bureaucratic patterns their prime attention, feminists have concentrated on the social constructions of gender. The accumulation of more and more evidence from more and more societies has made feminists increasingly confident in asserting that the omission of gender—femininity and masculinity—from any explanation of how militarization occurs not only risks a flawed political analysis; it risks, too, perpetually unsuccessful efforts to roll back militarization.

At this juncture in the historical evolution of feminism, "Rambo" has appeared. Its remarkable cross-cultural popular appeal—an appeal fueled by immense infusions of corporate capital—has seemed to confirm the feminist analysis. First, social constructions of masculinity—not just elite interests or state bureaucracies and their cosmologies—are serving to entrench and extend the grip of militarism. Second, militarism's reliance on particular forms of masculinity apparently exists in societies with otherwise different cultures and at different levels of industrialization. Third, militarizing masculinity cannot succeed without women also being made to play their parts in the militarizing process; although vital, those parts must be kept ideologically marginal.

I find these explanatory arguments persuasive. But I'm beginning to wonder whether they are enough. Specifically, I think we may need to test two new sets of hypotheses in our continuing exploration of how militarization works:

(1) All societies use, though each in its own way, ideas about masculinity and about femininity to organize themselves for state-controlled violence.

(2) It requires more than just one form of masculinity and more than one form of femininity to make militarization work in each setting.

In the following pages I will consider these hypotheses as they help reveal how militarization occurs in: (1) coping with the experience of wars past (won or lost); (2) the militarization of the Third World; (3) the internationalization of the military; (4) the militarization of sexuality; (5) the militarization of a society's civilian sector.

Rambo is not Steve Canyon. Steve Canyon may get a bit confused when he moves from comic strip World War II to comic strip war in 1950s Indochina. But he remains a character on a winning side. While somewhat of a maverick, he doesn't feel he's at war with his superiors. World War II, in this simplistic portrayal, seemed to involve a militarization of masculinity that served the state without depriving the white American male of his sense of individuality and his emotional attachment to women. The Rambo character is quite different. He openly defies his superiors. He tries to reopen a war that his state authorities want declared "over," if not won. He is so unconnected to either his fellow men or women that he rarely speaks in whole sentences. Rambo is a peculiarly "post-Vietnam" type of American militarized male. His message for men is about how to cope with national humiliation and elite betrayal: by resorting to individualistic military adventurism that defies official hierarchies but restores a nation's "pride" in its military.

But do men in other societies have the same responses to national humiliation? How have Belgian, Dutch, German, Chinese, Polish, Egyptian, Italian, Japanese, or French constructions of masculinity been affected by twentieth-century military losses? "Humiliation" is both a gendered and an enculturated emotion. So we might expect it to be militarized in quite dissimilar ways in different countries, with the consequence that "Rambo" will be absorbed (or rejected) in quite dissimilar ways.

The very definition of a war "lost" is problematic. As Finnish feminist Eva Isaksson asked, "Did you ever consider whether men in countries that lost their wars really think that they actually lost?" It may be that men and women in the same country ("on the same side") carry into contemporary political action quite contrary presumptions about whether there is anything to feel humiliated or repentant or defiant about. Moreover, men of different social classes may conceive of a war's outcome in ways so various that it produces quite dissimilar relationships between their senses of masculinity and its relationship to the state military.

Thus it is always useful to examine the current trend in militarizing masculinity in the context of what particular men imagine to be "the last war." For example, Klaus Theweleit, the German historian, has delved into the most intimate fantasies of men in the Freikorps. He argues that this particular group of men were militarized in large part by their desperate flight from the feminine. But this flight and the hatred for women it produced, which was so effectively manipulated by conservative authorities from 1918 through World War II, wasn't fueled by an ahistorical misogyny. According to Theweleit, it was rooted in these men's particular experience of a war lost, the First World War. In other words, to understand how the men in particular classes, ethnic groups, and nations adopt or reject notions of military humiliation and redemption we need to take seriously the militarization dynamics of "postwar" eras.

Let us take another example, one that is not idle speculation in 1989. How does military humiliation resonate among women and men in contemporary Japan? Despite U.S. government pressure on the Japanese to remilitarize and despite Prime Minister Nakasone's apparent desire to play down Japan's World War II errors and to revive the nation's military strength, Japanese popular notions of masculinity to date do not seem easily remilitarized. Yet Japanese feminists are closely monitoring what they believe are important, if subtle, efforts by the government to transform the postwar economistic model of Japanese masculinity in ways that will make it more amenable to a U.S.-backed military build-up.

Do men in other societies sift an alleged national humiliation through a militarized sieve in ways that make them respond to "Rambo" in precisely the same individualistically defiant way that American men seem to? I doubt it. In every country where "Rambo" seems to have become a cultural hero, students of militarization should look to see exactly what it is in the character and the narrative that is attractive to men. What do those tendencies, in turn, tell us about how men in those countries might be drawn to support militarism or reject it?

There is a second territory for our investigation of possible varieties of militarized masculinity: cross-national military training programs. Is "a drill sergeant a drill sergeant a drill sergeant"? The British government is an old hand at militarization. One of its successful empire-building strategies was to build armies out of local colonialized labor. To do that, British officials had to find ways to persuade local male rulers that their personal authority and status would be enhanced if they would allow the British to build them "proper" armies filled with "proper" soldiers. Then they had to persuade thousands of male peasants and nomadic herdsmen that their manhood would be enhanced within their own communities if they would enlist in the newly created British-controlled armies. There was nothing automatic about either of these processes. Creating modern armies out of traditional materials was never an easy task. It involved a subtle mix of persuasion and coercion, always varied by time and by place.

This complex historical process was more than a matter of exporting British notions of militarized manhood to different ethnic communities in India, Nigeria, and Malaysia. Reading old training manuals and eavesdropping on British colonial officials' reminiscences suggest that considerable adaptation had to go on to make this imperial strategy work. That is, masculinity could not be militarized in Scotland in exactly the same ways that it could be militarized in India or Nigeria. Furthermore, women in each of these countries—Britain, India, and Nigeria—were thought of as playing slightly different roles in order to sustain the "manly soldier" needed by the empire. This was rarely talked about in formal reports and typically is ignored entirely by military historians. But it was analyzed at length by feminist reformers in the 1880s, when, having won the repeal of the patriarchal Contagious Diseases Acts, they launched an international campaign to expose the British government's policies toward military prostitution in India. Campaigners writing in their journal *The Dawn* noted that British male officials believed that, for some reason, Indian male soldiers didn't use Indian women as prostitutes in the same ways as British male soldiers posted in India did. The bureaucratic debates over how to reduce venereal disease among British soldiers stationed abroad became a discussion of differences between British soldiers' and the empire's foreign soldiers' militarized sexuality.

World Wars I and II both were fought by major powers with men (and, less visibly, with women) from their respective colonies. The British government used Indian and Caribbean men as soldiers; the Japanese government used Korean men; the French used Vietnamese and North African men; the Germans used East African men; the Americans used Native American, Hawaiian, Puerto Rican, and Filipino men. Out of these wars male officials drew lessons about what sorts of masculinity "worked" in combined military operations. But, with few exceptions, we know little about how these men from the colonized societies experienced militarized standards of manhood or how such experiences shaped postwar nationalist movements and the relations between local men and women and imperial and colonized men. Nor have we been curious enough about how postcolonial military policies concerning training, leadership, sexuality, marriage, or weaponry have been molded in part by these World War I or II interactions between colonizing and colonized military men. Studies of the career patterns and military curricula of South Korea, the Philippines or Jamaica might be one place to start in understanding the varieties of military cultures around the world.

Training is rarely devoid of historically gendered "lessons." The British government, despite a shrunken empire, continues to energetically export its military training expertise. It is often an instrument for promoting the sale of military equipment. But it is more than that. In November 1986, the British government signed an agreement to start training Mozambiquan soldiers. Reports suggested that it was the Zimbabwean regime of Robert Mugabe, a supporter of the besieged Mozambiquan FRELIMO-led government, which smoothed the way (the western press called it "acting as the midwife") for this military training agreement. Evidently, Zimbabwean officials have been pleased with the British military programs impact upon its own military, a force that had to be rebuilt at the end of the Zimbabwean revolutionary war. Does this mean that contemporary British military strategies for turning 1980s British middle-class men into officers and working-class (often in fact unemployed) urban men into useful soldiers can be applied to rural Zimbabwean men of different ethnic groups with no adjustments?

What do officials of the importing governments hope to gain by subjecting their military men to foreign training? Perhaps such policy choices imply an elite's disappointment with their society's current constructions of masculinity. Perhaps the acceptance of British or United States—or French, Cuban, East German, or Israeli—military training teams suggests that a country's male officials imagine their own male citizens to be "undisciplined." That is, maybe they believe that the "traditional" construction of masculinity in their own societies (or at least in the ethnic communities from which they choose to recruit most of their soldiery) is too "wild" or "disorderly" to serve the regime's own goals of national unification, social order, and state security. Alternatively—or perhaps simultaneously—the present elite might imagine that the conventions of manhood among their male population are too dismissive of the sorts of modern weapons technology that requires literacy and patience. Thus they have concluded that American or British or East German men's approaches to militarizing masculinity will produce the kinds of soldiers they think they need. And the exporting officials are more than eager to comply.

Elites who invite foreign soldiers to train their men may go so far as to imagine that their own men, subjected to such manipulation, will return to civilian society after their military service as more productive male farmers, more loyal government supporters, more responsible fathers. Certainly all of these assumptions are encouraged in the exporting governments' own recruiting promotions. What do these same officials assume, then, about their women citizens' reactions to their fathers', husbands', and brothers' new attitudes?

The flow of consequences from the internalizations of military training has never been one-way, however. The men who have acted as colonial officers, international liaisons, or foreign advisors have returned home from their assignments with lasting notions about which masculine traits in their own societies make them, as men, "naturally" better, braver, more inventive, more professional, more disciplined—and better soldiers than the men from the other cultures they have been sent to train. Usually there is a strong element of ethnocentrism or outright racism mixed into these paternalistic militarized, masculinized memories. . . .

There also are growing differences among NATO's militaries concerning the alleged relationship between homosexuality and "national security." The Canadian parliament in 1986 was pressed by feminists to drop the exclusion of lesbians and gay men from the Canadian armed forces. In the United States, political mobilization among lesbians and gay men is light years ahead of where it stood in the 1940s. One consequence is that the U.S. government today faces multiple court actions brought by women's and civil liberties groups challenging the legality —and the logic—of discharging women and men accused of homosexuality.

In virtually every NATO military the constructions of masculinity and femininity—and the relationship of each to military preparedness and national security—are in flux. The Dutch, West German, U.S., French, and Italian governments—as dissimilar as they are in terms of historical memory and in contemporary strategic roles—in the late 1980s are all carrying on discussions about how to make more military use of "their" women: they are fretting about women's decisions to have fewer children, but they refuse fundamentally to alter their notions of military "manpower" needs. How each regime goes about resolving this gendered strategic dilemma will vary. Among the critical variables will be: 1) the strength of each country's women's movement and lesbian-gay movement; 2) the historic ties among civilian manhood, the conception of citizenship, and the state's military; 3) the current elite's definition of "national security"; 4) the availability of young men from the classes and ethnic groups that the military commanders trust. The gendered dynamics of an multinational military alliance such as NATO will be the product of each of these domestic relationships worked out through the unequal structure of NATO itself.

What would the Warsaw Pact's internal politics look like through similar lenses? Ethnic Russian men at the top of the Soviet military command structure worry more about their growing dependence on Asian Soviet men for rank-and-file soldiery. Historically, this seems to be a new worry. It derives not from the lessons these men have drawn from Soviet experiences in World War II, but from the meanings they are assigning to the Red Army's experiences in Afghanistan. Will they move toward using more women, especially "European" Soviet women, in uniformed military jobs? And if they do (there is evidence that this is already happening), and if they find they can control the dynamics of masculinity and femininity sufficiently not to damage their military performance, will they then encourage other Warsaw Pact regimes to recruit more women as a complement to and not a substitute for continued pressure on women from trusted ethnic groups to produce more future soldiers? Already Rumania and Yugoslavia make increased use of women in their national security formulas—especially in local militias and in the name of "home defense." This institutionalized rationale avoids fundamentally challenging existing ideological ties between manhood and militarism. But both of these regimes are outside the core of the Warsaw Pact, making their gendered military innovations less likely to affect intraalliance dynamics.

Joint maneuvers are feats of logistical and political management. They are also tests of militarized gender management. For the success or failure of any joint maneuver hangs on whether soldiers and officers of different cultures can learn to trust each other. And trust depends on some shared understandings of "bravery," "loyalty," "reasonableness," "reliability," and "skill." Each of these concepts is gendered. That is, each is infused with presumptions about proper behavior for "real men" and "real women." But are they each gendered in precisely the same way in each society whose soldiers are thrown together on a supposedly hostile battlefield? If they aren't, how do sergeants, majors, and generals try to reconcile those differences so that the joint maneuver will "work"?

It may be that different militarized masculinities are not fully reconciled; they only are band-aided over with misogyny. How often do Honduran and American men on "Big Pine" joint maneuvers camouflage their basic distrust of one another by trading jokes about the Honduran women working as prostitutes around their camps?

Military medicine is [another] site for making visible the historical processes involved in militarizing masculinity. In 1909, U.S. Army physicians conservatively estimated that two hundred men out of every one thousand troops were being hospitalized for venereal disease. According to historian Allan Brandt, between April 1917 and December 1919 the U.S. military as a whole recorded 383,706 male soldiers having been diagnosed with either syphillis, gonorrhea, or chancroid. By the end of World War I these numbers had set off a debate inside the American military establishment over which conceptualization of militarized masculinity best served the U.S. war effort in Europe.

Allan Brandt describes how Progressive reformers pressed the military to rely on the "cleansing influence of war" to restore the moral purity of American manhood. Following this policy, military officers would appeal to American male soldiers' sense of their own moral aspirations and to their capacities for self-control. But many military authorities were skeptical. Their notions of manhood in khaki were less optimistic. Instead of trusting the moral self-control of their troops, these commanders argued that they should be allowed to institute compulsory medical exams for soldiers and, much more controversial, that they should be authorized to distribute chemical prophylaxes to their men. They based their policy stance on the assumption that "men will be men," especially when taken away from the restraining influences of the feminized home environment. These military men cared less about promoting war's "cleansing influence" than about ensuring military victory.

Every military strategy for preventing sexually transmitted diseases among male soldiers has had as its companion a strategy for controlling women, local women and foreign women. One can read the political history of venereal disease and now AIDS as an account of how military officials have sought to control women and the idea of femininity for the sake of getting and keeping the kinds of militarized men they have wanted. Indoctrination and basic training courses for male soldiers have had to be carefully designed; those for women soldiers have had to be fashioned quite differently. Guidelines for the practice of military medicine and public health officials have had to be assessed with an eye to manpower and morale needs. Health department officials operating in the towns near military bases have had to be persuaded to conduct their business in ways that support the kinds of masculine and feminine behavior thought to enhance the military. Training courses and policies for "doughnut dollies" and other women volunteers have had to be fashioned so that those women's work bolsters rather than shakes militarized men's morale.

Civilian and uniformed policymakers have not found it easy to design policies that maintain the military's legitimacy in the eyes of the wider citizenry, with its own expectations about appropriate masculine and feminine behavior, while simultaneously ensuring a kind of soldiery presumed to optimize military effectiveness. Policymakers have worried over compulsory genital exams for their male soldiers, fearing they might jeopardize the men's morale. They have debated whether women in the military should be given the same access to contraceptives as men in the military. There have been twists and turns in military policy regarding whether to allow prostitutes on military bases and whether to leave the physical exams of suspected prostitutes to local civilian authorities. Policymakers have seemed to be in a perpetual state of uncertainty over whether marriage should be promoted among soldiers as a way of cutting down on the costly incidence of venereal disease, and, if so, whether that encouragement should extend to marriages between their own male soldiers and women from the foreign countries in which they are based. Finally, regardless of which policy options are chosen, there remains the thorny question of how the military and civilian officials should describe and justify these policies to the public.

Since the V-2 rockets were invented and launched over the English Channel, militaries in the most advanced industrialized societies have needed more than footsoldiers and generals. Their governments have believed they have needed underground missile silo technicians, cartographers, factory managers, engineers, and physicists.

Despite the increasing numbers of women being assigned to "noncombat" posts, most of these jobs in the militarized infrastructure are filled by men. Yet are the standards for masculinity the same in the various sectors of technology? While the frontline infantryman—or even an action-seeking lieutenant colonel sitting in the White House basement—may respond to the peculiarly Ramboesque mix of masculinity and militarization, will the scientist sitting at his laboratory computer designing a satellite laser weapon respond in the same way?

Most of our descriptions of civilian workers, business managers, scientists, and intellectuals in military contract work describe American men. For instance, William Broad has reported on the emerging subculture at the Lawrence Livermore Laboratories in California, the site of President Reagan's Strategic Defense Initiative's ("Star Wars") most esoteric research. His book, *Star Warriors*, is not feminist—he is only slightly curious about the women whose less dramatic labors or emotional validation sustain SDI research and political lobbying. Yet he does provide considerable information about how these male scientists talk, dream, and joke. Few of them are married or have girlfriends. Most of them seem to live at their computer terminals, except when they take breaks to drink coke or consume great quantities of ice cream. They don't appear to be particularly violent; they don't wear army surplus fatigues; they don't have rifles mounted on the backs of their pick-up trucks. They do have a penchant for boyish pranks. They do seem to thrive on competition and to see both the scientific world and the larger world as places where rivalry is the norm.

The latter is the ideological trait that seems to make them likely candidates for militarization. And in fact the men who recruited these young scientists made a point of playing upon their competitiveness to attract them to SDI weapons research. Still, they appear unlikely candidates for a military's basic training. They are too contemptuous of collective discipline. Their notions of action seem more cerebral than physical. And yet they clearly find deep reassurances about their own manhood in the militarized science they do. And the U.S. elites who see militarization as the bedrock of American security need for these men to feel those reassurances. That, as much as grant money, is what makes these male scientists militarizable. Admirers of Sylvester Stallone might hold these Livermore men in contempt, branding them "nerds," but they are no less critical for the 1980s militarizing of American society than M-16 wielding "grunts."

The men who lure scientists into militarized laboratory communities appear to have notions about their recruits' sexual needs not shared by their army or navy counterparts. For instance, institutionalized homophobia doesn't seem to send off warning sirens when a young male engineer eschews girls. Nor do the men responsible for the morale of the Livermore scientists seem to think they require brothels just outside the laboratory's gates. Has anyone suggested that these "Star Warriors" be sent to VD classes? Why not?

Richard Rhodes's new history of the making of the U.S. atomic bomb has been glowingly described as exhaustive and comprehensive. But when Rhodes turns his thoughts to the gendered dynamics of this militarized scientific enterprise and the peculiar community it fostered in the New Mexican desert, his curiosity suddenly wanes. Not just are the roles that women played outside his realm of historical curiosity, so are the principal male actors' notions about themselves as men interacting with women and with other men. For instance, Rhodes slips into a "lighthearted" section on the ways members of the Los Alamos community entertained themselves with a tantalizingly brief account of a debate over prostitution and "loose women." The discovery of regular visits being made by men to the single women's barracks set off an official discussion about the dangers of VD, the needs of men, and the authority of the army and civilian officials. "We did decide to continue it," one official told Rhodes. But we learn nothing more. Rhodes and his interviewee seem to share some unspoken cross-generational masculinized understanding that even in the Manhattan Project, "men will be men." That understanding shuts the door on what might have been a revealing exploration into the ways in which militarized male scientists match or diverge from their infantry counterparts. Rhodes's failure of curiosity also leaves it to a future historian to uncover how the male authorities conceptualized the sexual needs of male scientists. It may be that militarized masculinity takes one form when men are socialized into the world of nuclear warfare planning, while it takes quite a different form when men are socialized into the world of what is euphemistically called conventional warfare.

Carol Cohn is a feminist who has had the unusual opportunity to spend time inside a civilian think tank at the Massachusetts Institute of Technology devoted to strategic theorizing. She describes still another breed of militarized American masculinity that has emerged since World War II—the "defense intellectual." These men seem more likely to have social relations with women. More are married. Many of them seem able to turn on "the charm." Although all of their professional peers are men, they interact more regularly with the women who work for them as secretaries. As yet, though, we don't know much about what sorts of emininity their wives, lovers, and secretaries are pressed to adopt in order maintain smooth relationships with men who get satisfaction out of being defense intellectuals.

What Carol Cohn reveals, however, is the elaborate and often surprising linguistic and ideological formulas that these men construct to enable them to discuss death and destruction day after day. Some of the language is embarrassingly (at least to the feminist ear) phallic. They talk constantly about "penetrations," "thrusts." But Cohn finds that many of the terms these American men have created to discuss efficient death and destruction are unexpectedly domestic: they pat a missile not as if it were a sexual object, but as if it were a baby or a puppy. As Carol Cohn observes, "The creatures one pats are small, cute, harmless—not terrifyingly destructive. Pat it, and its lethality disappears." These men's subculture isn't quite as isolated as that of the men at Livermore Laboratory; but they have created a language and cosmology that seems to permit them to reduce their emotional investment in the actual outcomes of their abstract "scenarios."

This sort of militarized man, the defense intellectual, has come to play an increasingly influential role in those political systems that have—or wish to have—a regional or even global military role and that have technologically and industrially complex infrastructures to back up that role. It may be historically a new construction of masculinity, one that did not exist on the brink of either World War I or World War II. In societies with this brand of militarization, military planning has become too complex, presumably, for generals, politicians, and weapons producers.

Still to be written are feminist descriptions of how masculinity—and thus femininity—are constructed within companies and factories reliant on defense contracts. From Hilary Wainwright we do have a sense that at least some British women working today in the usually feminized electrical units of defense factories do not seem to get the ideological or monetary rewards that their male counterparts do from working on weapons. However, they may be encouraged to see themselves as supporting "our boys" as sort of surrogate militarized mothers. But what of white-collar middle managers and senior executives, the largely masculinized management strata of aerospace, armaments, and electronics companies who have made conscious decisions to pursue local and foreign defense contracts? Perhaps they get some boost to their sense of manhood from being involved with such products and from being in regular contact with military officers.

Women as wives and lovers have to make adjustments in order to support or validate these choices. Marriages are affected when men become more and more involved in secret work, when their business days are shaped by state security concepts, or when their professional colleagues are military professionals. When a corporate contractor's wife refuses to make these adjustments in her marriage she may send small tremors through her country's military-industrial complex.

I think it would be a mistake to imagine that, because each one of these cogs in the increasingly complex military machine appears to rely on notions of masculinity, all the parts automatically work together in smooth precision. "Grunts," "nerds," "defense intellectuals," "captains of industry," "the brass"—all may be masculinized, but those masculinizations may not create bonds of trust or respect. William Broad's SDI scientists and Carol Cohn's defense intellectuals both talk of the military officers and the civilian politicians they deal with quite contemptuously. Conversely, uniformed military men of various ranks may dismiss scientists and intellectuals as too removed from reality (as they see it). It would not be surprising if some of this mutual derision were translated into comments about the other's tenuous manliness and the other's failed relations with women.

So, once again, sorting out possible varieties of masculinity—here within a single militarized society—need not induce factor-juggling paralysis. It could equip feminists with more accurate portraits of the ideological requirements any technologically sophisticated and spatially interventionist militarizing government has to try to meet. It may shed light on tensions and contradictions within those military systems, exposing them as less impermeable, more fragile.

Yet we should avoid Americanizing our analysis. It doesn't follow that every militarizing society is constructing the same divisions of labor or the same varieties of masculinity to sustain its military system. The Soviet Union, France, Britain, Israel, and South Africa may come closest to replicating the current American masculinized, militarized division of labor. Each of these states has been trying to build its own scientific and industrial military infrastructure. Each prides itself on its capacity to absorb information and make plans. But are Soviet engineers afraid of other men calling them the Russian equivalent of "nerds" if they carry calculators clipped to their belts?

Are Israeli defense intellectuals as prone as their American counterparts to looking down upon uniformed military men? They—as well as Israeli men working as engineers in the country's large weapons industry—are said to be able to sympathize with their male counterparts in uniform because they too serve in the military as reservists until the age of fifty-five. Not many societies, however, have a conscription system that helps to ensure this empathy between men socialized into different forms of militarized masculinity.

Each country may be distinguished by its own sort of tension between militarized masculinities. Consequently, roles that different groups of women are pressured to play in order to reduce or mask those tensions in the name of a smoothly running military machine might be somewhat different.

Militarization is a tricky process. It occurs both during those periods of intense militarization that we call "war" and during periods that we refer to as "peace" or "prewar" or "postwar" or "interwar." Militarization is occurring when any part of a society becomes controlled by or dependent on the military or on military values. Virtually anything can be militarized: toys, marriage, scientific research, university curriculums, motherhood, fatherhood, AIDS, immigration, racism, shopping, or comic strips. Each one of these processes involves the transformation of meanings and relationships. Rarely does it happen without the use of public power and authority. Occasionally the process is reversed. Children's play seemed to be demilitarized in the early 1970s, as evidenced by "G.I. Joe's" sharp fall in sales. Those American, Canadian, European, and Japanese scientists who are refusing to take part in SDI research are trying to demilitarize their professions. Women in any country who refuse to see their sons' accepting conscription or voluntarily enlisting in the military as a way to cope with civilian unemployment are taking steps to demilitarize motherhood. University teachers who encourage their students to assign as much analytical "seriousness" to pacifist movements as to national security policymakers are demilitarizing at least a small part of their curriculum.

Whether one is tracing militarizing social processes or demilitarizing social processes, it is necessary to chart how women and men in any particular historical setting comprehend what it means to be "manly" and what it means to be "feminine." Government and military officials not only have been effected by their own perceptions of manliness and femininity; many of them have attempted to design policies to ensure that civilians and soldiers relate to one another in those gendered ways that ease the complicated process of militarization.

PART IV

Social Institutions

35
Hanging Tongues: A Sociological Encounter with the Assembly Line

WILLIAM E. THOMPSON

This story may sound familiar to many of you: What looks like a well-paying job and an avenue to the good life turns out to be a mirage. By the time we recognize the mirage for what it is, the alternative paths have become strewn with the boulders of debt and family commitments, creating walls that can prove nearly insurmountable.

This qualitative sociological study analyzes the experience of working on a modern assembly line in a large beef plant. It explores and examines a special type of assembly line work which involves the slaughtering and processing of cattle into a variety of products intended for human consumption and other uses.

Working in the beef plant is "dirty work," not only in the literal sense of being drenched with perspiration and beef blood, but also in the figurative sense of performing a low-status, routine, and demeaning job. Although the work is honest and necessary in a society which consumes beef, slaughtering and butchering cattle is generally viewed as an undesirable and repugnant job. In that sense, workers at the beef plant share some of the same experiences as other workers in similarly regarded occupations (for example, ditchdiggers, garbage collectors, and other types of assembly line workers). . . .

THE SETTING

The setting for the field work was a major beef processing plant in the Midwest. At the time of the study, the plant was the third largest branch of a corporation which operated ten such plants in the United States. . . .

The beef plant was organizationally separated into two divisions: Slaughter and Processing. This study focused on the Slaughter division in the area of the plant known as the *kill floor*. A dominant feature of the kill floor was the machinery of the assembly line itself. The line was composed of an overhead stainless steel rail which began at the slaughter chute and curved its way around every work station in the plant. Every work station contained specialized machinery for the job performed at that place on the line. Dangling from the rail were hundreds of stainless steel hooks pulled by a motorized chain. Virtually every part of the line and all of the implements (tubs, racks, knives, etc.) were made of stainless steel. The walls were covered with a ceramic tile and the floor was made of sealed cement. There were floor drains located at every work station, so that at the end of each work segment (at breaks, lunch, and shift's end) the entire kill floor could be hosed down and cleaned for the next work period.

Another dominant feature of the kill floor was the smell. Extremely difficult to describe, yet impossible to forget, this smell combined the smells of live cattle, manure, fresh beef blood, and internal organs and their contents. This smell not only permeated the interior of the plant, but was combined on the outside with the smell of smoke from various waste products being burned and could be smelled throughout much of the community. This smell contributed greatly to the general negative feelings about work at the beef plant, as it served as the most distinguishable symbol of the beef plant to the rest of the community. The single most often asked question of me during the research by those outside the beef plant was, "How do you stand the smell?" In typical line workers' fashion, I always responded, "What smell? All I smell at the beef plant is money." . . .

METHOD

The method of this study was nine weeks of full-time participant observation as outlined by Schatzman and Strauss (1973) and Spradley (1979; 1980). To enter the setting, the researcher went through the standard application process for a summer job. No mention of the research intent was made, though it was made clear that I was a university sociology professor. After initial screening, a thorough physical examination, and a helpful reference from a former student and part-time employee of the plant, the author was hired to work on the *Offal* crew in the Slaughter division of the plant. . . .

THE WORK

. . . The line speed on the kill floor was 187. That means that 187 head of cattle were slaughtered per hour. At any particular work station, each worker was required to work at that speed. Thus, at my work station, in the period of one hour, 187 beef tongues were mechanically pulled from their hooks; dropped into a large tub filled with water; had to be taken from the tub and hung on a large stainless steel rack full of hooks; branded with a "hot brand" indicating they had been inspected by a USDA inspector; and then covered with a small plastic bag. The rack was taken to the cooler, replaced with an empty one, and the process began again.

It would be logical to assume that if a person worked at a steady, continuous pace of handling 187 tongues per hour, everything would go smoothly; not so. In addition to hanging, branding, and bagging tongues, the worker at that particular station also cleaned the racks and cleaned out a variety of empty stainless steel tubs used to hold hearts, kidneys, and other beef organs. Thus, in order to be free to clean the tubs when necessary, the "tongue-hanger" had to work at a slightly faster pace than the line moved. Then, upon returning from cleaning the tubs, the worker would be behind the line (*in a hole*) and had to work much faster to catch up with the line. Further, one fifteen-minute break and a thirty-minute lunch break were scheduled for an eight-hour shift. Before the "tongue-hanger" could leave his post for one of these, all tongues were required to be properly disposed of, all tubs washed and stored, and the work area cleaned.

My first two nights on the job, I discovered the consequences of working at the line speed (hanging, branding, and bagging each tongue as it fell in the tub). At the end of the work period when everybody else was leaving the work floor for break or lunch, I was furiously trying to wash all the tubs and clean the work area. Consequently, I missed the entire fifteen minute break and had only about ten minutes for lunch. By observing other workers, I soon caught on to the system. Rather than attempting to work at a steady pace consistent with the line speed, the norm was to work sporadically at a very frenzied pace, actually running ahead of the line and plucking tongues from the hooks before they got to the station. With practice, I learned to hang two or three tongues at a time, perform all the required tasks, and then take an unscheduled two or three minute break until the line caught up with me. Near break and lunch everybody worked at a frantic pace, got ahead of the line, cleaned the work areas, and even managed to add a couple of minutes to the scheduled break or lunch.

Working ahead of the line seems to have served as more than merely a way of gaining a few minutes of extra break time. It also seemed to take on a symbolic meaning. The company controlled the speed of the line. Seemingly, that took all element of control over the work process away from the workers. . . . However, when the workers refused to work at line speed and actually worked faster than the line, they not only added a few minutes of relaxation from the work while the line caught up, but they symbolically regained an element of control over the pace of their own work. . . .

COPING

One of the difficulties of work at the beef plant was coping with three aspects of the work: monotony, danger, and dehumanization. While individual workers undoubtedly coped in a variety of ways, some distinguishable patterns emerged.

Monotony

The monotony of the line was almost unbearable. At my work station, a worker would hang, brand, and bag between 1,350 and 1,500 beef tongues in an eight-hour shift. With the exception of the scheduled fifteen-minute break and a thirty-minute lunch period (and sporadic brief gaps in the line), the work was mundane, routine, and continuous. As in most assembly line work, one inevitably drifted into daydreams (e.g., Garson, 1975; King, 1978; Linhart, 1981). It was not unusual to look up or down the line and see workers at various stations singing to themselves, tapping their feet to imaginary music, or carrying on conversations with themselves. I found that I could work with virtually no attention paid to the job, with my hands and arms almost automatically performing their tasks. In the meantime, my mind was free to wander over a variety of topics, including taking mental notes. In visiting with other workers, I found that daydreaming was the norm. Some would think about their families, while others fantasized about sexual escapades, fishing, or anything unrelated to the job. One individual who was rebuilding an antique car at home in his spare time would meticulously mentally rehearse the procedures he was going to perform on the car the next day.

Daydreaming was not inconsequential, however. During these periods, items were most likely to be dropped, jobs improperly performed, and accidents incurred. Inattention to detail around moving equipment, stainless steel hooks, and sharp knives invariably leads to dangerous consequences. Although I heard rumors of drug use to help fight the monotony, I never saw any workers take any drugs nor saw any drugs in any workers' possession. It is certainly conceivable that some workers might have taken something to help them escape the reality of the line, but the nature of the work demanded enough attention that such a practice could be ominous.

Danger

The danger of working in the beef plant was well known. Safety was top priority (at least in theory) and management took pride in the fact that only three employee on-the-job deaths had occurred in twelve years. Although deaths were uncommon, serious injuries were not. The beef plant employed over 1,800 people. Approximately three-fourths of those employed had jobs which demanded the use of a knife honed to razor-sharpness. Despite the use of wire-mesh aprons and gloves, serious cuts were almost a daily occurrence. Since workers constantly handled beef blood, danger of infection was ever present. As one walked along the assembly line, a wide assortment of bandages on fingers, hands, arms, necks, and faces could always be seen.

In addition to the problem of cuts, workers who cut meat continuously sometimes suffered muscle and ligament damage to their fingers and hands. In one severe case, I was told of a woman who worked in processing for several years who had to wear splints on her fingers while away from the job to hold them straight. Otherwise, the muscles in her hand would constrict her fingers into the grip position, as if holding a knife. . . .

When I spoke with fellow workers about the dangers of working in the plant, I noticed interesting defense mechanisms. . . . After a serious accident, or when telling about an accident or death which occurred in years past, the workers would almost immediately dissociate themselves from the event and its victim. Workers tended to view those who suffered major accidents or death on the job in much the same way that nonvictims of crime often view crime victims as either partially responsible for the event, or at least as very different from themselves (Barlow, 1981). "Only a part-timer," "stupid," "careless" or something similar was used, seemingly to reassure the worker describing the accident that it could not happen to him. The reality of the situation was that virtually all the jobs on the kill floor were dangerous, and any worker could have experienced a serious injury at any time. . . .

Dehumanization

Perhaps the most devastating aspect of working at the beef plant (worse than the monotony and the danger) was the dehumanizing and demeaning elements of the job. In a sense, the assembly line worker became a part of the assembly line. The assembly line is not a tool used by the worker, but a machine which controls him/her. A tool can only be productive in the hands of somebody skilled in its use, and hence becomes an extension of the person using it. A machine, on the other hand, performs specific tasks, thus its operator becomes an extension of it in the production process. . . . When workers are viewed as mere extensions of the machines with which they work, their human needs become secondary in importance to the smooth mechanical functioning of the production process. In a bureaucratic structure, when "human needs collide with systems needs the individual suffers" (Hummel, 1977: 65).

Workers on the assembly line are seen as interchangeable as the parts of the product on the line itself. An example of one worker's perception of this phenomenon at the beef plant was demonstrated the day after a fatal accident occurred. I asked the men in our crew what the company did in the case of an employee death (I wondered if there was a fund for flowers, or if the shift was given time off to go to the funeral, etc.). One worker's response was: "They drag off the body, take the hard hat and boots and check 'em out to some other poor sucker, and throw him in the guy's place." While employee death on the job was not viewed quite that coldly by the company, the statement fairly accurately summarized the overall result of a fatal accident, and importance of any individual worker to the overall operation of the production process. It accurately summarized the workers' perceptions about management's attitudes toward them. . . .

SABOTAGE

It is fairly common knowledge that assemblyline work situations often led to employee sabotage or destruction of the product or equipment used in the production process (Garson, 1975; Balzer, 1976; Shostak, 1980). This is the classic experience of alienation as described by Marx (1964a,b). . . . At the beef plant I quickly learned that there was an art to effective sabotage. Subtlety appeared to be the key. "The art lies in sabotaging in a way that is not immediately discovered," as a Ford worker put it (King, 1978:202). This seemed to hold true at the beef plant as well. . . .

The greatest factor influencing the handling of beef plant products was its status as a food product intended for human consumption. . . . Though not an explicitly altruistic group, the workers realized that the product would be consumed by people (even family, relatives, and friends), so consequently, they rarely did anything to actually contaminate the product.

Despite formal norms against sabotage, some did occur. It was not uncommon for workers to deliberately cut chunks out of pieces of meat for no reason (or for throwing at other employees). While regulations required that anything that touched the floor had to be put in tubs marked "inedible," the informal procedural norms were otherwise. When something was dropped, one usually looked around to see if an inspector or foreman noticed. If not, the item was quickly picked up and put back on the line.

Several explanations might be offered for this type of occurrence. First, since the company utilized a profit-sharing plan, when workers damaged the product, or had to throw edible pieces into inedible tubs (which sold for pet food at much lower prices), profits were decreased. A decrease in profits to the company ultimately led to decreased dividend checks to employees. Consequently, workers were fairly careful not to actually ruin anything. Second, when something was dropped or mishandled and had to be rerouted to "inedible," it was more time-consuming than if the product had been handled properly and kept on the regular line. In other words, if no inspector noticed, it was easier to let it go through on the line. There was a third, and seemingly more meaningful, explanation for this behavior, however. It was against the rules to do it, it was a challenge to do it, and thus it was fun to do it.

The workers practically made a game out of doing forbidden things simply to see if they could get away with it. . . . New workers were routinely socialized into the subtle art of rulebreaking as approved by the line workers. At my particular work station, it was a fairly common practice for other workers who were covered with beef blood to come over to the tub of swirling water designed to clean the tongues, and as soon as the inspector looked away, wash their hands, arms, and knives in the tub. This procedure was strictly forbidden by the rules. If witnessed by a foreman or inspector, the tub had to be emptied, cleaned, and refilled, and all the tongues in the tub at the time had to be put in the "inedible" tub. All of that would be a time-consuming and costly procedure, yet the workers seemed to absolutely delight in successfully pulling off the act. As Balzer (1976:90) indicates:

> Since a worker often feels that much if not all of what he does is done in places designated by the company, under company control, finding ways to express personal freedom from this institutional regimentation is important.

Thus, artful sabotage served as a symbolic way in which the workers could express a sense of individuality, and hence, self-worth.

THE FINANCIAL TRAP

Given the preceding description and analysis for work at the beef plant, why did people work at such jobs? Obviously, there are a multitude of plausible answers to that question. Without doubt, however, the key is money. The current economic situation, the lack of steady employment opportunities (especially for the untrained and poorly educated), combined with the fact that the beef plant's starting wage exceeded the minimum wage by approximately $5.50 per hour emerge as the most important reasons people went to work there.

Despite the high hourly wage and fringe benefits, however, the monotony, danger, and hard physical work drove many workers away in less than a week. During my study, I observed much worker turnover. Those who stayed displayed an interesting pattern which helps explain why they did not leave. Every member of my work crew answered similarly my questions about why they stayed at the beef plant. Each of them took the job directly after high school, because it was the highest-paying job available. Each of them had intended to work through the summer and then look for a better job in the fall. During that first summer on the job they fell victim to what I label the "financial trap."

The "financial trap" was a spending pattern which demanded the constant weekly income provided by the beef plant job. This scenario was first told to me by an employee who had worked at the plant for over nine years. He began the week after his high school graduation, intending only to work that summer in order to earn enough money to attend college in the fall. After about four weeks' work he purchased a new car. He figured he could pay off the car that summer and still save enough money for tuition. Shortly after the car purchase, he added a new stereo sound system to his debt; next came a motorcycle; then the decision to postpone school for one year in order to continue working at the beef plant and pay off his debts. A few months later he married;

within a year purchased a house; had a child; and bought another new car. Nine years later, he was still working at the beef plant, hated every minute of it, but in his own words "could not afford to quit." His case was not unique. Over and over again, I heard stories about the same process of falling into the "financial trap." The youngest and newest of our crew had just graduated high school and took the job for the summer in order to earn enough money to attend welding school the following fall. During my brief tenure at the beef plant, he purchased a new motorcycle, a new stereo, and a house trailer. When I left, he told me he had decided to postpone welding school for one year in order "to get everything paid for." I saw the financial trap closing in on him fast; he did too. . . .

Summary and Conclusions

There are at least three interwoven phenomena in this study which deserve further comment and research.

First is the subtle sense of unity which existed among the line workers. . . . The line both symbolically and literally linked every job, and consequently every worker, to each other. . . . A system of "uncooperative teamwork" seemed to combine simultaneously a feeling of "one-for-all, all-for-one, and every man for himself." Once a line worker made it past the first three or four days on the job which "weeded out" many new workers, his status as a *beefer* was assured and the sense of unity was felt as much by the worker of nine weeks as it was by the veteran of nine years. Because the workers maintained largely secondary relationships, this feeling of unification is not the same as the unity typically found on athletic teams, in fraternities, or among various primary groups. Yet it was a significant social force which bound the workers together and provided a sense of meaning and worth. Although their occupation might not be highly respected by outsiders, they derived mutual self-respect from their sense of belonging.

A second important phenomenon was the various coping methods . . . the beef plant line workers developed and practiced . . . for retaining their humanness. Daydreaming, horseplay and occasional sabotage protected their sense of self. Further, the prevailing attitude among workers that it was "us" against "them" served as a reminder that, while the nature of the job might demand subjugation to bosses, machines, and even beef parts, they were still human beings. . . .

A third significant finding was that consumer spending patterns among the beefers seemed to "seal their fate" and make leaving the beef plant almost impossible. A reasonable interpretation of the spending patterns of the beefers is that having a high-income/low-status job encourages a person to consume conspicuously. The prevailing attitude seemed to be "I may not have a nice job, but I have a nice home, a nice car, etc." This conspicuous consumption enabled workers to take indirect pride in their occupations. One of the ways of overcoming drudgery and humiliation on the job was to surround oneself with as many desirable material things as possible off the job. These items (cars, boats, motorcycles, etc.) became tangible rewards for the sacrifices endured at work.

The problem, of course, is that the possession of these expensive items required the continual income of a substantial paycheck which most of these men could only obtain by staying at the beef plant. These spending patterns were further complicated by the fact that they were seemingly "contagious." Workers talked to each other on breaks about recent purchases, thus reinforcing the norm of immediate gratification. A common activity of a group of workers on break or lunch was to run to the parking lot to see a fellow worker's new truck, van, car or motorcycle. Even the seemingly more financially conservative were usually caught up in this activity and often could not wait to display their own latest acquisitions. Ironically, as the workers cursed their jobs, these expensive possessions virtually destroyed any chance of leaving them.

Working at the beef plant was indeed "dirty work." It was monotonous, difficult, dangerous, and demeaning. Despite this, the workers at the beef plant worked hard to fulfill employer expectations in order to obtain financial rewards. Through a variety of symbolic techniques, they managed to overcome the many negative aspects of their work and maintain a sense of self-respect about how they earned their living.

REFERENCES

Balzer, Richard (1976). *Clockwork: Life In and Outside an American Factory.* Garden City, NY: Doubleday.

Barlow, Hugh (1981). *Introduction to Criminology.* 2d ed. Boston: Little, Brown.

Garson, Barbara (1975). *All the Livelong Day: The Meaning and Demeaning of Routine work.* Garden City, NY: Doubleday.

Hummel, Ralph P. (1977). *The Bureaucratic Experience.* New York: St. Martin's Press.

King, Rick (1978). "In the sanding booth at Ford." Pp. 199–205 in John and Erna Perry (eds.), *Social Problems in Today's World.* Boston: Little, Brown.

Linhart, Robert (translated by Margaret Crosland) (1981). *The Assembly Line.* Amherst: University of Massachusetts Press.

Marx, Karl (1964a). *Economic and Philosophical Manuscripts of 1844.* New York: International Publishing (1844).

———(1964b). *The Communist Manifesto.* New York: Washington Square Press (1848).

Schatzman, Leonard, and Anselm L. Strauss (1973). *Field Research.* Englewood Cliffs, NJ: Prentice-Hall.

Shostak, Arthur (1980). *Blue Collar Stress.* Reading, MA: Addison-Wesley.

Spradley, James P. (1979). *The Ethnographic Interview.* New York: Holt, Rinehart & Winston.

———(1980). *Participant Observation.* New York: Holt, Rinehart & Winston.

36
Automating Work

Thomas R. Ide and Arthur J. Cordell

The replacement of backbreaking jobs with machines has long been the dream of social visionaries. Today, we are seeing a proliferation of labor-saving technologies, with the savings in labor often going to the firm providing the service. For employees, "labor saving" often means fewer available jobs. Remaining jobs and new jobs created by new technologies can also mean greater inequality between workers, with potentially serious social consequences.

These are not the best of times. Disparity between the rich and poor has been increasing in the industrialized world and those in-between have become part of a shrinking middle class. The majority of new jobs are in the service sector and tend to be polarized between a relatively small number requiring high skills and low-paying retail and consumer-service areas.

Banking and financial services provide an interesting picture of what is occurring in the automated world of today. The ubiquitous automated teller machines are a constant reminder of the magnitude of the changes taking place before our eyes. As the young computer-literate generation moves into the wage-earning class, more and longer lines form in front of Green Machines, Blue Machines, and the multi-colored ones that cater to networks such as Circuit, Interac, Cirrus and Plus. Money can be obtained virtually anywhere at the push of a few buttons without the need of travellers checks, passports, or a knowledge of the local language. A plastic card does the trick along with an identification number and a bank account in good standing.

Accessibility is the attraction for the user. Open seven days a week, the machines are not only found at banks but are conveniently located in shopping malls or wherever people gather. Cheapness and efficiency recommend them to financial institutions since the need for human interfaces who must be paid salaries is greatly reduced. Only a few individuals are required to stock the boxes with cash and pick up any deposits or other paper. The amounts of the withdrawals and deposits are automatically debited or credited to the appropriate accounts along with the service charges.

The net result is a decrease in demand for workers, less need for costly negotiations over conditions of employment, and less friction between management and labor. Workers servicing automated tellers are primarily at lower income levels. But the erosion of jobs does not stop there. Fewer supervisors and accountants are needed and fewer individuals who are skilled in human relations to handle dissatisfied customers. Audits are enormously simplified as human error is reduced. Computers not only add, subtract, multiply, and divide without making mistakes, they are programmed to read, balance, and update accounts and transfer money.

Automation has also invaded upper and senior levels of management. A good example is the Toronto Dominion (TD) Bank's cash management services. The Toronto Dominion is among Canada's six largest chartered banks with assets of over 68.9 billion dollars. Though one of the most conservative financial institutions in Canada, it is a leader in innovative service to its clients. TD's trademarked Money Monitor system enables clients to manage cash flows more efficiently from their own computer terminals by accessing current account data in both Canadian and U.S. currencies; checking outstanding loan balances; monitoring current and historical account activities; transferring funds between accounts; and obtaining money market and foreign rates, and all of this without the need to call a branch for account information. . . .

The Toronto Dominion Bank is typical of what is happening in the industry. Indeed Canada, where 28 percent of payments are made electronically, lags well behind Japan and Germany where the percentages are 80 and 63 respectively. France has become a world leader in the use of "smart" or debit cards known as EFTPOS (Electronic Funds Transfer at the Point of Sale), a technology that has yet to make serious inroads elsewhere but seems sure to do so in the near future. The benefits are savings: costs of check production and reconciliation are eliminated; mailing costs are either eliminated or reduced; service charges are either lower or not as high as they might otherwise be; the time spent on administration is shortened; cash flow forecasting is enhanced; time and cost of preparing and handling invoices is eliminated; and bookkeeping is simplified. The drawbacks are primarily reduction of human contact and dehumanization of the process.

The benefits claimed for the Toronto Dominion Bank's cash management services are savings in the time spent by people in doing jobs that can now be accomplished more efficiently and in less time by machines. Citicorp is planning to launch a new generation home banking terminal designed for broad consumer use. Called the Enhanced Telephone, it is a hybrid device that looks like an overweight telephone with a small enhanced screen. The enhanced telephone is designed to stimulate the home banking market now stalled at about 100,000 users in the United States. These telephones will have the same functions as personal computers used for banking at home. They can pay bills, transfer funds, get a loan, review accounts and, in the future, get price quotes and trade securities. Enhanced telephones will be leased with a small installation charge and a modest monthly fee. The device will have a slot for insertion of a smart card. With this feature in place, customers will have the ultimate in home banking at their disposal. They will be able to get cash at home by transferring funds from their checking or savings accounts to their smart cards which can then be used for making purchases.

In the present trend toward a global economy with the accompanying need to become competitive, downsizing has become a buzzword. Downsizing is generally used to describe reductions in costs of operations and most of these are related to labor. This means, for financial institutions and their customers, a reduction in the number of (or less future demand for) employees such as tellers, clerks, supervisors, accountants, auditors, and managers.

Downsizing has become the trend. Many corporations are revamping their headquarters. They are moving away from a preoccupation with an edifice that is both monumental and complex to one that is flexible and smaller. This shift reflects a new strategy in the economy and in management style. Technology, the thinning of middle management, and new management philosophies are making the ideas behind the big buildings outdated. Lavish use of space tends to 'embarrass' corporations. One financial analyst said ". . . the institutional headquarters is a dodo. If I see a company building one, I sell my stock." Since the mid-1980s, as corporations have responded to global competition and technological change by merging and consolidating, downsizing or eliminating entire levels of management, some two million middle management positions have been permanently eliminated.

If financial institutions are one pillar of the service sector, transportation, communications, and utilities are the others. Telecommunications has undergone the most radical changes. Digitalization, lasers, and the development of fibre optics paved the way for the marriage of telephones and computers and a host of new services. Advanced voice, data and image communications included facsimile machines, cordless telephones, digital multiplex systems, mobile cellular telephones, international automatic credit card services, full-color video conferences and personal communication services whereby people are assigned telephone numbers rather than locations. All these developments are not without human costs. In Australia, Telecom has eliminated 17,000 positions in the last decade with about 6,000 of these within the last year. Furthermore, cut backs [sic], representing an additional 33⅓ percent, could be imposed over the next two to three years.

In the United States, AT&T plans to install computerized operator services allowing the close of thirty-one offices and elimination of one-third, or 6,000, of all operators. The operators will be replaced by "voice recognition" technology that responds to the caller's verbal prompts. Instead of talking to a human operator, callers will tell the computer the type of call they would like to make. The computer prompts the caller to say "collect", "third number", "person-to-person" or "calling card."

When placing a collect call the computer tells the called party "I have a collect call from Mr. So-and-So. Do you accept the call"? The computer can recognize "yes" or "no" and carries out the transaction based on the response from the called party. . . .

The effects of automation in the service sector go beyond the banking and telecommunications industry have been affected by automation in the service sector. All their customers are affected as well. Every new service means savings of one kind or another. Furthermore businesses that contract for a cash management or sophisticated electronic data system benefit in a material sense. Whether or not they employ tellers or operators, they do require the work of accountants, auditors, and record keepers, and it is these positions they are able to eliminate.

With instantaneous access to information about accounts receivable and payable, the need for large finance departments run by middle managers is reduced. Downsizing also means less demand for office space and hence less demand for construction workers, carpenters, plumbers, painters, designers and architects. Does this mean that fewer jobs are available and, with reduced payrolls, that there are fewer people with the income required to buy the products of the now more efficient and competitive retailers and manufacturers? The question is so important that it requires a much more comprehensive examination of the impact of automation on the service sector.

. . . [T]he service sector in Canada has grown dramatically. In the late 1940s, 60 percent of the Canadian labor force worked in the goods sector—natural resources, manufacturing and construction. Today over 70 percent of workers are employed in services. And the shift to services is not over. During the 1980s virtually all of the net job creation in Canada took place in the service sector. The service sector defies easy definition. Services usually refer to intangible, non-transferable and non-storable activities. However, there is a blurring between goods and services. In fact most goods are produced and sold as complex packages of services. . . .

New digital technologies plus modern telecommunications have led to a revolution in the way services are delivered. The equivalent of automated bank tellers is coming to the car rental industry. Budget Rent-a-Car is experimenting with remote rental booths in shopping malls and hotels. Customers use a video booth to dial a reservation agent then punch in charge card and driver's license information. The machine dispenses a car key for the rental car that can be found in a nearby parking lot.

A growing number of companies that are equipment suppliers diagnose customer problems from service centers hundreds or even thousands of miles away. And, increasingly, the remote diagnosis is followed up by a remote repair job. Among the companies that rely on long distance telephone lines for diagnosis and repair are Pitney Bowes for its FAX machines, General Electric for its body-scanning systems, and AT&T for business telephone exchanges. Remote diagnosis and repair systems allow equipment suppliers to reduce the number of service calls. They also cut the time spent on problems that must still be dealt with on site because the remote diagnosis allows the repairer to be dispatched with the proper tools and parts.

At Pitney Bowes' National Diagnostics Center in Florida, twenty-two engineers are on duty twenty-four hours a day. Between them they take close to 30,000 service calls a month. Most problems are small enough for the engineers to talk customers through the fix-up over the telephone. If service is needed, the diagnostic center can often fix the problem remotely. Through a telephone line the customer's machine is ordered to send an electronic status report covering 100 or more features. The report takes twenty seconds and is used to program a Florida FAX machine into a duplicate of the customer's.

Also received by telephone from the customer's machine is a list of the last twenty transactions. Problems show up with error codes attached to the transaction. The repairs are made to the software in the machine in Florida and the fixed software is sent back through the telephone lines. Consider the near future when problems affecting appliances, such as refrigerators, air conditioners, and washing machines can be diagnosed in the home by telephone. It is cheaper to determine the problem remotely and talk the home owner through a minor repair than to send a service person to the site. However, if necessary, the expert will arrive with the proper part and knows in advance what needs to be fixed.

Sometimes the labor that is saved by corporations is shifted to the consumer. A few years ago, the fast food chain McDonald's came up with the slogan "We do it all for you." In reality, at McDonald's, we do it all for them. We stand in line, take the food to the table, dispose of the waste, and stack our trays. As labor costs rise and technology develops, the consumer often does more and more of the work. Microprocessors allow for self-serve gas stations and automatic teller machines. Soon laser scanners in supermarkets will permit the consumer to pass the products over the scanner and save the cost of a cashier.

Already one telephone company is allowing the householder to become a telephone installer. A new resident in the State of Washington can obtain telephone service in a self-serve way by plugging a touchtone phone into a jack and pressing 811 on the key pad. A computer asks questions that can be answered by pressing more digits. The telephone is operating in less than twenty minutes compared with the usual two-day wait until a technician arrives. When university students returned to campus in September the "service-on-demand" system was able to handle a surge of 1,726 orders in two days instead of the usual two weeks. . . .

Sophisticated software packages are replacing humans throughout the corporate world at all levels. For example, expert systems or decision support software are now part of the everyday business world. Shearson Lehman uses neural networks to predict the performance of stocks and bonds. Merced County in California has an expert system that decides if applicants should receive welfare benefits. An American telephone company has a system that helps unskilled workers diagnose customer telephone problems. The U.S. Internal Revenue Service is testing software designed to read tax returns and detect fraud. American Airlines has an expert system that schedules the routine maintenance of its airplanes.

Many applications represent the knowledge transferred or embedded in the software. The opportunities are immense since most procedures and processes depend on an ever increasing level of expertise. One estimate is that the applied research related to how products are built and how they work makes up 70 percent of their development costs. For some applications in the service sector, for example the selling of mutual funds, this percentage rises to 90 percent. The incentive to transfer knowledge from human brains to computer software is very high indeed. Automating the service sector produces faster service and makes labor redundant. For example, the Merced County system is able to review a matrix of 6,000 government regulations to determine in seventy-two hours—versus as long as three months—if an applicant qualifies for benefits. Since the intelligence is in the machine, a smaller support staff and less skilled interviewers are needed. The system is reputed to save the county 4 million dollars per year in administrative and training costs. The county welfare agency has also been able to cut its staff by 28 percent and still serve the same client caseload. . . .

. . . New services are offered and the remaining workers are made much more productive. So why worry? Is it not nice to have our tastes and interests profiles lodged in a computer data base somewhere so that when we call a hotel for reservations the computer "remembers" that we want a particular type of room, located in a particular section of the hotel, and so on? Or, when renting a car, the rental agent has access to our previous rental file and gets us on the road in minutes? The worry is that automation of the service sector, while providing a dizzying array of new means of satisfying our wants and needs, it is also having its affect on the type of jobs that are available.

Simply stated, we are beginning to see the creation of a work force with a bi-modal set of skills. Highly trained people design and implement the technology, and unskilled workers carry out the remaining jobs. The resulting divide in the workforce is reflected in disturbing patterns of income. The middle class is shrinking, with only a few joining the upper class and many taking the step down. Added to the skill/income problem is a parallel rise in non-standard employment—part-time work, short-term work, and increasingly self-employment. Most part-time workers are classed as involuntary. This means that they would prefer regular jobs. In Canada non-standard jobs account for nearly half of all new jobs and now represent nearly 30 percent of total employment. Non-standard jobs tend to be non-union, and are less likely covered by employee benefits and pension plans.

Although it is not directly caused by the new information technology, much of non-standard employment is related to the trend to contract out work. With information technology certain kinds of work can be done anywhere and purchased as needed by other firms. The influence of labor unions is minimized, overhead costs are kept down, and the labor, when acquired, is cheaper since there are few, if any, employee benefits to pay.

The overall effect of automation of the service sector is still unclear. What is known is that for a variety of reasons, including automation, a polarization of incomes is taking place. In 1967, 27 percent of the Canadian workforce had annual earnings that were middle level (within 25 percent of the median on either side). By 1986 only 22 percent of the labor force fell within this group—a decline of 5 percent. The low income segment rose from 36 percent in 1967 to 40 percent in 1986. The high income segment went from 37 percent in 1967 to 39 percent in 1986. Clear evidence of a "declining middle." While the experts differ on why the middle class is in decline, all agree that a continuation of this trend threatens the social fabric.

Similar trends appear to be under way in the United States as well. Between 1970 and 1990 the share of all income received by the richest one-fifth of families grew by 3.3 percentage points to 43.7 percent. The share received by the poorest one-fifth fell to 4.6 percent. The income shares of families in the second and third quintile also fell and the share received by the fourth quintile—the fifth of families just beneath the richest—rose slightly.

When big corporations began laying off white-collar employees in the early 1980s, 90 percent were quickly re-employed in similar jobs in a large company at the same pay or better. In the late 1980s only 50 percent were rehired. Today, only 25 percent are able to come back into the corporate world. According to *Business Week*, quoting one executive hiring firm, "there just aren't those jobs any more, and they can't hope to ever get them again . . . they're going to have to think of other ways of being employed." While middle managers represent only 6 to 7 percent of the workforce in the United States, almost 17 percent of corporate layoffs came from their ranks between 1988 and 1991.

Technologies driven by microelectronics and concomitant developments in communications promised a new era for the 1990s, an era that would be highly productive, environmentally benign, and one where material goods would be accessible at prices so low that virtually all members of society could enjoy a quality of life never before possible.

What is more, work, which Stendahl said was "the essential ballast in the vessel of life," was to be transformed from a tedious, backbreaking activity to a rewarding experience that would meet not only the primary needs for food, clothing, and shelter but also those secondary, essentially human requirements for variety, recognition, and an experience of success.

But the microprocessor, thought to be "the engine of the eighties," must have sputtered slightly. As one writer in *Fortune* said, "No novelist would dare put into a book the most extreme of the dizzying contrasts of wealth and poverty that make up the ordinary texture of life in today's American cities."

In the developing countries, millions of people have fled their homes, infant mortality rates have been increasing, and poverty is at an all time high. The industrialized nations are experiencing the worst economic downturn since the Great Depression of the 1930s. Unemployment is rampant. Social unrest is increasing and many young people have given up hope of enjoying a standard of living equal to that of their parents or even their grandparents. Furthermore, as a recent report released by the United Nations said, "Environmental destruction is increasing."

Just as Hamlet declaimed, "To be or not to be: that is the question," we might well ask "what has gone wrong"? The allusion is not inappropriate for indecision is the predominant attribute of many of today's leaders. Traditional policies seem inadequate in light of the magnitude of the problems facing society.

But the problem is not just technological. It rather is a complex of economic, ideological, political, sociological, and psychological factors, and in part it is just bad luck. Debt, national and individual, is surely a contributing factor. Collectively and individually we tend to spend more than we can afford. The hands of politicians are tied in the major industrial nations because such a large portion of revenues goes to pay the interest on government debt. Corporations are similarly over extended. Individuals are seduced by advertisers and instant credit through plastic cards. Little or nothing is set aside for the proverbial rainy day.

Automation, whether in the goods or services sector, at least under the present circumstances, leads to more and more unemployment. As consumption decreases, inventories increase. Consumer confidence falls along with the purchasing power of larger and larger segments of the working classes. The economy experiences an on-going recession or depression. Shrinking numbers of people work in situations with lifetime employment with benefits and pensions. Part-time employment and other non-standard employment is the lot of increasing numbers. Corporate offices are staffed by a small corps of coordinators. Everyone else is under a personal contract or some indirect form of employment as through an intermediary agency supplying service on demand. As Peter F. Drucker proposed, the corporation of the future will look more like a symphony orchestra or a hospital with the central office conducting a group of players under contract.

As more individuals fall into the social security net designed to help them contend with a presumably relatively short transition period, the costs of such services rise and debt-ridden governments scramble to cope with the ever-increasing demands. Adding to the problem is the need for financial assistance to overextended corporations which, despite commitment to a system designed to reward winners, are reluctant to become losers. Governments of all political stripes are faced with the dilemma that if they do not help the corporations, massive numbers of jobs will be lost and the economic downturn will become more severe. . . .

. . . Automation of the service sector has resulted in a shrinking middle class, the group from which the largest share of tax revenues has come in the past. Larger levies on corporations are possible, but in a global market place companies can take their business, or declare their profits, elsewhere. Many do, moving not only head offices but factories, taking advantage of wage rates that are minuscule by comparison with those in the industrial world. The largest corporations are international and their allegiance is not to the countries that spawned them, but to shareholders that may live in any one of a number of countries anywhere in the global village. There is also a management agenda to be met. Increased earnings make the stock of the company more attractive and lead to stock offerings in the future. Stock option purchase packages, which are becoming more and more a part of the compensation of senior management, are increasing in value, thus enriching professional executives. Where the earnings are made and in what part of the world is irrelevant. . . .

Established social services, such as health care, education and libraries, are allowed to deteriorate or are placed on a user-pay basis. The principle of universal availability of services, one of the hallmarks of advanced societies, is gradually abandoned. The rich do very well in a world of private security systems, vacation resorts and so on. The poor are pretty much on their own, moving from one de-skilled job to another with little chance of breaking out of the poverty cycle. With the middle class disappearing as a way station to advancement, few incentives are left to even attempt to better oneself. The elite, either unwilling or unable to change, cling to outmoded ideologies. As the situation worsens, reactions become stronger and denial is the predominant mood.

The business-as-usual scenario may well be a likely one but it is far from promising. With little or no job security, we are essentially creating a new feudal system where Kafka-like authorities and a senior managerial class, with close ties to the government of the day, replace the landowner. The prospects for democracy, with advanced living conditions of a developed country, look increasingly dim. As frustrations increase, as the dream becomes a nightmare, rioting is in danger of becoming a normal phenomenon.

Law and order are politicians' watchwords, deemed best to reach and appeal to a shrinking number of constituents. That is until a new deliverer appears on the scene. It need not be a Hitler or an Idi Amin, but anybody carrying the alluring promise of security and full employment will find receptive ears. All that may be asked of us in exchange is our freedom.

37
The Jobs-Skills Mismatch

JOHN D. KASARDA

Manufacturing was once the primary activity of people in cities in the industrialized world. Increasingly, these jobs are going to Third World countries. As the urban environment changes, fewer manufacturing jobs requiring no more than a high-school education are available. New employment opportunities are in service jobs, many of these very low-skilled, but others requiring high levels of education and training. Yet the gap is growing between educational attainment and the skills needed to get and hold a good job. This is particularly the case for immigrants and minorities in the United States, Germany, and Britain.

The role of industrial cities in North America and Western Europe is being radically transformed by two trends in global economic restructuring: the growth of the service economy and the shift of production toward the less-developed countries. These trends are increasing the demand for higher skills among the labor force and causing intractably high rates of urban unemployment among less-skilled workers.

Between 1965 and 1987, the proportion of Gross Domestic Product accounted for by manufacturing in the US declined from 28 percent to 20 percent, while the proportion of the GDP accounted for by services rose from 57 percent to 68 percent.

Over the same time period, manufacturing in West Germany fell from 40 percent of the GDP to 33 percent, while services rose from 43 percent to 60 percent. Manufacturing shrunk from over one-third of the GDP to one-fourth in the United Kingdom while services expanded to 60 percent of the economy.

This shifting composition of economic activity translates directly into employment changes. From 1979 through 1986, the European Community lost manufacturing jobs at the rate of 2.2 percent per year. At the same time, service employment rose at the rate of 1.6 percent per year. Manufacturing job losses in the United Kingdom averaged 4.5 percent per year during this time period while those in the US and West Germany hovered around one percent per year.

In the last few years of this period, manufacturing employment losses have decelerated and service sector employment accelerated. The major exception to the pattern of manufacturing job loss was Japan, with annual gains of 1.1 percent through the early and mid-1980s.

By 1985, US steel industry employment was 46 percent of what it was a decade earlier. In Germany it was two-thirds of what it had been in 1974 and in the UK less than one-third.

As manufacturing jobs disappeared in Europe and North America, employment in Third World export-processing zones—where production is intended for immediate export—increased from approximately 500,000 in 1975 to almost 1.3 million in 1986. And much more export production is located outside these zones.

Increasingly, multinational manufacturers headquartered in the developed world are subcontracting out the entire production process to the third World—from tennis balls to fork-lift trucks, numerically controlled lathes and key telephone systems. Two of the top ten exporters of telecommunication equipment are in the Third World.

SKYSCRAPERS VS. SMOKESTACKS

The social effects of the trend toward increased service employment and decreased manufacturing employment is most evident in the metropolitan areas, where 80.3 percent of Americans, 92.5 percent of Britons and 87.3 percent of Germans reside.

Cities are increasingly shedding their function of production and becoming only centers of coordination and control. The production plant is no longer necessarily a few miles from company headquarters in a nearby industrial district; it may be on the next continent.

If US and Western European cities are to have a significant role in the global economy it will not be as production sites, but as hubs in a network of governmental, industrial, commercial and cultural organizations. They will house the headquarters of international organizations, banks and financial firms as well as the administrative headquarters of producer-service firms and Third World manufacturers.

This new urban role will require a new set of skills. The higher-level administrative functions which at least some US and Western European cities could fulfill require advanced schooling and specialized skills. Even below the "professional" level, accounting, management and R&D require relatively high levels of education. Increasingly, employers in these sectors require four-year college degrees for entry-level positions.

Yet at a time when increasing levels of education by workers in OECD[1] cities are required to match emerging high-skill jobs, their educational systems seem to be faltering, particularly in the US. Few OECD countries are increasing university enrollments at a significant pace. In the US, secondary schools are not doing an adequate job of retaining students or educating the ones that remain. Minorities, who are beginning to dominate the residential bases of major US cities, are experiencing high-school dropout rates in excess of 33 percent.

The under-education problem is particularly acute among blacks in

1. Organization for Economic Cooperation and Development. [Editor]

urban America and among new immigrants, particularly with respect to language skills.

The changing skill requirements, coupled with the ineffectiveness of educational systems, have resulted in the marginalization of these groups. Increasingly, underclass blacks and Hispanic immigrants in the US; and the ex-colonials, Africans and Mediterranean immigrants in Europe, are not integrated into the social or economic mainstream. Europe is coming to resemble America in the numbers of immigrants that now make up its population. In Frankfurt, for example, more than 20 percent of the residents are foreign born, mostly Turks and, more recently, Africans with limited educations.

NO MOBILITY WITHOUT SKILLS

The functional transformation of cities has radically affected the distribution of job opportunities based on levels of education. The data are already very clear for US cities. Available evidence suggests that Western Europe is following the same patterns as the US with a 10-to-15 year lag.

All major cities had consistent employment losses in industries with the lowest skill requirements. By far, the heaviest job losses occurred after 1970 when growth in urban underclass populations accelerated in the American industrial North.

New York City, for instance, lost only 9,000 jobs between 1953 and 1970 in those industries in which the educational level of the average jobholder was less than high-school completion. But it lost more than half-a-million jobs in these industries between 1970 and 1986. Philadelphia, Baltimore, and St. Louis have also lost substantial numbers of jobs since 1970 in industries typically requiring less than college education.

The four cities that accounted for the lion's share of the increase in concentrated poverty populations during the 1970s—New York, Chicago, Philadelphia, and Detroit—also experienced the lion's share of declines in jobs held by high-school dropouts and by those with only a high-school degree. Particularly affected were those large numbers of urban blacks who had not completed high school, especially younger ones. For city black youth, school drop-out rates ranged from 30 to 50 percent during the 1970s and early 1980s.

The educational disparities between black residents and skill levels needed for jobs in America's urban areas are dramatic. Despite their educational gains, black urban labor remains highly concentrated in the less-than-high-school education category where city employment has most rapidly declined since 1970. Blacks are greatly underrepresented in the college-graduate categories where urban employment is rapidly rising.

The structural mismatch between city jobs and the low level of education attained by black labor helps explain why policies based primarily on urban economic development have had limited success in reducing

urban black joblessness. The fact is that most blacks simply lack the education to participate in the new growth sectors of the urban economy.

While newly created urban jobs taken by college graduates have skyrocketed, the percentage of urban black males who have completed college remains extremely small. For those who are out of work, the
disparity at the higher-education end is even greater.

Decline in manufacturing jobs is by no means the only pertinent indicator of losses in traditional blue-collar employment, but it corresponds
to other indicators of the capacity of cities to sustain large numbers of
residents with limited educational attainment.

Further, between 1970 and 1980, there were dramatic drops across all
cities in the percentage of poorly educated black males who worked full
time and a leap in the percentage not working at all. By 1980, fewer than
half of the out-of-school black males in each city had full-time jobs. Conversely, the percentage not working at all rose in Baltimore from 24.7 to
45.0; in New York from 28.2 to 43.9; in Philadelphia from 26.7 to 50.6;
in St. Louis from 31.8 to 48.4, and in Washington, DC from 23.4 to 42.1.

Clearly, the loss of low-education-requisite jobs in traditional city industries accelerated black joblessness.

In sum, education-job opportunity mismatches are particularly acute
in those cities where declines in traditional blue-collar industries and the
growth of information-processing industries have been most substantial
since 1970.

So different are the skills used and the education required in these
growing, as opposed to declining, urban industrial sectors that adaptation by the poorly educated is exceedingly difficult. This difficulty is
concretely represented in the exceptionally high jobless rates of those
central-city residents who have not completed high school, regardless of
race, and rapid rises since 1970 in jobless rates of residents who are
poorly educated, even though they may have obtained a high-school
diploma.

SOCIAL DISTRESS

US, UK and West German cities are undergoing functional transformations from centers of goods processing to centers of information
processing.

The data for the US show that the education levels associated with
urban jobs have risen faster than that of the labor pool—particularly the
minority labor pool—to be found in those cities. The result is a labor-
job mismatch which stymies social progress.

The situation in the UK and Germany appears to be analogous. The
national, and urban, economies are losing manufacturing jobs while the
service sector takes on new importance. Many Europeans, both native
and immigrant, are poorly prepared educationally for the new roles cities
can play. Despite a diversity of ethnic groups, the minority populations

326   JOHN D. KASARDA

are, on the whole, less well prepared. This relative lack of education is reflected in higher unemployment rates. At the same time, the minority portion of the work force is growing.

These minority populations in the US and Europe were attracted by the economic opportunities cities had to offer. A dynamic of family re-unification and chain migration was set in motion that resulted in increasing minority populations, even after the opportunities had dwindled. The result has been high unemployment and social distress in our urban center.

38
The Second Shift: Employed Women Are Putting in Another Day of Work at Home

Arlie Hochschild

Despite the fact that a majority of American women are in the paid labor force and that more than 60 percent of women with school-age children are working outside the home, women continue to do the lion's share of household work. Based on interviews with and observations of fifty-two couples over an eight-year period, the author describes many forms of conflict: for example, how women should enact the role of paid worker; between the role of employed person and parent; between husbands and wives. This is symptomatic of the strain that two-job families are coping with, strain that requires society-wide solutions.

Every American household bears the footprints of economic and cultural trends that originate far outside its walls. A rise in inflation eroding the earning power of the male wage, an expanding service sector opening up jobs for women, and the inroads made by women into many professions—all these changes do not simply go on around the American family. They occur *within* a marriage or living-together arrangement and transform it. Problems between couples, problems that seem "unique" or "marital," are often the individual ripples of powerful economic and cultural shock waves. Quarrels between husbands and wives in households across the nation result mainly from a friction between faster-changing women and slower-changing men.

The exodus of women from the home to the workplace has not been accompanied by a new view of marriage and work that would make this transition smooth. Most workplaces have remained inflexible in the face of the changing needs of workers with families, and most men have yet to really adapt to the changes in women. I call the strain caused by the disparity between the change in women and the absence of change elsewhere the "stalled revolution."

If women begin to do less at home because they have less time, if men do little more, and if the work of raising children and tending a home requires roughly the same effort, then the questions of who does what at home and of what "needs doing" become a source of deep tension in a marriage.

Over the past 30 years in the United States, more and more women have begun to work outside the home, and more have divorced. While some commentators conclude that women's work *causes* divorce, my research into changes in the American family suggests something else. Since all the wives in the families I studied (over an eight-year period) worked outside the home, the fact that they worked did not account for why some marriages were happy and others were not. What *did* contribute to happiness was the husband's willingness to do the work at home. Whether they were traditional or more egalitarian in their relationship, couples were happier when the men did a sizable share of housework and child care.

In one study of 600 couples filing for divorce, researcher George Levinger found that the second most common reason women cited for wanting to divorce—after "mental cruelty"—was their husbands' "neglect of home or children." Women mentioned this reason more often than financial problems, physical abuse, drinking, or infidelity.

A happy marriage is supported by a couple's being economically secure, by their enjoying a supportive community, and by their having compatible needs and values. But these days it may also depend on a shared appreciation of the work it takes to nurture others. As the role of the homemaker is being abandoned by many women, the homemaker's work has been continually devalued and passed on to low-paid housekeepers, baby-sitters, or day-care workers. Long devalued by men, the contribution of cooking, cleaning, and care-giving is now being devalued as mere drudgery by many women, too.

In the era of the stalled revolution, one way to make housework and child care more valued is for men to share in that work. Many working mothers are already doing all they can at home. Now it's time for men to make the move.

If more mothers of young children are working at full-time jobs outside the home, and if most couples can't afford household help, who's doing the work at home? Adding together the time it takes to do a paid job and to do housework and child care and using estimates from major studies on time use done in the 1960s and 1970s, I found that women worked roughly 15 more hours each week than men. Over a year, they worked an extra month of 24-hour days. Over a dozen years, it was an extra year of 24-hour days. Most women without children spend much more time than men on housework. Women with children devote more time to both housework and child care. Just as there is a wage gap between men and women in the workplace, there is a "leisure gap" between them at home. Most women work one shift at the office or factory and a "second shift" at home.

In my research, I interviewed and observed 52 couples over an eight-year period as they cooked dinner, shopped, bathed their children, and in general struggled to find enough time to make their complex lives work. The women I interviewed seemed to be far more deeply torn between the demands of work and family than were their husbands. They talked more about the abiding conflict between work and family. They felt the second shift was *their* issue, and most of their husbands agreed. When I telephoned one husband to arrange an interview with him, explaining that I wanted to ask him how he managed work and family life, he replied genially, "Oh, this will *really* interest my *wife*."

Men who shared the load at home seemed just as pressed for time as their wives, and as torn between the demands of career and small children. But of the men I surveyed, the majority did not share the load at home. Some refused outright. Others refused more passively, often offering a loving shoulder to lean on, or an understanding ear, as their working wife faced the conflict they both saw as hers. At first it seemed to me that the problem of the second shift *was* hers. But I came to realize that those husbands who helped very little at home were often just as deeply affected as their wives—through the resentment their wives felt toward them and through their own need to steel themselves against that resentment.

A clear example of this phenomenon is Evan Holt, a warehouse furniture salesman who did very little housework and played with his four-year-old son, Joey, only at his convenience. His wife, Nancy, did the second shift, but she resented it keenly and half-consciously expressed her frustration and rage by losing interest in sex and becoming overly absorbed in Joey.

Even when husbands happily shared the work, their wives *felt* more responsible for home and children. More women than men kept track of doctor's appointments and arranged for kids' playmates to come over. More mothers than fathers worried about a child's Halloween costume or a birthday present for a school friend. They were more likely to think about their children while at work and to check in by phone with the baby-sitter.

Partly because of this, more women felt torn between two kinds of urgency, between the need to soothe a child's fear of being left at daycare and the need to show the boss she's "serious" at work. Twenty percent of the men in my study shared housework equally. Seventy percent did a substantial amount (less than half of it, but more than a third), and 10 percent did less than a third. But even when couples more equitably share the work at home, women do two thirds of the daily jobs at home, such as cooking and cleaning up—jobs that fix them into a rigid routine. Most women cook dinner, for instance, while men change the oil in the family car. But, as one mother pointed out, dinner needs to be prepared every evening around six o'clock, whereas the car oil needs to be changed every six months, with no particular deadline. Women do more child care than men, and men repair more household appliances. A child needs to be tended to daily, whereas the repair of household appliances can often wait, said the men, "until I have time." Men thus have more control over when they make their contributions than women do. They may be very busy with family chores, but, like the executive who tells his secretary to "hold my calls," the man has more control over his time.

Another reason why women may feel under more strain than men is that women more often do two things at once—for example, write checks and return phone calls, vacuum and keep an eye on a three-year-old, fold laundry and think out the shopping list. Men more often will either cook dinner *or* watch the kids. Women more often do both at the same time.

Beyond doing more at home, women also devote proportionately more of their time at home to housework than men and proportionately less of it to child care. Of all the time men spend working at home, a growing amount of it goes to child care. Since most parents prefer to tend to their children than to clean house, men do more of what they'd rather do. More men than women take their children on "fun" outings to the park, the zoo, the movies. Women spend more time on maintenance, such as feeding and bathing children—enjoyable activities, to be sure, but often less leisurely or "special" than going to the zoo. Men also do fewer of the most undesirable household chores, such as scrubbing the toilet.

As a result, women tend to talk more intensely about being overtired, sick, and emotionally drained. Many women interviewed were fixated on the topic of sleep. They talked about how much they could "get by on": six and a half, seven, seven and a half, less, more. They talked about who they knew who needed more or less. Some apologized for how much sleep they needed—"I'm afraid I need eight hours of sleep"—as if eight was "too much." They talked about how to avoid fully waking up when a child called them at night, and how to get back to sleep. These women talked about sleep the way a hungry person talks about food.

If, all in all, the two-job family is suffering from a speedup of work and family life, working mothers are its primary victims. It is ironic, then, that often it falls to women to be the time-and-motion experts of family life. As I observed families inside their homes, I noticed it was often the mother who rushed children, saying, "Hurry up! It's time to go," "Finish your cereal now," "You can do that later," or "Let's go!" When a bath needed to be crammed into a slot between 7:45 and 8:00, it was often the mother who called out, "Let's see who can take their bath the quickest!" Often a younger child would rush out, scurrying to be first in bed, while the older and wiser one stalled, resistant, sometimes resentful: "Mother is always rushing us." Sadly, women are more often the lightning rods for family tensions aroused by this speedup of work and family life. They are the villains in a process in which they are also the primary victims. More than the longer hours and the lack of sleep, this is the saddest cost to women of their extra month of work each year.

Raising children in a nuclear family is still the overwhelming preference of most people. Yet in the face of new problems for this family model we have not created an adequate support system so that the nuclear family can do its job well in the era of the two-career couple. Corporations have done little to accommodate the needs of working parents, and the government has done little to prod them.

The Reagan and Bush administrations say they are "pro-family" but confuse being pro-family with being against women's work outside the home. During a time when more than 70 percent of wives and mothers work outside the home (the rate is still climbing), the Reagan administration's Panel on the Family offered as its profamily policy only a package of measures against crime, drugs, and welfare. In the name of protecting the family, the Republicans proposed to legitimize school prayer and eliminate family-planning services. They did nothing to help parents integrate work and family life. We have to ask, when marriages continue to end because of the strains of this life, is it pro-family or anti-family to make life in two-job families so very hard? As working parents become an interest group, a voting block, and a swing vote in elections, the issue of policies to ease life in two-job families is likely to become a serious political issue in years ahead.

We really need, as sociologist Frank Furstenberg has suggested, a Marshall Plan for the family. After World War II we saw that it was in our best interests to aid the war-torn nations of Europe. Now—it seems obvious in an era of growing concern over drugs, crime, and family instability—it is in our best interests to aid the overworked two-job families right here at home. We should look to other nations for a model of what could be done. In Sweden, for example, upon the birth of a child every working couple is entitled to 12 months of paid parental leave—nine months at 90 percent of the worker's salary, plus an additional three months at about three hundred dollars a month. The mother and father are free to divide this year off between them as they wish. Working parents of a child under eight have the opportunity to work no more than six hours a day, at six hours' pay. Parental insurance offers parents money for work time lost while visiting a child's school or caring for a sick child. That's a true pro-family policy.

A pro-family policy in the United States could give tax breaks to companies that encourage job sharing, part-time work, flex time, and family leave for new parents. By implementing comparable worth policies we could increase pay scales for "women's" jobs. Another key element of a pro-family policy would be instituting fewer-hour, more flexible options—called "family phases"—for all regular jobs filled by parents of young children.

Day-care centers could be made more warm and creative through generous public and private funding. If the best form of day-care comes from the attention of elderly neighbors, students, or grandparents, these people could be paid to care for children through social programs.

In these ways, the American government would create a safer environment for the two-job family. If the government encouraged corporations to consider the long-range interests of workers and their families, they would save on long-range costs caused by absenteeism, turnover, juvenile delinquency, mental illness, and welfare support for single mothers.

These are real pro-family reforms. If they seem utopian today, we should remember that in the past the eight-hour day, the abolition of child labor, and the vote for women seemed utopian, too. Among top-rated employers listed in *The 100 Best Companies to Work for in America* are many offering country-club memberships, first-class air travel, and million-dollar fitness centers. But only a handful offer job sharing, flex time, or part-time work. Not one provides on-site day-care, and only three offer child-care deductions: Control Data, Polaroid, and Honeywell. In his book *Megatrends*. John Naisbitt reports that 83 percent of corporate executives believed that more men feel the need to share the responsibilities of parenting; yet only 9 percent of corporations offer paternity leave.

Public strategies are linked to private ones. Economic and cultural trends bear on family relations in ways it would be useful for all of us to understand. The happiest two-job marriages I saw during my research were ones in which men and women shared the housework and parenting. What couples called good communication often meant that they were good at saying thanks to one another for small aspects of taking care of the family. Making it to the school play, helping a child read, cooking dinner in good spirit, remembering the grocery list, taking responsibility for cleaning up the bedrooms—these were the silver and gold of the marital exchange. Until now, couples committed to an equal sharing of housework and child care have been rare. But, if we as a culture come to see the urgent need of meeting the new problems posed by the second shift, and if society and government begin to shape new policies that allow working parents more flexibility, then we will be making some progress toward happier times at home and work. And as the young learn by example, many more women and men will be able to enjoy the pleasure that arises when family life is family life, and not a second shift.

39
Religious Individualism and Fundamentalism

ROBERT N. BELLAH, RICHARD MADSEN, WILLIAM M. SULLIVAN, ANN SWIDLER, AND STEVEN M. TIPTON

Belief in God and regular church attendance is higher in the United States than in any other industrialized country. Religious tolerance and pluralism, however, are built into our laws and institutions, and reflect the nation's history of immigration and settlement. In this excerpt from one of contemporary sociology's most widely read books, the authors describe this pluralism by contrasting two different approaches to religion.

Religion is one of the most important of the many ways in which Americans "get involved" in the life of their community and society. Americans give more money and donate more time to religious bodies and religiously associated organizations than to all other voluntary associations put together. Some 40 percent of Americans attend religious services at least once a week (a much greater number than would be found in Western Europe or even Canada) and religious membership is around 60 percent of the total population.

In our research, we were interested in religion not in isolation but as part of the texture of private and public life in the United States. Although we seldom asked specifically about religion, time and again in our conversations, religion emerged as important to the people we were interviewing, as the national statistics just quoted would lead one to expect.

For some, religion is primarily a private matter having to do with family and local congregation. For others, it is private in one sense but also a primary vehicle for the expression of national and even global concerns. Though Americans overwhelmingly accept the doctrine of the separation of church and state, most of them believe, as they always have, that religion has an important role to play in the public realm. But as with every other major institution, the place of religion in our society has changed dramatically over time. . . .

THE LOCAL CONGREGATION

We may begin a closer examination of how religion operates in the lives of those to whom we talked by looking at the local congregation, which traditionally has a certain priority. The local church is a community of worship that contains within itself, in small, so to speak, the features of the larger church, and in some Protestant traditions can exist autonomously. The church as a community of worship is an adaptation of the Jewish synagogue. Both Jews and Christians view their communities as existing in a covenant relationship with God, and the Sabbath worship around which religious life centers is a celebration of that covenant. Worship calls to mind the story of the relationship of the community with God: how God brought his chosen people out of Egypt or gave his only begotten son for the salvation of mankind. Worship also reiterates the obligations that the community has undertaken, including the biblical insistence on justice and righteousness, and on love of God and neighbor, as well as the promises God has made that make it possible for the community to hope for the future. Though worship has its special times and places, especially on the Sabbath in the house of the Lord, it functions as a model or pattern for the whole of life. Through reminding the people of their relationship to God, it establishes patterns of character and virtue that should operate in economic and political life as well as in the context of worship. The community maintains itself as a community of memory, and the various religious traditions have somewhat different memories.

The very freedom, openness, and pluralism of American religious life makes this traditional pattern hard for Americans to understand. For one thing, the traditional pattern assumes a certain priority of the religious community over the individual. The community exists before the individual is born and will continue after his or her death. The relationship of the individual to God is ultimately personal, but it is mediated by the whole pattern of community life. There is a givenness about the community and the tradition. They are not normally a matter of individual choice.

For Americans, the traditional relationship between the individual and the religious community is to some degree reversed. On the basis of our interviews, we are not surprised to learn that a 1978 Gallup poll found that 80 percent of Americans agreed that "an individual should arrive at his or her own religious beliefs independent of any churches or synagogues." From the traditional point of view, this is a strange statement—it is precisely within church or synagogue that one comes to one's religious beliefs—but to many Americans it is the Gallup finding that is normal.

Nan Pfautz, raised in a strict Baptist church, is now an active member of a Presbyterian congregation near San Jose. Her church membership gives her a sense of community involvement, of engagement with issues at once social and moral. She speaks of her "commitment" to the church, so that being a member means being willing to give time, money, and care to the community it embodies and to its wider purposes. Yet, like many Americans, she feels that her personal relationship to God transcends her involvement in any particular church. Indeed, she speaks with humorous disdain of "churchy people" such as those who condemn others for violations of external norms. She says, "I believe I have a commitment to God which is beyond church. I felt my relationship with God was O.K. when I wasn't with the church."

For Nan, the church's value is primarily an ethical one. "Church to me is a community, and it's an organization that I belong to. They do an awful lot of good." Her obligations to the church come from the fact that she has chosen to join it, and "just like any organization that you belong to, it shouldn't be just to have another piece of paper in your wallet." As with the Kiwanis or any other organization, "you have a responsibility to do something or don't be there," to devote time and money, and especially to "care about the people." It is this caring community, above all, that the church represents. "I really love my church and what they have done for me, and what they do for other people, and the community that's there." Conceived as an association of loving individuals, the church acquires its value from "the caring about people. What I like about my church is its community."

This view of the church as a community of empathetic sharing is related to another aspect of Nan's thought. Despite her fundamentalist upbringing, her religiousness has developed a mystical cast. She sees the Christian tradition as only one, and perhaps not even the best, expression of our relationship to what is sacred in the universe. It is this mysticism and her sense of empathy with others, rather than any particularly Christian vision, that seems to motivate Nan's extraordinary range of social and political commitments. "I feel we have a commitment to the world, to animals, to the environment, to the water, to the whole thing. It all, in my opinion, is the stewardship of what God has loaned us. The American Indian religion is so fantastic, I think. All those Bible-pounding people came and told them that they were pagans, when they have such a better concept of what religion is all about." For Nan, empathy creates a sense of responsibility because she feels kinship, equality, perhaps even a kind of fusion with all others in the world, and so she suffers for their suffering. Her credo is, "We're all on this earth. Just because I was fortunate to be born in America and white doesn't make me any better than someone that's born in Africa and is black. They deserve to eat just as much as I deserve to eat. The boat people have the same feelings that I do. The same feelings—how can we say no to them?" . . .

There are thousands of local churches in the United States, representing an enormous range of variation in doctrine and worship. Yet most define themselves as communities of personal support. A recent study suggests that what Catholics look for does not differ from the concerns of the various types of Protestants we have been discussing. When asked the direction the church should take in future years, the two things that a national sample of Catholics most asked for were "personal and accessible priests" and "warmer, more personal parishes." The salience of these needs for personal intimacy in American religious life suggests why the local church, like other voluntary communities, indeed like the contemporary family, is so fragile, requires so much energy to keep it going, and has so faint a hold on commitment when such needs are not met.

RELIGIOUS INDIVIDUALISM

Religious individualism, evident in these examples of church religion, goes very deep in the United States. Even in seventeenth-century Massachusetts, a personal experience of salvation was a prerequisite for acceptance as a church member. It is true that when Anne Hutchinson began to draw her own theological conclusions from her religious experiences and teach them to others, conclusions that differed from those of the established ministry, she was tried and banished from Massachusetts. But through the peculiarly American phenomenon of revivalism, the emphasis on personal experience would eventually override all efforts at church discipline. Already in the eighteenth century, it was possible for individuals to find the form of religion that best suited their inclinations. By the nineteenth century, religious bodies had to compete in a consumers' market and grew or declined in terms of changing patterns of individual religious taste. But religious individualism in the United States could not be contained within the churches, however diverse they were. We have noted the presence of individuals who found their own way in religion even in the eighteenth century. Thomas Jefferson said, "I am a sect myself," and Thomas Paine, "My mind is my church." Many of the most influential figures in nineteenth-century American culture could find a home in none of the existing religious bodies, though they were attracted to the religious teachings of several traditions. One thinks of Ralph Waldo Emerson, Henry David Thoreau, and Walt Whitman.

Many of these nineteenth-century figures were attracted to a vague pantheistic mysticism that tended to identify the divine with a higher self. In recent times, what had been a pattern confined to the cultural elite has spread to significant sections of the educated middle class. Tim Eichelberger, a young Campaign for Economic Democracy activist in Southern California, is typical of many religious individualists when he says, "I feel religious in a way. I have no denomination or anything like that." In 1971, when he was seventeen, he became interested in Buddhism. What attracted him was the capacity of Buddhism to allow him to "transcend" his situation: "I was always into change and growth and changing what you were sort of born into and I was always interested in not having that control me. I wanted to define my own self." His religious interest involved the practice of yoga and a serious interest in leading a nonviolent life. "I was into this religious purity and I wanted the earth around me to be pure, nonviolence, nonconflict. Harmony. Harmony with the earth. Man living in harmony with the earth; men living in harmony with each other." His certainty about nonviolence eventually broke down when he had to acknowledge his rage after being rejected in a love relationship. Coming to terms with his anger made him see that struggle is a part of life. Eventually, he found that involvement in CED gave an expression to his ideals as well as his understanding of life as a struggle. His political concern with helping people attain "self-respect, self-determination, self-realization" continues his older religious concern to define his own self. But neither his religion nor his politics transcend an individualism in which "self-realization" is the highest aspiration.

That radical religious individualism can find its own institutional form is suggested by the story of Cassie Cromwell, a suburban San Diego volunteer a generation older than Eichelberger, who came to her own religious views in adolescence when she joined the Unitarian church. She sums up her beliefs succinctly: "I am a pantheist. I believe in the 'holiness' of the earth and all other living things. We are a product of this life system and are inextricably linked to all parts of it. By treating other living things disrespectfully, we are disrespectful of ourselves. Our very survival depends on the air 'god,' the water, sun, etc." Not surprisingly, she has been especially concerned with working for ecological causes. Like Eichelberger, she began with a benign view of life and then had to modify it. "I used to believe that man was basically good," her statement of her philosophy continues. "I didn't believe in evil. I still don't know what evil is but see greed, ignorance, insensitivity to other people and other living things, and irresponsibility." Unlike most of those to whom we talked, Cassie is willing to make value judgments about religion and is openly critical of Christianity. She believes that "the Christian idea of the superiority of man makes it so difficult to have a proper concern for the environment. Because only man has a soul, everything on the earth can be killed and transformed for the benefit of man. That's not right."

Commoner among religious individualists than criticism of religious beliefs is criticism of institutional religion, or the church as such. "Hypocrisy" is one of the most frequent charges against organized religion. Churchgoers do not practice what they preach. Either they are not loving enough or they do not practice the moral injunctions they espouse. As one person said, "It's not religion or the church you go to that's going to save you." Rather it is your "personal relationship" with God. Christ will "come into your heart" if you ask, without any church at all.

In the cases of Tim Eichelberger and Cassie Cromwell, we can see how mystical beliefs can provide an opening for involvement in the world. Nonetheless, the links are tenuous and to some extent fortuitous. Both had to modify their more cosmic flights in order to take account of evil and aggression and work for the causes they believe in. The CED provides a focus for Eichelberger's activities, as the ecology movement does for Cassie. But their fundamental views were formed outside those contexts and their relation to the respective groups, even Cassie's long-standing connection with the Unitarians, remains one of convenience. As social ideals, neither "self-realization" nor the "life system" provide practical guidance. Indeed, although both Tim and Cassie value "harmony with the earth," they lack a notion of nature from which any clear social norms could be derived. Rather, the tendency in American nature pantheism is to construct the world somehow out of the self. (Again, Emerson is a clue.) If the mystical quest is pursued far enough, it may take on new forms of self-discipline, committed practice, and community, as in the case of serious practitioners of Zen Buddhism. But more usually the languages of Eastern spirituality and American naturalistic pantheism are employed by people not connected with any particular religious practice or community.

INTERNAL AND EXTERNAL RELIGION

Radically individualistic religion, particularly when it takes the form of a belief in cosmic selfhood, may seem to be in a different world from conservative or fundamentalist religion. Yet these are the two poles that organize much of American religious life. To the first, God is simply the self magnified; to the second, God confronts man from outside the universe. One seeks a self that is finally identical with the world; the other seeks an external God who will provide order in the world. Both value personal religious experience as the basis of their belief. Shifts from one pole to the other are not as rare as one might think. . . .

Conversely, cosmic mysticism may seem too threatening and undefined, and in reaction a religion of external authority may be chosen. Larry Beckett was attracted to Hinduism and Buddhism in his countercultural stage, but found them just too amorphous. The clarity and authority that he found in the New Testament provided him with the structure that till then had been lacking in his life.

Howard Crossland . . . finds a similar security in his religion. He tends to view his Christianity as a matter of facts rather than emotion: "Because I have the Bible to study, it's not really relying on your emotions. There are certain facts presented and you accept the facts." Not surprisingly, Crossland is concerned about his own self-control and respects self-control in others. He never went through a countercultural phase, but he does have memories of a father who drank too much—an example of what can happen when control gets lost. In his marriage, in relation to his children, and with the several people who work under him, Crossland tries to be considerate and put the good of others ahead of his own. As he sees it, he is able to do that because of the help of God and His church: "From the help of other members of the congregation and with the help of the Holy Spirit, well, first of all you accept God, and then He gives you help to do good to your fellowman, to refrain from immorality, to refrain from illegal things." . . .

Since these two types of religion, or two ways of being religious, are deeply interrelated, if our analysis is correct, some of the obvious contrasts between them turn out to be not quite what they seem. It is true that the first style emphasizes inner freedom and the second outer control, but we cannot say that the first is therefore liberating and the second authoritarian, or that the first is individualistic and the second collectivist. It is true that the first involves a kind of radical individualism that tends to elevate the self to a cosmic principle, whereas the second emphasizes external authorities and injunctions. But the first sees the true self as benevolent and harmonious with nature and other humans and so as incompatible with narrow self-seeking. And the second finds in external authority and regulation something profoundly freeing: a protection against the chaos of internal and external demands, and the basis for a genuine personal autonomy. Thus, though they mean somewhat different things by freedom and individuality, both hold these as central values. And while the first is clearly more focussed on expressive freedom, the second in its own way also allows important opportunities for expressive freedom in intensely participatory religious services and through emphasis on love and caring. Finally, though conservative religion does indeed have a potential for authoritarianism, particularly where a magnetic preacher gathers inordinate power in his own hands, so does extreme religious individualism. Where a guru or other religious teacher is thought to have the secret of perfect personal liberation, he or she may gain excessive power over adherents.

The limitation for millions of Americans who remain stuck in this duality in one form or another is that they are deprived of a language genuinely able to mediate among self, society, the natural world, and ultimate reality. Frequently, they fall back on abstractions when talking about the most important things. They stress "communication" as essential to relationships without adequately considering what is to be communicated. They talk about "relationships" but cannot point to the personal virtues and cultural norms that give relationships meaning and value. It is true that religious conservatives go further in specifying content than the others we have discussed, but they, too, not infrequently revert to the popular language of therapy, and even when they are specific, there are often little more than the idealized norms of "traditional morality," accepted unreflectively, to fall back on. . . .

40
Christian Soldiers

SIDNEY BLUMENTHAL

What role should religion play in the government? In Iran and some other countries there is a close link between religion and politics. In the United States there is a much greater divide between the two. This does not keep the Catholic Church from being involved in the abortion controversy or many Protestant denominations from opposing the death penalty. The Christian Right has become increasingly visible in political affairs, raising again that age-old question of the separation of church and state.

Three years ago, Ralph Reed, the executive director of the Christian Coalition, wished not to be seen. "I want to be invisible," he said. "I do guerrilla warfare. I paint my face and travel at night. You don't know it's over until you're in a body bag. You don't know until Election Night." But on June 25th Reed played the expansive host at a luncheon given by the Coalition, the most influential group on the religious right, which was attended by hundreds of delegates to the Iowa Republican Party Convention. They were celebrating their victories in gaining control of the state Party's central committee, ousting moderate Republicans, and in dictating a platform that supported the teaching of creationism in the public schools and opposition to "secular humanism, political correctness, New Age concepts, the PETA (People for the Ethical Treatment of Animals) philosophy, one world government, situational ethics, and the teaching of homosexuality as an acceptable life style or behavior." Reed told the crowd, "I don't think it's the American way to oppose people with religious faith getting involved." . . .

For the religious right, invisibility is no longer possible. From South Carolina to Oregon, state parties are falling under its sway. The movement became a truly volatile and defining issue with the Virginia Republican Convention, held on June 3rd and 4th—the most clarifying political event to occur since the 1992 Presidential election. By itself, it may have seemed a sensational singularity, but it was not. Virginia was followed a week later by the Texas Republican Convention, a week after that by the one in Minnesota, and a week after that by Iowa. In Texas, the religious right took control of the state Party, enthusiastically electing one of their own as chairman and voting down a resolution, proposed by a benighted moderate, that read, "The Republican Party is not a church. . . . A Republican should never be put in the position of having to defend or explain his faith in order to participate in the party process." In Minnesota, the religious right overwhelmingly dominated the state Convention, pledging their support for governor to Allen Quist, a creationist and anti-abortion activist, who in 1985, after his first wife, who was six months pregnant, was killed in a car accident, had the fetus displayed in the open coffin. Quist's opponent at the Convention was the incumbent Republican governor, Arne Carlson, who is a moderate. Across the nation, the flag and the cross are becoming one.

The upsurge of the religious right at the 1992 Republican National Convention, in Houston, startled many, but the shifts in the G.O.P. that came into stark public view then are now flaring into open combat nationwide. In the 1992 Presidential election, Evangelical Protestants became the single largest constituency within the Republican Party, without which it would not have had even a minimally credible base within the electoral college. Consequently, a cultural and religious war is being waged within the Party between the mainline Protestants, who defined Republicanism, and the ascendant Evangelicals, whose claims on Party structures are depicted by the Old Guard as takeovers. Since 1992, the conservative movement has steadily folded itself into its one concentrated point of energy—the religious right. There may be another Republican Party, but it exists only in the irretrievable past. For now, the G.O.P. is gathering in a permanent Houston Convention.

The Richmond Convention was a far less diluted and mediated event than the one in Houston. Every side of the Richmond Coliseum—east and west, north and south—was plastered with signs reading "North." Fourteen thousand delegates to the Virginia Republican Party Convention, the largest deliberative body in American politics, were packed in from floor to rafters, coiled in anticipation. Suddenly, the thunderous chords of "Eye of the Tiger," the theme song from "Rocky III," crashed through the loudspeakers, stilling the eager humming of the crowd. The hall was thrown into darkness. On a thirty-foot-tall video screen, which was just behind the platform and was flanked by statues of trumpeting elephants, a huge black-and-white picture of Jane Fonda appeared. "*Boo!*" The fight song rumbled on, louder and louder. Jesse Jackson's face appeared. "*Boo!*" Then, ratcheting up the decibel level and the scale of demonology, came Dan Rather. "*Boo!*" After him, Sam Donaldson. "*Boo!*" Then Mephisto himself, Bill Clinton. "*Booo!*" Block letters filled the screen, asking the delegates, "WHOSE SIDE ARE YOU ON?"

Then, abruptly, the film began to solicit love for the hero who could save the delegates from their enemies. In tender tones, his friends and comrades, his wife and mother testified to his bravery, resolve, and fidelity. The hero himself, a Cincinnatus in jeans, strode toward the camera, with his farm as a backdrop, to explain that "family values" has become his "battle cry"—that he must give up the plow for the sword. The music pumped way up. The hero's name was chanted over and over.

Spotlights sweeping the arena converged in a pinpoint onstage. Oliver North, Republican candidate for the United States Senate, materialized within it. *"Ollie! Ollie!"*

North's rise from the shame of the Iran-Contra scandal to the respectability of the podium in Richmond may appear to be a hallucinogenic turn in a bizarre Virginia reel. But his nomination is neither a flashback nor a provincial sideshow. The transformation of Ollie North the witness, facing a phalanx of senators, into Ollie North the candidate for the Senate has required a drastic political mutation, not so much in him as in the Republican Party. Ollie has emerged as the most renowned figure of the most vital and aggressive movement within the national Party: the nominee as Christian soldier. . . .

The corridors of the Coliseum and the Richmond Centre, another convention hall, across the street, were lined with venders' booths—a bazaar of ideological objects. There were several sections promoting North. One booth sold North's books, "Under Fire: An American Story" and "One More Mission: Ollie North Returns to Vietnam." Another was manned by the Law Enforcement Coalition for Oliver North, whose director, James Jones, told me, "We expect eighty thousand members. I've never seen a person be so endorsed by a group. We even got people from the C.I.A. and the Capitol Hill police. . . . No doubt in my mind what happened in Iran-Contra. The man put himself out as a sacrificial lamb." A third booth sought recruits to the Ollie North "prayer network," a group that prays for him daily and "includes everyone from nuns in Texas to Ollie himself," according to an instruction sheet handed out to potential "Prayer Warriors." The sheet also stated that "prayer and submission to the Father's will and His guidance are the key to victory for Ollie" and includes a "program" that involves reading from Psalm 84: "O God, behold our shield, and look upon the face of Your anointed." . . .

. . . The Christian Coalition, from its stand, handed out free copies of its newspaper, *Christian American*, and recruited for its activist training school. "Think Like Jesus. Lead Like Moses. Fight Like David. Run Like Lincoln," read the cover of the recruiting brochure. Inside, it asked, "Can You Spare 12 Hours to Save Christians from Destruction?" A seminar promises to teach "how to elect candidates with Christian values," and aspirants are told, "Believe it or not, the Lord may even want you to run for office. Your availability is more critical than your lack of political ability." . . .

William Bennett, who under Reagan was a director of the National Endowment for the Humanities and then the Secretary of Education, addressed a fund-raising dinner during the Convention. In the post-Bush period, Bennett has become the toastmaster of the religious right. He is the G.O.P.'s favorite preacher on morals—an Eastern intellectual urging alignment with the Christian Coalition. Bennett's latest ventures as an authority on values are his editorship, in 1993, of a best-selling volume of uplifting stories and poems, "The Book of Virtues," and his compilation of a pamphlet, "The Index of Leading Cultural Indicators," which was originally published by the Heritage Foundation, and which quantifies the fall of virtue in America.

Bennett's big theme at the dinner was, as always, that traditional values are being undermined by liberalism. He spoke of giving a speech at Stanford University "to defend Western civilization," because "there was no one on the faculty who would do it." Social rot, he warned, was spreading. "Welfare is bad for people, whether they're poor, middle class, or wealthy," he said. Moral fibre was weakening. He gave many illustrations of anti-social behavior caused by liberalism. The last best hope, he concluded, was "the party of Lincoln." After his speech, he joined Ralph Reed at a Coalition reception. When he entered, there were excited cries of "Bennett in '96! Bennett in '96!"

The next day—the day of the balloting—Mike Farris, a prominent new-style Virginia Republican, stepped up to introduce the keynote speaker. Farris's eminence comes from his martyrdom: last year, everyone else on the Republican ticket was elected to statewide offices in a sweep; only Farris, the candidate for lieutenant governor, was defeated. (He carried forty-six per cent of the vote.) A number of Republican leaders refused to support him because he represents the religious right. Farris, who is forty-two and comes from Washington State, drifted across the country and through a host of organizations before winding up as one of the movement's tribunes in Virginia. In the early nineteen-eighties, he founded the Moral Majority chapter in Washington State, and a few years later he went on to found the Home School Legal Defense Association. He has argued that public schools are "unconstitutional," objected to the idea of separation of church and state, approved of discrimination against gays, and enjoined women not to work outside the home. His backers believed that his loss was attributable to betrayal by the Old Guard. . . .

Shortly thereafter, North's name was placed in nomination, and, in the spotlight, he spoke. His eyes glistened; his voice had a tremulous catch. North summoned the Republicans to a new battlefield: "Fifty years ago at this very minute, thirty-five hundred Virginians—the Stonewall Brigade of the 29th Infantry Division—were preparing to spearhead one of the most audacious operations in history. Their mission: to lead the way across Omaha Beach at dawn, on D Day. . . . Now, in this last decade of the twentieth century, Virginians are again being called upon to lead in another great test of resolve. This time the beach-head we need to seize is not on some distant shore. It is across the Potomac—in Washington." . . .

War, for North, is an all-consuming metaphor. He is a true Prayer Warrior, a charismatic Evangelical who has diligently made the rounds of all the religious-right groups. At a meeting in 1991, he explained, "Government has replaced God as a place we turn. Government couldn't help me. It wasn't even able to pay me my retirement. I had to turn to God." Now, for him, religion is politics, and politics is war. And when the delegates' votes were tallied North easily bested Miller. As the theme from "Rocky" blasted, the nominee strode to the platform to issue a challenge: "This is our government. They stole it. And we're coming to take it back!" . . .

In the 1992 Presidential election, conservative Evangelicals were revealed to be a large part of the Republican Party's irreducible base. Bush held on to only two voting blocs: those making more than seventy-five thousand dollars a year and white born-again Protestants. Sixty-two per cent of the latter bloc voted for Bush; indeed, twenty-eight per cent of all Bush voters were Evangelicals. No other group in the Republican column matched their size. They are more consistently Republican, more consistently conservative, and more self-motivated than any other group of voters, and their support for Bush grew through 1992 while the support of others shrank. Running against an unprecedented Democratic ticket of two Southern Baptists, Bush nonetheless received a greater percentage of the Evangelical vote than he did running against Michael Dukakis in 1988. The base was immovable. According to the Christian Coalition, forty-two per cent of the delegates at the 1992 Republican Convention were Evangelicals. In the two largest states that went Republican—Florida and Texas—sixty and seventy-two per cent, respectively, of Bush voters were Evangelicals. The only states that Bush won without them were the most sparsely populated Western ones.

The end of the Cold War and the dissolution of the Evil Empire created a vacuum on the right. Ever since the Cold War's advent, the disparate elements of the right wing had been tied together by the thread of anti-Communism. William F. Buckley, Jr.,'s expedient use of the term "fusionism" enabled the isolated and fractured conservative "remnant" to combine in the nineteen-fifties, not least through Buckley's *National Review*, and was a basis for the triumph of Reaganism three decades later. What had begun with squabbling sects of ideologues became a movement with national power. In 1992, Bush presided over the implosion of conservatism as we had known it. But it was not simply his political maladroitness or an economic downturn that unravelled it. The change occurred at "a more seismic level," Ralph Reed told me. "They were united by Communism and now they're not." In America, as in Europe, the removal of the bipolarity of the Cold War unleashed ethnic and religious tensions that had been mostly submerged for nearly half a century. Pat Buchanan's clarion call at the Houston Convention for "cultural warfare" was an instance of such post-Cold War atavism. "The truth is, the ends of wars bring the most divisive politics recorded in American history," Reed said. "The old.dichotomies of liberal-conservative, internationalist-isolationist, dove-hawk are breaking apart. There are some ideological categories being formed that don't have any history in the politics of the Cold War. The ends of wars don't bring stability. They bring chaos and recriminations. Postwar eras are periods of an enormous realigning of political lines."

"There's more than ten years of work here," Morton Blackwell, who was North's floor leader at the Convention, told me after North's nomination. In the post-civil-rights era, the enlistment of religion in the cause of politics began with efforts by Republican operatives to split off Southern Baptists from their allegiance to the Democratic Party on the basis of social issues. The intent was to gain a marginal vote. Religion itself was not part of the equation, except for a residual anti-Catholicism. Indeed, the roots of the religious right are surprisingly deep, stretching back at least as far as the Know-Nothing Party of nativists, in the eighteen-fifties. Reverend Lou Sheldon, the chairman of the Traditional Values Coalition, expressed the distilled nativist sentiment perfectly in 1993, when he told the San Francisco *Chronicle*, "We were here first. You don't take our shared common values and say they are biased and bigoted. . . . We are the keepers of what is right and what is wrong."

In 1978, the Internal Revenue Service ruled that Christian academies (whose origins were as "seg" academies, which enabled whites to escape school integration) would no longer have tax-exempt status. That ruling galvanized an element of the clergy connected with the conservative movement to organize against the Democrats. "It began in the nineteen-seventies, when conservative-movement activists made a conscious effort to involve theological leaders in politics," Blackwell said. "Most of the conservative ones were of the opinion that public affairs were not part of their calling." Jerry Falwell was recruited in this period by conservative operatives to head an organization they called the Moral Majority. By 1980, right-wing activists had organized Evangelical preachers into a group called the Religious Roundtable, and it was addressed by Ronald Reagan when he was running for the Presidency. "I want you to know that I endorse you and what you are doing," he told them.

Reagan supported the religious right rhetorically, but, somehow, divisive legislation always conveniently managed to get tabled. In the summer of 1984, for the first time, preachers of the religious right such as Falwell and Pat Robertson appeared on the podium at a Republican National Convention. It was a decisive moment in the shift of Evangelical voters. Blackwell said that "in terms of affecting elections at the grass roots, there was one technique: comparing church membership rolls with voters rolls. They discovered church members weren't registered and registered them." In 1984, Blackwell was serving as the liaison between the Reagan White House and the religious right. It was not his first service to the right wing of the Party: for the 1972 Republican National Convention, he had crafted delegate-selection rules that favored conservatives.

By its very nature, the religious right, rooted in Evangelical Protestantism, is sectarian and schismatic, tending to fall prey to controversies over doctrinal issues. Through the late nineteen-eighties, after the conviction of Jim Bakker for defrauding supporters of a hundred and sixty million dollars, Jimmy Swaggart's sobbing confession of adultery with a prostitute, and the electorate's rebuke of Pat Robertson, the movement suffered numerous fissures and seemed to break up. It was generally assumed that the Evangelicals had retreated into privatism, just as they had done after the humiliating Scopes trial, in 1925. Ralph Reed explained the resurgence of the movement in 1992: "There have been three significant Presidential campaigns that reoriented the political landscape: the Goldwater campaign, which transferred control from the Eastern-establishment wing of the Republican Party to the Southern and Western grassroots wing; the McGovern campaign, which transferred the Democratic Party from the old guard to the New Left, where it remains today; and, third, the Robertson campaign. It gave activists an advanced degree in hardball politics. We took a beating, dusted ourselves off, and got up for another round. The campaign was a midwife. It took a social-protest movement and made it a savvy movement of political veterans, enmeshed in the machinery of party politics."

After Robertson lost, he converted his mailing list of nearly two million names and organizational contacts into the Christian Coalition. For its executive director he hired Reed, who had been the executive director of the College Republicans and later a campaign staffer for Jack Kemp. The Christian Coalition was not the obvious campaign tool of a politician; it does not endorse or make contributions to candidates. "It's issue centered, not personality centered," Reed told me. "Unlike United We Stand, it's not designed to advance a personality. Whereas when Perot takes a beating the whole organization suffers, as long as issues are being advanced, the Christian Coalition advances." Robertson now presides over an expanding commercial and religious empire in Virginia Beach and plays a strong role in the work of the Coalition, which is based in Chesapeake, the next town. He still makes frequent political pronouncements. In 1993, for example, he said about the separation of church and state, "There is no such thing in the Constitution. It's a lie of the left, and we're not going to take it anymore." In Georgia, at a Christian Coalition rally on June 4th addressed by Robertson, House Minority Whip Newt Gingrich proclaimed deferentially that Robertson "would play a role" in helping the Republicans win majorities in Congress in the midterm elections.

The Christian Coalition, unlike the religious-right groups of the nine-teen-eighties, is not devoted mainly to spreading its message through television and radio shows. Instead, it runs training seminars for political cadres, at which participants are taught the rudiments of taking control of local Republican organizations from the bottom up. During the early nineteen-nineties, the Coalition operated quietly—even, as Reed advised, with ('stealth.") A draft of the Pennsylvania Christian Coalition manual, for instance, instructed, "You should never mention the name Christian Coalition in Republican circles." By the Republican Convention of 1992, it had gained dominance or significant leverage in about twenty state Parties and in numerous counties.

In 1993, Dr. Steven Hotze, who favors the death penalty for gays, was elected chairman of the advisory committee of the Harris County, Texas, Republican Party with the support of the Christian Coalition. The Oregon Citizens Alliance, which gained control of the Oregon G.O.P. with Coalition support, proposed an initiative in 1992 that would have classified homosexuality as "abnormal, wrong, unnatural, and perverse." In Washington State, the Republican Party, under the sway of the religious right, took an official stand against witchcraft and yoga. "We could not save George Bush from himself," Reed said after the campaign.

Bush's defeat was hardly a defeat for the Christian Coalition. Despite the often exotic causes of some of its local leaders, the strategy from Chesapeake is to forge alliances wherever it can with Republican candidates who do not necessarily share the Coalition's entire agenda, in order to get practical experience for its troops and a share of the spoils; its object in every campaign is to build an infrastructure to help promote itself in the long run. Even if a candidate loses, the organization grows. According to Reed, the Christian Coalition has a million two hundred thousand supporters, with more than half of them contributing fifteen dollars a year in dues. "We've organized them into precinct captains, providing a full menu of activities for them beyond giving money," he told me. He claims that at the moment there are eight hundred and seventy-two chapters, with at least one in every state, and that nineteen states have full-time field staffs who raise their own salaries. This year, the budget for the national organization is twenty million dollars.

The Christian Coalition has emerged as the political powerhouse of a large alternative culture that includes schools, institutes, newspapers, magazines, radio and television stations, and thousands of politically mobilized churches—a culture that religious-right leaders consciously see as a counterweight to a coherent liberal establishment and its institutions, which, Robertson has explained, "are firmly in the hands of secular humanists who are exerting every effort to debase and eliminate Bible-based Christianity from our society." For the activists of the religious right, politics is a post-millennialist battle for ultimate dominion over America.

The Coalition and its allies are conducting a long march through the Republican Party. In 1960, sixty-nine per cent of the nation's mainline Protestants, constituting about two-fifths of the total population, voted Republican. In all ways, they *were* the Republican Party. In 1992, only thirty-nine per cent of the mainline Protestants, who had declined to about one-fifth of the population, voted Republican. For the first time in the history of the G.O.P., they were no longer the Party's largest plurality—they had been displaced by the Evangelicals. "We have a 'Field of Dreams' strategy: Build it and they will come," Reed said. "The priority has always been to organize, to build a permanent infrastructure. We're looking twenty years ahead, not two years. If we build our movement only against Bill Clinton, once Clinton is gone, in either two or six years, then what will we say?"

Blackwell told me, "You can put together a winning coalition two or three times in a century. We did it in 1980. We're not going to put together a different one any time soon."

Yet each election cycle provides a chance for building. For instance, besides the victories in Virginia, Texas, Minnesota, and Iowa, a congressional seat in Kentucky that had been held in seeming perpetuity by the Democrats was won in a special election by a Republican—Ron Lewis, a Baptist minister and Christian-bookstore owner. The Christian Coalition was heavily involved and its efforts included distributing more than ninety thousand pieces of literature in the district. Religious-right groups and the national Republican Party worked to pump hundreds of thousands of dollars and numerous operatives into the campaign. In the midterm elections, the religious right is involved in hundreds of races, from the state level to the national. In California alone, its activists are working on dozens of legislative campaigns. (In 1992, a group of California millionaires associated with the religious right gave more than three million dollars to local candidates and causes, becoming the most generous political contributors in the state and exceeding the largesse of any political-action committee there. More than two-thirds of their candidates won Republican primaries.)

In the aftermath of the Virginia Convention, all possibility of the religious right's maintaining a "stealth" strategy in any important campaign is obviously foreclosed. An obstacle for them may be that their religion will be seen as a form of political partisanship limited to one faction of one party. For other Republicans, the religious right will pose an uncomfortable political quandary, by obliging them to define themselves in relation to the growing movement. . . .

. . . Former Vice-President Dan Quayle, whose recently published political memoir, "Standing Firm," is filled with professions of Evangelical faith, is also out on the hustings. In January, he spoke at a training conference of religious-right activists in Fort Lauderdale, whose theme was

"Reclaiming America," and before the event began he stood at attention as the crowd of more than two thousand rose, faced a flag with a cross on it, and, with hands on hearts, recited in unison, "I pledge allegiance to the Christian flag, and to the Saviour, for whose Kingdom it stands, one Saviour, crucified, risen, and coming again, with life and liberty for all who believe."

41
Domestic Networks

CAROL B. STACK

How far do family ties and responsibilities extend? For the typical African-American family they extend beyond parents and children to cousins, aunts, uncles, and even fictive kin. Decades of discrimination and institutional racism have left many people with few resources to draw on in times of need, and so helping relationships have remained a critical feature of the extended family.

In The Flats the responsibility for providing food, care, clothing, and shelter and for socializing children within domestic networks may be spread over several households. Which household a given individual belongs to is not a particularly meaningful question, as we have seen that daily domestic organization depends on several things: where people sleep, where they eat, and where they offer their time and money. Although those who eat together and contribute toward the rent are generally considered by Flat's residents to form minimal domestic units, household changes rarely affect the exchanges and daily dependencies of those who take part in common activity.

The residence patterns and cooperative organization of people linked in domestic networks demonstrate the stability and collective power of family life in The Flats. Michael Lee grew up in The Flats and now has a job in Chicago. On a visit to The Flats, Michael described the residence and domestic organization of his kin. "Most of my kin in The Flats lived right here on Cricket Street, numbers sixteen, eighteen, and twenty-two, in these three apartment buildings joined together. My mama decided it would be best for me and my three brothers and sister to be on Cricket Street too. My daddy's mother had a small apartment in this building, her sister had one in the basement, and another brother and his family took a larger apartment upstairs. My uncle was really good to us. He got us things we wanted and he controlled us. All the women kept the younger kids together during the day. They cooked together too. It was good living."

Yvonne Diamond, a forty-year-old Chicago woman, moved to The Flats from Chicago with her four children. Soon afterwards they were evicted. "The landlord said he was going to build a parking lot there, but he never did. The old place is still standing and has folks in it today. My husband's mother and father took me and the kids in and watched over them while I had my baby. We stayed on after my husband's mother died, and my husband joined us when he got a job in The Flats."

When families or individuals in The Flats are evicted, other kinsmen usually take them in. Households in The Flats expand or contract with the loss of a job, a death in the family, the beginning or end of a sexual partnership, or the end of a friendship. Welfare workers, researchers, and landlords have long known that the poor must move frequently. What is much less understood is the relationship between residence and domestic organization in the black community.

The spectrum of economic and legal pressures that act upon ghetto residents, requiring them to move—unemployment, welfare requirements, housing shortages, high rents, eviction—are clear-cut examples of external pressures affecting the daily lives of the poor. Flats' residents are evicted from their dwellings by landlords who want to raise rents, tear the building down, or rid themselves of tenants who complain about rats, roaches, and the plumbing. Houses get condemned by the city on landlords' requests so that they can force tenants to move. After an eviction, a landlord can rent to a family in such great need of housing that they will not complain for a while.

Poor housing conditions and unenforced housing standards coupled with overcrowding, unemployment, and poverty produce hazardous living conditions and residence changes. "Our whole family had to move when the gas lines sprung a leak in our apartment and my son set the place on fire by accident," Sam Summer told me. "The place belonged to my sister-in-law's grandfather. We had been living there with my mother, my brother's eight children, and our eight children. My father lived in the basement apartment 'cause he and my mother were separated. After the fire burned the whole place down, we all moved to two places down the street near my cousin's house."

When people are unable to pay their rent because they have been temporarily "cut off aid," because the welfare office is suspicious of their eligibility, because they gave their rent money to a kinsman to help him through a crisis or illness, or because they were laid off from their job, they receive eviction notices almost immediately. Lydia Watson describes a chain of events starting with the welfare office stopping her sister's welfare checks, leading to an eviction, co-residence, overcrowding, and eventually murder. Lydia sadly related the story to me. "My oldest sister was cut off aid the day her husband got out of jail. She and her husband and their three children were evicted from their apartment and they came to live with us. We were in crowded conditions already. I had my son, my other sister was there with her two kids, and my mother was about going crazy. My mother put my sister's husband out 'cause she found out he was a dope addict. He came back one night soon after that and murdered my sister. After my sister's death my mother couldn't face living in Chicago any longer. One of my other sisters who had been adopted and raised by my mother's paternal grandmother visited us and persuaded us to move to The Flats, where she was staying.

All of us moved there—my mother, my two sisters and their children, my two baby sisters, and my dead sister's children. My sister who had been staying in The Flats found us a house across the street from her own."

Overcrowded dwellings and the impossibility of finding adequate housing in The Flats have many long-term consequences regarding where and with whom children live. Terence Platt described where and with whom his kin lived when he was a child. "My brother stayed with my aunt, my mother's sister, and her husband until he was ten, 'cause he was the oldest in our family and we didn't have enough room—but he stayed with us most every weekend. Finally my aunt moved into the house behind ours with her husband, her brother, and my brother; my sisters and brothers and I lived up front with my mother and her old man."

Kin-Structured Local Networks

The material and cultural support needed to absorb, sustain, and socialize community members in The Flats is provided by networks of cooperating kinsmen. Local coalitions formed from these networks of kin and friends are mobilized within domestic networks; domestic organization is diffused over many kin-based households which themselves have elastic boundaries.

People in The Flats are immersed in a domestic web of a large number of kin and friends whom they can count on. From a social viewpoint, relationships within the community are "organized on the model of kin relationships." . . . Kin-constructs such as the perception of parenthood, the culturally determined criteria which affect the shape of personal kindreds, and the idiom of kinship, prescribe kin who can be recruited into domestic networks.

There are similarities in function between domestic networks and domestic groups which [one scholar] characterizes as "workshops of social reproduction." Both domains include three generations of members linked collaterally or otherwise. Kinship, jural and affectional bonds, and economic factors affect the composition of both domains and residential alignments within them. There are two striking differences between domestic networks and domestic groups. Domestic networks are not visible groups, because they do not have an obvious nucleus or defined boundary. But since a primary focus of domestic networks is child-care arrangements, the cooperation of a cluster of adult females is apparent. Participants in domestic networks are recruited from personal kindreds and friendships, but the personnel changes with fluctuating economic needs, changing life styles, and vacillating personal relationships.

In some loosely and complexly structured cognatic systems, kin-structured local networks (not groups) emerge. Localized coalitions of persons drawn from personal kindreds can be organized as networks of kinsmen.

Goodenough . . . correctly points out that anthropologists frequently describe "localized kin groups," but rarely describe kin-structured local
groups. . . . The localized, kin-based, cooperative coalitions of people
described in this chapter are organized as kin-structured domestic networks. For brevity, I refer to them as domestic networks. . . .

GENEROSITY AND POVERTY

The combination of arbitrary and repressive economic forces and social behavior, modified by successive generations of poverty, make it
almost impossible for people to break out of poverty. There is no way
for those families poor enough to receive welfare to acquire any surplus
cash which can be saved for emergencies or for acquiring adequate appliances or a home or a car. In contrast to the middle class, who are
pressured to spend and save, the poor are not even permitted to establish
an equity.

The following examples from Magnolia and Calvin Waters' life illustrates the ways in which the poor are prohibited from acquiring any
surplus which might enable them to change their economic condition or
life style.

In 1971 Magnolia's uncle died in Mississippi and left an unexpected
inheritance of $1,500 to Magnolia and Calvin Waters. The cash came
from a small run-down farm which Magnolia's uncle sold shortly before
he died. It was the first time in their lives that Magnolia or Calvin ever
had a cash reserve. Their first hope was to buy a home and use the
money as a down payment.

Calvin had retired from his job as a seasonal laborer the year before
and the family was on welfare. AFDC alloted the family $100 per month
for rent. The housing that the family had been able to obtain over the
years for their nine children at $100 or less was always small, roach
infested, with poor plumbing and heating. The family was frequently
evicted. Landlords complained about the noise and often observed an
average of ten to fifteen children playing in the household. Magnolia
and Calvin never even anticipated that they would be able to buy a
home.

Three days after they received the check, news of its arrival spread
throughout their domestic network. One niece borrowed $25 from Mag-
nolia so that her phone would not be turned off. Within a week the
welfare office knew about the money. Magnolia's children were immediately cut off welfare, including medical coverage and food stamps.
Magnolia was told that she would not receive a welfare grant for her
children until the money was used up, and she was given a minimum
of four months in which to spend the money. The first surplus the family
ever acquired was effectively taken from them.

During the weeks following the arrival of the money, Magnolia and
Calvin's obligations to the needs of kin remained the same, but their

ability to meet these needs had temporarily increased. When another uncle became very ill in the South, Magnolia and her older sister, Augusta, were called to sit by his side. Magnolia bought round-trip train tickets for both of them and for her three youngest children. When the uncle died, Magnolia bought round-trip train tickets so that she and Augusta could attend the funeral. Soon after his death, Augusta's first "old man" died in The Flats and he had no kin to pay for the burial. Augusta asked Magnolia to help pay for digging the grave. Magnolia was unable to refuse. Another sister's rent was two months overdue and Magnolia feared that she would get evicted. This sister was seriously ill and had no source of income. Magnolia paid her rent.

Winter was cold and Magnolia's children and grandchildren began staying home from school because they did not have warm winter coats and adequate shoes or boots. Magnolia and Calvin decided to buy coats, hats, and shoes for all of the children (at least fifteen). Magnolia also bought a winter coat for herself and Calvin bought himself a pair of sturdy shoes.

Within a month and a half, all of the money was gone. The money was channeled into the hands of the same individuals who ordinarily participate in daily domestic exchanges, but the premiums were temporarily higher. All of the money was quickly spent for necessary, compelling reasons.

Thus random fluctuations in the meager flow of available cash and goods tend to be of considerable importance to the poor. A late welfare check, sudden sickness, robbery, and other unexpected losses cannot be overcome with a cash reserve like more well-to-do families hold for emergencies. Increases in cash are either taken quickly from the poor by the welfare agencies or dissipated through the kin network.

Those living in poverty have little or no chance to escape from the economic situation into which they were born. Nor do they have the power to control the expansion or contraction of welfare benefits . . . or of employment opportunities, both of which have a momentous effect on their daily lives. In times of need, the only predictable resources that can be drawn upon are their own children and parents, and the fund of kin and friends obligated to them.

42
Love, Arranged Marriage, and the Indian Social Structure

Giri Raj Gupta

For most of you the idea of marrying someone you do not love seems absurd. In many societies, however, arranged marriages are common and result in lasting and satisfying bonds between husband and wife. Marital success is dependent not only on how partners feel toward one another. The social supports for their partnership and family are critical. In a Hindu society, such as is found in India, the family not only plays a major role in arranging a marriage but in making the marriage a success.

Marriage is an immemorial institution which, in some form, is found everywhere. Mating patterns are closely associated with marriage, more so with the social structure. It's not the institution of marriage itself, but the institutionalization of mating patterns which determine the nature of family relationships in a society. Primitive societies present a wide array of practices ranging from marriage by capture to mutual love and elopement. Yet, the people who marry through customary practice are those who are eligibles, who consciously followed the established norms, and who did the kind of things they were supposed to do. The main purpose of marriage is to establish a family, to produce children, and to further the family's economic and social position. Perhaps, there are some transcendental goals too. Generally, women hope for kind and vigorous providers and protectors and men for faithful mothers and good housekeepers; both undoubtedly hope for mutual devotion and affection too. Irrespective of the various ways of instituting marriage, most marriages seem to have these common goals.

There are few works commenting on mating patterns in India. Though some monographs on tribal and rural India have treated the subject, nevertheless, serious sociological attention has only infrequently been given. The present paper attempts to explain the variables as a part of the cultural system which help in promotion and sustenance of the arranged marriage, particularly in the Hindu society in India. In addition, the paper also critically analyzes the present-day mating patterns which relate to precautionary controls working against the potentially disintegrative forces of change; especially those endangering family unity, religious structure, and the stratification system.

ROMANTIC LOVE VERSUS CONJUGAL LOVE

One is intrigued by the cultural pattern in India where the family is characterized by arranged marriage. Infatuation as well as romantic love, though, is reported quite in abundance in the literature, sacred books, and scriptures, yet is not thought to be an element in prospective marital alliance (see Meyer 1953: 322–39).

Sanskrit or Hindi terms like *sneh* (affection) and *prem* or *muhbbat* carry two different meanings. *Sneh* is nonsensual love, while *prem* is a generic term connoting love with god, people, nation, family, [neighbor], and, of course, lover or beloved. In fact, there is a hierarchy of relationships. In Urdu literature, concepts like *ishque ruhani* (love with the spirit), *ishque majazi* (love with the supreme being), and *ishque haqiqi* (love with the lover or beloved) are commonly referred to love relationships. Interestingly, the humans supposedly reach the highest goal of being in love with god through the love they cherish among humans. Great love stories in mythology and history illustrate the emotion, as opposed to reason, which characterize the thoughts and acts of persons in love. The quality of the emotions may be characterized best by the altruistic expressions of a person for the person in love. Most people in India do not go around singing their love as one might imagine after watching Indian movies and dramatic performances. Even the proximity, intimacy, freedom, and permissiveness characterized in such media are rarely commonplace in the reality of the day-to-day life. In general, to verbalize and manifest romantic expressions of love is looked upon as a product of poets' or novelists' fantasies. Yet, at least theoretically, to be in love with someone is a highly cherished ideal.

In one of the most ancient scriptures, Rgveda, it was wished that a person's life be of a hundred-year duration. The Hindu sages in their theory of *purusharthas* suggested four aims of life: *dharma*, righteousness, which provides a link between animal and god in man; *artha*, acquisitive instinct in man, enjoyment of wealth and its manifestations; *kama*, instinctive and emotional life of man and the satisfaction of sex drives and aesthetic urges; and *moksha*, the end of life and the realization of an inner spirituality in man (see Kapadia 1966: 25).

The Hindu scriptures written during 200 B.C. to 900 A.D. mention eight modes of acquiring a wife known as Brahma, Daiva, Arsha, Prajapatya, Asura, Gandharva, Rakshasa, and Paisacha. Only the first four are known as *dharmya*, that is, according to religion. An exchange of gifts between the subjects' families marks the wedding ceremony, but no dowry is paid. In the Asura form payment of the bride price is the main element, while Rakshasa and Paisacha, respectively, pertain to the abduction and seduction of a girl when she is unconscious. The Gandharva marriage refers to a marriage by mutual choice. The Hindu lawgivers differ in their opinions and interpretations of this kind of marriage; some called it the best mode of marriage, while others viewed it stigmatic on religious and moral grounds. However, there is no reliable data to support or justify the popularity of any one of these modes of marriage. The first four kinds pertain to arranged marriages in which the parental couple ritually gives away the daughter to a suitable person, and this ideal continues to be maintained in the Hindu society. Opposed to these are four others, three of which were objected to by the scriptwriters in the past and viewed as illegal today, though nevertheless, they happen. The Gandharva mode, though opposed to the accepted norm, is nearest to what may be variously termed as "free-choice," "romantic," or "love" marriage. Yet through the ages Hindu revivalism and other socioreligious and economic factors discredited the importance of Gandharva marriage.

Diversified sects of Muslims and Christians view marriage as a civil contract as opposed to a sacrament. However, marriages are arranged most often with the consent of the subjects. The Muslims, at least theoretically, permit polygamy according to Islamic law; however, they prefer monogamy. As opposed to Hindu and Christian communities it is customary that the boy's party initiates a marriage proposal (see Kapadia 1966: 209–14; Kurian 1974: 357–58, 1975).

Most Indian marriages are arranged, although sometimes opinions of the partners are consulted, and in cases of adults, their opinions are seriously considered. Another aspect of this pattern is that individuals come to believe that their life mate is predestined, their fate is preordained, they are "right for each other," they are helpless as far as choice is concerned and therefore must succumb to the celestial forces of the universe. That the entire syndrome, typical for the society, represents a complex set of forces working around and upon the individual to get married to a person whom one is destined to love. It is also believed to be good and desirable that critical issues like the choosing of a life partner should be handled by responsible persons of family and kin group. However, it is generally possible that persons in love could marry if related prohibitions have been effectively observed.

Generally, love is considered a weak basis for marriage because its presence may overshadow suitable qualities in spouses. Therefore, arranged marriages result from more or less intense care given to the selection of suitable partners so that the family ideals, companionship, and co-parenthood can grow, leading to love. Ernest Van Den Haag writes about the United States:

A hundred years ago, there was every reason to marry young—though middle-class people seldom did. The unmarried state had heavy disadvantages for both sexes. Custom did not permit girls to be educated, to work, or to have social, let alone sexual, freedom. . . . And, though, less restricted than girls shackled to their families, single men often led a grim and uncomfortable life. A wife was nearly indispensable, if only to darn socks, sew, cook, clean, take care of her man. (1973: 181)

Goode views romantic love paradoxically, and calls it the antithesis of "conjugal love," because marriage is not based upon it, actually a couple strives to seek it within the marital bond (1959: 40). The latter, presumably, protect the couple against the harmful effects of individualism, freedom, and untoward personality growth. It may be worthwhile here to analyze the structural conditions under which mating relationships occur and to see how they relate to various values and goals in Indian society.

A study conducted in 1968, on 240 families in Kerala, a state which has the highest literacy rate in India, reveals that practical consideration in the selection of mates rather than free-choice or romantic love becomes the basis of marriage. In order of importance, the study reports that the major qualities among the girls considered important are: good character, obedience, ability to manage home, good cook, should take active part in social and political affairs, educated, religious, depending entirely on husband for major decisions, fair complexion, good companion with similar intellectual interests, and beauty (Kurian 1974: 335). Among the boy's qualities, his appearance, charm, and romantic manifestation do not count much, while the social and economic status of his family, education, and earning potential overshadow his personal qualities (Kurian 1974: 355; see also Ross 1961: 259).

The Kerala study further illustrates some interesting trends, such as: that only 59 percent of the respondents thought that meeting the prospective wife before marriage contributes to marital happiness. The parental preferences about the nature of choice of spouse of their children showed that 5.8 percent wanted to arrange the marriage without consulting sons and daughters, while 75.6 percent wanted to arrange the marriage with the consent of sons and daughters, 17.3 percent were willing to allow free choice to their children with their approval, and only 1.3 percent will allow freedom of choice without parental interference (Kurian 1974: 358). In fact, what Srinivas observed over three decades ago in Mysore was that "romantic love as a basis of marriage is still not very deep or widely spread in the family mores of India today," has not yet changed much (see Srinivas 1942: 60).

The dilemma of a boy who had fallen in love with a girl from a lower caste is reported from a study of Bangalore, a city of about a million people:

My love affair has caused me great trouble, for my intense love of the girl and the devotion to my parents cannot be reconciled. My parents don't like our engagement, and I cannot displease them, but on the other hand I cannot give up my girl who has done so much for me. She is responsible for progress and the bright future which everyone says is ahead of me. The problem is my greatest headache at the present time. (Ross 1961: 269)

During my own fieldwork during 1963–67, in Awan, a community of about three thousand people in Rajasthan state, having extensive and frequent urban contacts, it took me no time to figure out that a question inquiring about "romantic" or "love" marriage would be futile, because people simply laughed it away. Parental opinion was reinforced by several other considerations. One man, a community elite, remarked:

> Young people do not know what love is; they are, if at all, infatuated which is very transitory and does not entail considerations of good marital life. If my son marries, I wish to see that the girl is well-raised, obedient, preserves the family traditions, ready to bear the hardships with us, and to nurse us in our old age.

Love, a premarital manifestation, is thus thought to be a disruptive element in upsetting the firmly established close ties in the family, a transference of loyalty from the family of orientation to a person, and a loss of allegiance of a person, leaving the family and kin group in disdain for personal goals.

Continued loyalty of the individual to the family of orientation and kin group is the most cherished ideal in the Indian family system. To preserve this ideal, certainly the simplest recourse is child marriage or adolescent marriage. The child is betrothed, married, and most often placed in a job and generally provides the deference demanded by the elders. Though this pattern does not give much opportunity to the individual to act freely in matrimonial affairs, it maintains a close link of the couple with the father's household which requires much physical, social, and emotional care throughout the family cycle and particularly in old age. The relationships in the extended joint family are all-important.

The Hindu scriptural texts prescribe that a person should go through *grahstashrama* (a stage of householder's life) which includes procreation of children. The status system gives high prestige to the parents of large families. Kinship and religious values stress the need for a male heir. Large families provide security, both in economic and social terms, for the old and the destitute and the ill in a country where old-age pensions, disability, sickness benefits, and unemployment as well as medical insurance are either nonexistent or inadequate. When a family has several children, their marriages have to be spaced for economic as well as social reasons, which in turn necessitates early marriages.

Similar to other indigenous civilizations, a high value is placed upon chastity, especially female virginity in its ideal form. Love as play or premarital activity is not encouraged. Rather, elders consider it as their most important duty to supervise nubile girls. Marriage is an ideal, a duty, and a social responsibility usually preceded by highly ritualized ceremonial and festive events illustrating gradual involvement, especially of the female preparatory to the initiation of her marital role. Interestingly, all these ritual activities are role oriented (such as contributing to the long and prosperous life of the prospective husband) rather than person oriented (such as taking vows for the success of a person who is in love). This is one of those most pertinent factors which infuses longevity to the marital bond. The upper caste ideal that a girl could be ritually married only once in her lifetime and destined to marry the same person in lives to come continues to determine explicit and categorical aversion among girls to premarital interactions with strangers. Paradoxically, though, there is an implicit assumption that a person's marriage to a person of the opposite sex is governed by supreme celestial forces; in actual practice, mundane realities usually settle a marriage.

The early marriage of the person does not permit much personal independence and is further linked with another structural pattern in which the kinship rules define a class (caste, subcaste, regional group) of eligible future spouses. In other words, in the interest of homogamy and sanctity of the kin group, marriage should occur early. Thus, this would eliminate the chances of an unmarried adult to disregard a link with his or her kin group and caste. Problems arise at times when a person goes across the narrow limits of a group, often losing his chances of obtaining the usual support from the family, the kin group, and the caste. However, transgressions of basic family norms by an individual which may cause loss of identity, rejection, and an aggravated departure from the value system are rare. Often it is circumventing rather than contradicting the system which provides clues to change. Under such a pattern, elders negotiate and arrange marriages of their children and dependents with a likelihood of minimum generational conflict reinforcing greater chances of family unity. Adolescent physical and social segregation is marked by a greater emphasis on the learning of discrete sex roles idealizing, at least theoretically, parental roles.

As found in Western cultures, the youth culture frees the individual from family attachments thus permitting the individual to fall in love; and love becomes a substitute for the interlocking of kinship roles. The structural isolation of the Western family also frees the married partners' affective inclinations, that they are able to love one another (Parsons 1949: 187–89). Such a pattern is absent in the Indian family system.

Contrary to this, in India, marriage of a boy indirectly strengthens his bonds with the family of orientation. It is one of the major crises which marks his adulthood and defines his responsibilities towards his parents and the kin group. His faith and sentimental involvement in the family of orientation is an acknowledgment of the usual obligations incurred in his raising and training. A pervasive philosophy of individualism appears to be spreading and suggests a trend toward free mate choices, equality for women, equal divorce rights, and taking up of traditionally known ritually inferior but lucrative occupations; this militantly asserts the importance of the welfare of the person over any considerations of the continuity of the group. The trend toward conjugal family systems, widespread as it is, is generally confined to the urbanized regions (Gore 1958; Kapur 1970). Moreover, these changes where they appear on one hand, are viewed as social problems and as symptoms of the breakdown of time-honored ways; on the other, they are looked at as indicators of personal achievement, individual fulfilment, and family prestige.

SOCIALIZATION

The cultural pattern demands that a child in India cannot isolate himself from his parents, siblings, and other members of the extended family.

The maturation process is rarely fraught with problems or turmoil associated with parent and adolescent children as they all learn to play new roles and feel new feelings. A child's expanding world gradually gives a mature sense of responsibilities to share in most of the important decisions in his life cycle. Covert parent-child conflict is shadowed by affection and sentimental ties helping the adolescents to achieve desirable balance between rebellion and conformity, individual wishes and feelings of the parents. Occasionally, this causes some problems. Since parents make decisions about most significant aspects of the family, including the marriage of their children, passive, indifferent, and sometimes negative feelings develop in the children as they seek to be dependent on other members of the family.

The family in India is known for its cohesive function, especially providing for the emotional needs of its members. Most often, this function is effectively performed by the extended kin group which, in fact, is a segment of the caste or subcaste. Adults, as well as children, must have love and security in order to maintain emotional stability under the stresses of life and in order to meet the emotional demands made upon them by the crises. In addition to providing the positive emotional needs of its members by personal sacrifices done by the members on a regular basis throughout the life cycle of the family, it also provides a safe outlet for negative feelings. Conflicts arising from interpersonal relations are generally handled by the older members, and care is taken by them to ensure that roles and responsibilities are clearly defined. Conflicts are resolved and mitigated by a general concern in the group favoring the emotional satisfaction of the individual. A person throughout his adolescence is never isolated from the family. Thus, not only generations, but extended and local units of kin groups are forced into a more intensive relationship. The affectional ties are solidified by mutual care, help in crisis situations, and assistance provided. This often destroys negative feelings. Several rituals, rites, and ceremonial occasions reinforce the unity of the family (Dube 1955: 131–58; Gupta 1974: 104–16). In general, a person substantially invests his emotions and feelings in his family and kin group, denial of which may be hazardous to his psyche. Such a deep involvement of the individual causes his emotional dependence on the family and acceptance to its wishes in most of the crucial decisions and events in his life, including marriage.

Premarital Interaction and Mate Selection

India is perhaps the only subcontinent which provides a wide variety of mate selection processes from an open to a very closed system, from marriage by capture in the primitives to the arranged marriage among Hindus and Muslims. Moreover, rules prohibiting certain classes of persons from marrying one another also vary, such as three to four clan avoidance rules in central and northern parts to preferential cross-cousin or maternal uncle and niece marriages in the south. In other words, rules regarding the definition of incest or areas of potential mates vary substantially. Most people in the Northern states, for example, prohibit marriage between persons of similarly named clans and extend this rule to several other related clans, such as of mother's clan, mother's mother clan, and father's mother clan. The people bearing these clan names may be living several hundred miles away . . . but are usually thought to be related. From this point of view, then, the ideal mate for any person could also be a stranger, an outsider, but an individual related to him in distant terms. . . . A person living across a state belonging to one's caste has a greater chance of being an eligible for a prospective mate than a person belonging to some other caste living next door. Caste is thus an extended kin group and, at least theoretically, membership in which is related through various kinds of kinship ties. Marriage alliances within the *jati* (caste or subcaste) reinforce kinship and family ties and cause a sort of evolution of the class system. Class generally determines future marital alliances within the caste. The resources assessed by a family in seeking a marital alliance from another family play a crucial role in determining the decision about the alliance. The voices of the significant members of the family are crucial in making a marriage since newlywed couples are barely into adulthood and have neither the material nor psychological resources to start a household of their own. Later in their married life when they have resources, they may still consider the opinions of the significant members because the disadvantages of not adhering to such opinions are greater than the annoyances of living together.

A Sociological Paradigm of Arranged Marriages

Recent research on the changing aspects of the family in India (Collver 1963; Conklin 1974; Desai 1964; Gore 1965; Gould 1968; Gupta 1974; Hooja 1968; Kapur 1970; Kurian 1961, 1974; Orenstein 1959, 1961, 1966; Ross 1961; Shah 1974; Singer 1968) suggests that there has been little change in the joint family system in India, which is a vanguard of the arranged marriage.

The above discussion gives us to understand that what is needed in our approach to arranged marriage is a frame of reference which is more fully on the sociological level. As a step toward this goal, a general theoretical approach to the arranged marriage or "conjugal love" relationship has been formulated which, it is believed, takes account of the historical, cultural, and psychological levels, and brings into central focus the sociological level. The following tentative theoretical formulation is proposed only as a first attempt to outline what sociological factors are generally responsible to the growth of "conjugal love" as opposed to "romantic love." By any conservative estimate, love marriages occur in only less than 1 percent of the population.

1. It is important to note that arranged marriages are closely associated with "closed systems" wherein the hierarchies are very intricate and more than one factor such as historical origins, ritual positions, occupational affiliations, and social distance determinants play significant roles in defining the in-group and the outgroup, particularly in marital alliances. In such systems, group identity is marked by strong senses of esoteric values, and such values are preserved and reinforced by attributes which distinguish a group in rank and its interaction with others. That is, most proximate ties of the individuals ought to be within their own group.

2. Continuity and unity of the extended family is well-preserved since all the significant members of the family share the mate-selection decision make-up which involves several persons who are supposedly known to have experience and qualifications to find a better choice as against the free choice of the subject. Obviously, this leads to lower age at marriage and, in turn, strengthens the predominance of the family over the individual choice.

3. Any possible problems emerging from a couple's functioning in marital life become problems for the whole family. Advice and counseling from the members of the extended family to improve the couple's relationship, weathering life's storms, or even sharing in crises are reinforced by the shared responsibilities. This is also partly responsible for denouncing the idea of divorce and forces working against it. This is not to say that this, in fact, resolves all the conflicts in marriage.

4. As long as the social system is unable to develop a value system to promote individualism, economic security outside the family system, and a value system which advances the ideals of nuclear family, the individuals in such a system continue to demand support from the family which, in turn, would lead to reemphasizing the importance of arranged marriage. Forces of modernization supporting the "romantic ideal" would continue to find partial support in such a system as long as the sources of moral and material support for the individual are based in the extended/joint family system.

364 GIRI RAJ GUPTA

5. It is difficult to assume that arranged marriage is related to the low status of a woman since man is also a party to it. If the concept of "free choice" is applicable to either sex, perhaps it will not support the ideal of arranged marriage. Apparently, an individual who opts for free choice or a "love marriage" is likely to dissociate from his/her family, kin group, caste, and possibly community, which he/she cannot afford unless he/she has been ensured tremendous support from sources other than these conventional institutions.

6. Arranged marriages, in general, irrespective of caste or class categories, help in maintaining closer ties with several generations. Families in such a system are an insurance for the old and the orthodox, a recluse for the devout and the defiant, a haven for the invalid and the insipid.

7. The demographic situation in India, as in most developing societies, is also a contributing factor, among others, to the early arranged marriages. After independence, India has made many advancements in science, technology, and medicine. . . . life expectancy, which was 29 years in 1947, is now 54 years. However, the vicious circle of early child marriage, early pregnancy, high mortality rate, and replacement of the population are closely interwoven to ensure society from extinction. While the value system notoriously maintains this chainwork, the declining mortality rate further accentuates early marriages to shelve off the economic burden of the family by spacing weddings. The family protects and insulates from ruining itself by arranging marriages as early as possible and for using its resources for status aggrandizement.

Since the changes in Indian society often present a welter of traditional and modern, conventional as well as prestige and [glamor]-oriented marital role models with significant changes in the value system, it is quite probable that in the long run, "romantic ideal" will pervade the system. Whether such changes will be a part of a continuum, that is, revitalization of the mythological past or acceptance of the ideals of the modern West, preserving tenacity and positive elements of its own against the swaggering forces of change, has yet to be seen.

REFERENCES

CHEKKI, D. A. (1968). Mate selection, age at marriage and propinquity among the Lingayats of India. *Journal of Marriage and the Family*, 30 (November): 707–11.

COLLVER, A. (1963). The family cycle in India and the United States. *American Sociological Review*, 28: 86–96.

CONKLIN, G. H. (1974). The extended family as an independent factor in social change: A case from India. *Journal of Marriage and Family*, 36 (November): 798–804.

CORMACK, M. (1953). *The Hindu woman*. New York: Bureau of Publications, Columbia University.

DESAI, I. P. (1964). *Some aspects of family in Mahuva.* Bombay: Asia Publishing House.

DUBE, S. C. (1955). *Indian village.* New York: Cornell University Press.

GOODE, W. J. (1959). The theoretical importance of love. *American Sociological Review,* 24: 38–47.

——— (1963). *World revolution and family patterns.* New York: Free Press.

GORE, M. S. (1968). *Urbanization and family change.* Bombay: Popular Prakashan.

GUPTA, G. R. (1974). *Marriage, religion and society: Pattern of change in an Indian village.* New York: Halsted Press.

HATE, C. A. (1970). Raising the age at marriage. *The Indian Journal of Social Work,* 30: 303–09.

HOOJA, S. (1968). Dowry system among the Hindus in North India: A case study. *The Indian Journal of Social Work,* 38: 411–26.

KAPADIA, K. M. (1966). *Marriage and family in India,* 3rd ed. London: Oxford University Press.

KAPUR, P. (1970). *Marriage and the working woman in India.* Delhi: Vikas Publications.

KARVE, I. (1965). *Kinship organization in India.* Bombay: Asia Publishing House.

KLASS, M. (1966). Marriage rules in Bengal. *American Anthropologist,* 68: 951–70.

KURIAN, G. (1961). *The Indian family in transition.* The Hague: Mouton.

——— (1974). Modern trends in mate selection and marriage with special reference to Kerala. In G. Kurian, Ed., *The Family in India—A Regional View* (pp. 351–67). The Hague: Mouton.

——— (1975). Structural changes in the family in Kerala, India. In T. R. Williams, Ed., *Psychological Anthropology.* The Hague: Mouton.

MADAN, T. N. (1965). *Family and kinship: A study of the Pandits of rural Kashmir.* New York: Asia Publishing House.

MANDELBAUM, D. G. (1970). *Society in India,* vol. I & II. Berkeley: University of California Press.

MEYER, J. J. (1953). *Sexual life in ancient India.* New York: Barnes & Noble.

ORENSTEIN, H. (1959). The recent history of the extended family in India. *Social Problems,* 8: 341–50.

——— (1961). The recent history of family in India. *Social Problems,* 8 (Spring): 341–50.

——— (1966). The Hindu joint family: The norms and the numbers. *Pacific Affairs,* 39 (Fall-Winter): 314–25.

PARSONS, T. (1949). *Essays in sociological theory.* Glencoe, Illinois: Free Press.

ROSS, A. D. (1961). *The Hindu family in its urban setting.* Toronto: University of Toronto Press.

SHAH, A. M. (1974). *The household dimension of family in India.* Berkeley: University of California Press.

SINGER, M. (1968). The Indian joint family in modern industry. In M. Singer & B. S. Cohn, Eds., *Structure and change in Indian society.* Chicago: Aldine Publishing Co.

SRINIVAS, M. N. (1942). *Marriage and family in Mysore.* Bombay: New Book Co.

VAN DEN HAAG, E. (1973). Love or marriage. In M. E. Lasswell & Thomas E. Lasswell, Eds., *Love, marriage and family: A developmental approach* (pp. 181–86). Glenview, Illinois: Scott, Foresman and Co.

VATUK, S. (1972). *Kinship and urbanization.* Berkeley: University of California Press.

43
Why France Outstrips the United States in Nurturing Its Children

FRED M. HECHINGER

It would be difficult to argue that parents in one society love their children more than parents in another do. Across societies, however, children are treated in radically different ways. Culture explains some of this, but institutional arrangements also play a part. In France a government more closely involved in economic affairs makes sure that both public and private corporate resources are used to provide children with the things they need and helps families cope with the stress of working and raising their children.

In a contest between child care in France and the United States, American children are the losers.

"Why don't you change it? It is incredible for a large rich country to accept the terrible infant-mortality rate. It's crazy."

That was how a woman who helps oversee child-care and preschool education in France reacted to the way America treats its infants and children. The official, Solange Passaris, special counselor on early childhood and motherhood to the Ministry of Health and Social Protection said in an interview that because Europe was no longer in economic crisis it could now deal with children's welfare as part of a country's economic well-being.

She said she did not understand how the United States could accept ranking 19th in the world in the prevention of infant deaths while France ranked fourth.

National commitment may be at the heart of the matter. Even discounting the French passion for dramatic style, there is a political message in President François Mitterrand's statement that "France will blossom in its children." Or, as the president of the French-American Foundation, Edward H. Tuck, said more prosaically in a recent report by the foundation, "A Welcome for Every Child," France's success is attributable to "national policies focused on children, highly trained staffs, clearly defined responsibilities among agencies and a committed leadership at all levels of government."

Child care in France enjoys strong support from business and industry. "We try to create a partnership between business, the unions and government," Mrs. Passaris said.

Maternal leaves with pay begin six weeks before birth and continue for 10 weeks after delivery. Corporate leaders do not appear to be concerned over any possible negative effect on productivity and profits.

By contrast, American business interests lobbied so successfully against legislation that would have provided 10 weeks of *unpaid* maternity leaves that President Bush vetoed it.

To strengthen the family, French parents may take off two years without pay after a child's birth, knowing that their jobs remain protected. On major issues, this is truly a tale of two countries.

Pre- and postnatal health care, lacking for so many poor women and their babies in the United States, is firmly anchored in French national policy. So is immunization, which in the United States has become increasingly erratic, leading to the revival of children's diseases that had been considered virtually extinct.

French educators, health experts and politicians appreciate the close link between preventive health care and children's future success in school and life.

In the United States, millions of children are exposed to unlicensed day care. In high-quality centers, the cost is high. That creates great disparities in the lives of rich and poor children.

In France, the cost of care for children up to the age of 3 ranges from $195 a year for the poorest families to a maximum of $4,700 for the wealthiest.

Preschool for 3-to-5-year-olds is free, and 98 percent of the children attend it, more than three times the American percentage. Safe and nurturing places for young children of working parents are available from early morning to late afternoon.

In the United States, low pay and low status severely hamper the staffing of child-care centers. According to a recent report by the General Accounting Office, 40 percent of the workers in child-care centers in the United States leave each year.

French preschool teachers hold the equivalent of a master's degree in early childhood and elementary education. The directors of child-care centers are pediatric nurses, with additional training in public health and child development. Staff members have the equivalent of two years of college plus a two-year course in child development and early childhood education.

As an incentive, France offers students of preschool education free college tuition plus a stipend in return for a pledge to work in the field for at least five years after graduation.

Home care, which allows families to take in three children in addition to their own, is also licensed. In addition to daily compensation, family daycare providers are covered by Social Security, disability and unemployment insurance.

The home-care system is augmented with small-group centers to allow the children to mingle with others once a week.

A look at child care in industrial societies suggests that under regulated capitalism, as in France, or in social democracies, as in Scandinavia, children's welfare is protected because it is viewed as crucial to the children's and the nations' futures.

By contrast, leaving child care exposed to the uncertainties of a largely unregulated free market, as in the United States and Britain, has created conditions that Mrs. Passaris calls crazy. The practice leaves many children with inadequate care and permanently damaged, a costly liability to society.

44
Colonialized Leisure, Trivialized Work

Stanley Aronowitz

The author, himself a manual worker turned writer, is highly critical of the educational system in the United States. He sees the lessons it imparts in its structure as more important than the lessons imparted in its classrooms. Linking educational process to the organization of labor in capitalist societies, Aronowitz shows us how we "learn to labor" from the day we pass through the schoolyard gate.

In contrast to the relative freedom afforded children in early childhood to construct their own play society, the grammar school introduces a new constraint on play. Learning the prescribed curriculum is called "work," and play is assigned to a special time in the day, called "recess" but supervised by adults. Thus the institution simultaneously legitimizes play as one of its regular functions, but rationalizes it as a break from the *real* activity of children within the institution—school "work." Play in this context is meant to rejuvenate the child in order to make it more ready for "learning."

Indeed, the child learns in school. But the content of the curriculum is far less important than the structure of the school itself. The child learns that the teacher is the authoritative person in the classroom, but that she is subordinate to a principal. Thus the structure of society can be learned through understanding the hierarchy of power within the structure of the school. Similarly, the working class child learns its role in society. On one side, school impresses students as a whole with their powerlessness since they are without the knowledge required to become citizens and workers. On the other, the hierarchy of occupations and classes is reproduced by the hierarchy of grade levels and tracks within grades. Promotion to successive grades is the reward for having mastered the approved political and social behavior as well as the prescribed "cognitive" material. But within grades, particularly in large urban schools, further distinctions among students are made on the basis of imputed intelligence and that in turn is determined by the probable ability of children to succeed in terms of standards set by the educational system.

Students placed in lower tracks within the grades learn early in their school careers that these tracks represent their failure. Even if they succeed in terms of the "subject matter," the labels assigned to lower tracks restrict their horizon of future occupations. During the course of school- ing these children find themselves in homogeneous groupings based on evaluations of their intelligence that appear to be a function of heredity rather than class. By the time the child reaches junior high school or high school he knows where he is going. His destination is the factory, the office, the retail store, and he will become an operative rather than a manager, a worker rather than an owner. And the school conveys the message, not only in the system of guidance that reinforces the decisions made by educators in the lower grades, but by its structure. In New York City, the junior high school was created overnight when the school leaving age was raised by law. These institutions were nakedly designed as holding pens for those who would have otherwise left school. The junior high school is fashioned neither on the family model of the ele- mentary school nor the factory model of the high school. It is a hybrid with no essential rationale except as a container. Its lack of educational philosophy has produced instances of disorder since students are certain that there is no learning going on and even teachers are not certain why children are there.

By high school the classroom is no longer an attempt to replicate the home; it is rather an attempt to replicate the factory. More men have become teachers than in the lower grades; the decorations are gone and replaced by maps, charts, bulletin boards; the student no longer remains in the classroom the whole day—instead education is now departmen- talized, ostensibly to offer a wide range of choices of subjects as well as instructors. The notion of "free time" becomes "study hall." Play is now structured into games that are bureaucratized beyond being put in time slots. The high school has a phalanx of official teams that compete with those of other schools. These are the important, socially recognized forms of play, while the voluntary forms, such as intramural sports, are denigrated.

The classroom has symbolically been represented as the real world, and even large portions of leisure-time activities are organized by the institution. Friendships remain independent of institutions to some ex- tent, but many are now found in various institutionally sponsored activ- ities such as sports, newspapers, and clubs. However, the working class high school students are employed after school and on weekends so that they are unable to participate to much of an extent in extracurricular life. For them, the reality principle organizes life. The centrality of school to work opportunities, the requirement that they work after school in order to help support themselves and their families as a condition for remain- ing in school, and the confinement of play to Saturday night, make adults of them at an early age.

The curricula of high schools reinforce the three broad tracks to which students have been assigned: academic, vocational, and general diploma students take different classes, develop different friends and other social contacts, and learn that their expectations are limited by the character of their education. Even for those assigned to the academic track, school demands that life consist in continuous work. Homework assignments can occupy most of the afternoon and evening. Parents are mobilized to keep the pressure on students to finish their assignments before they engage in any play, peer relationships, or television watching. Rarely is the substance of the assignments challenged by parents, since the object of their completion is to assure the grades required for admittance to colleges and universities. Just as the reality principle for working class children is represented by the need to work after school, children of professionals, business persons, and skilled workers who are funneled into the academic track learn that their "careers" come first and that autonomy must be subordinated to the goal of college admission.

For the most part, the specter of rejection by college has been sufficient to keep academic-track students in line. They have been introjected with the values of school and parents and engage in other activities when they should be performing their homework tasks only at the price of discomfort and guilt. They know that they should study, even if they are unable to rationalize either the activity or the substance of the homework in terms of the intrinsic worth of the content assimilated. They come to view learning as something outside of themselves—as instrumental to goals that are extrinsic to the questions of interpretation of specific mathematics or literature problems. Children learn in school to become acceptable to others. They know that the bright student is defined in terms of the curriculum, that rewards are given to those who can tolerate its boredom and its demands.

Students unable to tolerate school are those whose earlier life has not been disciplined to the regime of homework and learning "things." Their intelligence is irrelevant to the larger society, at best, and subversive to its values at worst. They are sometimes impatient with school because they are unable to adapt successfully to its demands. If they have broken the linguistic code required for reading, they rebel against the sort of reading required by school. In other cases, learning to read represents a surrender to the school bureaucracy, so some students fail to master the essentials of reading until they have left school and can find a good reason to learn them.

From the point of view of the educational hierarchy, the social legitimation of the school is deeply intertwined with the reading program. It is believed that if children learn nothing else in school, at least they have a chance to master reading. Yet most schools have adopted the empiricist view of language learning, that is, the notion that knowledge of language forms is acquired through the senses and by conditioning. In public schools, reading is typically taught through repetition of atomized pieces of information that are accorded differential status in the knowledge hierarchy and are arranged arbitrarily according to conceptions of child development that assume the progressive character of learning capacity. . . .

The implicit content of the school curriculum in almost every instance, has little to do with its explicit educational goals. One need not prove that schools are organized deliberately to thwart learning to recognize the tenuousness of their educational claims. . . .

For working class children who know that social mobility is an ideology, and that they are probably fated to end up in manual occupations, the effort is to endure school rather than participate. Their energy and their sense of self are preserved by tuning out the rigors of reading and mathematics, since they do not regard these activities as important to their lives. Instead, the curriculum is perceived as a means of pressure to force them to abandon their secret world—to learn to regard their relationships with their peers as less significant than those with teachers. Many children who "fail" in school are trying to cling to childhood because they know it is the moment in their lives, however fleeting, in which authority has least power over them.

The rebellious students' awareness that school represents the end of innocence is quickly transformed into guilt and regret for not having listened to their teachers early in life. By high school the failing students have developed a self-image that corresponds to their class position. They begin to doubt their rejection of mobility, and of school as a significant institution in the process of ascending the class structure. Many working class students become ambivalent about their own choice and live the rest of their lives in simultaneous regret and resentment. The anti-intellectualism prevalent among many workers is wrought of complex motives. On the one hand, they are cynical about the American dream that promises advancement through education. On the other hand, they are not sure that their cynicism is justified. This uncertainty is generated, in part, by the rapidly changing character of the American occupational structure, which has replaced unskilled and semiskilled jobs in manufacturing by unskilled and semiskilled jobs in service industries. In the largest growth areas in the service occupations, public employment and distributive trades, the idea of craft or manual skill is largely eliminated. Persons entering these occupations merely require knowledge of how to read, and how to follow bureaucratic procedures. Most jobs in retailing require the minimum of skills, except "human relations" skills that cannot be learned in school anyway. Public employees are perfectly trained by schools if [one scholar] is right in his assertion that the curriculum consists chiefly in understanding the structure of domination and hierarchy.

The rise of the service industries has been accompanied by the emergence of an ideology of meritocracy according to which the achievement of credentials actually creates mobility. The reality that the new service sector represents a deterioration of skills rather than their development is obscured by the welter of prerequisites for transition from the blue to the white collar. Another factor contributing to the reinforcement of mobility ideology as the rationale for school attendance is the fact that many children of factory workers are now offered white-collar jobs, a step that seems to signal a fundamental change, even though wages for the new jobs are often significantly lower than for factory or transportation occupations.

Aaron Cicourel has demonstrated that the process of class differentiation is facilitated by decision-makers in the educational process whose image of each child tends to correspond to his or her class background rather than imputed intelligence or academic achievement. His study of administrative attitudes and behavior in an urban high school shows that the key influential staff are not aware of the class criteria upon which they evaluate the chances of students to gain college entrance. On the contrary, their belief that they develop guidance techniques on the basis of evaluation of a student's record of intelligence and achievement is belied by evidence that they have acted on evaluative criteria according to which working class students are *a priori* less able to cope with the demands of colleges.

Thus high school is the critical point in a person's life in terms of probable class and occupational affiliations. The tendency of schools is to strengthen the class structure by assimilating elitist ideologies into the decision-making apparatus while retaining the overarching ideology in which school is seen as the vehicle of class leveling and social mobility. The paradox here parallels the paradox of early school reform: Educational achievement is said to make possible a democratic society freed of class differentiation. However, the promise that educational achievement is a path to social mobility in itself implies the existence of class differences. Schools actually cannot deliver equality of opportunity much less equality *per se*. The IQ test, administered in the second grade, prefigures the differential opportunities that will be offered students, for assignments to different tracks will be made on the basis of the labels derived from test results. These labels attached to students are carried from grade to grade until the student experiences himself as the reflection of the label.

The educational ideologies developed over the past hundred years are more than rationalizations for the role of schools as a traffic police for the prevailing social division of labor and more than the means of justifying the large expenditures of society for school support. They also serve to impress upon the child that his failure to climb the occupational ladder or rise beyond his parents' social class is a function of his own lack of intelligence or effort. The notion of equality of opportunity through universal compulsory schooling places responsibility on the individual for social failure while attributing successes to the institutions.

In grade school, the teacher as the surrogate parent and significant adult in the child's educational experience tells the student daily how he/she is perceived by the school system. In smaller communities where there is only one class to each grade, "bright" children in grammar school are placed in the front of the classroom, are accorded recognition from teachers, and are encouraged to become important actors in aspects of school life such as newspapers, drama groups, and the "monitoring" system where students learn to administer discipline to one another. "Dumb" children or "bad" children are lumped together as the ineducables and are relegated to the back of the classroom and are asked to do nothing except keep quiet. In large urban schools where Black and working class children constitute the majority of the school population the distinctions between the tracks within each grade serve the purpose of selecting out those children for whom school remains chiefly custodial and those who are deemed eligible for possible professional and technical occupations and school experience that may increase the chance of success.

The child may be able to reject these messages through the influence of parents and peers. First, parents' own perception of the child may mitigate the school's label. But often parents are themselves unable to resist the judgments of school officials, which they accept as honest and accurate since they are made by "professionals." In turn, the professional assumes the unwavering accuracy of the intelligence test as a measure of "potential" and a guide for making professional decisions as to the child's future educational experiences.

The strength acquired by becoming recognized as a worthy person by peers is certainly a locus of possible resistance to the imposition from above of the image of failure. Peer interaction, as we have argued, is predicated on the assumption of equality. In play and friendship children experience themselves as persons to be respected and their social environment as characterized by cooperation. Even though factors of geographic and class segregation make reasonable the idea of life chances determined by class the autonomous world of children allows for the process of individuation and the subjectively experienced expectation of dignity.

The child has to assimilate two rather conflicting systems. The battering received by the young from parents and school to force them to adapt to the expected mode of behavior is viewed by them as an imperative to be resisted, but one to which they will ultimately surrender. The form of surrender, however, cannot merely be passive acquiescence, if the social system is to reproduce itself vigorously. Children must make internal, incorporate in their self-system, the ideas of social mobility and social equality. They must learn how to cooperate with authority and with one another, but to compete at the same time for the rewards offered by the adult world. They must retain their "drive" to excel, but this drive must be sublimated by sports, school work, and self-discipline. They must learn to take pleasure in deprivation and reserve their leisure for prescribed periods that are viewed by adults as providing a "release" from the necessary routines of daily life and labor. Under capitalism, as Marx pointed out more than a century ago, the worker only can be allowed to live his own life after labor has been performed. Thus labor must become instrumental for the enjoyment of leisure time, it is not viewed as intrinsically satisfying except by those whose work remains close to the older artisan mode of production where the worker owned his own tools and saw the relationship between his skill and the product resulting from the expenditure of labor time. It is only in artisanship that the aesthetic element of work is preserved.

As we have seen, capitalism forces children to regard play and most adults to regard their leisure as the core of their self-controlled lives. It is here alone that the chance remains to escape domination.

In early adolescence girls have evolved the ritual known as a "slumber" party. It is not a game, but an explicit statement of autonomous relationship that takes the form of a group of girls sleeping at the house of one of their friends. The whole activity consists in being together, sharing with one another their experiences with boys, parents, and teachers. It is a ritual of autonomy because it requires that the parents understand that they are not to interfere with the girls' time together. Boys increasingly spend more time away from home and form peer relationships that are implicitly antiadult and conspiratorial.

Teenagers often adopt popular culture to serve the purpose of strengthening their solidarity. This is especially the case in the era of rock and roll when the music is often raucous and the words refer to such "counter-cultural" phenomena as drugs, political opposition, and other themes that are not socially approved or even understood by their parents. The music of groups such as the Rolling Stones, the Grateful Dead, and the Jefferson Airplane and the lyrics of Bob Dylan and Janis Joplin are particularly illustrative of the contradiction in mass culture between its conservative and radical aspects. The enormous interest by working class high school and college youth in learning how to play guitar, drums, and other musical instruments indigenous to rock music expresses the yearning for participation rather than spectatorship, and the desire for activity that is truly independent of institutional life.

Within schools, both for boys and for girls, the bathroom becomes one of the few places where autonomy can be found. The bathroom is much more than its explicitly intended function would suggest. For high school students it is the place where forbidden activity can be undertaken in relative privacy, except for the occasional raids by teachers. Smoking, horseplay, exchange of pornographic information through graffiti—as well as exchange of novels and other written material and talk about sex and other topics which the classroom has specifically excluded except in their most alienated forms—provide elements of autonomous interaction even in schools that rigidly circumscribe student freedom. The schools are quick to recognize the bathroom as a locus of the resistance of students to total administration. Increasingly, teachers and school guards are assigned to patrol the facility in search of children seeking refuge from the wonders of the classroom. Loitering must be expunged from the daily routine of the school lest students receive information that conflicts with the approved curriculum and learn habits that undermine the ethic of work and subordination.

Yet play is not viewed as serious activity since it is voluntary and is pursued for its own sake. Symbolically its voluntary character makes it "frivolous" in the sense that it neither produces anything that is socially useful nor constitutes a particularly important way to instill values and goals that are consistent with the reproduction of labor. When adults "play" cards, go bowling, or throw a ball around for no particular reason other than pleasurable exercise, they assert their autonomy from institutions that claim their energies in daily life. When games are institutionalized, however, when the players are relegated to the role of spectators of others engaged in the "act" of performing game rituals, one witnesses the perversion of play. As Johann Huizinga has remarked, "Play to order is no longer play: it could at best be a forcible imitation of it."

Within the last decade, higher education has occupied a more crucial position as one of the options available to working-class youth. Post–secondary school education is now more common among working class youth for several reasons. The most important is that, as the productivity of industrial labor has increased because of technological change and the accelerated pace of labor, there are fewer available jobs for which a high school diploma is a sufficient credential. Moreover, the proliferation of the service occupations that have replaced industrial jobs has failed to create jobs requiring new skills. Under these conditions, higher education is one of the alternatives to unemployment or acceptance of a low-paying job (if it can be found) in government and other service industries.

As another option the young person may join the armed forces, and during those years of service learn a trade which may result in a skilled civilian job. However, this decision brings with it the disadvantage of possible active duty in a war zone, and there is no real assurance that voluntary enlistment will result in a marketable skill unless the economy is actually expanding. There is ample evidence, in fact, that the presumption of economic growth is no longer identical with the goal of full employment, especially in manual and technical occupations, since capital investment is concentrated in areas that are both labor- and capital-saving. Nevertheless, many Black and white rural and Southern youths have joined the armed forces rather than face unemployment or dead-end, low-paying jobs in the garment and service industries. In states where free college education is offered only to veterans service in the armed forces becomes for Blacks a prelude to social and occupational advancement.

Other youths enter two-year and four-year colleges precisely to escape the probability of being drafted; others to avoid alienated unskilled labor in a manufacturing or service industry, or the pervasiveness of drugs and petty crime that dominates the streets of some working class and Black neighborhoods.

The armed forces have proven to be no solution for these youths. The promise of learning a trade is often broken by the simple device of flunking students out of mechanical and technical programs using traditional criteria of tests, even when the criterion of aptitude is waived. The hidden history of the Vietnam War, a story only dimly disseminated and understood, is that the termination of U.S. ground fighting resulted as much from the mutinous spirit of the soldiers as it did from international power considerations. The infrequent press reports of refusals by whole companies to engage in combat, widespread use of drugs among both enlisted men and officers, and group desertion from the battlefield, obscured the extent of indiscipline among members of the U.S. armed forces. Combined with the substantial number of young people who refused enlistment and left the country, were excused for mental and physical reasons, or are languishing in jail, the numbers of those rejecting military service in one way or another is huge. I have spoken to veterans attending community college who describe vividly cases where the low morale of American soldiers literally crippled the capacity of U.S. combat forces in the field. Even when the U.S. intensified the air war in Southeast Asia because of its ineffectiveness on the ground, rebellion did not cease. *The New York Times* reported several cases of flight crews and individuals who were "quietly sent home" after declining combat missions.

In late 1972, the rebellion spread to the ships. At first naval officials responded to sailors' protests having to do with racist attitudes of officers and poor food and working conditions; there were promises to improve the situation. But many conservatives in the naval bureaucracy and in Congress were unhappy with this solution. Instead, after conducting a congressional investigation into the rebellion, the chairman of the committee explained that those who participated in the protests were low-IQ, malcontents, mostly Black, unable to master the intricacies of modern naval technology, and recommended that they be released from the service. Shortly thereafter, in early 1973, the naval high command announced that it would discharge "up to 6000" of these men from the Navy and would tighten entrance requirements in the future.

The end of the draft and the national administration's program for an all-volunteer army is directly related to the now open, now hidden, rebellions in the armed forces against the traditional absolute power of the officer corps over enlisted men. The fundamental democratic concept that lay behind the notion of a citizen army, that is, one where all people share the responsibility for national defense, was behind the draft policy during the Civil War. Nixon's program for the professionalization of the armed forces may be welcomed by large numbers of young people who hate the military and have no wish to participate in it. But the impact of the draft on the course of the Vietnam War bears witness to its utility as an instrument of opposition. By making soldiers dependent upon the hierarchy of rank, by transforming the whole military from a "service" to a "profession," a dangerous weapon for suppressing popular movements has been seized by the state. The rebellion in the armed forces has been one of the most important recent manifestations of working class discontent and social actions. Unless understood as part of the same impulse that produced Lordstown and the high school rebellions of 1969–71, an important dimension of its significance is lost. The military revolt attests to the refusal of young people to mindlessly follow the admonition perpetrated by the public school system that citizenship consists in the belief, "My country right or wrong." The ideological role of school in providing the intellectual categories of social cohesion has been seriously questioned by students who have perceived the irrationality of the prevailing authority relations within the institutions.

Beyond the avoidance incentive, the two-year colleges in particular seem to hold out the promise that the ideology of equal educational opportunity can be realized. The past five years have been marked by dramatic expansion in the number of two-year colleges, the enrollment of high school graduates in these institutions, and the expansion of federal and state support for them. In the earlier periods of American higher education these schools were designed to absorb middle and upper class youth who could not qualify for private and state universities; the modern community college movement, however, is aimed at the absorption of working class youth who have been tracked for vocational and general diplomas as well as the lower half of the academic graduates who did not qualify for four-year colleges. Like the armed forces, two-year colleges are institutions of masked unemployment—institutions of containment for youths who cannot be integrated into the labor force in the unskilled and semiskilled job areas, but who nonetheless must be instilled with the ideologies of social advancement.

Community colleges now have an enrollment of nearly two and one-half million, about one third of the total full-time enrollment in post–secondary educational institutions. These schools are the fastest growing sector among all institutions of higher education. Community colleges were first proposed in the late 1950s as training grounds for workers who perform technical labor that requires less than professional credentials. However, in the past few years, with the relatively large unemployment of technical and scientific labor caused by cutbacks in some defense industries and the advancement of technologies, technical training has diminished as the primary focus of these institutions. Instead we can observe a gradual rise in liberal arts curricula, a *de facto* recognition that the community college is no longer a distinct institution providing specific kinds of occupational training.

The rise of liberal arts in the junior colleges can be viewed within the context of the rise of service industries. In the new service sector, workers are required to have no specific knowledge. The important skill required to function within public service bureaucracies is preeminently the toleration of boredom. Community colleges provide ample training for this feature of bureaucratic work. Unlike four-year colleges that prepare students for entrance into graduate schools or for the low-level and middle-level managerial occupations within bureaucracies and industry, community colleges are really an extension of high schools. While the four-year colleges perpetuate the separation of social sciences into a series of discrete disciplines such as sociology, economics, political science, etc., on the presumption that their students are likely to enter teaching occupations or at least require some degree of detailed knowledge of an academic discipline in order to develop the necessary skills of bureaucratic thinking, typically, the two-year colleges avoid the separation of the social sciences and languages. But the integration of the social sciences or the physical sciences is not an expression of any intellectual realization that such fragmentation is theoretically and educationally unsound. Rather, the "social studies" department of the community college is characterized by a plethora of survey courses in which theory is subsumed by historical empiricism, where issues are not sharpened, and where the object is to provide students with the most superficial information to be regurgitated on end-term examinations.

The basis of the community college curriculum (and the first two years of state university) is the task of maintaining the educational experience as alienated activity. The student is further socialized to the work-world by such means as lecture halls containing four hundred students for a course in psychology in which various approaches to the "subject" are handed down by the teacher in bewildering succession. The successful student is the one who endures the massification of his education and manages to pass the exam. The others are either academically dismissed on the basis of their short tolerance or placed on probation and advised to take courses that are oriented exclusively to the practical applications of the sciences, social sciences, or humanities.

The job of the community colleges and the first two years of state and city universities is to screen out those students who are deemed academically unfit. The dreadful curriculum may be a product of the limited intellect of school planners, the large classes may reflect the impoverishment of the school budget, but the objective role of the school is not unrelated to these phenomena. The success of the community college and junior college may be measured by the number of students who have dropped out of college and have internalized their decision as a failure to measure up to academic standards. Since higher education is presumed to be qualitatively different from secondary school insofar as it claims to provide concrete professional or preprofessional training, its standards are held determined by the criteria that are external to its institutional decision-making process.

The life of the university is understood to consist in the content of the curriculum, a program normally divided into specialized fields of inquiry corresponding to the division of technical and intellectual labor. Typically, teaching is an activity engaged in by a person of no particular pedagogic skills since his employment is ordinarily dependent on the acquiring of credentials and the publication of books and of papers in recognized professional and scientific journals. In contrast to lower schools, colleges and universities accord ambivalent status and powers to the administration, often considered a necessary evil rather than a source of academic authority. This tendency to hold to the ideology of the university as a "community of scholars" has suffered some erosion in recent years with the entrance of a large number of Blacks, veterans, and other groups ordinarily deemed unfit for higher learning. "Compensatory" education has asserted the importance of teaching as opposed to meticulous scholarship and lecturing methods. But the old guard will not abandon the image of the university as the repository of objective knowledge independent of all political and bureaucratic considerations. This myth is maintained in the midst of the most comprehensive transition in the role of the universities since their inception.

The curious alliance between minority students, including women, and college administrations has resulted from the perception of formerly excluded groups that the old academic standards are maintained, to a large degree, to perpetuate their exclusion. Thus the "Black Power" revolt in the colleges has had the anomalous effect of strengthening anti-intellectual currents in American life even as it asserts democratic values. Movements for loosening entrance requirements and effecting curriculum reform within higher education are profoundly important means of challenging elitism. Yet the danger is real that they will become instruments for battering down the last ramparts of serious scholarship within colleges and help accelerate the tendencies toward mass education. Increasingly, the broad objective of critical thinking has been submerged in liberal arts curricula, and students are advised that these disciplines must be viewed from the standpoint of their occupational utility. Even in areas such as humanities and social sciences that have no direct links to the prevailing technical division of labor within corporations and public agencies, these disciplines are still understood, in part, as training grounds for teachers and research workers.

The instrumental character of American higher education has been engendered by its massification and its specific economic role as an institution of deferred labor. As a consequence the stratification of higher education parallels the tracking system within elementary and secondary schools that, in turn, reflects the social and technical division of labor in capitalist society as a whole. The elite universities from which corporate and political managers are drawn are institutions that permit the widest range of cultural and intellectual choices and experiences available in capitalist educational institutions. Like the "academies" of ruling class socialization (e.g., Exeter, Andover, Groton), the real curriculum is not the specific subject matter offered in the classroom, but the social and political networks established among peers who understand that they are destined to occupy positions at the pinnacle or at least on the higher levels of corporate/political hierarchies. Radical ideas are given the widest possible range for expression because the assumption is that these ideas are functional to training persons who are required to possess a flexibility sufficient to integrate a broad range of alien views within the dominant culture. The condition of success of capitalist culture is its ability to thwart the development of alternatives. This task can only be achieved by exposing the new elites to their negations and assisting them to find ways to make any negation an instrument of domination.

The community college, in contrast, is typically bereft of liberal culture. Where the play element is particularly stressed at ruling class universities in order to train elites for occupational and social roles that demand the widest degree of imagination and invention, even if these qualities are put to questionable uses, imagination is held in low esteem in the state schools and community colleges, where training replaces education and programmed response overcomes thought.

The community college student becomes aware that he is receiving an inferior training, much less education, by the content of the courses, the cultural poverty of campus life, and the dreary physical surroundings. Many urban colleges are located in storefronts, converted office buildings, trailers, barracks, and makeshift facilities of varied assortment. Since a preponderance of students hold part-time jobs provided directly by the college through federally aided programs such as "work/study" or sling hamburgers in chain restaurants like McDonald's and Burger Chef, there is little time for reflection. The lecture character of many courses, the limited opportunity for interaction between students and faculties created by the heavy teaching loads and large number of students in each class, all contribute to the sense of futility shared by many who may have entered these schools with some expectations of learning something.

The student does learn that he has been deceived once more. The endless waiting in the lower grades for a different education that was supposed to be fulfilled by college is followed by the recognition that college is not meant to be a fount of wisdom, but is, at best, a credential for a job. When this illusion too is smashed by the high levels of unemployment among those who have completed four-year colleges, the student realizes that college beats working at McDonald's and that its main value consists in postponing for a while the bleak job prospects that lie ahead. At best, the community college graduate may become a manager at McDonald's rather than a short-order cook, who is typically only a high school graduate.

PART V

Social Change in the Modern World

45
The Rise and Fall of Mass Rail Transit

JOE R. FEAGIN AND

ROBERT PARKER

There are more automobiles than people in Los Angeles. Is this a reflection of the preferences and choices of individual consumers, or is it a consequence of structured choices? The authors show that far-sighted corporations found common cause in organizing transportation that would suit their interests, and the romance of Americans and their cars began a new chapter.

... [M]ost U.S. cities have become *multinucleated*, with major commercial, industrial, and residential areas no longer closely linked to or dependent upon the downtown center. Decentralization has become characteristic of our cities from coast to coast. Essential to decentralization has been the development and regular extension of an automobile-dominated transportation system serving businesses and the general citizenry, but mostly paid for by rank-and-file taxpayers. With and without citizen consent, corporate capitalists, industrialists and developers, and allied political officials have made key decisions fundamentally shaping the type of transportation system upon which all Americans now depend.

THE AUTO-OIL-RUBBER INDUSTRIAL COMPLEX

The auto-oil-rubber industrial complex has long been central to both the general economy and the urban transportation system in the United States. Automobile and auto-related industries provide a large proportion, sometimes estimated at one-sixth, of all jobs, although this proportion may be decreasing with the decline and stagnation in the auto industry over the last two decades. An estimated one-quarter to one-half of the land in central cities is used for the movement, storage, selling, and parking of automobiles, trucks, and buses. The expanding production of automobiles and trucks has been coordinated with the expansion of highways and freeways and has facilitated the bulging suburbanization around today's cities.

Because of the dominance of autos and trucks in the U.S. transportation system, the traditional social scientists ... have typically viewed that transportation system as preordained by the American "love" for the automobile. For example, in a recent book on Los Angeles, historian Scott Bottles argues that "America's present urban transportation system largely reflects choices made by the public itself"; the public freely chose the automobile as a "liberating and democratic technology." Conventional explanations for auto-centered patterns focus on the response of a market system to these consumers. Auto-linked technologies are discussed as though they force human decisions: Thus "the city dweller, especially in recent times, has been a victim of the technological changes that have been wrought in transportation systems." . . . [T]raditional ecologists and other social scientists view the complexity and shape of cities as largely determined by technological developments in transportation—a reasonable view—but these technologies are not carefully examined in terms of their economic contexts, histories, and possible technological alternatives. For example, unlike the United States, numerous capitalist countries in Europe, including prosperous West Germany, have a mixed rail transit/automobile transport system. There interurban and intraurban rail transit remains very important. For this reason, the U.S. system cannot be assumed to be simply the result of "free" consumer choices in a market context. The capitalistic history and decision-making contexts that resulted in the positioning of automobiles at the heart of the U.S. transportation system must be examined.

EARLY MASS RAIL TRANSIT

Rural and urban Americans have not always been so dependent on automobiles for interurban and intraurban transport. In the years between the 1880s and the 1940s many cities had significant mass transit systems. By 1890 electric trolleys were in general use. Indeed, electric trolley routes, elevated railroads, and subways facilitated the first urban expansion and decentralization. Some investor-owned rail transit companies extended their trolley lines beyond existing urbanized areas out into the countryside in an attempt to profit from the land speculation along the rail lines. Glenn Yago has documented how transit owners and real estate speculators worked together to ensure the spatial and economic development of cities by private enterprise. Transit companies were a significant force in urban sprawl. The suburban spread of Los Angeles, for example, got its initial push from the expansion of trolley rail lines. Not initially laid out as an automobile city, this sprawling metropolis developed along streetcar tracks; only later was the streetcar network displaced by automobiles.

The reorganization and disruption of mass rail transit that took place in the early 1900s did not result just from the challenge of improved automobile technology. Rather, capitalist entrepreneurs and private corporations seeking profits reorganized and consolidated existing rail transit systems. Electrification of horse-drawn streetcars increased investment costs and stimulated concentration of ownership in larger "transit trusts" of landowning, finance, and utility entrepreneurs. Mergers of old transit firms and the assembly of new companies were commonplace, and there was much speculation in transit company stock. Yago has provided evidence on the corrupt accounting practices, over-extension of lines for real estate speculation, and overcapitalization which led to the bankruptcy of more than one-third of the private urban transit companies during the period 1916–1923. Sometimes the capitalists involved in the transit companies were too eager for profits. "These actions in turn," Charles Cheape notes, "drained funds, discouraged additional investment, and contributed significantly to the collapse and reorganization of many transit systems shortly after World War I and again in the 1930s."

Ironically, one consequence of the so-called "progressive" political reform movement in cities in the first decades of the twentieth century was that supervision of rail transit systems was often placed in the hands of business-dominated regulatory commissions, many of whose members were committed to the interests of corporate America (for example, transit stock manipulation for profit), rather than to the welfare of the general public. In numerous cases the extraordinary profits made by rail transit entrepreneurs, together with their ties to corrupt politicians, created a negative public image—which in turn made the public less enthusiastic about new tax-supported subsidies and fare hikes for the troubled rail transit systems. Moreover, as the profits of many of the private transit firms declined, public authorities in some cities, including Boston and New York, were forced to take over the transit lines from the poorly managed private companies in response to citizen pressure for mass transportation. This fact suggests that there has long been popular *demand* for publicly owned rail transit that is reliable, convenient, and inexpensive. Indeed, during the period 1910–1930 a *majority* of Americans either could not afford, because of modest incomes, or could not use, because of age or handicap, an automobile.

A Corporate Plan to Kill Mass Transit?

By the late 1910s and 1920s the ascension of the U.S. auto-oil-rubber industrial complex brought new corporate strategies to expand automobile markets and secure government subsidies for road infrastructure. Mass rail transit hindered the profit-oriented interests of this car-centered industrial complex, whose executives became involved not only in pressuring governments to subsidize roads but also in the buying up of mass transit lines. For example, in the early 1920s, Los Angeles had the largest and most effective trolley car system in the United States. Utilizing more than a thousand miles of track, the system transported millions of people yearly. During World War II, the streetcars ran 2,800 scheduled runs a day. But by the end of that war, the trolleys were disappearing. And their demise had little to do with consumer choice. As news analyst Harry Reasoner has observed, it "was largely a result of a criminal conspiracy":

The way it worked was that General Motors, Firestone Tire and Standard Oil of California and some other companies, depending on the location of the target, would arrange financing for an outfit called National City Lines, which cozied up to city councils and county commissioners and bought up transit systems like L.A.'s. Then they would junk or sell the electric cars and pry up the rails for scrap and beautiful, modern buses would be substituted, buses made by General Motors and running on Firestone Tires and burning Standard's gas.

Within a month after the trolley system in Los Angeles was purchased, 237 new buses arrived. It is important to realize that, for all the financial and management problems created by the private owners of the rail transit firms, the old transit systems were still popular. In the year prior to the takeover, the Los Angeles electric lines made $1.5 million in profits and carried more than 200 million passengers. The logic behind the corporate takeover plan was clear. The auto-related firms acted because a trolley car can carry the passengers of several dozen automobiles.

During the 1930s GM created a holding company through which it and other auto-related companies channeled money to buy up electric transit systems in 45 cities from New York to Los Angeles. As researcher Bradford Snell has outlined it, the process had three stages. First, General Motors (GM) helped the Greyhound corporation displace long-distance passenger transportation from railroads to buses. Then GM and other auto-related companies bought up and dismantled numerous local electric transit systems, replacing them with the GM-built buses. Moreover, in the late 1940s, GM was convicted in a Chicago federal court of having conspired to destroy electric transit and to convert trolley systems to diesel buses, whose production GM monopolized. William Dixon, the man who put together the criminal conspiracy case for the federal government, argued that individual corporate executives should be sent to jail. Instead, each received a trivial $1 fine. The corporations were assessed a modest $5,000 penalty, the maximum under the law. In spite of this conviction, GM continued to play a role in converting electric transit systems to diesel buses. And these diesel buses provided more expensive mass transit: "The diesel bus, as engineered by GM, has a shorter life expectancy, higher operating costs, and lower overall productivity than electric buses. GM has thus made the bus economically noncompetitive with the car also." One source of public discontent with mass transit was this inferiority of the new diesel buses compared to the rail transit cars that had been displaced without any consultation with consumers. Not surprisingly, between 1936 and 1955 the number of operating trolley cars in the United States dropped from about 40,000 to 5,000.

In a lengthy report GM officials have argued that electric transit systems were already in trouble when GM began intervening. As noted above, some poorly managed transit systems were declining already, and some had begun to convert partially to buses before GM's vigorous action. So from GM's viewpoint, the corporation's direct intervention only accelerated the process. This point has been accented by Bottles, who shows that GM did not single-handedly destroy the streetcar systems in Los Angeles. These privately controlled systems were providing a lesser quality of service before GM became involved. The profit milking and corruption of the private streetcar firms in Los Angeles were not idiosyncratic but were common for privately owned mass transport in numerous cities.

Also important in destroying mass transit was the new and aggressive multimillion-dollar marketing of automobiles and trucks by General Motors and other automobile companies across the United States. And the automobile companies and their advertisers were not the only powerful actors involved in killing off numerous mass transit systems. Bankers and public officials also played a role. Yago notes that "after World War II, banks sold bankrupt and obsolete transit systems throughout the country at prices that bore no relation to the systems' real values." Often favoring the auto interests, local banks and other financial institutions tried to limit government bond issues that could be used to finance new equipment and refurbish the remaining rail transit systems.

Because of successful lobbying by executives from the auto-oil-rubber complex, and their own acceptance of a motorization perspective, most government officials increasingly backed street and highway construction. They cooperated with the auto industry in eliminating many mass transit systems. Increased governmental support for auto and truck transportation systems has meant systematic disinvestment in mass transit systems. Over the several decades since World War II, governmental mass transit subsidies have been small compared with highway subsidies. This decline has hurt low- and moderate-income people the most. Less public transit since World War II has meant increased commuting time in large cities where people are dependent on the automobile, which is especially troublesome for moderate-income workers who may not be able to afford a reliable car; less mass transit has also meant increased consumer expenditures for automobiles and gasoline. Auto expansion has frustrated the development of much mass transit because growing street congestion slows down buses and trolleys, further reducing their ridership. As a result, governmental funding for public rail transit has been cut, again chasing away riders who dislike poorly maintained equipment. And fares have been increased. Riders who can use automobiles do so. And the downward spiral has continued to the point of extinction of most public rail transit systems.

Mass transit was allowed to decline by the business-oriented government officials in most cities. Consumer desires were only partly responsible for this. Consumers did discover the freedom of movement of autos, and even in cities with excellent rail transit systems many prefer the auto for at least some types of travel. But consumers make their choices *from the alternatives available*. With no real rail transportation alternative to the automobile in most urban areas, consumers turned to it as a necessity.

Ironically, as the auto and truck congestion of the cities has mounted between the 1950s and the 1980s, more and more citizens, and not a few business leaders, have called for new mass transit systems for their cities. . . .

MASS TRANSIT IN OTHER CAPITALISTIC COUNTRIES

Comparative research on U.S. and German transportation systems by Yago has demonstrated the importance of looking at corporate power and economic structure. Mass rail transport developed in Germany before 1900. In the 1870s and 1880s the German national and local governments became interested in mass transit; at that time the coal, steel, iron, chemical, and electrical manufacturing companies were dominant in German capitalism. Interestingly, corporate executives in these industries supported the development of rail transportation; by 1900 the national and local governments had subsidized and institutionalized intraurban and interurban rail transport systems, which served the transport needs not only of the citizenry but also of the dominant coal, steel, chemical, and electrical industries. These industries also supplied equipment and supplies for the rail networks. In contrast, in the United States early transport companies were involved in manipulation and land speculation; transit service was rarely the central goal of the early rail transit firms. In contrast to Germany, dominance of U.S. industry by a major economic concentration did not come to the United States until after 1900, and when it did come, the auto-oil-rubber industrial complex was dominant. There was no other integrated industrial complex to contest this dominance of the auto-related firms, and governmental intervention was directed at support of motorization and the automobile. In Germany governmental intervention for mass rail transit had preceded this dominance of the motorization lobby. This suggests that the *timing* of the implementation of technological innovations in relation to corporate development is critical to their dominance, or lack of dominance, in cities and societies.

Interestingly, it was the Nazi interest in motorization and militarization in the 1930s that sharply increased the role of auto and truck transport in Germany. Adolf Hitler worked hard to motorize the military and the society. After World War II, the German auto lobby increased in power, and an auto transport system was placed alongside the rail transport system. However, the West German government and people have maintained a strong commitment to both systems; and the OPEC-generated oil crises of the 1970s brought an unparalleled revival of mass transit in Germany, whereas in the United States there was a more modest revival. The reason for the dramatic contrast between the two countries was that Germany had retained a rail passenger transport system, one that is still viable and energy conserving to the present day.

46

Population, Poverty and the Local Environment

PARTHA S. DASGUPTA

We often imagine that environmental destruction follows on the heels of population pressure and the inability of the environment to support its animal and human population. The author reverses this image, showing in several ways how environmental damage stimulates insupportable population growth. This puts the concern for the environment at the forefront of the issue of population growth and control.

As with politics, we all have widely differing opinions about population. Some would point to population growth as the cause of poverty and environmental degradation. Others would permute the elements of this causal chain, arguing, for example, that poverty is the cause rather than the consequence of increasing numbers. Yet even when studying the semiarid regions of sub-Saharan Africa and the Indian subcontinent, economists have typically not regarded poverty, population growth and the local environment as interconnected. Inquiry into each factor has in large measure gone along its own narrow route, with discussion of their interactions dominated by popular writings—which, although often illuminating, are in the main descriptive and not analytical.

Over the past several years, though, a few investigators have studied the relations between these ingredients more closely. Our approach fuses theoretical modeling with empirical findings drawn from a number of disciplines, such as anthropology, demography, ecology, economics, nutrition and political science. Focusing on the vast numbers of small, rural communities in the poorest regions of the world, the work has identified circumstances in which population growth, poverty and degradation of local resources often fuel one another. The collected research has shown that none of the three elements directly causes the other two; rather each influences, and is in turn influenced by, the others. This new perspective has significant implications for policies aimed at improving life for some of the world's most impoverished inhabitants.

In contrast with this new perspective, with its focus on local experience, popular tracts on the environment and population growth have usually taken a global view. They have emphasized the deleterious effects that a large population would have on our planet in the distant future. Although that slant has its uses, it has drawn attention away from the economic misery endemic today. Disaster is not something the poorest have to wait for: it is occurring even now. Besides, in developing countries, decisions on whether to have a child and on how to share education, food, work, health care and local resources are in large measure made within small entities such as households. So it makes sense to study the link between poverty, population growth and the environment from a myriad of local, even individual, viewpoints.

The household assumes various guises in different parts of the world. Some years ago Gary S. Becker of the University of Chicago was the first investigator to grapple with this difficulty. He used an idealized version of the concept to explore how choices made within a household would respond to changes in the outside world, such as employment opportunities and availability of credit, insurance, health care and education.

One problem with his method, as I saw it when I began my own work some five years ago, was that it studied households in isolation; it did not investigate the dynamics between interacting units. In addition to understanding the forces that encouraged couples to favor large families, I wanted to understand the ways in which a reasoned decision to have children, made by each household, could end up being detrimental to all households.

In studying how such choices are made, I found a second problem with the early approach: by assuming that decision making was shared equally by adults, investigators had taken an altogether too benign view of the process. Control over a family's choices is, after all, often held unequally. If I wanted to understand how decisions were made, I would have to know who was doing the deciding.

Power and Gender

Those who enjoy the greatest power within a family can often be identified by the way the household's resources are divided. Judith Bruce of the Population Council, Mayra Buvinic of the International Center for Research on Women, Lincoln C. Chen and Amartya Sen of Harvard University and others have observed that the sharing of resources within a household is often unequal even when differences in needs are taken into account. In poor households in the Indian subcontinent, for example, men and boys usually get more sustenance than do women and girls, and the elderly get less than the young.

Such inequities prevail over fertility choices as well. Here also men wield more influence, even though women typically bear the greater cost. To grasp how great the burden can be, consider the number of live babies a woman would normally have if she managed to survive through her childbearing years. This number, called the total fertility rate, is between six and eight in sub-Saharan Africa. Each successful birth there involves at least a year and a half of pregnancy and breast-feeding. So in a society where female life expectancy at birth is 50 years and the fertility rate is, say, seven, nearly half of a woman's adult life is spent either carrying a child in her womb or breast-feeding it. And this calculation does not allow for unsuccessful pregnancies.

Another indicator of the price that women pay is maternal mortality. In most poor countries, complications related to pregnancy constitute the largest single cause of death of women in their reproductive years. In some parts of sub-Saharan Africa as many as one woman dies for every 50 live births. (The rate in Scandinavia today is one per 20,000.) At a total fertility rate of seven or more, the chance that a woman entering her reproductive years will not live through them is about one in six. Producing children therefore involves playing a kind of Russian roulette.

Given such a high cost of procreation, one expects that women, given a choice, would opt for fewer children. But are birth rates in fact highest in societies where women have the least power within the family? Data on the status of women from 79 so-called Third World countries display an unmistakable pattern: high fertility, high rates of illiteracy, low share of paid employment and a high percentage working at home for no pay—they all hang together. From the statistics alone it is difficult to discern which of these factors are causing, and which are merely correlated with, high fertility. But the findings are consistent with the possibility that lack of paid employment and education limits a woman's ability to make decisions and therefore promotes population growth.

There is also good reason to think that lack of income-generating employment reduces women's power more directly than does lack of education. Such an insight has implications for policy. It is all well and good, for example, to urge governments in poor countries to invest in literacy programs. But the results could be disappointing. Many factors militate against poor households' taking advantage of subsidized education. If children are needed to work inside and outside the home, then keeping them in school (even a cheap one) is costly. In patrilineal societies, educated girls can also be perceived as less pliable and harder to marry off. Indeed, the benefits of subsidies to even primary education are reaped disproportionately by families that are better off.

In contrast, policies aimed at increasing women's productivity at home and improving their earnings in the marketplace would directly empower them, especially within the family. Greater earning power for women would also raise for men the implicit costs of procreation (which keeps women from bringing in cash income). This is not to deny the value of public investment in primary and secondary education in developing countries. It is only to say we should be wary of claims that such investment is a panacea for the population problem.

The importance of gender inequality to overpopulation in poor nations is fortunately gaining international recognition. Indeed, the United Nations Conference on Population and Development held in Cairo in September 1994 emphasized women's reproductive rights and the means by which they could be protected and promoted. But there is more to the population problem than gender inequalities. Even when both parents participate in the decision to have a child, there are several pathways through which the choice becomes harmful to the community. These routes have been uncovered by inquiring into the various motives for procreation.

LITTLE HANDS HELP . . .

One motive, common to humankind, relates to children as ends in themselves. It ranges from the desire to have children because they are playful and enjoyable, to the desire to obey the dictates of tradition and religion. One such injunction emanates from the cult of the ancestor, which, taking religion to be the act of reproducing the lineage, requires women to bear many children [see "High Fertility in Sub-Saharan Africa," by John C. Caldwell and Pat Caldwell; *Scientific American*, May 1990].

Such traditions are often perpetuated by imitative behavior. Procreation in closely knit communities is not only a private matter; it is also a social activity, influenced by the cultural milieu. Often there are norms encouraging high fertility rates that no household desires unilaterally to break. (These norms may well have outlasted any rationale they had in the past.) Consequently, so long as all others aim at large families, no household on its own will wish to deviate. Thus, a society can get stuck at a self-sustaining mode of behavior that is characterized by high fertility and low educational attainment.

This does not mean that society will live with it forever. As always, people differ in the extent to which they adhere to tradition. Inevitably some, for one reason or another, will experiment, take risks and refrain from joining the crowd. They are the nonconformists, and they help to lead the way. An increase in female literacy could well trigger such a process.

Still other motives for procreation involve viewing children as productive assets. In a rural economy where avenues for saving are highly restricted, parents value children as a source of security in their old age. Mead Cain, previously at the Population Council, studied this aspect extensively. Less discussed, at least until recently, is another kind of motivation, explored by John C. Caldwell of the Australian National University, Marc L. Nerlove of the University of Maryland and Anke S. Meyer of the World Bank and by Karl-Göran Mäler of the Beijer International Institute of Ecological Economics in Stockholm and me. It stems from children's being valuable to their parents not only for future income but also as a source of current income.

Third World countries are, for the most part, subsistence economies. The rural folk eke out a living by using products gleaned directly from plants and animals. Much labor is needed even for simple tasks. In addition, poor rural households do not have access to modern sources of domestic energy or tap water. In semiarid and arid regions the water supply may not even be nearby. Nor is fuelwood at hand when the forests recede. In addition to cultivating crops, caring for livestock, cooking food and producing simple marketable products, members of a household may have to spend as much as five to six hours a day fetching water and collecting fodder and wood.

Children, then, are needed as workers even when their parents are in their prime. Small households are simply not viable; each one needs many hands. In parts of India, children between 10 and 15 years have been observed to work as much as one and a half times the number of hours that adult males do. By the age of six, children in rural India tend domestic animals and care for younger siblings, fetch water and collect firewood, dung and fodder. It may well be that the usefulness of each extra hand increases with declining availability of resources, as measured by, say, the distance to sources of fuel and water.

. . . But at a Hidden Cost

The need for many hands can lead to a destructive situation, especially when parents do not have to pay the full price of rearing their children but share those costs with the community. In recent years, mores that once regulated the use of local resources have changed. Since time immemorial, rural assets such as village ponds and water holes, threshing grounds, grazing fields, and local forests have been owned communally. This form of control enabled households in semiarid regions to pool their risks. Elinor Ostrom of Indiana University and others have shown that communities have protected such local commons against overexploitation by invoking norms, imposing fines for deviant behavior and so forth.

But the very process of economic development can erode traditional methods of control. Increased urbanization and mobility can do so as well. Social rules are also endangered by civil strife and by the takeover of resources by landowners or the state. As norms degrade, parents pass some of the costs of children on to the community by overexploiting the commons. If access to shared resources continues, parents produce too many children, which leads to greater crowding and susceptibility to disease as well as to more pressure on environmental resources. But no household, on its own, takes into account the harm it inflicts on others when bringing forth another child.

Parental costs of procreation are also lower when relatives provide a helping hand. Although the price of carrying a child is paid by the mother, the cost of rearing the child is often shared among the kinship. Caroline H. Bledsoe of Northwestern University and others have observed that in much of sub-Saharan Africa fosterage is commonplace, affording a form of insurance protection in semiarid regions. In parts of West Africa about a third of the children have been found to be living with their kin at any given time. Nephews and nieces have the same rights of accommodation and support as do biological offspring. In recent work I have shown that this arrangement encourages couples to have too many offspring if the parents' share of the benefits from having children exceeds their share of the costs.

In addition, where conjugal bonds are weak, as they are in sub-Saharan Africa, fathers often do not bear the costs of siring a child. Historical demographers, such as E. A. Wrigley of the University of Cambridge, have noted a significant difference between western Europe in the 18th century and modern preindustrial societies. In the former, marriage normally meant establishing a new household. This requirement led to late marriages; it also meant that parents bore the cost of rearing their children. Indeed, fertility rates in France dropped before mortality rates registered a decline, before modern family-planning techniques became available and before women became literate.

The perception of both the low costs and high benefits of procreation induces households to produce too many children. In certain circumstances a disastrous process can begin. As the community's resources are depleted, more hands are needed to gather fuel and water for daily use. More children are then produced, further damaging the local environment and in turn providing the household with an incentive to enlarge. When this happens, fertility and environmental degradation reinforce each other in an escalating spiral. By the time some countervailing set of factors—whether public policy or diminished benefits from having additional children—stops the spiral, millions of lives may have suffered through worsening poverty.

Recent findings by the World Bank on sub-Saharan Africa have revealed positive correlations among poverty, fertility and deterioration of the local environment. Such data cannot reveal causal connections, but they do support the idea of a positive-feedback process such as I have described. Over time, the effect of this spiral can be large, as manifested by battles for resources [see "Environmental Change and Violent Conflict," by T.F. Homer-Dixon, J.H. Boutwell and G. W. Rathjens; *Scientific American*, February 1993].

The victims hit hardest among those who survive are society's outcasts—the migrants and the dispossessed, some of whom in the course of time become the emaciated beggars seen on the streets of large towns and cities in underdeveloped countries. Historical studies by Robert W. Fogel of the University of Chicago and theoretical explorations by Debraj Ray of Boston University and me, when taken together, show that the spiral I have outlined here is one way in which destitutes are created. Emaciated beggars are not lazy; they have to husband their precarious hold on energy. Having suffered from malnutrition, they cease to be marketable.

Families with greater access to resources are, however, in a position to limit their size and propel themselves into still higher income levels.

It is my impression that among the urban middle classes in northern India, the transition to a lower fertility rate has already been achieved. India provides an example of how the vicious cycle I have described can enable extreme poverty to persist amid a growth in well-being in the rest of society. The Matthew effect—"Unto every one that hath shall be given, and he shall have abundance: but from him that hath not shall be taken away even that which he hath"—works relentlessly in impoverished countries.

BREAKING FREE

This analysis suggests that the way to reduce fertility is to break the destructive spiral. Parental demand for children rather than an unmet need for contraceptives in large measure explains reproductive behavior in developing countries. We should therefore try to identify policies that will change the options available to men and women so that couples choose to limit the number of offspring they produce.

In this regard, civil liberties, as opposed to coercion, play a particular role. Some years ago my colleague Martin R. Weale and I showed through statistical analysis that even in poor countries political and civil liberties go together with improvements in other aspects of life, such as income per person, life expectancy at birth and infant survival rate. Thus, there are now reasons for thinking that such liberties are not only desirable in themselves but also empower people to flourish economically. Recently Adam Przeworski of the University of Chicago demonstrated that fertility, as well, is lower in countries where citizens enjoy more civil and political freedom. (An exception is China, which represents only one country out of many in this analysis.)

The most potent solution in semiarid regions of sub-Saharan Africa and the Indian subcontinent is to deploy a number of policies simultaneously. Family-planning services, especially when allied with health services, and measures that empower women are certainly helpful. As societal norms break down and traditional support systems falter, those women who choose to change their behavior become financially and socially more vulnerable. So a literacy and employment drive for women is essential to smooth the transition to having fewer children.

But improving social coordination and directly increasing the economic security of the poor are also essential. Providing cheap fuel and potable water will reduce the usefulness of extra hands. When a child becomes perceived as expensive, we may finally have a hope of dislodging the rapacious hold of high fertility rates.

Each of the prescriptions suggested by our new perspective on the links between population, poverty and environmental degradation is desirable by itself, not just when we have those problems in mind. It seems to me that this consonance of means and ends is a most agreeable fact in what is otherwise a depressing field of study.

47
The Pro-Choice Movement: Confrontation and Direct Action

SUZANNE STAGGENBORG

The women's movement that emerged in the 1960s and continues today has focused on a wide array of issues, involved hundreds of organizations, and ranged across the political and ideological spectrum of American society. One facet of the women's movement is the pro-choice movement, which originally sought to make abortions legal (the U.S. Supreme Court's decision in Row v. Wade *recognized this right) and has subsequently worked to maintain this right. The following reading focuses specifically on the pro-choice movement in the Chicago area and its use of direct action and confrontation to win support for its cause.*

By 1970, the women's liberation movement was a national phenomenon. Feminists were attracting media and public attention by staging demonstrations and raising controversial demands. Abortion was a central feminist issue that was dramatized through direct action: In New York in 1969 the feminist Redstockings held "counter-hearings" to protest the biased state legislative hearings on abortion reform. In Detroit in 1970 a "funeral march" was held by women's liberation activists to protest the deaths of women killed by back-alley abortionists while the legislature debated abortion reform. In Chicago, feminists disrupted the convention of the American Medical Association to protest the AMA's lack of support for abortion law repeal. Throughout the country, feminists staged street theater, "speak-outs," and other demonstrations for abortion rights. . . .

For all of its conventional pressure-group tactics, the movement to legalize abortion was very much a part of the protest cycle of the 1960s. Direct-action tactics such as demonstrations had become part of the repertoire of movement participants, and the grass-roots constituents of the population and women's movements could be mobilized to participate in such tactics. The opportunities for direct action and the strong obstacles to achieving legalized abortion through institutionalized channels alone ensured that no movement organization limited its activities solely to institutionalized arenas.

Use of the direct-action tactics of "outside" challengers was facilitated in part by the same organizational characteristics that limited the movement's capacity for influence through established channels. Although formalized organizational structures help movement organizations operate in the world of conventional pressure-group politics, such structures make it more difficult to take quick action and to bypass disputes over radical positions and confrontational tactics. The movement's informal organization in the years before the legalization of abortion allowed movement organizations to take advantage of opportunities for confrontation and direct action, which often involved an element of risk. . . .

To understand fully the movement's strategies and tactics in these years, it is necessary to go beyond a strictly organizational analysis to an examination of the feminist approach to abortion, which was an important part of the movement. Women's liberation groups saw themselves as part of a larger movement that was challenging basic social, economic, and political institutions. Their goal was to create participatory democratic institutions that would serve human needs rather than corporate interests. The women's health movement that developed within the younger branch of the women's movement wanted to create a nonprofit, high-quality health care delivery system and to challenge the hierarchical doctor-client relationship, demanding that women participate in their own health care. . . . It was in this larger context that the women's liberation movement addressed the abortion issue.

THE CREATION OF A NEW CONSCIOUSNESS

Although a movement's "success" is typically measured in terms of substantive reforms, movements can also succeed in bringing about changes in "collective consciousness." . . . In the case of the women's liberation movement, changes occurred in the way in which women thought about their sexuality, their health, and their reproductive rights. To achieve this change in women's consciousness, the movement bypassed established organizational channels to reach women directly through new kinds of educational forums.

In Boston, a group of women—which became the Boston Women's Health Collective—began doing its own research on abortion, childbirth, and other women's health issues and offering an informal course to share the information with other women. In 1970, the group put together a book entitled *Women and Their Bodies* (later called *Our Bodies, Our Selves*) which was published by a local non-profit press. . . . The book, which was distributed through women's centers and other movement networks, became the basis for "Women and Their Bodies" courses conducted by women's liberation groups across the country. Such courses were part of a larger "self-help" movement in which women sought to empower themselves by gaining access to information about their bodies and control over health care services.

In Chicago, a "Women and Their Bodies" course became part of the CWLU's[1] Liberation School for Women. Abortion was discussed in this course in the context of broader concerns about women's health care and women's control of their bodies. Moreover, the Liberation School was more than simply an educational forum. It exposed many women for the first time to the ideas of the women's liberation movement, and also helped recruit new women into the Union. On some occasions, women from the "Women and Their Bodies" classes even attended demonstrations for abortion rights and other CWLU activities as a group.

Another public forum for discussion of abortion created by women's liberation groups throughout the country was the "speak-out," a public event at which individual women talked about their own personal experiences with abortion. In Chicago, a speak-out held by the CWLU in 1970 "to provide a women's liberation point of view on a subject which has received so much media attention" . . . was a key event for mobilizing activity on abortion (interviews with CWLU activists, 1983). This kind of educational activity was very successful for the CWLU because it relied solely on the willingness of activists to talk about their personal experiences, something they were quite prepared to do. Speak-outs were often genuinely moving events that served to recruit women to the movement and to attract media attention to the feminist perspective on abortion. These movement organizations were thus able to create their own means of reaching audiences with radical demands.

The feminist perspective that was articulated in such alternative forums was distinctly different from that of single-issue repeal groups. In contrast with the cautious approach of activists in groups like Illinois Citizens for the Medical Control of Abortion, feminists were publicly declaring the social acceptability of abortion and asserting an unconditional right to legal abortion. Participants in the women's liberation movement brought a different set of experiences to the abortion issue than did persons with backgrounds in family-planning organizations and traditional voluntary associations. Many CWLU members were students and former students who had participated in other protest movements and who had experienced something of a "sexual revolution" on college campuses in the late 1960s. Although some of my informants confessed a bit of embarrassment in looking back at their own rhetoric, at the time a "revolution" seemed to be under way. The rapidly growing women's movement appeared to offer an opportunity for bringing about far-reaching social changes.

Given their backgrounds—and the fact that groups like ICMCA[2] were around to give a more moderate voice to the movement—CWLU participants saw no reason to limit their demands on abortion. Indeed, they saw their status as outsiders to the political establishment as an asset

---

1. Chicago Women's Liberation Union. [Editor]
2. Illinois Citizens for the Medical Control of Abortion. [Editor]

rather than a liability. The CWLU's activities were targeted mainly at women because part of the whole purpose of the Union was to build a larger and more powerful women's movement capable of bringing about radical social change. Based on their own experiences, CWLU activists thought that women would respond to more radical demands on issues like abortion and that controversial demands would help raise women's "consciousness." As a former CWLU activist explained when asked in an interview about the call for "abortion on demand":

> I think we felt that "abortion on demand" was the thing that would appeal to most people, most women . . . in the course of their lives, every single woman has probably had a chance or thought about an abortion. . . . We felt that that demand would bring more people in. . . . And part of it was just breaking out. Just changing something, breaking out from things. The most far-out thing was the one that you wanted to advocate because you felt that people would say, "You're right," you know, and break out—because everyone was feeling so repressed.

As this response indicates, there was an expressive element . . . to the CWLU abortion demands, but there was also a belief that the expression of feelings would serve the more instrumental purpose of mobilizing more women. For women's liberation groups, legal abortion was not an end in itself, but part of a broader fight for "women's control of their bodies" and a responsive health care system (which was, in turn, part of a long-term challenge to other capitalist institutions). Although CWLU activists were concerned about the availability and legal status of abortion, the issue was also a means by which women could be mobilized and larger concerns raised. It seemed likely to CWLU activists that abortion would be legalized, especially after the progress made by the repeal movement in 1970, but they wanted more than just legalization. As another CWLU activist told me in an interview about the CWLU's approach to the abortion issue:

> Particularly after the New York stuff happened [including the emergence of for-profit referral services], we wanted to make it clear to people that although getting abortion legalized was a step in the right direction, it certainly wasn't the answer to any of the problems, because there were a lot of problems which have been *created* by legalization, and we wanted a situation where abortion was not only available on demand but ultimately where we had a health care system which did not allow profiteering on people's abortions, etc., etc., so it was couched in terms which would set up a debate which would allow all of these issues which we thought were consciousness raising to be elaborated.

An important reason, then, for the use of confrontational demands and noninstitutionalized protest tactics was that the women's liberation movement organizations had much broader social change goals than just legal abortion that required different kinds of strategies and tactics. Given the perceptions of the momentum of social change during this period, it did not seem unrealistic to expect that these broader goals could be achieved through confrontational tactics. . . .

Whereas [some] activists . . . employed [radical] tactics as a way of getting the movement off the ground, single-issue groups like ICMCA turned to public education out of frustration with the lack of progress in institutionalized arenas. In 1967, after the defeat of a bill to establish a commission for the study of abortion in Illinois, ICMCA made a decision to spend the next two years on an educational campaign to convince the public of the need for repeal. . . . Similarly, after the defeat of a 1970 abortion reform bill, ICMCA decided to concentrate on educational work along with work in the political arena. . . . Although ICMCA worked through established organizations like churches, on numerous occasions the group also initiated public discussions of the abortion issue. These discussions were often held in settings such as university campuses, in order to reach the student constituency that was critical to both the population and the women's liberation movements. ICMCA also worked through women's rights organizations like Chicago NOW,[3] which held an educational forum on abortion for its members in February 1970, with speakers from ICMCA and the Clergy Consultation Services participating. . . .

Like Lana Clarke Phelan and other early abortion activists, ICMCA activists felt that they were making an important contribution simply by discussing abortion openly in these various forums. This sentiment was also shared by Rev. Howard Moody, who recently reflected about the role of the clergy service in talking freely about abortion: "It was to free that word up. To free it from the silence, from the whispered things. People need to be able to say things. But abortion was so underground, so hidden, that to use that word openly—and then to explain it, what it really was—." . . .

Use of the Mass Media

Although not all public education tactics involved media attention, the mass media were frequently used to gain direct access to constituents, a strategy that encouraged dramatic presentations of confrontational demands. One of Chicago NOW's major activities on the abortion issue in 1970, for example, was a Mother's Day press conference at the city morgue . . . to dramatize the dangers of illegal abortion. . . . Although feminist groups attracted much of the media attention, single-issue abortion movement organizations were quite actively trying to get media attention for the cause. . . .

NARAL[4] was able to attract a good deal of media attention as a result of both the controversial nature of its positions and the public relations skills of NARAL leaders. Lawrence Lader, a key architect of the NARAL strategy during this period, had already been making many media appearances and giving press conferences on the subject of abortion after

3. National Organization for Women. [Editor]
4. National Abortion Rights Action League. [Editor]

the publication in 1966 of his controversial book *Abortion*. . . . Under Lader's leadership, NARAL held several demonstrations and press conferences at which controversial announcements often were made in order to create publicity for the organization and win new advantages in the fight for repeal. On many occasions, NARAL successfully combined the public relations know-how of its leaders with the willingness of feminists to participate in confrontational or theatrical kinds of activities.

Like ICMCA, NARAL also spent a good deal of time debating the opposition, in part because this was a way to get media attention. For example, in the early 1970s NARAL developed materials, including a "Debating the Opposition" manual and a "Portrait of the Opposition" document, in order to train local activists and to expose the Catholic Church's backing of the anti-abortion movement. NARAL speakers debated "Right to Life" opponents on local television and radio shows across the country. The initial NARAL strategy, like that of ICMCA, was to respond to anti-abortion arguments and fetus pictures with "fact and reason." . . . After advertisements employing pictures of fetuses were successfully used to defeat the 1972 abortion repeal referendum in Michigan, however, "militants" in NARAL used their influence to adopt a confrontational strategy similar to that of the opposition. As Lawrence Lader explained:

> Logic is not very powerful against those pictures. . . . We had to do something, so we decided we would come in with the same thing. . . . We were able to get highly documented [material] from sheriffs, hospitals; we were able to get these pictures together. We had a number of pictures of dead women on the floor in motels, killed during an abortion, from a hack doctor in prelegal days, and we had these blown up. So I would always call up a news station and say, "Look, we've got these pretty frightening pictures and we'll show them to you ahead of time if you want, but if they're going to come in with their pictures, we will demand equal right, and you've got to be aware of this. We prefer no pictures." So a lot of shows banned them. I can remember Channel 5 in New York had me on a show there, and they showed their pictures and I had a few horrible pictures and there were all these gasps from the audience, and that's the last time I recall using them. They did their job. . . .

Overall, NARAL's mobilization tactics were more confrontational than those of ICMCA. Part of the reason for this was its greater use of the media to push proactive demands as well as to educate the public. Given the media's attraction to conflict, it was not difficult to get coverage by debating the opposition, but it was another matter to get coverage at press conferences. In order to do so, NARAL had to make "news." . . .

Service Projects

Not only did the movement promote a women's rights perspective on abortion through the media and through the creation of new kinds of educational forums, but alternative institutions also were created as movement activists began offering abortion-related services to women, particularly abortion referrals. . . . A number of individuals began making referrals to women for abortions in the 1960s, before the founding of most abortion movement organizations. By the late 1960s, their ranks were joined by feminists, clergy, and other activists who began organizing abortion referral services throughout the country. . . .

For the women's liberation movement, projects such as abortion referral services were both responses to the immediate needs of women and part of a longterm strategy of creating alternative institutions that would empower women. In Chicago, the Chicago Women's Liberation Union had its hand in a number of abortion-related service projects, including the Women's Liberation Abortion Counseling Service, known as "Jane" . . . Like other referral services around the country, Jane began by providing referrals for abortions. But members of the Abortion Counseling Service ended up performing abortions themselves after learning to do so by assisting at abortions and after they learned that one of the abortionists they had been using was not himself a licensed doctor. . . . Thus, the women literally took control of the technology, creating a service that they felt was nonhierarchical and sensitive to the needs of women.

As part of the same strategy of empowering women with information and access to technology, the CWLU created pregnancy-testing services that were conducted at several locations in Chicago, including a working-class southwest side location. . . .

There were numerous debates in the CWLU as to the value of these service projects. Advocates of the projects argued that they were not merely providing services but also building alternative institutions that allowed women to control their bodies rather than rely on male-oriented, for-profit health care services. The Abortion Counseling Service, for example, made a deliberate attempt to create a supportive, female-oriented atmosphere for women having abortions. Supporters also contended that the services allowed the CWLU to reach minority, poor, and working-class women—and in fact the Abortion Counseling Service and pregnancy-testing projects did serve many minority and economically disadvantaged women, some of whom were recruited to the Union or at least were exposed to the women's liberation movement. Critics of the service projects complained, however, that they were not political enough and that they drained resources from other Union projects. . . .

There were several reasons why the Abortion Counseling Service and the pregnancy-testing services continued to function. In the case of Jane, it was abundantly clear that the service was needed by women who could not otherwise afford abortions. The risk in providing the service and the real needs that were so obviously being served created a strong sense of solidarity and commitment among the women in the Jane collective. Moreover, the decentralized structure of the Union . . . allowed both the Abortion Counseling Service and the pregnancy-testing services to operate independently, despite whatever debate occurred within the Union. As with all CWLU work projects, women who were not official members of the CWLU could still participate in the projects, thereby making it easier to recruit enough workers. Both Jane and the pregnancy-testing services required little more than the commitment of activists, as both charged small fees that covered the costs of the services and required skills learned on the job. The attempt at establishing a free health clinic failed, on the other hand, because it would have needed far more resources than the Union was able to mobilize, particularly given the mixed feelings about service projects among CWLU activists. . . .

FEMINIST MOBILIZATION AND DIRECT ACTION

Given the limited support for abortion law repeal from established organizations, the presence of the women's movement was by far the most positive feature of the political environment of the abortion movement in the years following NARAL's founding in 1969. The women's movement was growing rapidly, and the news media were interested in both the abortion issue and the women's movement. In addition to tactics like referral services that were aimed at women, feminists initiated direct-action tactics such as demonstrations that were targeted at established power holders. They also provided support for direct-action tactics initiated by single-issue abortion movement organizations.

Demonstrations by women's movement activists sent a message of public support for abortion rights to established organizations and authorities and served an expressive function for participants. Organizations like the Chicago Women's Liberation Union organized a number of demonstrations that were targeted at representatives of the "establishment," such as the American Medical Association, as well as government officials. . . .

NARAL frequently did take advantage of the availability of feminist groups to organize demonstrations. As a result of close ties between NOW and NARAL, NOW helped launch NARAL through strong participation in NARAL's first national action, a day of "Children by Choice" demonstrations held in conjunction with press conferences in eleven cities on Mother's Day in 1969. Because NOW was growing rapidly in terms of members and chapters in the early 1970s, NOW was able to participate on a number of occasions in demonstrations for abortion law repeal in cooperation with NARAL. Chicago NOW joined other NOW chapters and local women's liberation groups in organizing or participating in demonstrations for abortion law repeal and related issues. . . .

NARAL's adoption of radical demands and controversial tactics was due to internal organizational factors in addition to the influence of the women's movement. With regard to the organizational resources needed to advocate such positions, Lawrence Lader and other key leaders had experience in providing abortion referrals and knew the legal risks and public relations benefits of doing so. . . .

Most importantly, NARAL's organizational structure allowed those leaders of NARAL who advocated confrontational positions to push their strategies. NARAL was centrally controlled by its executive committee in the pre-1973 period, and its operating procedures were informal. . . . There was no system of rotating individuals off the executive committee every few years, thereby allowing the "militants" . . . who had a majority on the executive committee, to control the nominating committee. The NARAL board of directors, which was representative of a broader range of the NARAL constituency, may have chosen a more cautious approach, but it was an unwieldy body of up to ninety members that met only once a year and therefore did not control the real decision making in the organization. When those leaders on the NARAL executive committee who favored radical demands and confrontational tactics wanted to take action (e.g., call a press conference or a demonstration), they simply picked up the phone to obtain approval from a majority of the executive committee. In this way, action could be taken which bypassed bureaucratic procedures that might have limited NARAL to the adoption of less confrontational tactics. For these reasons, the informal, centralized NARAL organization facilitated the use of tactics favored by the "militants" in the leadership. . . .

The strategies of another major organization in the pre-1973 abortion repeal movement, Zero Population Growth, were similarly influenced by the growth of the women's movement in the late 1960s and the early 1970s and by internal organizational characteristics. Like NARAL and NOW, ZPG adopted the demand for repeal, rather than reform, of abortion laws, advocating legal abortion as a component of the "basic human right to limit one's own reproduction." . . . ZPG's primary concern, of course, has always been overpopulation, and abortion was advocated, along with contraception and sterilization, as a "means of birth control" that would help bring down the birthrate. Sensitive to the concerns of feminists about its potential coercion of women, however, ZPG conspicuously stressed the voluntary nature of its demands for abortion, sterilization, and contraception and, from the start, expressed its support for women's rights.

ZPG took a "women's rights" approach to abortion in part as a result of overlaps in the national leadership of ZPG and groups like NARAL and NOW. The organization was also influenced by its numerous chapters, many of which consisted of students who were strongly interested in abortion and women's rights. In the early years in Chicago, for example, a number of campus-based ZPG chapters were working for repeal alongside feminists. Although there was also a more conservative element in ZPG's local constituency . . . , the organization's decision-making structure allowed national leaders, who tended to be sympathetic to women's rights, to maintain control over ZPG's positions.

In general, the presence of the women's movement was a strong influence on the strategic and tactical choices of the abortion movement. Not only did women's movement organizations initiate many direct-action tactics, but various other kinds of organizations also sought to use both the energies of feminists and the repertoire of tactics associated with the women's movement and other movements of the 1960s. NARAL frequently mobilized feminist support for its actions. . . .

Even the more staid Illinois Citizens for the Medical Control of Abortion (ICMCA) engaged in demonstrations, although they were less confrontational than those in which feminists typically participated, and, significantly, they were targeted at legislators. In 1970, ICMCA sent a few busloads of women, accompanied by sympathetic reporters, to a small demonstration in Springfield to call attention to an abortion reform bill before the state legislature. And in 1971, ICMCA again bused supporters to Springfield for a demonstration in support of a repeal bill. Chicago-area ZPG supporters lent some needed bodies to these and other orderly ICMCA demonstrations, which were typically combined with more institutionalized tactics.

Conclusion

Before 1973, the confrontational direct-action tactics of political "outsiders" were as much a part of the movement to legalize abortion as were the conventional means of influence used by seasoned activists. The presence of the women's movement in the expanded social movement sector of the 1960s was an important factor prompting the use of these tactics. Feminists took to the streets to demand abortion rights, but they also worked to create a new social consciousness about women's rights to abortion. Although direct-action tactics did not have the direct impact that litigation had on the legalization of abortion, they helped bring the abortion issue to public attention and created an atmosphere of support for legal abortion. Moreover, the alternative institutions and cultural changes created by the women's health movement would have an important influence on subsequent collective action.

48
Science, Technology, and Political Conflict: Analyzing the Issues

Dorothy Nelkin

As the twentieth century draws to a close, many people are skeptical about the ability of science to improve their lives. It often seems complex beyond their understanding. The laboratories of giant corporations seem focused only on making science profitable. Most importantly, the unintended consequences of science and technology have made doubters of many people. Science and technology are not neutral phenomena, and their future direction will be determined by decisions made either by all of us or by a powerful elite.

In the spring of 1977 at a forum on recombinant DNA research, protest groups invaded the austere quarters of the National Academy of Sciences singing: "We shall not be cloned." During that same spring, thousands of people camped at a reactor site in Seabrook, New Hampshire, to protest the construction of a nuclear power plant. Fundamentalists are increasingly open in their objections to the teaching of evolution in the public school system. Right-to-life groups bring lawsuits against scientists for fetal research. Citizens protest the decision to ban laetrile as a cancer therapy and question mandatory automobile safety devices as examples of government paternalism. Industrial practices of toxic waste disposal have generated local citizen action. And the standards established by scientists to regulate chemical substances are a source of public dispute. Indeed controversy seems to erupt over nearly every aspect of science and technology as decisions once defined as technical (within the province of experts) have become intensely political.

The development of science and technology had remained largely unquestioned during the period of rapid economic growth that followed World War II. But belief in technological progress has been tempered by awareness of its ironies. Technological "improvements" may cause disastrous environmental problems: drugs to stimulate the growth of beef cattle may cause cancer; "efficient" industrial processes may threaten worker health; biomedical research may be detrimental to human subjects; and a new airport may turn a neighborhood into a sonic garbage dump. Even efforts to control technology may impose inequities, as new standards and regulations pit quality of life against economic growth and the expectation of progress and prosperity.

Thus the past decade has been remarkable for political action directed against science and technology. Issue-oriented organizations have formed to obstruct specific projects; scientists have called public attention to risks; and many groups demand greater accountability and public participation in technical policy decisions. . . .

Science has always faced ambivalent public attitudes. The acceptance of the authority of scientific judgment has coexisted with mistrust and fear, revealed, for example, in the response to innovations such as vaccination or research methods such as vivisection. The romantic view of the scientist as "a modern magician, a miracle man who can do incredible things" parallels negative images of:

> Dr. Faustus, Dr. Frankenstein, Dr. Moreau, Dr. Jekyll, Dr. Cyclops, Dr. Caligari, Dr. Strangelove. . . . In these images of our popular culture resides a legitimate public fear of the scientist's stripped down, depersonalized conception of knowledge—a fear that our scientists will go on being titans who create monsters.

Even as attacks against science increase, public attitude surveys suggest that science and technology are favorably perceived as instrumental in achieving important social goals. About 70% of Americans believe that science and technology have changed life for the better. Furthermore, the standing of scientists relative to other occupations has continually improved. In the United States scientists rank second only to physicians in occupational prestige (they were fifth in 1966). Similarly, in Europe a survey by the Commission on the European Communities finds widespread consensus that "science is one of the most important factors in the improvement of daily life."

What then is the significance of the flare-up of disputes over science and technology? Are the recent controversies a manifestation of the "crisis of authority" associated with the 1960s, or are they simply local protests against decisions that affect particular and immediate interests? Do the disputes express widely shared ideological and political concerns, or do they simply reflect antiscience sentiments and resistance to technological change?

From one viewpoint, the activities of protest groups resemble nineteenth-century Luddism—a wholesale rejection of technological change. Zbigniew Brzezinski calls such opposition "the death rattle of the historically obsolete." But from another perspective, protest is a positive and necessary force in a society that, Theodore Roszak claims, "has surrendered responsibility for making morally demanding decisions, for generating ideals, for controlling public authority, for safeguarding the society against its despoilers. Thus while most of us are "frozen in a position of befuddled docility," protest groups fight to preserve the values lost in the course of technological progress.

Many controversies arise when citizens in a community become aware that they must bear the costs of a project that will benefit a different or much broader constituency. Airports, power plants, and highways serve large regions, but near neighbors bear the environmental and social burden. Normally such projects are planned and sites selected on the basis of economic efficiency and technical criteria. But community protests raise basic questions of distributive justice: can any reduction in some citizens' welfare be justified by greater advantages to others? can the magnitude or intensity of costs borne by neighbors of a major project be reasonably incorporated into cost-benefit calculations? . . .

A second source of controversy over science and technology is the fear of potential health and environmental hazards. We are deluged with warnings about "invisible" hazards (PCBs, freon, radiation, cyclamates —the list is long and growing), so the fear of risk is inevitable. This fear is aggravated by the often poorly understood nature of risk. How does one really know, for example, if a nuclear waste storage facility is adequately protected against long-term radiation leakage? Assessing risk is complicated. For often, while an accident could be catastrophic, the chances of one are small and difficult to calculate. In the case of nuclear waste disposal, it is the fear of an unlikely but potentially devastating catastrophe that sustains conflict. In other cases, risks are known but must be weighed against potential benefits; then dispute focuses on balancing competing priorities in decisions about regulation (for example, in setting worker safety standards).

New technology has increased our capability to detect potential risks, but technical uncertainties leave considerable leeway for conflicting interpretation. . . . Moreover the possibility of risk poses the political question of how to regulate and control science and technology without imposing unreasonable constraints. . . .

A third kind of controversy involves questions of freedom of choice when government regulates. Laetrile is banned, airbags are mandatory; both decisions infringe on freedom of choice—the freedom to choose one's own medication, the freedom to take one's own risks. If a water supply is fluoridated, airbags mandated, or universal vaccination required, everyone must partake of the decision and its consequences. And if the sale of laetrile or saccharin is prohibited, those who want these products are denied the right to buy them. Governments impose regulations on the assumption that individual choices have social costs or that individuals may fail to make rational and enlightened choices on their own behalf.

Such constraints, however, also may be viewed as protection of professional privilege, as unnecessary government paternalism, or as a violation of individual rights. These are the perceptions that have maintained the laetrile dispute. . . .

Finally, conflict occurs when science or technology is perceived to flaunt traditional values. Controversies over research procedures and over science education reflect a renewed concern with moral and religious values in American society. At a time when accomplishments of science have fostered in some a faith in rational explanations of nature, there are concerted efforts by others to reinvest educational systems with traditional faith. And even as biomedical research brings about dramatic improvements in medical care, there are always critics seeking to block research and to question areas of science that challenge traditional values.

For protest groups in such disputes, it is the moral implications of science and the potential for misuse of scientific findings that shape their dissent. They fear that science may change the normal state of nature, alter the genetic structure of mankind, or threaten deeply held beliefs about free will and self-determination. A major source of concern with respect to recombinant DNA research, for example, is the potential for removing the obstacles to genetic engineering by allowing scientists to transfer hereditary characteristics from one strain to another. This evokes images of eugenics and leads directly to questions about the wisdom of seeking certain kinds of knowledge at all. Thus the effort to defend moral values poses a threat to freedom of scientific inquiry, a deeply held value in itself. . . .

Controversy as a Political Challenge

Critics of science and technology perceive a vast distance between technology and human needs—indeed between the governing and the governed. They question the ability of representative institutions to serve their interests. They resent the concentration of authority over technology in private bureaucracies and public agencies responsible for technological change. And they challenge assumptions about the importance of technical competence as the basis for legitimate decision-making authority.

Sources of Opposition

Those who live in the vicinity of an airport, a nuclear waste disposal facility, or who work in a vinyl chloride plant, have practical reasons to protest. They are directly impacted by land appropriation, noise, immediate risks, local economic or social disruption, or by some encroachment on their individual rights. Others, including many environmentalists, creationists, and laetrile supporters, protest out of adherence to a "cause." And there are people not directly affected by a specific project or controversy who oppose science and technology because of global political concerns. Some nuclear critics, for example, see science as an instrument of military or economic domination and oppose technology for ideological reasons.

These conflicts over science and technology draw support from sharply contrasting social groups. Most active are middle-class, educated people with sufficient economic security and political skill to participate in decision-making. But conservative fundamentalists in California and Arkansas, seeking to influence a science curriculum, share concern about local control with citizens in a liberal university community seeking to influence the siting of a power plant.

Finally, an important source of criticism has been the scientific community itself. Many young scientists became politicized during the 1960s. At that time, they focused on antiwar activities, on university politics, and on the issue of military research in universities. More recently, their attention has turned to the environment, energy, biomedical research, and harmful industrial practices. These scientists often initiate controversies by raising questions about potential risks in areas obscured from public knowledge.

The Political Role of Experts

Technical expertise is a crucial political resource in conflicts over science and technology. For access to knowledge and the resulting ability to question the data used to legitimize decisions is an essential basis of power and influence. The cases will suggest the important role of the activist-scientist in formulating, legitimizing, and supporting the diverse concerns involved in the controversies. Scientists were the first to warn the public about the possible risks of recombinant DNA research. They were the first to call the public's attention to the problems of developing nuclear power before solving the problem of radiation disposal techniques. As various controversies develop, scientists are called upon to buttress political positions with the authority of their expertise. The willingness of scientists to expose technical uncertainties and to lend their expertise to citizen groups constitutes a formidable political challenge.

The authority of scientific expertise rests on assumptions about scientific rationality. Interpretations and predictions made by scientists are judged to be rational because they are based on data gathered through rational procedures. Their interpretations therefore serve as a basis for planning and as a means for defending the legitimacy of policy decisions.

The cases demonstrate how protest groups also exploit technical expertise to challenge policy decisions. Power plant opponents have their own scientists who legitimize their concerns about thermal pollution. Environmentalists hire their own experts to question the technical feasibility of questionable projects. Laetrile supporters have their own medical professionals. Even fundamentalists seeking to have the Biblical account of creation taught in the public schools present themselves as scientists and claim "creation theory" to be a scientific alternative to evolution theory.

Whatever political values motivate controversy, the debates usually focus on technical questions. The siting controversies develop out of concern with the quality of life in a community, but the debates resolve around technical questions—the physical requirements for the facility, the accuracy of the predictions establishing its need, or the precise extent of environmental risk. Concerns about the freedom to select a cancer therapy devolve into technical arguments about the efficacy of treatment. Moral opponents of fetal research engage in scientific debate about the precise point at which life begins.

This is tactically effective, for in all disputes broad areas of uncertainty are open to conflicting scientific interpretation. Decisions are often made in a context of limited knowledge about potential social or environmental impacts, and there is seldom conclusive evidence to reach definitive resolution. Thus power hinges on the ability to manipulate knowledge, to challenge the evidence presented to support particular policies, and technical expertise becomes a resource exploited by all parties to justify their political and economic views. In the process, political values and scientific facts become difficult to distinguish.

The debates among scientists documented in these cases show how, in controversial situations, the value premises of the disputants color their findings. The boundaries of the problems to be studied, the alternatives weighed, and the issues regarded as appropriate—all tend to determine which data are selected as important, which facts emerge. The way project proponents or citizen groups use the work of "their" experts reflects their judgments about priorities or about acceptable levels of risk. Whenever such judgments conflict, this is reflected in the selective use of technical knowledge. Expertise is reduced to one more weapon in a political arsenal.

When expertise becomes available to both sides of a controversy, it further polarizes conflict by calling attention to areas of technical ambiguity and to the limited ability to predict and control risks. The very existence of conflicting technical interpretations generates political activity. And the fact that experts disagree, more than the substance of their disputes, fires controversy. After hearing 120 scientists argue over nuclear safety, for example, the California State Legislature concluded that the issues were not, in the end, resolvable by expertise. "The questions involved require value judgments and the voter is no less equipped to make such judgments than the most brilliant Nobel Laureate." Thus the role of expertise in these disputes leads directly to demands for a greater public role in technical decision-making.

The Participatory Impulse

Most of the controversies described [were] provoked by specific decisions: to expand an airport; to ban a drug; to site a power plant or highway; to develop a new weapon. Those who propose these projects define the decision and the issues involved primarily as technical—subject to objective criteria based on energy forecasts, studies of environmental impact, accident statistics, or predictions of future needs. Opposition groups, on the other hand, perceive such decisions in a political light. They use experts of their own, but mainly for tactical purposes—to prove that technical data are at best uncertain and subject to different interpretations. They try to show that important questions involve political choices and that these can be obscured by technical criteria. In the end, they seek a role in making social choices.

The cases suggest that the nature of public opposition depends on a number of circumstances. If a project in question (for example, an airport) directly affects a neighborhood, local activists are relatively easy to organize on the basis of immediate interests. Many issues (such as recombinant DNA research or the automobile airbag or a new weapon) have no such natural constituency. Risks may be diffuse. Affected interests may be hard to define, or so dispersed as to be difficult to organize. Or the significant affected interests may be more concerned with employment than with their environment and therefore willing to accept certain risks. In such cases, participation is limited and the controversies involve mainly scientists or professional activists. Even in these conflicts, however, political protest can be maintained only if the leadership can count on support among a wider group of people who, though generally inactive, will lend support at public hearings, demonstrations, and other key events.

What channels do these groups exploit as they try to influence technology policy? First, they seek to capture technical resources. But those who oppose a project must also organize their activities to develop maximum public support. Expanding the scope of conflict is necessary to push decisions commonly defined as technical out into the political arena. Thus dramatic and highly publicized media events often are important. Tactics in the controversies described . . . range from routine political actions like lobbying or intervention in public hearings to litigation, referenda, and political demonstrations. These channels of participation depend on the institutional framework or political system in which opposition takes shape. In the United States litigation has become a major means for citizens to challenge technology. The role of the courts has expanded through the extension of the legal doctrine of standing—private citizens without alleged personal economic grievances may bring suit as advocates of the public interest. The courts have been used by citizens not only in environmental cases, but in challenging research practices as well, as we see in the litigation over fetal research.

The participatory impulse has also forced elected representatives seeking to maintain their popular support to consider technical issues that are normally beyond their political jurisdiction. For example, the Cambridge City Council and local government bodies in a number of other university communities claim the authority to judge the adequacy of safety regulations in biology laboratories. Local townships forbid the transport and disposal of radioactive materials within their jurisdiction. And referenda on specific technologies such as nuclear power are increasingly common.

Such events evidence a changing relationship between science and the public. But it should not be assumed that demands for participation imply antiscience attitudes. More often they suggest a search for a more appropriate articulation between science and those affected by it. In its report on recombinant DNA research, the Cambridge Review Board thoughtfully expressed a prevailing view.

> Decisions regarding the appropriate course between the risks and benefits of potentially dangerous scientific inquiry must not be adjudicated within the inner circles of the scientific establishment. . . . We wish to express our sincere belief that a predominantly lay citizens' group can face a technical, scientific matter of general and deep public concern, educate itself appropriately to the task, and reach a fair decision.

This view sees science and technology policy as no different from other policy areas, subject to political evaluation that includes intense public debate. This, indeed, is the political challenge posed by the current state of controversy over science and technology, and it has profound implications for their resolution.

THE RESOLUTION OF CONFLICT

How one perceives science and technology reflects special interests, personal values, attitudes toward risk, and general feelings about science and authority. The social and moral implications of science and technology, the threat to human values, may assume far greater importance than any details of scientific verification. Perceptions therefore differ dramatically.

- Is recombinant DNA research a potential boon to medical progress, or a risky procedure continued only because of vested interests among scientists?
- Is nuclear power a solution to the energy problem or a destructive force perpetuated because of existing industrial commitments?
- Is the air bag a solution to the problem of automobile safety, or a paternalistic mandate violating freedom of choice?
- Are binary weapons systems a boon for national security or an unnecessary risk to fragile international negotiations?

Resolution of a dispute depends on the nature of just such underlying perceptions. If the question at issue is merely one of specific interests, compensation measures could reduce conflict. But where more basic ideological principles or attitudes are at stake, no direct solutions will satisfy all protagonists—in the creationist controversy and in the debate over fetal research, all efforts to compromise have failed.

Nor is there much evidence that technical arguments change anyone's mind. In the disputes over fetal research and even in the various siting controversies no amount of data could resolve value differences. Each side used technical information mainly to legitimate a position based on existing priorities. Ultimately, dramatic events or significant political changes had more effect than expertise. For example, the growing base of technical information about the dangers of existing conditions in vinyl chloride plants did not lead to more stringent standards of occupational safety until the dramatic announcement of the death of several workers.

In some cases, increased knowledge may eventually depoliticize an issue by helping to separate facts from values or by clarifying the technical constraints that limit policy choices. But even in the old conflict over compulsory vaccination, changing attitudes toward governmental regulation had more to do with reducing opposition than the obvious benefit of the vaccination program.

The outcome of many disputes depends on the relative political power of competing interests. In some cases industrial interests prevail; chemical firms were clearly influential in framing the principles that were to shape safety standards for the vinyl chloride industry. In other cases, powerful protest groups exercise sufficient economic leverage to determine the outcome; the ability of environmentalists to impose costly delays in the power plant siting controversy affected the ultimate decision not to build. In still other cases, external political factors are decisive. The election of minority governments in Ontario and Ottawa influenced the outcome of the Toronto airport controversy. Federal, state, and local government relationships affect decisions in the nuclear field. And because of the protracted nature of many controversies (for example, the air bag dispute), outcomes are influenced by changes in the political environment over time.

But ultimately the implementation of policies involving science and technology depend on public acceptance. Efforts to foster greater acceptance of science and technology are numerous. United States legislation has provided greater public access to information, expanded public hearing procedures, and extended opportunities for intervention in rule-making and adjudicatory procedures. We shall see how these procedures operate in the controversies discussed in this book. Citizens are also appointed to advisory committees and institutional review boards, and public involvement is required in environmental impact statements. Standing advisory commissions (such as the National Commission for the Protection of Human Subjects of Biomedical Research) have been established to interpret, clarify, and assure the quality of technical opinion and to gather information on public concerns as well. In the recombinant DNA case, we shall see the creation of a Citizens Review Board, formed to evaluate conflicting evidence about the adequacy of NIH guidelines for the research and advise on the wisdom of allowing a research facility in Cambridge, Massachusetts.

Whether such efforts will eventually help to resolve conflict remains to be seen, but many difficulties are apparent as we see these participatory mechanisms developed and used. Assessing science and technology may call for specialized knowledge, in turn creating problems for the layman. The vagueness of the boundaries between the technical and political dimensions of policies concerning science and technology—between questions of technical feasibility and political acceptability—itself enhances the difficulty of finding appropriate means to expand public choice. There are also problems in determining who should be involved in a decision—who is really representative of public interests. And finally the effect of a greater public role on the development of science and technology, on administrative efficiency, and on citizens' attitudes, is difficult to predict.

In the 1980s increasing governmental and industrial concern about scientific and technological competition has reduced opportunities for participation. Access to information is increasingly difficult, public officials are muzzled, citizen participation on commissions and committees is curtailed. However, controversies over science and technology persist. They continue to develop over competing political, economic and ethical values, reflecting a dialectic between the desire for efficiency and the demands of a democratic technology. The tendency to place a high value on efficiency leads to defining inherently political problems as technical. Yet technical planning limits public choice and threatens the widely held assumption that people should be able to influence decisions that affect their lives. And this assumption has considerable and increasing salience. Indeed of all the questions raised in the disputes over science and technology, the most pervasive have been: who should control? what is the relevant expertise? is responsibility for decisions to rest with those with technical knowledge or with those who bear the impact of technological choices? Does one rely on professionals to assess the impact of their research or on those who may be affected? Assumptions are changing about the importance of technical competence to assess science and technology. This challenging of authority is the most striking aspect of the many recent disputes. . . .

But even as these individual conflicts quiet down, the same tensions recur in other contexts and in other places. Controversies erupt over the bans on saccharin and cyclamates, fluoridation, weather modification programs, research on the XYY chromosome, the swine flu vaccine, toxic dumps, the use of pesticides, and genetic screening techniques. . . . Older controversies reemerge, often in similar form. Indeed, few conflicts involving social and political values are ever fully resolved. The persistence of controversy [reveals] a significant movement to reassess the social values, the priorities, and the political relationships that are always present in technical decisions.

49
Jihad vs. McWorld

BENJAMIN R. BARBER

There are many social forces creating a more interconnected world. They are breaking down barriers of geography, politics, culture, and economics and opening up possibilities for sharing and mutual support. But the richer and more powerful of the world are also exploitating the poorer and less powerful. In response many peoples of the world are looking inward and seeking to erect protective barriers against the forces that would draw them into a global marketplace of goods, services, ideas, and culture. The future for democracy in either case is not good, but neither is it hopeless.

Just beyond the horizon of current events lie two possible political futures—both bleak, neither democratic. The first is a retribalization of large swaths of humankind by war and bloodshed: a threatened Lebanonization of national states in which culture is pitted against culture, people against people, tribe against tribe—a Jihad in the name of a hundred narrowly conceived faiths against every kind of interdependence, every kind of artificial social cooperation and civic mutuality. The second is being borne in on us by the onrush of economic and ecological forces that demand integration and uniformity and that mesmerize the world with fast music, fast computers, and fast food—with MTV, Macintosh, and McDonald's, pressing nations into one commercially homogenous global network: one McWorld tied together by technology, ecology, communications, and commerce. The planet is falling precipitantly apart *and* coming reluctantly together at the very same moment.

These two tendencies are sometimes visible in the same countries at the same instant: thus Yugoslavia, clamoring just recently to join the New Europe, is exploding into fragments; India is trying to live up to its reputation as the world's largest integral democracy while powerful new fundamentalist parties like the Hindu nationalist Bharatiya Janata Party, along with nationalist assassins, are imperiling its hard-won unity. States are breaking up or joining up: the Soviet Union has disappeared almost overnight, its parts forming new unions with one another or with like-minded nationalities in neighboring states. The old interwar national state based on territory and political sovereignty looks to be a mere transitional development.

The tendencies of what I am here calling the forces of Jihad and the forces of McWorld operate with equal strength in opposite directions, the one driven by parochial hatreds, the other by universalizing markets, the one re-creating ancient subnational and ethnic borders from within, the other making national borders porous from without. They have one thing in common: neither offers much hope to citizens looking for practical ways to govern themselves democratically. If the global future is to pit Jihad's centrifugal whirlwind against McWorld's centripetal black hole, the outcome is unlikely to be democratic—or so I will argue.

McWorld, or the Globalization of Politics

Four imperatives make up the dynamic of McWorld: a market imperative, a resource imperative, an information-technology imperative, and an ecological imperative. By shrinking the world and diminishing the salience of national borders, these imperatives have in combination achieved a considerable victory over factiousness and particularism, and not least of all over their most virulent traditional form—nationalism. It is the realists who are now Europeans, the utopians who dream nostalgically of a resurgent England or Germany, perhaps even a resurgent Wales or Saxony. Yesterday's wishful cry for one world has yielded to the reality of McWorld.

The market imperative. Marxist and Leninist theories of imperialism assumed that the quest for ever-expanding markets would in time compel nation-based capitalist economies to push against national boundaries in search of an international economic imperium. Whatever else has happened to the scientistic predictions of Marxism, in this domain they have proved farsighted. All national economies are now vulnerable to the inroads of larger, transnational markets within which trade is free, currencies are convertible, access to banking is open, and contracts are enforceable under law. In Europe, Asia, Africa, the South Pacific, and the Americas such markets are eroding national sovereignty and giving rise to entities—international banks, trade associations, transnational lobbies like OPEC and Greenpeace, world news services like CNN and the BBC, and multinational corporations that increasingly lack a meaningful national identity—that neither reflect nor respect nationhood as an organizing or regulative principle.

The market imperative has also reinforced the quest for international peace and stability, requisites of an efficient international economy. Markets are enemies of parochialism, isolation, fractiousness, war. Market psychology attenuates the psychology of ideological and religious cleavages and assumes a concord among producers and consumers—categories that ill fit narrowly conceived national or religious cultures. Shopping has little tolerance for blue laws, whether dictated by pub-closing British paternalism, Sabbath-observing Jewish Orthodox fundamentalism, or no-Sunday-liquor-sales Massachusetts puritanism. In the context of common markets, international law ceases to be a vision of justice and becomes a workaday framework for getting things done—

enforcing contracts, ensuring that governments abide by deals, regulating trade and currency relations, and so forth.

Common markets demand a common language, as well as a common currency, and they produce common behaviors of the kind bred by cosmopolitan city life everywhere. Commercial pilots, computer programmers, international bankers, media specialists, oil riggers, entertainment celebrities, ecology experts, demographers, accountants, professors, athletes—these compose a new breed of men and women for whom religion, culture, and nationality can seem only marginal elements in a working identity. Although sociologists of everyday life will no doubt continue to distinguish a Japanese from an American mode, shopping has a common signature throughout the world. Cynics might even say that some of the recent revolutions in Eastern Europe have had as their true goal not liberty and the right to vote but well-paying jobs and the right to shop (although the vote is proving easier to acquire than consumer goods). The market imperative is, then, plenty powerful; but, notwithstanding some of the claims made for "democratic capitalism," it is not identical with the democratic imperative.

The resource imperative. Democrats once dreamed of societies whose political autonomy rested firmly on economic independence. The Athenians idealized what they called autarky, and tried for a while to create a way of life simple and austere enough to make the polis genuinely self-sufficient. To be free meant to be independent of any other community or polis. Not even the Athenians were able to achieve autarky, however: human nature, it turns out, is dependency. By the time of Pericles, Athenian politics was inextricably bound up with a flowering empire held together by naval power and commerce—an empire that, even as it appeared to enhance Athenian might, ate away at Athenian independence and autarky. Master and slave, it turned out, were bound together by mutual insufficiency.

The dream of autarky briefly engrossed nineteenth-century America as well, for the underpopulated, endlessly bountiful land, the cornucopia of natural resources, and the natural barriers of a continent walled in by two great seas led many to believe that America could be a world unto itself. Given this past, it has been harder for Americans than for most to accept the inevitability of interdependence. But the rapid depletion of resources even in a country like ours, where they once seemed inexhaustible, and the maldistribution of arable soil and mineral resources on the planet, leave even the wealthiest societies ever more resource-dependent and many other nations in permanently desperate straits.

Every nation, it turns out, needs something another nation has; some nations have almost nothing they need.

The information-technology imperative. Enlightenment science and the technologies derived from it are inherently universalizing. They entail a quest for descriptive principles of general application, a search for universal solutions to particular problems, and an unswerving embrace of objectivity and impartiality.

Scientific progress embodies and depends on open communication, a common discourse rooted in rationality, collaboration, and an easy and regular flow and exchange of information. Such ideals can be hypocritical covers for power-mongering by elites, and they may be shown to be wanting in many other ways, but they are entailed by the very idea of science and they make science and globalization practical allies.

Business, banking, and commerce all depend on information flow and are facilitated by new communication technologies. The hardware of these technologies tends to be systemic and integrated—computer, television, cable, satellite, laser, fiber-optic, and microchip technologies combining to create a vast interactive communications and information network that can potentially give every person on earth access to every other person, and make every datum, every byte, available to every set of eyes. If the automobile was, as George Ball once said (when he gave his blessing to a Fiat factory in the Soviet Union during the Cold War), "an ideology on four wheels," then electronic telecommunication and information systems are an ideology at 186,000 miles per second—which makes for a very small planet in a very big hurry. Individual cultures speak particular languages; commerce and science increasingly speak English; the whole world speaks logarithms and binary mathematics.

Moreover, the pursuit of science and technology asks for, even compels, open societies. Satellite footprints do not respect national borders; telephone wires penetrate the most closed societies. With photocopying and then fax machines having infiltrated Soviet universities and *samizdat* literary circles in the eighties, and computer modems having multiplied like rabbits in communism's bureaucratic warrens thereafter, *glasnost* could not be far behind. In their social requisites, secrecy and science are enemies.

The new technology's software is perhaps even more globalizing than its hardware. The information arm of international commerce's sprawling body reaches out and touches distinct nations and parochial cultures, and gives them a common face chiseled in Hollywood, on Madison Avenue, and in Silicon Valley. Throughout the 1980s one of the most-watched television programs in South Africa was *The Cosby Show*. The demise of apartheid was already in production. Exhibitors at the 1991 Cannes film festival expressed growing anxiety over the "homogenization" and "Americanization" of the global film industry when, for the third year running, American films dominated the awards ceremonies. America has dominated the world's popular culture for much longer, and much more decisively. In November of 1991 Switzerland's once insular culture boasted best-seller lists featuring *Terminator 2* as the No. 1 movie, *Scarlett* as the No. 1 book, and Prince's *Diamonds and Pearls* as the No. 1 record album. No wonder the Japanese are buying Hollywood film studios even faster than Americans are buying Japanese television sets. This kind of software supremacy may in the long term be far more important than hardware superiority, because culture has become more potent than armaments. What is the power of the Pentagon compared with Disneyland? Can the Sixth Fleet keep up with CNN? McDonald's in Moscow and Coke in China will do more to create a global culture than military colonization ever could. It is less the goods than the brand names that do the work, for they convey life-style images that alter perception and challenge behavior. They make up the seductive software of McWorld's common (at times much too common) soul.

Yet in all this high-tech commercial world there is nothing that looks particularly democratic. It lends itself to surveillance as well as liberty, to new forms of manipulation and covert control as well as new kinds of participation, to skewed, unjust market outcomes as well as greater productivity. The consumer society and the open society are not quite synonymous. Capitalism and democracy have a relationship, but it is something less than a marriage. An efficient free market after all requires that consumers be free to vote their dollars on competing goods, not that citizens be free to vote their values and beliefs on competing political candidates and programs. The free market flourished in junta-run Chile, in military-governed Taiwan and Korea, and, earlier, in a variety of autocratic European empires as well as their colonial possessions.

The ecological imperative. The impact of globalization on ecology is a cliché even to world leaders who ignore it. We know well enough that the German forests can be destroyed by Swiss and Italians driving gas-guzzlers fueled by leaded gas. We also know that the planet can be asphyxiated by greenhouse gases because Brazilian farmers want to be part of the twentieth century and are burning down tropical rain forests to clear a little land to plough, and because Indonesians make a living out of converting their lush jungle into toothpicks for fastidious Japanese diners, upsetting the delicate oxygen balance and in effect puncturing our global lungs. Yet this ecological consciousness has meant not only greater awareness but also greater inequality, as modernized nations try to slam the door behind them, saying to developing nations, "The world cannot afford *your* modernization; ours has wrung it dry!"

Each of the four imperatives just cited is transnational, transideological, and transcultural. Each applies impartially to Catholics, Jews, Muslims, Hindus, and Buddhists; to democrats and totalitarians; to capitalists and socialists. The Enlightenment dream of a universal rational society has to a remarkable degree been realized—but in a form that is commercialized, homogenized, depoliticized, bureaucratized, and, of course, radically incomplete, for the movement toward McWorld is in competition with forces of global breakdown, national dissolution, and centrifugal corruption. These forces, working in the opposite direction, are the essence of what I call Jihad.

JIHAD, OR THE LEBANONIZATION OF THE WORLD

OPEC, the world bank, the united nations, the International Red Cross, the multinational corporation . . . there are scores of institutions that reflect globalization. But they often appear as ineffective reactors to the world's real actors: national states and, to an ever greater degree, subnational factions in permanent rebellion against uniformity and integration—even the kind represented by universal law and justice. The headlines feature these players regularly: they are cultures, not countries; parts, not wholes; sects, not religions; rebellious factions and dissenting minorities at war not just with globalism but with the traditional nation-state. Kurds, Basques, Puerto Ricans, Ossetians, East Timoreans, Quebecois, the Catholics of Northern Ireland, Abkhasians, Kurile Islander Japanese, the Zulus of Inkatha, Catalonians, Tamils, and, of course, Palestinians—people without countries, inhabiting nations not their own, seeking smaller worlds within borders that will seal them off from modernity.

A powerful irony is at work here. Nationalism was once a force of integration and unification, a movement aimed at bringing together disparate clans, tribes, and cultural fragments under new, assimilationist flags. But as Ortega y Gasset noted more than sixty years ago, having won its victories, nationalism changed its strategy. In the 1920s, and again today, it is more often a reactionary and divisive force, pulverizing the very nations it once helped cement together. The force that creates nations is "inclusive," Ortega wrote in *The Revolt of the Masses*. "In periods of consolidation, nationalism has a positive value, and is a lofty standard. But in Europe everything is more than consolidated, and nationalism is nothing but a mania. . . ."

This mania has left the post–Cold War world smoldering with hot wars; the international scene is little more unified than it was at the end of the Great War, in Ortega's own time. There were more than thirty wars in progress last year, most of them ethnic, racial, tribal, or religious in character, and the list of unsafe regions doesn't seem to be getting any shorter. Some new world order!

The aim of many of these small-scale wars is to redraw boundaries, to implode states and resecure parochial identities: to escape McWorld's dully insistent imperatives. The mood is that of Jihad: war not as an instrument of policy but as an emblem of identity, an expression of community, an end in itself. Even where there is no shooting war, there is fractiousness, secession, and the quest for ever smaller communities. Add to the list of dangerous countries those at risk: In Switzerland and Spain, Jurassian and Basque separatists still argue the virtues of ancient identities, sometimes in the language of bombs. Hyperdisintegration in the former Soviet Union may well continue unabated—not just a Ukraine independent from the Soviet Union but a Bessarabian Ukraine independent from the Ukrainian republic; not just Russia severed from the defunct union but Tatarstan severed from Russia. Yugoslavia makes even the disunited, ex-Soviet, nonsocialist republics that were once the Soviet Union look integrated, its sectarian fatherlands springing up within factional motherlands like weeds within weeds within weeds. Kurdish independence would threaten the territorial integrity of four Middle Eastern nations. Well before the current cataclysm Soviet Georgia made a claim for autonomy from the Soviet Union, only to be faced with its Ossetians (164,000 in a republic of 5.5 million) demanding their own self-determination within Georgia. The Abkhasian minority in Georgia has followed suit. Even the good will established by Canada's once promising Meech Lake protocols is in danger, with Francophone Quebec again threatening the dissolution of the federation. In South Africa the emergence from apartheid was hardly achieved when friction between Inkatha's Zulus and the African National Congress's tribally identified members threatened to replace Europeans' racism with an indigenous tribal war. After thirty years of attempted integration using the colonial language (English) as a unifier, Nigeria is now playing with the idea of linguistic multiculturalism—which could mean the cultural breakup of the nation into hundreds of tribal fragments. Even Saddam Hussein has benefited from the threat of internal Jihad, having used renewed tribal and religious warfare to turn last season's mortal enemies into reluctant allies of an Iraqi nationhood that he nearly destroyed.

The passing of communism has torn away the thin veneer of internationalism (workers of the world unite!) to reveal ethnic prejudices that are not only ugly and deep-seated but increasingly murderous. Europe's old scourge, anti-Semitism, is back with a vengeance, but it is only one of many antagonisms. It appears all too easy to throw the historical gears into reverse and pass from a Communist dictatorship back into a tribal state.

Among the tribes, religion is also a battlefield. ("Jihad" is a rich word whose generic meaning is "struggle"—usually the struggle of the soul to avert evil. Strictly applied to religious war, it is used only in reference to battles where the faith is under assault, or battles against a government that denies the practice of Islam. My use here is rhetorical, but does follow both journalistic practice and history.) Remember the Thirty Years War? Whatever forms of Enlightenment universalism might once have come to grace such historically related forms of monotheism as Judaism, Christianity, and Islam, in many of their modern incarnations they are parochial rather than cosmopolitan, angry rather than loving, proselytizing rather than ecumenical, zealous rather than rationalist, sectarian rather than deistic, ethnocentric rather than universalizing. As a result, like the new forms of hypernationalism, the new expressions of religious fundamentalism are fractious and pulverizing, never integrating. This is religion as the Crusaders knew it: a battle to the death for souls that if not saved will be forever lost.

The atmospherics of Jihad have resulted in a breakdown of civility in the name of identity, of comity in the name of community. International relations have sometimes taken on the aspect of gang war—cultural turf battles featuring tribal factions that were supposed to be sublimated as integral parts of large national, economic, postcolonial, and constitutional entities.

THE DARKENING FUTURE OF DEMOCRACY

These rather melodramatic tableaux vivants do not tell the whole story, however. For all their defects, Jihad and McWorld have their attractions. Yet, to repeat and insist, the attractions are unrelated to democracy. Neither McWorld nor Jihad is remotely democratic in impulse. Neither needs democracy; neither promotes democracy.

McWorld does manage to look pretty seductive in a world obsessed with Jihad. It delivers peace, prosperity, and relative unity—if at the cost of independence, community, and identity (which is generally based on difference). The primary political values required by the global market are order and tranquillity, and freedom—as in the phrases "free trade," "free press," and "free love." Human rights are needed to a degree, but not citizenship or participation—and no more social justice and equality than are necessary to promote efficient economic production and consumption. Multinational corporations sometimes seem to prefer doing business with local oligarchs, inasmuch as they can take confidence from dealing with the boss on all crucial matters. Despots who slaughter their own populations are no problem, so long as they leave markets in place and refrain from making war on their neighbors (Saddam Hussein's fatal mistake). In trading partners, predictability is of more value than justice.

The Eastern European revolutions that seemed to arise out of concern for global democratic values quickly deteriorated into a stampede in the general direction of free markets and their ubiquitous, television-promoted shopping malls. East Germany's Neues Forum, that courageous gathering of intellectuals, students, and workers which overturned the Stalinist regime in Berlin in 1989, lasted only six months in Germany's mini-version of McWorld. Then it gave way to money and markets and monopolies from the West. By the time of the first all-German elections, it could scarcely manage to secure three percent of the vote. Elsewhere there is growing evidence that *glasnost* will go and *perestroika*—defined as privatization and an opening of markets to Western bidders—will stay. So understandably anxious are the new rulers of Eastern Europe and whatever entities are forged from the residues of the Soviet Union to gain access to credit and markets and technology—McWorld's flourishing new currencies—that they have shown themselves willing to trade away democratic prospects in pursuit of them: not just old totalitarian ideologies and command-economy production models but some possible indigenous experiments with a third way between capitalism and socialism, such as economic cooperatives and employee stock-ownership plans, both of which have their ardent supporters in the East.

Jihad delivers a different set of virtues: a vibrant local identity, a sense of community, solidarity among kinsmen, neighbors, and countrymen, narrowly conceived. But it also guarantees parochialism and is grounded in exclusion. Solidarity is secured through war against outsiders. And solidarity often means obedience to a hierarchy in governance, fanaticism in beliefs, and the obliteration of individual selves in the name of the group. Deference to leaders and intolerance toward outsiders (and toward "enemies within") are hallmarks of tribalism—hardly the attitudes required for the cultivation of new democratic women and men capable of governing themselves. Where new democratic experiments have been conducted in retribalizing societies, in both Europe and the Third World, the result has often been anarchy, repression, persecution, and the coming of new, noncommunist forms of very old kinds of despotism. During the past year, Havel's velvet revolution in Czechoslovakia was imperiled by partisans of "Czechland" and of Slovakia as independent entities. India seemed little less rent by Sikh, Hindu, Muslim, and Tamil infighting than it was immediately after the British pulled out, more than forty years ago.

To the extent that either McWorld or Jihad has a *natural* politics, it has turned out to be more of an antipolitics. For McWorld, it is the antipolitics of globalism: bureaucratic, technocratic, and meritocratic, focused (as Marx predicted it would be) on the administration of things—with people, however, among the chief things to be administered. In its politico-economic imperatives McWorld has been guided by laissez-faire market principles that privilege efficiency, productivity, and beneficence at the expense of civic liberty and self-government.

For Jihad, the antipolitics of tribalization has been explicitly antidemocratic: one-party dictatorship, government by military junta, theocratic fundamentalism—often associated with a version of the *Führerprinzip* that empowers an individual to rule on behalf of a people. Even the government of India, struggling for decades to model democracy for a people who will soon number a billion, longs for great leaders; and for every Mahatma Gandhi, Indira Gandhi, or Rajiv Gandhi taken from them by zealous assassins, the Indians appear to seek a replacement who will deliver them from the lengthy travail of their freedom.

THE CONFEDERAL OPTION

How can democracy be secured and spread in a world whose primary tendencies are at best indifferent to it (McWorld) and at worst deeply antithetical to it (Jihad)? My guess is that globalization will eventually vanquish retribalization. The ethos of material "civilization" has not yet encountered an obstacle it has been unable to thrust aside. Ortega may have grasped in the 1920s a clue to our own future in the coming millennium.

> Everyone sees the need of a new principle of life. But as always happens in similar crises—some people attempt to save the situation by an artificial intensification of the very principle which has led to decay. This is the meaning of the "nationalist" outburst of recent years. . . . things have always gone that way. The last flare, the longest; the last sigh, the deepest. On the very eve of their disappearance there is an intensification of frontiers—military and economic.

Jihad may be a last deep sigh before the eternal yawn of McWorld. On the other hand, Ortega was not exactly prescient; his prophecy of peace and internationalism came just before blitzkrieg, world war, and the Holocaust tore the old order to bits. Yet democracy is how we remonstrate with reality, the rebuke our aspirations offer to history. And if retribalization is inhospitable to democracy, there is nonetheless a form of democratic government that can accommodate parochialism and communitarianism, one that can even save them from their defects and make them more tolerant and participatory: decentralized participatory democracy. And if McWorld is indifferent to democracy, there is nonetheless a form of democratic government that suits global markets passably well—representative government in its federal or, better still, confederal variation.

With its concern for accountability, the protection of minorities, and the universal rule of law, a confederalized representative system would serve the political needs of McWorld as well as oligarchic bureaucratism or meritocratic elitism is currently doing. As we are already beginning to see, many nations may survive in the long term only as confederations that afford local regions smaller than "nations" extensive jurisdiction. Recommended reading for democrats of the twenty-first century is not the U.S. Constitution or the French Declaration of Rights of Man and Citizen but the Articles of Confederation, that suddenly pertinent document that stitched together the thirteen American colonies into what then seemed a too loose confederation of independent states but now appears a new form of political realism, as veterans of Yeltsin's new Russia and the new Europe created at Maastricht will attest.

By the same token, the participatory and direct form of democracy that engages citizens in civic activity and civic judgment and goes well beyond just voting and accountability—the system I have called "strong democracy"—suits the political needs of decentralized communities as well as theocratic and nationalist party dictatorships have done. Local neighborhoods need not be democratic, but they can be. Real democracy has flourished in diminutive settings: the spirit of liberty, Tocqueville said, is local. Participatory democracy, if not naturally apposite to tribalism, has an undeniable attractiveness under conditions of parochialism.

Democracy in any of these variations will, however, continue to be

428 BENJAMIN R. BARBER

obstructed by the undemocratic and antidemocratic trends toward uniformitarian globalism and intolerant retribalization which I have portrayed here. For democracy to persist in our brave new McWorld, we will have to commit acts of conscious political will—a possibility, but hardly a probability, under these conditions. Political will requires much more than the quick fix of the transfer of institutions. Like technology transfer, institution transfer rests on foolish assumptions about a uniform world of the kind that once fired the imagination of colonial administrators. Spread English justice to the colonies by exporting wigs. Let an East Indian trading company act as the vanguard to Britain's free parliamentary institutions. Today's well-intentioned quick-fixers in the National Endowment for Democracy and the Kennedy School of Government, in the unions and foundations and universities zealously nurturing contacts in Eastern Europe and the Third World, are hoping to democratize by long distance. Post Bulgaria a parliament by first-class mail. Fed Ex the Bill of Rights to Sri Lanka. Cable Cambodia some common law.

Yet Eastern Europe has already demonstrated that importing free political parties, parliaments, and presses cannot establish a democratic civil society; imposing a free market may even have the opposite effect. Democracy grows from the bottom up and cannot be imposed from the top down. Civil society has to be built from the inside out. The institutional superstructure comes last. Poland may become democratic, but then again it may heed the Pope, and prefer to found its politics on its Catholicism, with uncertain consequences for democracy. Bulgaria may become democratic, but it may prefer tribal war. The former Soviet Union may become a democratic confederation, or it may just grow into an anarchic and weak conglomeration of markets for other nations' goods and services.

Democrats need to seek out indigenous democratic impulses. There is always a desire for self-government, always some expression of participation, accountability, consent, and representation, even in traditional hierarchical societies. These need to be identified, tapped, modified, and incorporated into new democratic practices with an indigenous flavor. The tortoises among the democratizers may ultimately outlive or outpace the hares, for they will have the time and patience to explore conditions along the way, and to adapt their gait to changing circumstances. Tragically, democracy in a hurry often looks something like France in 1794 or China in 1989.

It certainly seems possible that the most attractive democratic ideal in the face of the brutal realities of Jihad and the dull realities of McWorld will be a confederal union of semi-autonomous communities smaller than nation-states, tied together into regional economic associations and markets larger than nation-states—participatory and self-determining in local matters at the bottom, representative and accountable at the top. The nation-state would play a diminished role, and sovereignty would lose some of its political potency. The Green movement adage "Think globally, act locally" would actually come to describe the conduct of politics.

This vision reflects only an ideal, however—one that is not terribly likely to be realized. Freedom, Jean-Jacques Rousseau once wrote, is a food easy to eat but hard to digest. Still, democracy has always played itself out against the odds. And democracy remains both a form of coherence as binding as McWorld and a secular faith potentially as inspiriting as Jihad.

Acknowledgments

Paul F. Lazarsfeld, "What Is Obvious?" *Public Opinion Quarterly*, 13 (Fall 1949), pp. 378–80.

C. Wright Mills, *The Sociological Imagination* (New York: Oxford University Press, 1959), pp. 3–8.

Leslie Marmon Silko, "The Border Patrol State," *The Nation* (October 17, 1994), pp. 412–16. Copyright © 1994 by Leslie Marmon Silko. First published in *The Nation*. Reprinted with the permission of Wylie, Aiken & Stone, Inc.

Herbert J. Gans, "The Positive Functions of Poverty," *American Journal of Sociology* 78, no. 2 (September 1972), pp. 275–88. A sequel to this article appears in the author's *War Against the Poor: The Underclass and Antipoverty Policy* (New York: Basic Books, 1995), pp. 91–102. Herbert J. Gans is the Robert S. Lynd Professor of Sociology at Columbia University.

Allan M. Brandt, "Racism and Research: The Case of the Tuskegee Syphilis Study," *Hastings Center Report*, (December 1978), pp. 21–29. Reproduced by permission © The Hastings Center.

Ned Polsky, *Hustlers, Beats, and Others*, revised ed. (Chicago: University of Chicago Press, 1969), pp. 34–47.

Patricia A. Gwartney-Gibbs and Denise H. Lach, "Sociological Explanations for Failure to Seek Sexual Harassment Remedies," *Mediation Quarterly* 9, no. 4 (Summer 1992), pp. 365–74. Copyright © 1992 by Jossey-Bass Inc., Publishers.

Robert Temple, *The Genius of China* (New York: Simon and Schuster, 1986), pp. 9–12.

Pico Iyer, "The Global Village Finally Arrives," *Time* 142, no. 21 (Fall 1993), pp. 86–87. Copyright © 1993 Time, Inc. Reprinted by permission.

John A. Hostetler, *Amish Society* (Baltimore: Johns Hopkins University Press, 1980), pp. 3–12. Copyright © 1980. Reprinted by permission of the Johns Hopkins University Press.

Reprinted from *Promises Not Kept: The Betrayal of Social Change in the Third World*, Second Edition, by John Isbister (West Hartford, Conn: Kumarian Press, Inc., 630 Oakwood Avenue, West Hartford, CT 06110 USA, 1993) from Chapter 4, pp. 87–96.

Clyde Kluckholm, *Mirror for Man* (University of Arizona Press, 1968), pp. 24–33.

Clifford Geertz, "Deep Play: Notes on a Balinese Cockfight" reprinted by permission of *Daedalus*, Journal of the American Academy of Arts and Sciences, from the issue entitled, "Myth, Symbol, and Culture," Winter 1972, Volume 101, Number 1.

Jan Harold Brunvand, *The Vanishing Hitchhiker: American Urban Legends and Their Meanings* (New York: W. W. Norton, 1981). Reprinted with the permission of W. W. Norton & Company, Inc. Copyright © 1981 by Jan Harold Brunvand.

E. Richard Sorenson, "Growing up as a Fore is to be 'in touch' and free," *Smithsonian* 8 (May 1977), pp. 107–14.

Erving Goffman, *Encounters: Two Studies in the Sociology of Interaction* (New York: Allyn & Bacon, 1961). Copyright © 1961. All rights reserved. Reprinted by permission of Allyn & Bacon.

Greta Foff Paule, *Dishing It Out: Power and Resistance among Waitresses in a New Jersey Restaurant* (Philadephia: Temple University Press, 1991), pp. 23–29.

Elizabeth W. Fernea and Robert A. Fernea, "A Look behind the Veil," from *Human Nature*. Copyright © 1979 by Human Nature, Inc. Reprinted by permission of Harcourt, Brace & Company.

William J. Chambliss, "The Saints and the Roughnecks," *Society* 11 (1973), pp. 24–31. Copyright © 1973. All rights reserved. Reprinted by permission of Transaction Publishers.

Barbara Katz Rothman, "Recreating Motherhood," *New Perspectives Quarterly* 7, no. 1 (Winter 1990), pp. 53–57.

Ruth Sidel, "Mixed Messages" from *On Her Own*. Copyright © 1990 by Ruth Sidel. Used by permission of Viking Penguin, a division of Penguin Books USA Inc.

Michael Messner, "Masculinities and Athletic Careers," *Gender & Society* 3 (March 1989), pp. 71–88. Copyright © 1989. Reprinted by permission of Sage Publications, Inc.

Barbara Sinclair Deckard, "Sexual Stereotypes as Political Ideology" from *The Women's Movement*. Copyright © 1983 by Harper & Row, Publishers, Inc. Reprinted by permission of HarperCollins Publishers, Inc.

Merrill Goozner, "Private Lives," *Chicago Tribune* (June 5, 1995). Tempo section, p. 1. Copyright © Chicago Tribune Company. All rights reserved. Used with permission.

Mantsios, Gregory, "Media Magic: Making Class Invisible," Paula Rothenberg in *Race, Class and Gender*, 3rd ed., ed. Paula Rothenberg (New York: St. Martin's Press, 1995), pp. 409–17. Courtesy of Gregory Mantsios.

Robert B. Reich, "As the World Turns," *The New Republic* 200, no. 18 (May 1, 1989), pp. 23–28. Copyright © 1989, The New Republic, Inc. Reprinted by permission of *The New Republic*.

Holly Sklar, "Imagine a Country," *Z Magazine* (November 1992), pp. 21–24.

Elliot Liebow, "Men and Jobs" from *Tally's Corner*. Copyright © 1967 by Little, Brown and Company. By permission of Little, Brown and Company.

Karl Marx and Friedrich Engels, "Manifesto of the Communist Party," in *Marx-Engels Reader*, 2nd ed., ed. Robert Tucker (New York: W. W. Norton, 1978).

Richard Rodriguez, "On Becoming a Chicano." Copyright © 1975 by Richard Rodriguez. Reprinted by permission of Georges Borchardt, Inc.

Douglas S. Massey and Nancy A. Denton, from *American Apartheid: Segregation and the Making of the Underclass* (Cambridge, Mass.: Harvard University Press). Copyright © 1993 by the President and Fellows of Harvard College. Reprinted by permission of the publishers.

George Ritzer, *The McDonaldization of Society*, pp. 9–17, copyright © 1993 by Pine Forge Press. Reprinted by permission of Pine Forge Press.

Boye De Mente, *Japanese Etiquette and Ethics in Business*, 5th ed., (Lincolnwood, Ill.: NTC Business Books, 1987), pp. 71–89.

Enloe, Cynthia, "Beyond Steve Canyon and Rambo: Feminist Histories of Militarized Masculinity," in *The Militarization of the Western World*, ed. John R. Gillis. Copyright © 1989 by Rutgers, The State University. Reprinted by permission of Rutgers University Press.

William E. Thompson, "Hanging Tongues: A Sociological 'Encounter with the Assembly Line,' " *Qualitative Sociology* 6, (1983).

Thomas R. Ide and Arthur J. Cordell, "Automated Work," *Society* (September/October 1994), pp. 65–71. Copyright © 1994. All rights reserved. Reprinted by permission of Transaction Publishers.

John D. Kasarda, "The Jobs-Skills Mismatch," *New Perspectives Quarterly* 7, no. 4 (Fall 1990), pp. 34–37.

Arlie Hochschild and Ann Machung, "UTNE Reader Selection" from *The Second Shift*. Copyright © 1989 by Arlie Hochschild. Used by permission of Viking Penguin, a division of Penguin Books USA Inc.

Robert N. Bellah, Richard Madsen, William M. Sullivan, Ann Swidler, and Steven M. Tipton, *Habits of the Heart: Individualism and Commitment in American Life* (Berkeley: University of California Press, 1985), pp. 219–22.

Sidney Blumenthal, "Christian Soldiers," *The New Yorker* (July 18, 1994). Copyright © 1994.

Carol B. Stack, "Domestic Networks," from *All Our Kin: Strategies for Survival in a Black Community*, pp. 90–94, 105–107. Copyright © 1974 by Carol B. Stack. Reprinted by permission of HarperCollins Publishers, Inc.

Giri Raj Gupta, "Love, Arranged Marriage, and the Indian Social Structure," in *Cross-Cultural Perspectives of Mate-Selection and Marriage*, ed. George Kurian (Westport, Conn.: Greenwood Publishing Group). Copyright © 1979. Reprinted with permission of Greenwood Publishing Group, Inc.

Fred M. Hechinger, "Why France Outstrips the United States in Nurturing Its Children," *The New York Times* (Wednesday, August 1, 1990), p. B8. Copyright © 1990 by The New York Times Company. Reprinted by permission.

Stanley Aronowitz, "Colonialized Leisure, Trivialized Work," from *False Promises* (New York: McGraw-Hill, Inc., 1973), pp. 75–91. Courtesy of Stanley Aronowitz.

Joe R. Feagin and Robert Parker, *Building American Cities: The Urban Real Estate Game*, 2nd ed. (Upper Saddle River, NJ: Prentice Hall, 1990), pp. 154–59. Reprinted by permission of Prentice Hall.

Partha S. Dasgupta, "Population, Poverty and the Local Environment," *Scientific American* (February 1995), pp. 40–45. Copyright © 1995 by Scientific American Inc. All rights reserved. Reprinted with permission.

Suzanne Staggenborg, "The Pro-Choice Movement: Confrontation and Direct Action," from *The Pro-Choice Movement: Organization and Activism in the Abortion Conflict*, pp. 43–54. Copyright © 1991 by Oxford University Press, Inc. Reprinted by permission.

Dorothy Nelkin, "Science, Technology, and Political Conflict: Analyzing the Issues" from *Controversy: Politics of Technical Decisions*, 2nd ed., ed. Dorothy Nelkin (Beverly Hills, Calif.: Sage Publications, 1984), pp. 9–24. Copyright © 1984. Reprinted by permission of Sage Publications, Inc.

Benjamin R. Barber, "Jihad vs. McWorld," published originally in the March 1992 issue of *Atlantic Monthly*. Benjamin R. Barber is Whitman Professor of Political Science and Director of the Whitman Center at Rutgers University.